MORE PEOPLE,
LESS EROSION

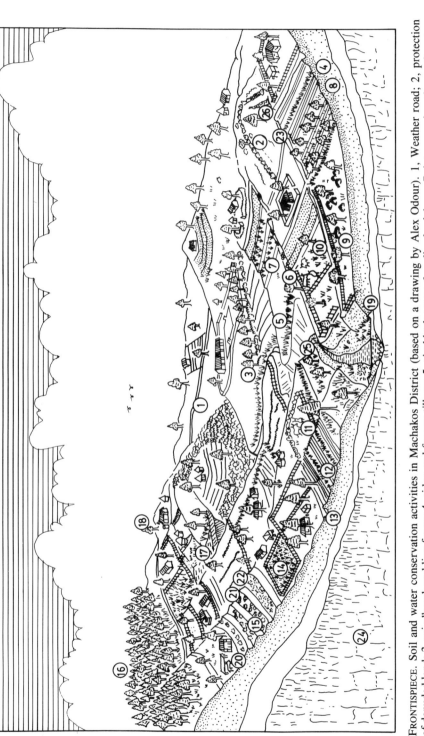

FRONTISPIECE. Soil and water conservation activities in Machakos District (based on a drawing by Alex Odour). 1, Weather road; 2, protection of denuded land; 3, windbreak and live fence; 4, ridge and furrow tillage; 5, sisal hedgerow; 6, gully checkdams; 7, intercropping; 8, agroforestry; 9, woodlot; 10, paddocking; 11, improved pasture; 12, forward sloping benches; 13, cut-off drain; 14, pasture establishment; 15, excavated level bench terraces; 16, gazetted forest; 17, earth dam; 18, roof water catchment; 19, river bank protection; 20, stall feeding; 21, coffee plantation; 22, crop residue management; 23, waterway; 24, soil profile; 25, river or stream; 26, gully erosion

MORE PEOPLE, LESS EROSION

Environmental Recovery in Kenya

MARY TIFFEN

MICHAEL MORTIMORE
Overseas Development Institute, London, UK

and

FRANCIS GICHUKI
Department of Agricultural Engineering, University of Nairobi, Kenya

JOHN WILEY & SONS
Chichester · New York · Brisbane · Toronto · Singapore

Copyright © 1994 by OVERSEAS DEVELOPMENT INSTITUTE
Published by John Wiley & Sons Ltd.
        Baffins Lane, Chichester,
        West Sussex PO19 1UD, England
        Telephone (+44) (243) 779777

Reprinted with corrections July 1994
Reprinted March 1995

Other Wiley Editorial Offices

John Wiley & Sons, Inc., 605 Third Avenue,
New York, NY 10158-0012, USA

Jacaranda Wiley Ltd, 33 Park Road, Milton,
Queensland 4064, Australia

John Wiley & Sons (Canada) Ltd, 22 Worcester Road,
Rexdale, Ontario M9W 1L1, Canada

John Wiley & Sons (SEA) Pte Ltd, 37 Jalan Pemimpin #05-04,
Block B, Union Industrial Building, Singapore 2057

Library of Congress Cataloging-in-Publication Data
Tiffen, Mary.
  More people, less erosion: environmental recovery in Kenya / Mary
Tiffen, Michael Mortimore, and Francis Gichuki.
    p.   cm.
  Includes bibliographical references and index.
  ISBN 0-471-94143-3
  1. Soil conservation — Kenya — Machakos (District) 2. Water
conservation — Kenya — Machakos (District) 3. Land use, Rural — Kenya
— Machakos (District) — Management. 4. Arid regions — Kenya — Machakos
(District) — Management.   I. Mortimore, M. J., 1937–
II. Gichuki, Francis. III. Title.
S625.K4T54 1994
333.76'16'096762 — dc20   93-2192
                                                  CIP

British Library Cataloguing in Publication Data

A catalogue record for this book is available from the British Library

ISBN 0-471-94143-3

Typeset in 10/12pt Times from author's disks by MHL Typesetting Ltd, Coventry
Printed and bound in Great Britain by Redwood Books Ltd, Trowbridge, Wiltshire

Contents

PART IV WHAT WORKED AND WHY

Acronyms and Currencies

ACZ	Agro-climatic zone
ADC	African District Council
ADEC	African Development and Economic Consultants Ltd
AEZ	Agro-ecological zone
ALDEV	African Land Development Board (later Land Development Board — non-scheduled areas)
ALUS	African Settlement and Land Utilisation
AMREF	African Medical Research Foundation
AP	Air Photography
ASAL	Arid and Semi-Arid Lands
CARE	Cooperative for Assistance and Relief Everywhere
CBS	Central Bureau of Statistics
CD	Community Development
CDA	Community Development Assistant
CHEK	Council for Human Ecology — Kenya
DAO	District Agricultural Officer
DC	District Commissioner
DI	Drought Index
DO	Divisional Officer
DoA	Department of Agriculture
FAO	Food and Agriculture Organization of the United Nations
K£	Kenya Pound = Ksh20. This unit is still used in some government reports, although it is no longer in the currency
KANU	Kenya African National Union
KFA	Kenya Farmers Association
KNA	Kenya National Archives
Ksh	Kenya shilling
LNC	Local Native Council
LR	Long Rains
LU	Livestock Unit
MALD	Ministry of Agriculture and Livestock Development
MIDP	Machakos Integrated Development Programme
MKS	Machakos (file abbreviation)

MoA	Ministry of Agriculture
MRDASW	Ministry for the Reclamation and Development of Arid and Semi-Arid Lands and Wastelands
NCPB	National Cereals and Produce Board
NGO	Non-Governmental Organisation
ODI	Overseas Development Institute
RC	Roman Catholic
RH	Rhodes House, Oxford
SIDA	Swedish International Development Agency
SR	Short Rains
SRF	Systematic Reconaissance Flight
SU	Stock Unit — informal unit, in which 1 zebu cow = 5 sheep or goats
UNCED	United Nations Conference on Environment and Development
USAID	United States Agency for International Development

Note on currency:
Prices are quoted in Ksh. 1990 values: US$1 = Ksh 22.9 = UK£0.56 = Ecu 0.79.

Note on weights and measures:
Metric weights and measures are used throughout, unless otherwise stated.

Foreword

The genesis for the Bank's interest in a study of the type reported here was its need to distil the lessons of projects in dryland areas. It soon became apparent that the short span of time involved in most of these interventions was not sufficient to enable one to differentiate between the longer run forces which might be supporting change and the part played by the 'project' interventions. This was a particular concern in dryland areas, where longer run climatic cycles may create fundamental changes in conditions under which rural households attempt to keep body and soul together. We, therefore, decided to try to find a semi-arid region where data existed on agricultural development for, we hoped, fifty years or more. There needed also to be sufficient written material for a study of the condition of the land resource and of development and change in land resource management practices to be feasible.

It was then that we learned that the Overseas Development Institute (ODI), specifically Mary Tiffen, had a similar interest, and we agreed on Machakos as our preferred site. We, frankly, looked upon this study as a pilot, as an attempt to see what could be gleaned from the historic record and supporting field work by a team led by experienced field researchers. The general interest and enthusiasm with which the study has been received indicates the success of the effort, and argues for its replication.

Another reason for interest on our side was a feeling that one of the traps into which most of us working in the development field fall, is an excessive focus on the problems of the moment and an expectation that actions can be taken which will assist in solving them in the relatively short term. This focus tends to blind us to the longer term trends which are continuing beneath our feet. Hindsight is always cheap, but going back to reports written twenty or thirty years ago often indicates that the view of the time did not recognise certain changes which were already occurring. This type of study reminds us how, over a relatively short period, continued incremental, adaptive changes, many of which are hardly noticed at the time, can add up to substantial change in the aggregate.

In this regard there has been much discussion recently of the need to evolve sustainable agricultural systems but very little consensus on how that might be done. There is a tendency to be concerned that changes which are underway, such as a shortening of fallow periods, will lead to undesirable outcomes. Similarly, in rangeland management, there have been predictions at regular intervals that the high stocking rate systems would collapse. In the same vein there have been successive predictions of a fuelwood crisis in Machakos and loss of trees, but no such crisis has occurred. This suggests that lessons can be learned on the conditions which enabled these systems to be adapted to changing economic and social circumstances without collapsing, and to continue to be productive, even if at a low level.

But, perhaps most important of all, a study of this type reminds us that the most important factor in development is the ability of individuals, groups, and nations to adapt to changing circumstances and to organise themselves to address problems and identify and implement appropriate measures. It suggests that we should focus a little more on the general conditions which promote such adaptation and on what can be done to assist groups to adapt in this way, as the people of Machakos District have done, and a little less on the minutiae of what individuals are doing at a particular point in time.

We should note here the immeasurable benefit that the study derived from the efforts of the team of Kenyan collaborators from the University of Nairobi and of the farmers and others from Machakos who gave of their time to assist the initial field investigations and subsequently in the 1991 workshop. Without their efforts much less would have been achieved. Perhaps, in a subtle way, the spirit of openness and enquiry with which the study team was received in the district reflects one of the reasons why successful adaptation was possible in this area and is likely to continue.

Washington, February 1993   John English
                                                        Principal Economist, World Bank
                                  Policy and Research Division, Environment Department

Acknowledgements

This study was initiated in 1990 as an element in the World Bank's Dryland Management Research Programme. Funding was provided by the Bank's Environment Department (drawing on a grant from the Government of Norway for research into the problems of dryland areas in the Sudano-Sahelian Region), the British Government's Overseas Development Administration and the Rockefeller Foundation (for the University of Nairobi component). It was sponsored in Kenya by the Ministry of Reclamation and Development of Arid, Semi-Arid Areas and Wastelands (MRDASW).

The aim of the first phase of the study was to quantify change in Machakos District, Kenya, where there was a good database, as accurately as possible, in a series of profiles which would give a sound foundation for developing policy lessons. This was carried out through collaboration between researchers at the Overseas Development Institute (ODI) and a team of scientists at the University of Nairobi. The project was led at ODI by Mary Tiffen, in association with Michael Mortimore, who took particular charge of coordinating the environmental studies. Kate Wellard (ODI) assisted the initial study of technology change. The University of Nairobi team were (in the order in which their contributions appear):

- Rainfall: Dr S. K. Mutiso, Department of Geography.
- Land use: Professor R. S. Rostom, Professor in the Department of Surveying and Photogrammetry. He was assisted by J. K. Yego and G. C. Mulaku. The photo-interpretation and photogrammetric and cartographic work was undertaken by the staff of the Department, assisted by Mr J. O. Ojuok (Ministry of Water Resources, Machakos District).
- Agricultural production: Professor A. C. Ackello-Ogutu and Dr S. G. Mbogoh, Department of Agricultural Economics.
- Soil fertility: Dr J. P. Mbuvi, Department of Soil Science.
- Soil erosion: Professor D. B. Thomas, Department of Agricultural Engineering. We owe him particular thanks for sharing his experience of the District since the 1950s, and for his substantial contributions to the photographic record.
- Vegetation: Dr Kassim O. Farah, Department of Range Management.
- Institutions and land tenure: Professor Judith Mbula Bahemuka, Department of Sociology, Mr J. W. Kaluli, Department of Agricultural Engineering, Jomo Kenyatta University College of Agriculture and Technology, researched the work of NGOs in soil and water conservation.
- Soil and water conservation: Dr F. N. Gichuki, Department of Agricultural Engineering.

Their initial studies were published as a series of ODI Working Papers, as indicated in the appropriate chapters and in the bibliography, which contain more detail than can be included in this book. These include the preliminary studies carried out by the ODI team: population and farming systems (Mary Tiffen); technology and tree management (Michael Mortimore).

The team was particularly fortunate that Professor Philip Mbithi, then Vice-Chancellor of the University of Nairobi, spared time not only to share his deep knowledge of his home district, but also to review first drafts. We are grateful to Mr George Mbate, Principal Economist at MRDASW, and formerly Programme Officer for the Machakos Integrated Development Programme (MIDP), for his assistance and advice, and for the help he and his staff gave in organising the workshop for government and local organisation staff, the researchers and representative farmers, at the Five Hills Hotel in Machakos in September 1991, which concluded the first phase of the study. Mr Peter Muasya, then District Community Development Assistant for Masaku County Council, was the third of this team of Akamba advisers, whose contributions by his own knowledge of the District and by his excellent arrangements for meetings with men and women community leaders, were invaluable. Mr P. M. Kimuli, Programme Officer for MIDP, facilitated meetings with District government officers. Our thanks go also to all the men and women in Machakos who answered our questions and took part in field discussions.

Following this first phase, Dr Gichuki came to London to participate in a second workshop (which was memorable for the contributions of many distinguished people in the United Kingdom who have worked in Machakos in the past), and to join in the planning of this book. The three main authors have synthesised and summarised the original material, filled it out with further research, and developed its theoretical meaning and policy implications. They have been assisted by comments and contributions from colleagues at ODI and elsewhere, individually or in seminars, who are almost too numerous to mention. However, very special thanks must go to John English, of the Environment Department of the World Bank, who throughout provided intellectual support, who attended both the Machakos and London workshops and who took the lead in the first summary (John English, Mary Tiffen and Michael Mortimore: Resource Management in Machakos District, Kenya, 1930–1990, Bank Environment Paper Number 5). We are also very grateful to John Peberdy, also in the Bank until his recent retirement, who was always ready to answer questions about his time as District Agricultural Officer in Machakos, 1954–1961.

We are grateful to the Kenya National Archives for permission to make copies of photographs in R. O. Barnes' original 1937 report on the status of soil erosion in the District, and for the help of its staff throughout the study. Rhodes House Library, Oxford, gave permission for quotations from the Maher papers. Dr F. N. Owako kindly gave permission for the use of photographs and other materials from his 1969 PhD thesis for the University of London.

We owe a special debt to T. E. Downing, Environmental Change Unit, University of Oxford, for making available data collected for his study of rainfall in eastern Kenya. We are also grateful to Dr Michael Norton-Griffiths, formerly Director of Ecosystems Ltd. for making reports of their 1981 and 1985 surveys of the District available.

Beth Smith provided secretarial, editorial and administrative back up with admirable thoroughness. John Antwi (Department of Geography, Bayero University, Kano, Nigeria) was responsible for the cartographic illustrations, excluding those in Chapter 5.

The three principal authors have tried to represent fairly the findings of their colleagues, which have been rewritten to shorten them and to integrate them into this connected story. They alone are responsible for any faults of emphasis which may remain.

PART I

INTRODUCTION

1

Machakos Then and Now

In February 1937, Colin Maher introduced his report on soil erosion and land use in the Ukamba Reserve,[1] Kenya, with the following despairing words in which he echoes Thomas Malthus:

> The Machakos Reserve is an appalling example of a large area of land which has been subjected to uncoordinated and practically uncontrolled development by natives whose multiplication and the increase of whose stock has been permitted, free from the checks of war and largely from those of disease, under benevolent British rule.
>
> Every phase of misuse of land is vividly and poignantly displayed in this Reserve, the inhabitants of which are rapidly drifting to a state of hopeless and miserable poverty and their land to a parching desert of rocks, stones and sand. (RH: Maher, 1937: 3. Reproduced by permission of Rhodes House Library, Oxford)

During the 1930s, official concern for what was admitted to be a long-standing problem reached its peak, with no less than eight official visits, reports, or recommendations commissioned between 1929 and 1939 (listed in Pole-Evans (1939) and discussed in Chapter 7). The Government's ambitious plans to arrest the cycle of degradation were then rudely interrupted by World War II, which severely constrained the resources available. But this clutch of reports provides not only a guide to the official consensus about the nature of the 'Machakos problem' and its remedy, but also baseline descriptions of the District when environmental management was at its nadir. Accepting all the ambiguities implicit in contemporary value judgements of native land use and management, we take this period — the 1930s — as our starting point.

The 'Machakos problem', in the general view, was rooted in the colonial history of Kenya. Four years before Maher, the Kenya Land Commission set up in 1932 ruled on the inevitable conflict between colonialist and colonised. Areas reserved for European settlement, known as the Scheduled Areas or White Highlands, bordered the 'Native' Reserve on two sides, and the Akamba had consistently claimed that their grazing lands were taken. These grazings, though unsettled, had been important for the survival of the herds when the rains and pastures failed in the homelands. On the other two sides, the Akamba confronted newly designated Crown Lands, whose use the Government felt entitled to control, and which, in the south-east, were so infested by the tsetse fly as to be almost useless (Figure 1.1). Thus encircled, the Akamba grew in numbers, and in livestock, while clearing extra land for shifting cultivation of food crops, and chopping down trees for fuel burning and construction of their homes. The implications for the management of the drylands should have been obvious, but the Government, from the beginning, was more concerned about political containment:

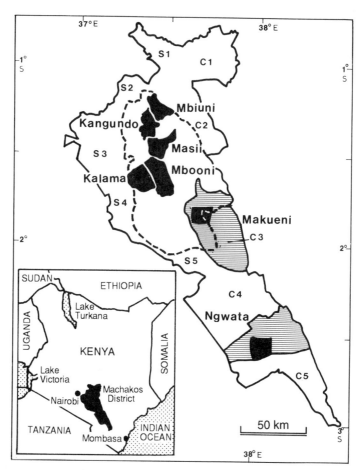

FIGURE 1.1. Machakos District, showing (shaded black) study locations (in Makueni and Ngwata, field studies were limited to the areas shown black). The boundary of the former Ukamba Reserve is shown with a broken line. C, Former Crown Lands: C1, North Yatta; C2, Yatta Plateau; C3, Lower Makueni; C4, Kikumbulyu; C5, Tsavo game reserve. S, Former settled areas: S1, Ward 10; S2; Ward 8; S3, Ward 11; S4, Ward 12; S5, Simba Ranch

> It would be impolitic weakness, now to open the question of [additional] grazing lands. Instead, every inducement should be made to encourage the sale of surplus stock. (*Annual Report*, Ukamba Province, 1912; quoted in Otieno, 1984: 61.)

And ten years later,

> It cannot be denied that the position is serious and that large numbers of native cattle die annually, literally from starvation. The granting of privileges outside the Reserve is however open to objection ... it is certain that the more facilities the Akamba obtain, the more they will need in future. (*Annual Report*, Ukamba Province, 1922; quoted in Otieno, 1984: 62.)

The link between colonial land appropriation and environmental degradation is conventional wisdom in the critical literature about the history of Machakos.[2]

Another linkage was clearly perceived in the official mind, connecting environmental misuse with the scourge of famine. Failures in rainfall were common in the District. In less than a century of recorded rainfall in the two rainy seasons of each year, there have been 90 droughts of light, moderate or severe degree. (The terms are defined, and the data analysed, in Chapter 3.) They often occurred in runs.

In 1928 both seasons recorded light droughts with crop failures, and in the following year the long rains failed severely. Locusts invaded, and the Quelea birds attacked the standing crops. The famine was called locally *Yua ya nzalukangwe*, meaning 'looking everywhere to find food'. Denudation of the grasslands was reported, and cattle died, but an appeal for famine relief was dismissed by the Governor. Worse followed. During 1933–1936, six droughts were recorded in eight seasons, three of them severe. Again locusts invaded, erosion intensified, cattle died, and food became desperately scarce. This time the Government could not stand aside. Maize and pigeon peas were distributed and the cattle tax was suspended. Efforts were intensified to induce destocking, and to introduce erosion control measures. They were seen to be the Government's logical response, and the only form of insurance against a repetition of disaster. However, with the return of better rains, the District was able to export some food crops during 1936–1939. The real low point appears to have been the 1940s, with small maize and bean exports only in 1942, and famine relief required during 1943–1946 and 1949–1951.

Soil erosion was, and continues to be, a difficult process to quantify. Many assessments rely on verbal descriptions to make their impact. Eye-witnesses seldom saw the need to measure areas, volumes and rates; to do so would have required technical resources that were not available. They did, however, often take photographs, relying on the impact of images of erosion gullies, denuded slopes, and decapitated soils to convey the severity of the problem and the need for interventions. Many things are missing from such photographs — in particular, the owners and the managers of the soil, their perceptions, their technologies and rationales. But photographs can provide objective reference points, against which later change can be assessed.

From R. O. Barnes' report of 1937 (KNA: Barnes, 1937), the authors have selected five such scenes for matching with contemporary landscapes (Figures 1.2–1.11). Taken 11 years before the first available vertical air photography, they permit a visual assessment of the changes that occurred over half a century. During that period, it should be observed, the population of the District grew fivefold, from about 240 000 to almost 1 400 000, and the numbers of livestock from an estimated 330 000 units (1930) to 593 000 (1989), while the area that was cultivated grew from about 15% of the Reserve in 1930 to between 50 and 80% in 1978.

FROM BADLANDS TO FARMLANDS

In the first photo pair (Figures 1.2 and 1.3), the Kalama Hills stand as background to the deeply dissected upland slopes of Kivandini, 5 km east from Machakos town. These slopes used to be called the 'Badlands' of the Reserve. Barnes' photograph (Figure 1.2) shows the exposed rock bed of a tributary stream, plunging towards the canyon of the Ikiwe River. Irregular patches of bare soil are visible on the slopes in the middle distance, and gullied treeless slopes and ridges in the far distance. A few banana plants grow near the stream and a patch of scrub woodland has been protected on the middle slope. No houses or permanent farms can be seen. In 1991 (Figure 1.3), the aspect is strikingly different. Densely scattered homesteads occupy the foreground and middle distance; carefully terraced fields, and boundary fences, cover the once denuded slopes; and on them grow a rich mixture of fruit and other useful trees (including mangos,

FIGURE 1.2. Kalama Hills from Kivandini, June—July(?) 1937. Map Sheet 162/2, GR 3104E, 98302N; Brg. 145°. (Photo: KNA: R. O. Barnes, 1937, photo 1. Reproduced by permission of Kenya National Archives.)

FIGURE 1.3. Kalama Hills from Kivandini, September 1991. Map Sheet 162/2, GR 3104E, 98302N; Brg. 145°. (Photo: M. Mortimore)

bananas, pawpaws and eucalyptus). Part of the scrubland has been converted into an amply wooded, terraced farm.

HUSBANDRY ON THE HILLSIDE

The southern slopes of the Iveti Hills (Figures 1.4 and 1.5) display a change no less remarkable. In 1937 some early efforts of the Forestry Department in afforesting the summits could be seen above the largely treeless lower slopes. On these slopes, Barnes remarked that 'numerous small gullies can be seen starting out of abandoned or closed native shambas'. The rills and gullies fed unchecked into the scarred and rocky stream channels. Settlements were sparse. However, a start had been made with planted hedges and woodlots. Most of these were still there in 1991. Trees and houses are now ubiquitous, and only one substantial area of uncultivated land survives. Apart from this area, the gullies have become revegetated. All cultivated land is terraced. Among the trees, the range in size suggests they are regenerating.

OLD AND NEW IN KYAMUNYUU

The slopes of Kyamunyuu (Figures 1.6 and 1.7) portray a mosaic of old and new that indicates the way in which the transformation (or capitalisation) of the landscape has come about. In 1937, a great deal of exposed rock or soil is visible in the stream channels, and the slopes of the Kalama Hills in the background are covered with erosion scars. Now, between the manicured perimeters of contoured fields, each with its homestead farm, the scrub woodland still betrays some evidences of erosion and neglect — stripped soils and outcropping rock — but on a reduced scale. Apart from some ridge-top reafforestation, accomplished after 1937, the vegetation on the grazing lands looked strikingly the same in 1991 as in 1937 — neither worse nor better. But the stable, terraced farmlands give the lie to the belief, often expressed in the 1930s, that cultivable topsoils were being stripped, and degradation was irreversible. The domestication of the wilderness, then, is visibly connected with the history of the individual family farm. The transformation of the distant slopes is equally impressive.

TRANSFORMATION OF THE FRONTIER

The plains of Iuni (Figures 1.8 and 1.9) bear witness to the growth of the settlement frontier, in five decades. Substantial areas of wooded grazing lands remain, but the noticeable feature is the occupation of a once empty plain and its transformation into family farms. In 1937 the fore slopes showed erosion and there were scars on the hills. There is no visible evidence of serious erosion anywhere in 1991. Even gentle slopes are terraced. This prospect is representative of newly settled lowland areas in Machakos. Yet the movement of farming households into the drier ecological zones of Kenya is sometimes claimed to have a deleterious impact on the environment. It need not.

GUARDIANS OF THE SLOPES

The north-east slope of Kiima Kimwe Hill shows, at close hand, the quality and comprehensiveness of conservation work (Figures 1.10 and 1.11). Woodlots (one already established in 1937) and farm boundaries carry quick-growing exotic trees, but on the terraces

FIGURE 1.4. Southern slopes, Iveti Hills, June–July(?) 1937. Map Sheet 162/2. GR 3083E, 98300N; Brg. 25°. (Photo: KNA: R. O. Barnes, 1937, photo 17. Reproduced by permission of Kenya National Archives.)

FIGURE 1.5. Southern slopes, Iveti Hills, January 1991. Map Sheet 162/2, GR 3083E, 98300N; Brg. 25°. (Photo: M. Mortimore)

FIGURE 1.6. Kyamunyuu, from Mumandu (Mbevo S.) hill, June—July(?) 1937. Map Sheet 162/2, GR 3096E, 98175N; Brg. 90°. (Photo: KNA: R. O. Barnes, 1937, photo 7. Reproduced by permission of Kenya National Archives.)

FIGURE 1.7. Kyamunyuu, from Mumandu (Mbevo S.) hill, January 1991. Map Sheet 162/2, GR 3096E, 48175N; Brg. 90°. (Photo: M. Mortimore)

FIGURE 1.8. Plains of Iuni, from Mumandu (Mbevo S.) hill, June–July(?) 1937. Map Sheet 162/2, GR 3096E, 98175N; Brg. 140°. (Photo: KNA: R. O. Barnes, 1937, photo 22. Reproduced by permission of Kenya National Archives.)

FIGURE 1.9. Plains of Iuni, from Mumandu (Mbevo S.) hill, January 1991. Map Sheet 162/2, GR 3096E, 98175N; Brg. 140°. (Photo: M. Mortimore)

FIGURE 1.10.Kiima Kimwe Hill (NE slope), June–July(?) 1937. Map Sheet 162/2, GR 3085E, 98296N; Brg. 110°. (Photo: KNA: R. O. Barnes, 1937, photo 18. Reproduced by permission of Kenya National Archives.)

FIGURE 1.11.Kiima Kimwe Hill (NE slope), January 1991. Map Sheet 162/2, GR 3084E, 98295N; Brg. 110°. (Photo: M. Mortimore)

appear bananas and other fruits. Embankments are maintained with care and patches of grassland are not eroded. Prosperous looking homesteads give a hint of productivity, and also house the labour — mostly women's — that bears the credit for this transformation, from what was largely a treeless slope (of 25° or more) in 1937.

These photographs encapsulate the paradox of Machakos. Dryland farming, then (and now) so commonly perceived to entail degradation — with growing numbers of people and of livestock — has been turned towards a new logic of sustainability. In this book we attempt to answer the questions: when, how and why?

NOTES

1 The Akamba are a Bantu tribe who form the main inhabitants of Machakos and Kitui Districts.
2 See, for example: Munro (1975), Wisner (1977), Otieno (1984), Silberfein (1989). However, Kimambo, (1970, quoted in Wisner, 1977) admits the possibility of vegetational degradation in pre-colonial Kitui: 'After about a century and a half . . . of hunters' fire, of grazing by Galla and Kamba herds, and through the inexhaustible hunger of elephant hordes, the vegetation of Kitui began to decline.' While the compression of the Akamba into a narrow Reserve undoubtedly contributed to the environmental crisis of the 1930s and 1940s, we shall show that other factors were also at work, including long-term weather cycles and population growth unaccompanied by market stimuli.

2

The District and the Study

OBJECTIVES

This book explores the relationship between increasing population density, productivity and environmental degradation, through a case study of Machakos District, in south-east Kenya, over the period 1930−1990. It seeks to measure the changes that have taken place, to interpret them in the context of a development theory, and to derive policy lessons that may have relevance elsewhere. Its principal findings are that population increase is compatible with environmental recovery from the degradation illustrated in Chapter 1, provided that market developments make farming profitable. There has been an approximate threefold increase in the value of output per capita, and a tenfold increase in the value of output per hectare. Population growth with new market opportunities has stimulated investment and innovation, but in a semi-arid area some of the necessary capital has had to be generated outside agriculture.

These findings are important in the context of the debates generated by the United Nations Conference on Environment and Development (UNCED) at Rio de Janeiro in 1992. They are at odds with some common assumptions, generally made on the basis of studies that have covered a shorter period, which assume that there has been little increase in agricultural productivity in Africa; that increased commercial production harms food supplies; that out-migration is all negative; that development depends overwhelmingly on government initiatives and aid support; and that population growth means fewer trees and harms the environment. The study shows the need for government facilitation of development by farmers and other rural entrepreneurs through policies which aid information flows (education as well as extension) and raise farm-gate prices (for example, transport improvements and minimisation of marketing costs), and through the types of consultation that secure dialogue between local people and government experts in diagnosing constraints and in removing impediments to innovation and change. It shows that population growth in agricultural areas renders change in farming and income systems inevitable since the old systems are not viable in the new circumstances. Farmers can adapt by innovation and investment and can develop new sustainable systems, but government policies can either impede or assist this process. Where there is a high degree of market integration there is also diversification of the local economy and an expansion of non-farm income-earning opportunities.

In such a study it is important to define the meaning given to such terms as development, sustainability and conservation. Our definitions are therefore set out in the Appendix to this chapter

There are two major schools of thought on environmental *degradation*. The first is primarily concerned with the natural environment and species diversity. In this sense, natural climax vegetation is good, and its replacement by farming is bad. There is no doubt that this replacement has taken place in Machakos, and that the rhinoceros has been displaced by man. However, there are two large national parks bordering the District, and a third small one within it, which conserve the natural fauna and flora. The second position, which we take, considers that degradation is the degeneration of the natural resource base to a point where the costs of restoring it to a level where it can support people at a reasonable standard of living become prohibitively high. This school of thought accepts that there is a natural resilience in the environment, which can be destroyed in certain circumstances. Variation in productive capacity over the short term may arise from physical, economic or social causes, for example, short-term changes in rainfall; changing market conditions which mean that investments to restore fertility levels become uneconomic; warfare, etc. Good farming is an activity which regularly depletes, then restores or improves fertility. In economic terms, the replacement of natural vegetation by sustainable farming systems, which over time maintain an adequate level of nutrient replacement, and which conserve soil and water in forms useful to man, is not degradation, but *development*, as we have defined it. The aim of policy then becomes the design of conditions in which the necessary investments in maintaining the productivity of the natural resource base are made.

Our focus is on a semi-arid environment. In the wake of the African droughts of the 1970s and 1980s, the setting up of the United Nations Environment Programme with its Desertification Branch on African soil, and the widespread publicity given by the international media to the desertification hypothesis, sustainability has come to challenge productivity as a stated objective of rural development, especially in drylands. Two overriding questions arise concerning (i) the compatibility of sustainable resource management with rapid population growth, and (ii) the possibility of turning a degradational cycle towards conservation under such conditions. Our definition of *sustainable management* as given in the Appendix stresses the maintenance or improvement of the properties of land and water, by methods which include *conservation*.

Alongside the sustainability debate goes a new politico-economic agenda which calls for the withdrawal of the state from many forms of direct action, in favour of creating an 'enabling environment' for private and community initiative. The rural landscape is managed by large and small farmers, as well as government, and we include all these in our definition of *dryland management*. A further question, therefore, concerns the necessary role for the state in the successful reversal of environmental degradation. At one extreme lies compulsion, at the other laissez-faire. In between lie a range of activities from subsidies and food-for-work schemes to the simple provision of education and the kind of infrastructure which makes private investment profitable. The policy debate continues against a background of widespread ignorance of the processes of change in the past, and of the part played by natural forces such as cyclical weather patterns on the one hand, and human activities on the other.

There has long been a belief that a given agro-ecological zone has a population-supporting capacity which cannot be exceeded without environmental degradation. Since Allan (1965) discussed this in relation to Africa it has been modified to incorporate different levels of agricultural technology (see, for example, Higgins et al, 1982) and, more rarely, by the supposition that part of the population will be supported by non-farm occupations. The dangers of exceeding this 'scientifically' assessed carrying capacity are used to justify government intervention to regulate land use. It is clear that agricultural output per unit of land varies according to agro-ecological zone if technology, crop mixes and capital investment are held constant. However, rising population density combined with access to new knowledge means that these things do not stay constant; rising population density facilitates access to new markets, new knowledge and new technologies.

Population growth in Kenya, which has been amongst the highest in the world, has led to fears that, even if there is some ability to adapt to the changes made necessary by changed land/labour ratios, farmers cannot cope when annual growth rates are far above the 1−2% per annum experienced in Western countries in the past. This was already noted in the 1960s:

> Though African populations have shown a certain capacity to adjust spontaneously to changing conditions as they perceive them, the fact of the matter is that today they are not adjusting satisfactorily to the slow but steady deterioration of their natural environment. In the face of gradually increasing population pressure and rising standard of living expectations, timely government action is absolutely essential (de Wilde, 1967, Vol.1: 225. Reproduced by permission of The Johns Hopkins University Press)

That conclusion, and the emphasis on the necessity of direct government action, would still be accepted by many. Looking back over six decades of such interventions in Machakos, there seem to have been three stages implicit in the way the Government sought to do this.

(1) Diagnosis. It was characteristic of recorded experience in Machakos that the Government and its technical officers, and not farmers or community leaders, took the dominant role in identifying problems.
(2) Prescription. Technical considerations took priority over economic in prescribing the solutions. (The labour, cost and price factors were rarely investigated thoroughly before promotion, for example, of terrace construction, and cotton production.)
(3) Intervention. Extension had to be top-down, to persuade the farmers to adopt the new technologies. (Frustration resulted if the promoted technologies were regarded by the farmers, as they sometimes were, as inappropriate solutions to inaccurately diagnosed problems.)

Failure of this diagnosis−prescription−intervention model, criticised by Mbithi (1971a), led predictably to a fourth stage, a search for culpability, usually resulting in the identification of exogenous factors, such as growth of population, colonial marginalisation, inherited cultural attitudes. Blame was also put on the inadequacy of the available government resources.[1] Yet government expenditures have been high, and have only been sustained by foreign aid. Government and external observers repeatedly made an assessment of failure, or at best, only very limited success. Thus, after the considerable government investments of funds and skilled personnel in the period 1946−1962, P. F. M. McLoughlin (the main author of the Machakos case study in de Wilde's (1967) study) concluded:

> ... standards of agriculture have remained very low over most of the district; virtually no improvement has taken place in animal husbandry. The Kamba who inhabit the district have often been reproached for their lack of interest in agriculture and their unresponsiveness to government efforts to change them. (de Wilde, 1967, Vol.2: 84.)

> ... The record in Machakos has not been one of unmitigated failure. The partial rehabilitation of land resources, coupled probably with some improvements in agricultural practices, has enabled the district to cope more effectively with the problem of feeding its growing population. In the higher areas coffee has provided a growing source of cash income; in the dryer areas sisal planting has given people some insurance against crop failure and enabled them to earn substantial cash income when sisal prices are high. Here and there other signs of progress may be noted. By and large, however, the record has been disappointing. Development has encountered many difficulties. (de Wilde, 1967, Vol 2: 117−18. Reproduced by permission of The Johns Hopkins University Press.)

Entry into the world economy and 'marginalisation' were blamed by other observers for the overflow of population into the more arid areas of the District, which was predicted to lead to man-made famine (Wisner, 1977). Another study saw failures in land resource management evidenced by various indicators, including the breakdown of the old indigenous farming systems (Bernard, in Consortium, Report 6, 1978), a breakdown we have interpreted positively as the evolution of new systems.

The diagnosis—prescription—intervention model has so dominated the history of dryland management in Machakos since 1930 that it is important to emphasise, at the outset, the different perspective of the present study. Our starting hypothesis is that during the period 1930—1990, a trend of degradation was turned towards sustainability in resource management. The long view — 60 years — directs analytical attention away from an *intervention—response* framework, to a confrontation with the *processes* of economic and environmental change. Such an attempt is regrettably rare in the development studies literature and tradition. When economic history is undertaken, the environmental variables may receive inadequate attention and the interactions between the economic, institutional and environmental variables are poorly understood. (This reflects the professional polarisation of the social and natural sciences, and not — as any field observer can appreciate — the experience of those who live on and work the land.) There is as yet no discipline of environmental history, and the concepts, models and techniques of reconstruction are patchily developed. Even on the ground, successive visitors and even resident staff were rarely able clearly to perceive the tone and pace of change. Those who could — in this case, the Akamba elders — were not often asked. Merely documenting change, in any case, is not enough. A 'process focus' implies a search for theory, with which this book concludes.

WHY CHOOSE MACHAKOS DISTRICT?

Our objective was to test hypotheses on the relationship between population growth and environmental conservation or degradation in a specific area where data were available for objective measurements of change over at least three long cycles in rainfall (i.e. about 60 years). The longitudinal perspective was essential because conclusions based on short periods could be vitiated by rainfall effects. Machakos District, Kenya, recommended itself because of its relevance to the questions under study and because of the information and data available. In particular, reports from the 1930s provided a baseline. Studies during the period 1958—1964, especially those of Peberdy (1958, 1961), Heyer (1966), de Wilde (1967) and Owako (1969), provide a mid-point record, which coincided with the important political and economic changes of Independence in 1963.

Lele and Stone in their comparative study of agricultural intensification at the *national* level in several African countries, identified Kenya as a country where a shift of policy emphasis to higher value crops and more productive land has been successfully supported by agricultural pricing, marketing, land reform and crop research policies. They attribute Kenya's relative economic success to these policies and associated government interventions, rather than to the free response of farmers to the market forces associated with population growth (Lele and Stone, 1989: 7). They consider that Kenya has, correctly, given priority to the development of its high-potential areas. We examine, at *district* level, an area with a high proportion of what in Kenyan terms is low-potential or marginal land within the same general national policy environment. The major limitation of analysis at the macro level is that farming systems having entirely different land per capita ratios and agro-ecological and technical characteristics are merged. Intensification may be demonstrable statistically but this may tell us little of the functional evolution of the systems, the process which policy seeks to direct.

Ultimately, a study of this kind is justified by the replicability of the experience elsewhere. Here we must steer cautiously between extremes. Unproven generalisation has always been an enemy of deeper understanding of Africa's environmental problems. De Wilde (1967) argued the case for agricultural development solutions to be tailored to time and place. All places are unique, and perhaps few more so than Machakos, with its special combination of dryness, bimodal rainfall, altitude, relatively good access to major cities (Nairobi and Mombasa), and cultural characteristics. Yet some lessons in dryland management have application outside the District. Our objective in Part IV of this book is to identify these lessons, and to set them in the context of a coherent theory of development under conditions of population growth.

Before setting out the structure of the study and the methodology we have employed, we provide some basic information about the District.

MACHAKOS DISTRICT

Early history, boundaries and administrative structures

The Akamba people are believed to have first occupied some uplands of Machakos during the 17th and 18th centuries. They lived by raising livestock (especially cattle) and cultivating shifting fields of grain and pulses, and by trade, their caravans linking them with coastal Akamba communities and with the Kikuyu. In 1889 the Europeans arrived, and a treaty was signed. Soon after, a British East Africa Company fort was built, and mission stations followed. In 1895, the British Protectorate of East Africa was declared, and in 1899 its capital was moved from Machakos to Nairobi. Chiefs began to be paid in 1897, and in 1901 the hut tax was imposed. In 1906, the Native Reserve was created, putting a barrier to the expansionary tendencies of the Akamba, as depicted in Figure 1.1. The Akamba particularly resented some further losses during 1908−1910 of small but useful amounts of land which they had understood to be assigned to them in 1906 (Munro, 1975: 77−79). They recovered the disputed land after 1962 (Chapter 4). Part of the Tsavo National Park was excised from the southern part after 1969.

The District forms part of Kenya's Eastern Province (and in the 1950s, was part of what was called Southern Province). It is in the charge of a District Commissioner (DC) and is sub-divided into Divisions, each headed by a Divisional Officer (DO), Locations (headed by a government-appointed Chief) and Sub-locations with an Assistant Chief. Increases in the number of locations, and changes in their divisional groupings, have occurred from time to time. In 1992 the southern part became the separate Makueni District. We have taken the administrative situation as given in the 1979 census as our standard for most purposes. Figure 2.3 identifies the 1979 Locations. Our study therefore relates to the District as defined between 1962 and 1992, unless the specific reference is to the Reserve. The District contained a population of about 1.4 million in 1989, of whom about 8% were urbanised, living in Machakos Township, Athi River (really an outpost of Nairobi) and a few smaller townships. The District remains mainly dependent on agriculture, but its population derives substantial income from non-farm earnings inside and outside the boundary.

Topography, rainfall and agro-ecological zones

The centre of the District contains several hill masses rising steeply to 1800—2100 m, which are surrounded by a plateau, in places deeply dissected, which slopes gradually downwards from about 1700 m in the north-west to 700 m in the south-east (Figure 2.1). In the north the isolated mountain, Ol Doinyo Sabuk, rises to 2144 m and, in the south, the Chyulu volcanic range reaches 2392 m. On the east side of the Athi River, the Yatta Plateau (a volcanic lava flow) forms an escarpment, backed by a gently inclined eastward-sloping surface. Other than the volcanic formations, the hills are mostly formed of granitic rocks of the Basement Complex, schists and gneisses. The soils are deeply weathered, except where eroded on steep slopes, or where unweathered rock outcrops in the hill escarpments. As would be expected in an area of such topographical and climatic diversity, the soils are varied (Sombroek et al, 1982). Most of the tributaries of the Athi are seasonal. The limited availability of perennial domestic and livestock water has influenced settlement patterns.

Precipitation patterns are critically important for farming and livestock production, and for recharging the groundwater and river systems. Average annual rainfall increases with altitude, and also declines, from the central hills outwards, from 1200 mm at nearly 2000 m altitude in the Mbooni Hills to less than 600 mm in the lowlands of the south-east and the dry plains of the extreme north-west (see Figure 2.2). The regime is bimodal, with rainy seasons normally occurring in March—May (the 'long' rains) and October—December (the 'short' rains). Two agricultural seasons occur, therefore, both of short duration.

Evaporation increases with temperatures downslope, so that a complex pattern of climatic or ecological zones has evolved. These are important for understanding the agricultural activity. Two classifications are available in Kenya — that of Sombroek et al, (1982), called *agroclimatic zones* (ACZ), and that of Jaetzold and Schmidt (1983), called *agro-ecological zones* (AEZ). In addition to rainfall, temperature and evaporation, the AEZ system also takes soil properties into account, and is related to the length and intensity of the growing season for crop and livestock production. It has therefore been adopted for the present study but we have amalgamated the number of zones in Machakos to form three groups, described as 2/3, 4 and 5/6.[2] These are shown in Figure 2.3. Each Location was assigned to its predominant AEZ, so that socio-economic data could be related to agro-ecological conditions. The variability and small amount of rainfall means that water conservation has a strong effect on productivity.

Under undisturbed conditions (now rare), the natural vegetation of the greater part of the District consists of thorny woodland dominated by *Acacia* spp., or *Commiphora* spp. The woodland contains thickets and develops into gallery forest along streams. On higher sites, *Combretum* woodland takes over, and on the tops of the hills, evergreen forest used to be found. Grassland occurs on black clay soils and areas of impeded drainage (KNA: Parsons, 1952; KNA: Trapnell, 1958). These communities have been removed (for cultivation) or modified (under grazing and woodcutting) over wide areas.

The economic and political environment

Even today, the best road and the only railway skirt the western boundary of the District, serving the former European farmed areas with their low population densities rather than the densely settled African areas (Figure 2.4). An improved road from Nairobi reached the northern Reserve boundary near Kangundo in the 1950s, which also had a connection to Thika, a centre for food

19

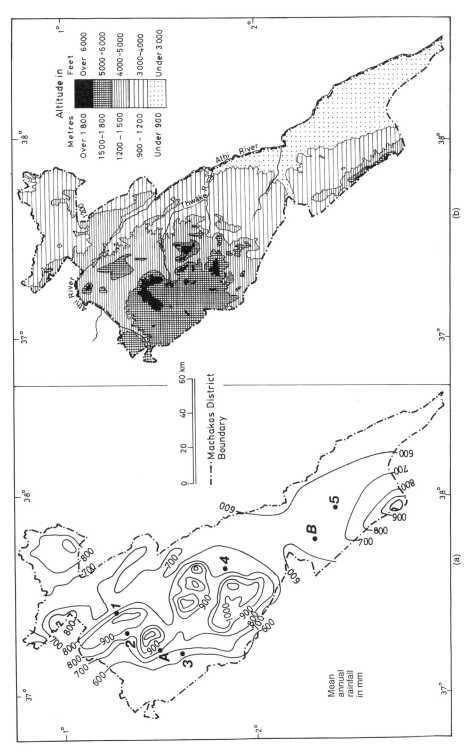

FIGURE 2.1. (a) Rainfall and (b) relief. Rainfall stations: A, Machakos; B, Makindu; 1, Kabaa; 2, Kangundo; 3, Katumani; 4, Kampi ya Mawe; 5, Kibwezi

20

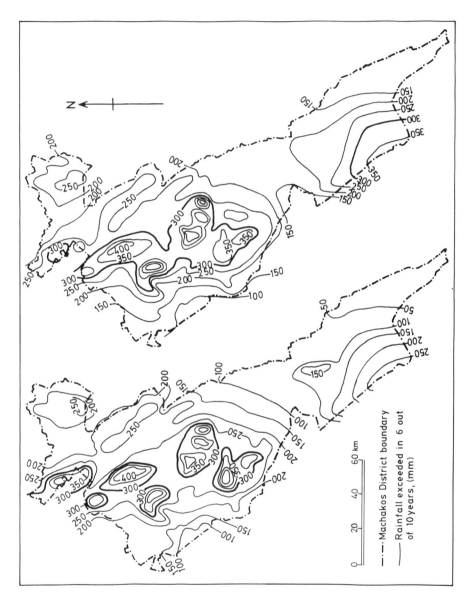

FIGURE 2.2. Rainfall probability in the long rains (left) and short rains (right) (after Jaetzold and Schmidt, 1983)

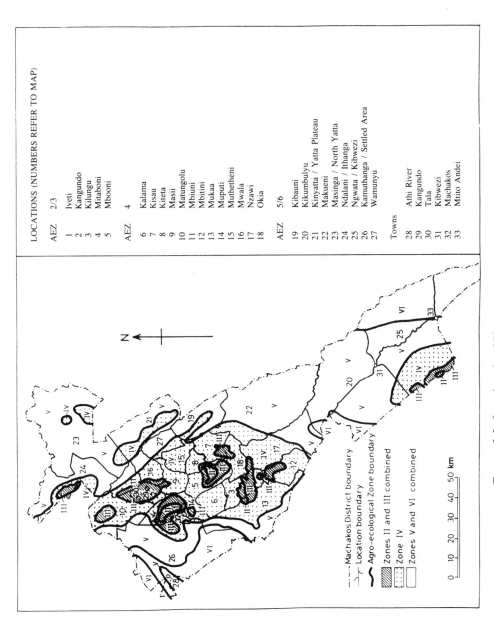

LOCATIONS (NUMBERS REFER TO MAP)

AEZ 2/3

1 Iveti
2 Kangundo
3 Kilungu
4 Mitaboni
5 Mbooni

AEZ 4

6 Kalama
7 Kisau
8 Kiteta
9 Masii
10 Matungolu
11 Mbiuni
12 Mbitini
13 Mukaa
14 Muputi
15 Muthetheni
16 Mwala
17 Nzawi
18 Okia

AEZ 5/6

19 Kibauni
20 Kikumbulyu
21 Kinyatta / Yatta Plateau
22 Makueni
23 Masinga / North Yatta
24 Ndalani / Ithanga
25 Ngwata / Kibwezi
26 Kamuthanga / Settled Area
27 Wamunyu

Towns

28 Athi River
29 Kangundo
30 Tala
31 Kibwezi
32 Machakos
33 Mtito Andei

----- Machakos District boundary
Location boundary
Agro-ecological Zone boundary

Zones II and III combined
Zone IV
Zones V and VI combined

0 10 20 30 40 50 km

FIGURE 2.3. Locations in 1979 and agro-ecological zones (AEZ)

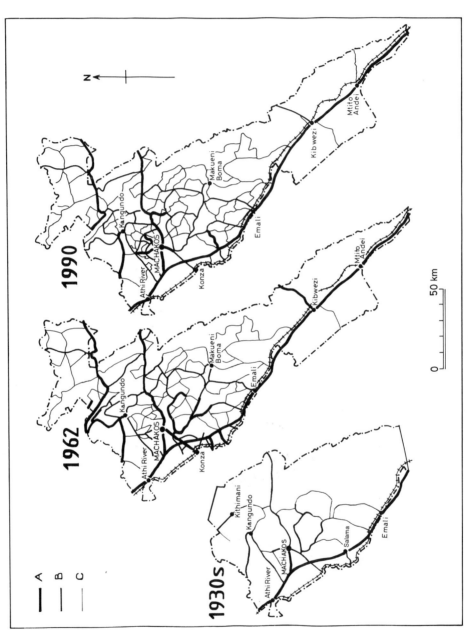

FIGURE 2.4. Roads and railway development. A: All weather roads, bonded (1930s), class 1 (1962), tarred (1990). B: All weather roads, loose (1930s), class 2 (1962), gravel (1990). C: Other roads and tracks. Sources: Morgan (1962), Forbes Munro (1975: 175), ADEC (1986) and others.

processing and tanning industries. Classified roads became a central government responsibility after 1963. There was surprisingly little change from 1963 to 1989.[3] Development in Machakos remains constrained by bad internal roads.

The early 1930s found a dual economy in Kenya, in which strict territorial demarcation gave European settlers and African smallholders unequal access to land and markets. It was also an economy in depression. Driven by the export prices of agricultural commodities (mostly produced in the European large-scale sector), the collapse of these prices led to a reduction in purchasing power which depressed the prices of output for the domestic market, much of it produced by the African smallholder sector. In particular, cattle prices during 1932–1934 fell to a fifth of their level ten years earlier, according to indices compiled by Stanmer in Kitui (van Zwanenberg, 1974). Cattle were the most important element in contemporary Akamba farming systems.

The colonial government's land policies were subject to two lobbies. The settlers, and their United Kingdom backers, wanted the utmost security for European land holdings, and if possible, their expansion. But some people in the United Kingdom, at times with the predominant influence in the Colonial Office, regarded colonies as trusteeships where the rights of the 'natives' had to be protected. The allocation of land was therefore always a contentious issue. (See Peberdy (1958), Munro (1975), Silberfein (1989), Wisner (1977), Anderson (1984) and Throup (1987). The latter two are particularly useful in showing the way conservation issues were used by the settlers to promote their cause in agricultural policy debates.) The Kenya Land Commission (Carter Commission), which visited Machakos in 1932, did not satisfy Akamba claims, and maintained government control over the unsettled Crown Land. The Akamba remained acutely suspicious of the Government's intentions.

Akamba tenure was already notably individualised in so far as land once cultivated was concerned, and also permitted exclusive temporary rights of use of grazing areas (see Chapter 5). After the publication of the Swynnerton Plan in 1954, the government encouraged consolidation of scattered plots and individually registered titles (Swynnerton, 1954). The start of registration was delayed in Machakos until 1968 because of opposition to consolidation. However, land titling was not a prior condition of agricultural development because Akamba traditional law already protected individual investment.

The 1960 Lancaster House conference, which envisaged independence for Kenya, resulted in an exodus of many Europeans. The Million Acre Scheme, providing for the orderly division of large mixed farms into smallholdings, was launched in 1962, but applied only to the small Mua hills area of Machakos, since most European land in the District had been ranches, for which the policy was to retain them as large-scale units. The main land change in Machakos was an unplanned, unsupervised surge of families into the Crown Lands.

Government control over African land was justified by its concern about the degradation which was increasingly apparent as human and livestock populations grew in the limited Reserve area. A succession of reports and visits to Machakos from 1929 onwards, led up to an attempted forceful destocking by compulsory cattle sales in 1938, which had to be reversed after an Akamba sit-down in Nairobi. After World War II a further attack on land degradation was made with the drawing up of a Ten Year Development Plan and large government investments during the period 1946–1962. Machakos received the lion's share of funds devoted to African lands. Compulsory communal work was organised for terracing and grass-planting, and large areas were closed to grazing. The transition to voluntary, farmer-led investments in a technology of their own choice is described in Chapter 11.

With Independence in 1963 the Kenya African National Union party (KANU) came to power with a policy of 'African socialism'. Nevertheless, its manifesto stated 'Every farmer must be sure of his land rights'. Free enterprise and foreign investment were encouraged in the commercial and industrial sectors, although there were natural moves to encourage Africanisation. Independence resulted in 'more hope, more confidence and more social mobility' which translated into a greater readiness to invest in agricultural productivity (Ruthenberg, 1966: 106–107) and to develop self-help. The beginnings of the new confidence in Machakos can be traced back to the return of 11 000 Akamba soldiers from the war in 1945 (Chapter 9).

War-time controls on marketing were retained by both the colonial and independent governments, resulting in the formation of statutory, centralised marketing organisations with monopoly control of most export crops, excluding horticulture, and some important domestic commodities. However, the Boards controlling the grain and livestock trades co-existed with a lively uncontrolled trade in the rural districts. The fostering of co-operatives began after the war and was the subject of a major Nordic-assisted effort after 1968. Kenya has been unusual in that most of its Marketing Boards have not aimed at price stabilisation, and pass a large share of the world market price to the farmer, after the deduction of marketing and initial processing costs. However, the take of the Boards and the Government increased in the 1980s (Chapter 15).

While most policies operate on a nation-wide basis, there have from time to time been differences in the amounts of resources directed to the large (or ex-European) farm sector as compared to the small farm sector, or as between the high potential and the semi-arid lands. At least until 1945, the European farmers secured most government attention, not only in marketing policies, but also in free veterinary services, and agricultural research directed at commodities such as tea and coffee which they produced. Drought, land degradation and the necessity for expensive famine relief impelled the provision of resources to the semi-arid areas, such as Machakos, in a major government investment in African land development (ALDEV) over the period 1946–1962. However, the 1954 Swynnerton Plan began a switch of resources to the higher-potential areas, which could provide quicker pay-offs, and this was accelerated by the Million Acre Scheme, which absorbed considerably more than half of all government expenditure on agriculture during the 1960s. The 1974–1976 drought returned attention to the lower-potential areas. Since 1978 different overseas agencies have committed funds in support of integrated rural development programmes for different semi-arid districts. Although Machakos secured the first of these, the European Community-financed Machakos Integrated Development Programme (MIDP) in 1978, funding was in the middle rank compared with other semi-arid districts (Chapter 15).

Kenya has witnessed several swings of the pendulum between the relative power of central and local government. The late 1920s saw the establishment of Local Native Councils (LNC) as rudimentary local authorities. The 1930s saw a more coercive approach when the LNC was obliged to divert some of its small funds to the central government's conservation priorities. From 1946 the Colonial Office in London promoted local government councils, community development, and co-operatives. The LNC ultimately evolved into a County Council, as an elected body raising local taxes to pay for government services and development. However, in 1969, President Kenyatta, wanting to strengthen central control through the Provincial Commissioners, transferred the major revenue source of the County Councils, together with control over primary education, health services and most roads, to the central government. Without major funds except some taxes on produce, County Councils were marginalised and had difficulty in carrying out their remaining duties in respect of minor roads, markets and community development, but they remain the only elected political body at the District level (Wallis, 1990).

Under President Moi the Central Government expanded its services at District level. The MIDP served as a model for a new policy of District Focus, announced in 1983. This was effective only in relation to special funds allocated to the District, mostly provided by external donors. Government budgets remained in the hands of policy-makers at headquarters in Nairobi, and were increasingly characterised by a high expenditure on staff and inadequate resources for operating and maintaining services.

Our story closes, as it began, with the District and national economy in depression, due in part to unfavourable world market conditions and in part to diminishing government effectiveness in delivering services while its take in taxes has increased. However, despite mistakes, policies have been, as Lele and Stone (1989) point out, sufficiently favourable to the small farmer to allow much to have been achieved in 60 years. The people of Machakos are able to face current difficulties from an enhanced resource base, not merely in terms of their physical environment, but also in terms of their own knowledge and skills. The steady development of that knowledge, in part a result of government and mission policies, but in part a result of their own determination to see their children educated, is one of the reasons why the successes achieved in Machakos cannot simply be ascribed to government action. To a considerable extent they have been, as we shall show, the result of individual and village-level investments and initiatives, in which some of the greatest government contributions have been indirect, via education, the keeping of the peace, and the provision of roads and water supplies.

STRUCTURE AND METHODOLOGY OF THE STUDY

Both the longitudinal nature of the study, and its major objective of learning from past experience, called for an interdisciplinary team (mainly from the University of Nairobi) working in collaboration with the co-ordinators (Overseas Development Institute, London). It included specialists in the following fields: agricultural economics; engineering and extension; climatology; economic history; geography; photogrammetry and surveying; range management; sociology; soil science and erosion. Others could justifiably have been included, since the number of insights that can be beneficial in such a multi-variate study appears to be almost infinite. It was found that interaction amongst the specialists generated fresh ideas, whose value to the study significantly extended that of their individual contributions.[4] The study also benefited significantly from the contribution of practical policy-makers at different levels, ranging from the Environment Department at the World Bank to the Ministry of Reclamation of Arid and Semi-Arid Lands and Wastelands in Kenya and the head of the community development services of the County Council. Community leaders were involved in five sample areas, where individual farmers were also visited and questioned. (The purpose of the interviews was to supplement, on a small scale, the earlier studies and not to embark on large socio-economic sample surveys. We therefore made sparing use of the farm-level data, but found the group-leader interviews very valuable.) The study began in July 1990 and concluded in Kenya with a workshop at Machakos in September 1991, which was attended by the study team, representatives of national, district and local government, and members of the farming community. The workshop was structured to ensure that all made inputs. It may be observed here that many farmers in Machakos — not only the 'progressive' ones — were found to be articulate enough to make individually significant contributions at all of these levels. Finally, a workshop was held in London to solicit feedback to preliminary results from other people whose experience in Kenya was relevant. (The preliminary results were published in a series of *ODI Working Papers* in 1991 and 1992, and consolidated in a shorter World Bank *Environment Paper* (English et al, in press)).

The study is divided into four parts, the first being this Introduction. Part II, 'Profiles of Change', quantifies as far as possible changes in rainfall; population; land tenure and use; agricultural production; soil erosion and fertility; and natural vegetation. From our analytical viewpoint, rainfall and population are treated as essentially independent variables, while the remainder are clearly management-dependent.

Profiles of change require reliable statistical series, or (if such are not available) baseline data against which subsequent changes may be measured. If neither are available, the best use must be made of indirect or piecemeal information from archival or other sources. Statistical measures of trends or cycles, which would allow change to be quantified, can be constructed only for a few variables. They are available from official sources for rainfall, population, and agricultural production, but the time intervals and reliability of these series varies. Rainfall data (other climatic data are peripheral to our objectives) are relatively accurate and can support full statistical analysis. Population data are relatively accurate but are, of course, only available for decennial censuses, and inter-census change must be inferred from the crude differences. Some production data are available annually but are known to be relatively inaccurate, and in view of this consideration, have to be used with care. For the remaining variables, there are no statistical series. Land use and vegetation change is estimated mainly from sequences of air photographs — three in number, approximately 15 years apart, during 30 years. For the soil, the most critical variable in our analysis, the database is weakest. Soil fertility investigations using baseline samples turned out to be inconclusive, and resort was made to a spatial analogue approach. The results are provisional. The difficulties experienced in constructing some of the profiles of change show the need for data series that permit the monitoring of change more accurately, more especially in environmental variables (other than the rainfall) where the work reported here provides, we hope, a starting point.

Our concern with the impact of population growth in land-use systems differs from the terms of the traditional debate about *output*, in being primarily concerned with resource *management*. But the two are closely related, so the terms of this debate, as originally set by Boserup (1965) and applied to farming systems by Ruthenberg (1980), Binswanger and McIntyre (1987), Pingali et al (1987) and others, are still relevant to us. Since management is concerned with the choice of technologies, we are also interested in the relationships between population growth and the rate of adoption of new technologies, as discussed by Simon (1986) and others. New technologies frequently demand new investments of labour and capital, and so we are concerned with incentives to invest, the mechanisms for raising capital and the information flows that assist in the evaluation of alternatives. Part III looks at institutional change amongst the managers (the Akamba and the Government) and at the evolution of management in relation to farming and income systems, and conservation of land, water and vegetation. It includes the conflict which has sometimes occurred between the different management parties in relation to both objectives and methods. The story of soil conservation is well documented but water conservation much less so. Soil and water conservation are at the heart of the study, and their relative success (albeit after many early failures) provides the District with its claim to fame in the conservation literature. By contrast, the realm of tree management (Chapter 13) received less attention until recently. Technological change (Chapter 14) is considered selectively, because the number of candidate technologies is great, in the light of current understanding of the sources and diffusion of technologies.

A large variety of sources have been used in order to reconstruct the profiles of management. These include: government and consultancy reports, theses, archives, published and unpublished papers; interviews with knowledgeable people; photographs; and field observations. The 30-year rule restricts access to archival materials, so government files since 1960 have not been seen. In any case, government files can only preserve the government view. The interviews with elderly community leaders, both men and women, in five sub-locations of Kangundo, Mbooni, Masii, Makueni and Ngwata Locations proved extremely valuable in understanding the Akamba view of change in their farming systems and community structures.

Having measured change quantitatively, and having found many changes to be positive, the final section, Part IV, deals with what worked and why, in terms of practical policy lessons and the theory of growth. The growth of population was the major changing variable throughout our period: in quantitative terms (a fivefold increase during six decades), in spatial terms (as older settled nuclei sent off branches to uninhabited land, Crown Lands were filled, and scheduled areas subdivided and resettled), and in economic terms (as the labour force grew in size and skills, diversified in occupations and participated in urban migration). It is entirely logical, therefore, to accord a central place to demographic growth in a developmental model for Machakos.

The only other variable whose impact is as far reaching is the rainfall, but no long-term trend has been found in the records (see Chapter 3). However, the average rainfall varies spatially, and when combined with altitude (or temperature) gives rise to the agro-ecological zones noted above. For the purpose of our development model, however, only two conditions need to be distinguished, higher- and lower-potential areas (on the gradient from AEZs 2 to 5). The model (Figure 2.5) derives essentially from Boserup (1965, 1981, 1990), but is adapted to take account of agro-ecological zonation. Population is first attracted to the higher-potential areas, where livelihoods can be earned with least effort. As the rural population grows, land per capita diminishes, the average farm becomes smaller, and household food sufficiency is threatened as farm incomes decline. The land degrades under extensive technology, as fallows shorten. A Malthusian outcome can be avoided by three strategies:

A. Permanent or short-term migration (circulation) to urban areas, or to non-agricultural occupations such as the police and the army. The main cost of this strategy is the private and social capital invested in schooling for the qualifications, if any, needed for employment. Security for personal movement is a precondition.

B. Permanent migration to lower-potential agricultural areas, maintaining the same agricultural technologies, but varying the mix of enterprises (for example, more livestock in drier zones). This strategy is costly, because the household will need farm equipment, new family housing and the means of surviving until the first harvest. Access to farmland, water and adequate security from wild animals are other preconditions. In time, as population grows and vacant land disappears, the conditions will be recreated for another choice of A, B or C.

C. Sustainable development *in situ*. This strategy breaks down into two options:

  (i) Agricultural intensification, including both farming and livestock production technologies, and accompanied by measures to conserve the land and water resources. For this option, capital is needed for land improvements, new technologies, and improved livestock. Not all of these investments can be created by extra family labour, so transfers of capital from members of the household who have earlier adopted option A can facilitate

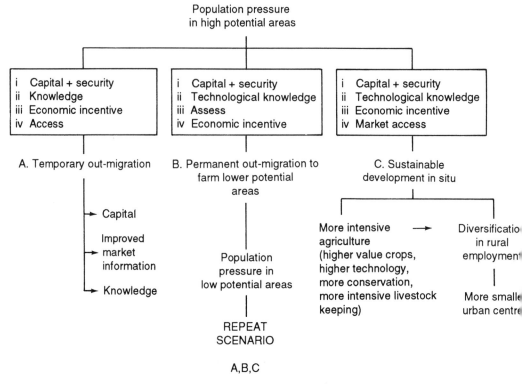

FIGURE 2.5. A developmental model for Machakos

this choice. Given the level of investment and enhanced value of the land, cash incomes must be generated, so crops are grown for sale. This needs market access. Investment also requires a secure form of tenure.

(ii) Income diversification, linked to market growth and the opportunities for employment in the processing, trading and transporting of farm output, and to service provision as living standards slowly rise.

The link between the adoption of conservation technology and intensification (option C(i)) is particularly important for the present study. According to the logic of the model, conservation pays when land becomes scarce under existing technological conditions. The construction of terraces, for example, if left to farmers' choice, should follow agricultural colonisation with a time-lag determined by the build-up of land scarcity. (The land per capita ratio *per se* is not the governing variable since every holding must if possible include grazing land in order to support draft animals and other stock. A shortage therefore becomes acute when cultivated land is still a small proportion of the whole (say 30%). However, this depends on both the agro-ecological zone and the technology used in livestock feeding.)

It is argued in this study that the growth of population, working conjointly through an increase in the labour force and the growth of markets, has driven agricultural intensification on the smallholdings, and that this intensification has characteristically taken the form of investments in sustainable technologies and management. Investment funds transferred from other sectors have themselves been generated by a diversification of incomes, made possible — and necessary — by high household fertility. Population growth, in so far as it reflects individual decisions on fertility, was (for much of our period) a rational response to the opportunities created by the urbanising, export-oriented, land-rich economy of Kenya. The strength of Akamba claims to land has added to its growing scarcity, so that its long-term conservation — rather than degradation — has become a necessary outcome of demographic growth. Technological change has been governed by this process, and the success or failure of a government's or others' interventions in either conservationary or productive technologies can best be understood in terms of congruence between the government's development objectives and the needs of farming households. Other technological change has been introduced as a result of people's own observations, experiments and exchanges of information.

We suggest, therefore, that a diagnosis–prescription–intervention mode is inadequate on its own (and more so if a top-down stance is taken); that the time-scale appropriate to the management of drylands is in decades, not in years; that a process mode is inescapable if change is to be understood and interventions are to succeed in promoting sustainable management; and that this will come about only with the participation of the local population in policy formulation and the identification of appropriate technologies.

APPENDIX: DEFINITIONS

- *Agricultural intensification* is increased average inputs of labour or capital on a smallholding, either on cultivated land alone, or on cultivated and grazing land, for the purpose of increasing the value of output per hectare. Value to the farmer may be for either consumption or marketing.
- *Development* is understood to mean the growth of real incomes and welfare; agricultural development is the growth in farm output and productivity.
- *Conservation* is taken to mean the retention of soil and water in places useful to man. It can be by the creation of structures, whether temporary or permanent, or by other methods.
- *Degradation* includes both the loss of soil by erosion and losses of soil productivity under cultivation or grazing by failure to replace nutrients or the modification of its physical properties. The term 'desertification' is not employed in the present study. Apart from the controversy surrounding its use (see Warren and Agnew, 1988; Mortimore, 1989a; Nelson, 1990) its inappropriateness to Machakos arises from the dominance of water (rather than wind) erosion in dictating the agenda for dryland management, and the lack of any proximate desert.
- *Dryland management* includes land management by smallholders, large landholders, or government in areas defined as arid or semi-arid.
- *Sustainable management* is the maintenance or improvement, over several years (of fluctuating rainfall), of soil chemical and physical properties on cultivated land, of pasture productivity on grazing land, of farm trees and regenerating woodland communities, and of groundwater recharge, compared with conditions at a chosen baseline (or the commencement of a period of study or observation). Such a functional definition does not call for an estimation of the biological productivity of the pristine ecosystem, or the biological properties of the soils, both of which may be impossible and which are, in practical terms, irrelevant to management objectives.

NOTES

1 The de Wilde study concluded that the staff and resources were never adequate to the need for patient efforts to diagnose what the farmers' problems were; to devise the proper solutions for these problems; and to persuade the farmers to adopt them (de Wilde, 1967, Vol.2: 99).

2 The Jaetzold classification takes the form of a matrix of seven altitudinal (temperature) strata upon seven precipitation strata. Of the cells, 10 occur in Machakos District. We have grouped these into three simplified zones as follows: LH2 and 3 + UM2 and 3 = AEZ 2/3, LM3 + UM4 + LM4 = AEZ 4, UM5 and 6 + LM5 and 6 = AEZ 5/6 (Jaetzold and Schmidt, 1983).

3 By the latter date Machakos had only 0.04 km of bitumen roads, and 0.2 km of roads of all grades per km^2 (Kenya, Ministry of Planning, 1988). This compares with about 2 km of roads per km^2 in Scotland, which has a lower population density.

4 Multidisciplinary collaboration, if it is to result in more than parallel but independent specialist contributions, requires (in our experience) formal and informal opportunities for interaction (e.g. workshops/working groups with defined agendas; joint investigations in the field).

PART II

PROFILES OF CHANGE

3

Rainfall[1]

INTRODUCTION

Environmental change in the study area can be represented in the form of positive or negative trends over time or as random or cyclical variability. It can result from the operation of both exogenous and endogenous factors. Critical among the first group is the rainfall, over which neither people nor government can exercise any control. We need to be able to distinguish the effects of rainfall variation from those resulting from the interacting decisions of individuals, households, communities and government, if we are to interpret environmental change in the past, and assess policy interventions for the future.

In this chapter, the records for five stations are examined in conjunction with earlier published studies. They reveal no evidence of a long-term trend in rainfall, but clear evidence of inter-annual and within-season variability. This random variability, which is the principal characteristic of the rainfall from a management perspective, was (since records began in 1892) superimposed on cycles of 9–11 years (for the long rains) and 16–22 years (for the short rains). The profile of rainfall indicates that this critical variable is neither better nor worse today than in the past; low and erratic rainfall remains the overwhelming constraint on dryland management. A chronology of droughts is constructed, using a rainfall (or drought) index, which provides a consistent measure of drought severity in the area as a whole.

The hilly terrain strongly influences rainfall distribution (Mutiso, 1988), favouring the central hill masses (see Figure 2.1). The rainfall in Machakos District, like other areas of eastern Kenya, is characterised by small total amounts, strongly seasonal distribution, and high temporal and spatial variation from year to year and from season to season. The easterly trade winds and the intertropical convergence (ITC) are the major rain-producing agents. The NE trades blow from December to February, with a maximum development in January; and the SE trades blow from May to September, with a maximum in July. Usually, there is a strong association of the ITC with rainfall and of the trade winds with dry conditions. The movements of the ITC result in two distinct wet seasons, namely the short rains (October–December), and the long rains (March–May), with a comparatively dry period between them.

TRENDS AND CYCLES

Downing and his colleagues (1988a: 154–163) carried out an investigation of secular rainfall trends in Machakos together with two neighbouring Districts (Kirinyaga and Embu). Four station series were used: for Embu, Kerugoya, Machakos Town and Makindu. Eleven-year running means were plotted to smooth the series. They found, taking all four stations together:

> There does not appear to be a widespread general trend in the smoothed series. In every case, the range of annual rainfall is much greater than the difference between one average mean and the next. Thus, there is no evidence on the time scale of the next decade or so of significant changes in the climatic parameters. (Downing et al, 1988a: 155.)

In order to test this conclusion at a larger number of stations within the District, the rainfall series for the years 1957–1990 were plotted for five additional stations (shown as 1–5 on Figure 2.2). These range from AEZ 3 (Kangundo, with over 900 mm annual rainfall) through Kabaa (731 mm) to AEZ 4 (Katumani and Kampi ya Mawe, with 717 and 698 mm), and AEZ 5 (Kibwezi, with 641 mm). Regressions of seasonal rainfall on year produced a range of values, but no evidence of a generalised, significant trend (Mutiso et al, 1991).

In Sahelian Africa a significant reduction in mean annual rainfall occurred after 1970 (Farmer and Wigley, 1985), amounting to over 30% in some areas, for example, northern Nigeria (Mortimore, 1989a). To test this possibility in Machakos District, mean seasonal rainfall during the periods 1957–1971 (15 years) and 1972–1990 (19 years) was compared for the five stations. The differences between the two periods are randomly variable and not significant (Mutiso et al, 1991).

With regard to cycles, Downing et al (1988a) found little conclusive evidence in the rainfall pattern, when analysed through an 11-year running mean. We derived five-year running means, for 1959–1988 from the rainfall records for October–December and March–May, 1957–1990, at the five stations used in the present study, and also for Makindu (one of the stations used by Downing). Figure 3.1 shows these. Without having recourse to statistical analysis, the running means display unmistakable evidence of a cycle of 9–11 years in the long rains at all six stations, with two completed cycles having peaks in 1967–1968 and 1977–1979, and troughs in 1973 and 1982–1985. In the short rains the six station series conform to a longer cycle of 16–22 years, declining from a peak in 1962–1963 to a trough in 1970–1974, and rising again to a peak in 1984 (1988 at one station). A longer series is needed in order to confirm the existence of the 16–22 year cycle. Figure 3.2 shows the 5-year running mean for each season separately at Machakos Town from 1892 to 1986, confirming both cycles over a longer period. However, the differences between the running means and the values for individual seasons confirm the conclusion of Downing and his colleagues that such cycles have limited predictive value for agricultural practice. Variability, and not long-term change, is the important characteristic of the rainfall.

VARIABILITY

The statistical properties of recorded rainfall are the best guide to expectations (see Figure 2.2). Rainfall reliability in each of the two seasons — the long rains and the short rains — closely resembles the spatial pattern of annual rainfall. The seasonal probabilities and those for the agricultural year (October to September) at Machakos and Makindu are summarised in Table 3.1 (after Downing et al, 1988a: 156). The majority of crops are single-season annuals. But it should be noted that some long-season crops, notably pigeon pea, are planted in the short rains and harvested after the long rains, with an agricultural year, therefore, extending from October to May of the following calendar year. What is clear is that only a small proportion

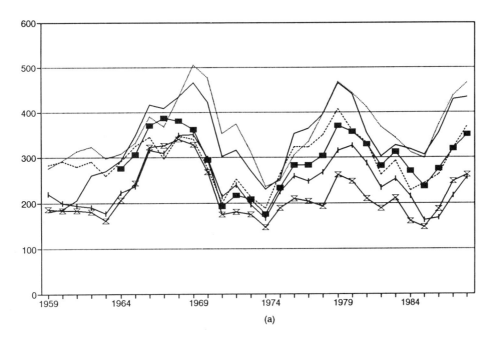

(a)

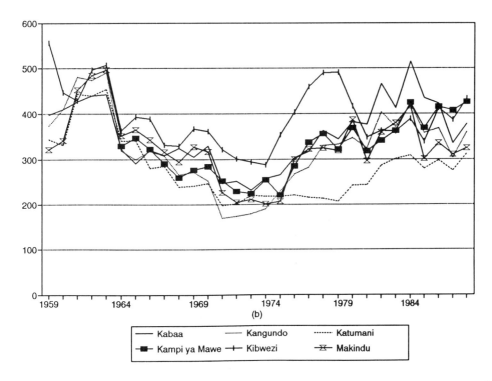

(b)

—— Kabaa	⋯⋯ Kangundo	⋯⋯⋯ Katumani
■—■ Kampi ya Mawe	+— Kibwezi	⨯—⨯ Makindu

FIGURE 3.1. Seasonal rainfall at five stations, 1957−1988 (five-year running means). (a) Long rains (March−May); (b) short rains (October−December)

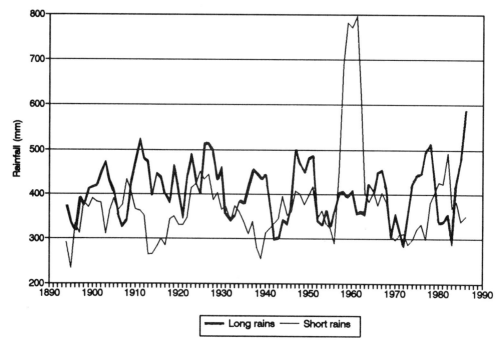

FIGURE 3.2. Seasonal rainfall at Machakos Town, 1894—1988 (five-year running means). Data provided by T. E. Downing

TABLE 3.1. Rainfall probabilities (30 years) for the seasons and agricultural year, at Machakos and Makindu[1]

		Rainfall (mm)	
Season		Machakos	Makindu
Mar.—May	(long) rains		
	10% probability	590.1	327.5
	Median	396.5	175.2
	90% probability	211.3	94.6
	98% probability	133.0	23.6
Oct.—Dec.	(short) rains		
	10% probability	670.5	603.0
	Median	344.0	260.5
	90% probability	240.0	148.9
	98% probability	198.0	102.7
Oct.—Sept.	(agricultural year)		
	10% probability	1377.3	1016.3
	Median	904.7	552.5
	90% probability	645.0	330.5
	98% probability	581.0	208.9

[1]Probabilities are cumulative probabilities of exceeding the stated total
Source: Downing et al (1988a: 156). Reproduced by permission of Kluwer Academic Publishers

of the District can expect more than 250 mm in either season in six or more years out of ten (Jaetzold and Schmidt, 1983). This is the barest minimum for producing a crop of maize even assuming a satisfactory distribution within the season.

The seasonal and annual figures take no account of the distribution of rainfall during the growing season, evapotranspiration, and losses to run-off and percolation. Detailed models are necessary for predicting soil moisture and thereby agricultural potential in a given area. The use of climatic data on a daily, decadal, monthly or seasonal basis, for drought prediction and crop planning in semi-arid Kenya, has been attempted by a number of researchers, notably Stewart and his collaborators (Stewart, 1991), who developed a method of 'response farming' which, under experimental conditions, allowed the optimal management of variable rainfall. Response farming has not been taken up by smallholders, however (Potter, 1988).

A CHRONOLOGY OF DROUGHTS

If farming systems are adapted to local average rainfall conditions, the impact of a drought (or a flood) on those systems can be approximated as the deviation of seasonal rainfall from normal. Such a procedure necessarily blurs the distinction between meteorological and agricultural drought.

Following Downing et al (1988a), the drought index (DI) is defined as:

$$DI = \frac{P - \bar{X}}{S}$$

where P = seasonal precipitation, $\bar{X}$ = the long-term average for that season, and S = the seasonal standard deviation from P.

The DI is normalised with a mean of 0 and a standard deviation of 1. (However, given a skewed distribution in the short rains and at the driest station (Makindu), the DI is considered to overemphasise slightly the drought situation for the short rains, and for the drier areas.) Seasonal drought probabilities, using three arbitrarily defined classes of severity (light, moderate and severe), are shown in Table 3.2 for Machakos and Makindu (using the series of Downing et al) and for our five stations. The table shows that, except at two stations, a severe drought can be expected one year in four or five, both in the long and the short rains. There is little evidence to support the popular view that the short rains are more reliable. The rainfall (or drought) indices for each season are year averaged to produce a combined series from 1894 to 1990.[2] The series is plotted in Figure 3.3.[3]

Other factors combined with droughts to produce food shortages. Table 3.3 reconstructs a chronology of drought in the District. It also collects, from several published sources, contemporary reports of the impact, causes and government responses to food and fodder shortages.

Droughts occur characteristically in runs rather than singly. Such runs created food and fodder crises long remembered in the District. Of 90 light, moderate and severe seasonal droughts in our series, 70 occurred in runs of two or more seasons, and only 20 occurred singly. The longest runs of consecutive drought seasons were in 1897−1899, 1949−1950 and 1974−1976 (all including four moderate or severe droughts). If single non-drought seasons are disregarded, the early 1970s were the worst period on record, with 10 moderate or severe droughts out of 16 seasons between 1969 and 1976. The years 1931 − 1936 had six moderate or severe droughts in 12 seasons.

TABLE 3.2. Seasonal drought probabilities using a drought index[1] (percentage of years)

Season	Machakos	Makindu	Kabaa	Kangundo	Katumani	Kampi ya Mawe	Kibwezi	Average[2]
No. of years	90	80	34	34	34	29	34	86
Long rains (Mar.–May)								
Light drought or worse	43	51	47	50	38	45	38	44
Moderate drought or worse	39	40	38	38	26	28	29	40
Severe drought	24	23	26	24	26	24	24	29
Short rains (Oct.–Dec.)								
Light drought or worse	60	58	44	50	59	41	50	57
Moderate drought or worse	30	41	38	32	38	34	38	35
Severe drought	7	21	21	24	6	24	26	10

[1]Light drought: $DI \leq -0.2$; moderate drought: $DI \leq -0.5$; severe drought: $DI \leq -0.8$
[2]Using a single series of drought indices constructed from available station series (see Figure 3.3)

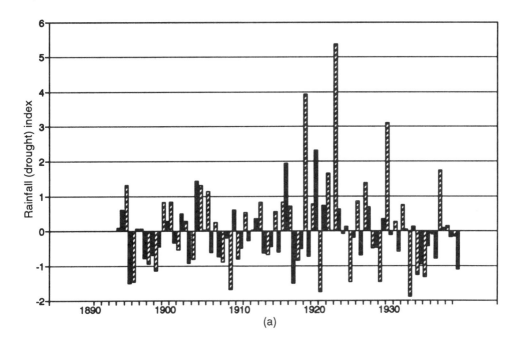

(a)

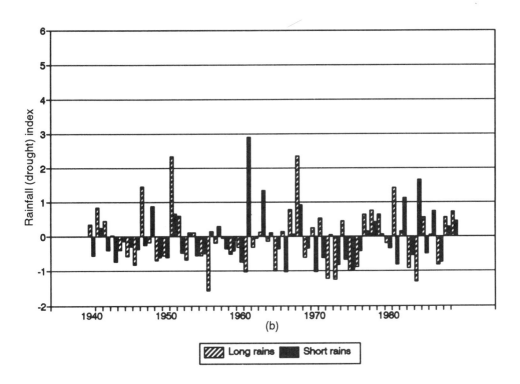

(b)

Long rains   Short rains

FIGURE 3.3. Rainfall (drought) index for Machakos District, 1894–1990

TABLE 3.3. A chronology of droughts[1] and drought runs[2] in Machakos

Year	Drought index		Impact[3]	Causes understood of food/fodder crisis	Intervention by Government and others
	LR	SR			
1895	−1.47(S)		'Yoa ya ngali' (= the carriage or Uganda Railway famine). 'Muvunga' (= sacks) Human deaths (est.) up to 50−75% of population.	Drought, smallpox, war, railway construction	None
1896		−1.51(S)			
1897		−0.78(M)			
1898	−0.94(S)	−0.69(M)			
1899	−1.14(S)	−0.44(L)			
1903		−0.93(S)	No record		None
1904	−0.81(S)				
1907		−0.74(M)	'A minor famine' (Lindblom)	Drought	
1908	−0.89(S)				
1909	−1.68(S)				
1910	−0.80(S)	−0.49(L)			
1913		−0.63(M)	Food shortages	Drought (coincided with Sahelian famine)	None
1914	−0.67(M)	−0.44(M)			
1917		−1.51(S)	No record		
1918	−0.84(S)	−0.50(M)			
1928	−0.49(L)	−0.47(L)	'Kakuti' 'Yua ya nzalukangye' (looking everywhere to find food); food shortage, denudation of grassland; cattle deaths	Drought, locusts, Quelea birds	Appeal for famine relief dismissed by the Governor
1929	−1.47(S)				
1933	−1.90(S)	−0.96(S)	Food shortages, cattle deaths Reports of intensified erosion	Drought, locusts	Maize and pigeon peas distributed; cattle tax suspended
1934	−1.26(L)	−0.43(L)			
1935	−1.32(S)				
1936		−0.78(M)			
1939	1.11(S)		Food shortage	Drought, conscription (Italian/Somali war)	Maize imports; (crop exports banned)
1943		−0.73(M)	25% foods needs produced	Drought, locusts,	Maize imports Food relief
1944	−0.40(L)				

Year	DI	DI	Effects	Cause	Response
1945	−1.58(S)	−0.30(L)	Human mortality (low)	smallpox, military demands	Famine relief, intensified soil conservation
1946	−0.83(S)	−0.37(L)			
1949	−0.70(M)	−0.61(M)	'Makonge' (= sisal — sold to buy food)		Famine relief, soil conservation, resettlement
1950	−0.56(M)	−0.60(M)	Food shortage	Drought	
1954	0.55(M)	−0.49(L)	Reduced exports by 20–25%; increased labour migration	Drought	Conservation, resettlement, dam building
1955	−0.55(M)				
1956	−1.57(S)				
1960	−0.74(M)	(+2.91)	'Ya mafuriko, na ndeke' (floods and aeroplanes)	Drought followed by floods	£1 million spend on food aid; air drops
1961	−1.03(S)		Food shortage, cattle deaths, (70%–80% among Maasai)		
1965	−0.36(L)		Food and fodder shortages	Drought	Large food imports, cattle movements
1969	−0.61(M)	−0.34(M)	No record		
1971	−0.62(M)				
1972	−1.21(S)		Food and fodder shortages cattle deaths (up to 80% among Maasai)	Drought	Government food aid, drought-resistant crops, stock improvement schemes
1973	−1.24(S)	−0.82(S)			
1974	−0.67(M)				
1975	−1.00(S)	−0.96(S)			
1976	−0.88(L)	−0.41(L)			
1980	−0.47(L)		Food shortage	Drought, depletion of maize stocks by early exports	NGO food for work programmes
1981	−0.80(S)				
1983	−0.92(S)	−0.54(M)	'Nikw'a ngwete' (I am dying with cash in my hands) Food shortage, cattle deaths	Drought, high prices	MIDP and other terracing programmes, international aid, yellow maize imports
1984	−1.31(S)				
1987	−0.82(M)	−0.75(M)			

Sources: Downing et al (1988b: 130); Mutiso (1988); Owako (1969); Lindblom (1920: 24–25); Thomas (1974: 13); Peberdy (1958: 10); Silberfein (1989)

L = Light drought (DI= ≤ −0.2); M = moderate drought (DI= ≤ −0.5); S = severe drought (DI= ≤ −0.8)

[1] In selecting years for entry into this table, a drought is defined as two or more successive seasons having moderate or severe droughts. Single seasons are excluded on the ground that under a bimodal rainfall regime, it takes two meteorological droughts to create a food and fodder shortage. However, this principle may not be infallible. In 1925, a DI of −1.46 in the long rains generated widespread migration from lowland areas (Silberfein, 1989: 83)

[2] The duration of a drought run (shown in groups of consecutive years) is defined as including successive years in which one or both seasons had a light, moderate or severe drought, provided that not more than one non-drought season separated two drought seasons in the sequence.

[3] The impact of a drought in the short rains is usually felt in the following calendar year

The 1940s were the last time that human mortality resulting from food shortage was reported on a significant scale in Kenya. Livestock mortality attributed to drought continued to occur on a significant scale in the District up to the drought run of 1983–1984.

LINKING DROUGHT WITH FOOD PRODUCTION

A rather poor correlation between the drought index and records of food shortages is to be expected in view of the following considerations:

(1) records of food shortages are inadequate, especially for the earlier periods;
(2) total seasonal rainfall does not necessarily provide a guide to crop or fodder production, which is also determined by its distribution;
(3) the effects of drought (or flood, in at least one year) may have been compounded by other factors, such as war requisitions, maize marketing failures, or pests.

A linkage between agricultural drought and food production may be attempted by means of production models which relate rainfall to output on the basis of experimental results. Konijn (1988) used such a model for the hybrid Katumani composite B maize, comparing the yields estimated with the model and the agroclimatic index, r/Eo (r = rainfall, Eo = potential evaporation), and using the values for 1974–1977 and 1984. (These 10 seasons were selected to represent a range of rainfall conditions.) A clear relation was demonstrated, with estimated yields increasing with the r/Eo ratio. However, on seven farmers' fields, estimated yields exceeded the observed yields in five seasons (in 1981–1983) by factors ranging from about 4.5 to 10. We may also note that farmers grew local and crossed varieties of maize in addition to Katumani B. It is clear that the maize model used by Konijn offers, at best, only an approximate indicator of food production in drought conditions, as recorded in the rainfall profile.[4] Keating et al (1990a) carried modelling a stage further with an application of the CERES-Maize model to the results from eight experiments (all except one on research stations). They found that the model simulated results better under water than under nitrogen constraints, and was unable to deal adequately with managed changes in soil properties and other factors affecting yields such as weeds, pests and diseases. It is thus unreasonable to expect an exact correlation between rainfall characteristics and crop yields.

We may conclude therefore that agricultural drought is still difficult to define in terms that accurately predict (or describe) crop production, especially in relation to farming systems in the semi-arid areas. In the drought of 1984–1985, the Government of Kenya relied on administrative and agricultural officers' reports for early warning of the food shortage (Borton, 1989; Mwanjila, 1989).

CONCLUSION

An examination of selected data on rainfall reveals no evidence of a generalised trend to support a hypothesis linking climatic with environmental change.

Variability, rather than long-term change, was the most important characteristic of rainfall behaviour in Machakos District during the period 1894–1990. Over the period clear long-term cycles appear. Drought events have contributed in a major way to food shortages and fodder crises. Droughts characteristically occur in runs of two or more seasons, and this amplifies their social, economic and environmental consequences. But agricultural drought is still difficult to define in terms that accurately describe (or predict) crop and livestock production.

NOTES

1 This chapter has been developed from initial research by S. K. Mutiso; see ODI Working Paper 53.
2 The series for Machakos and Makindu were provided by T. E. Downing, Environmental Change Unit, University of Oxford.
3 Variability is itself subject to change in the medium term (as pointed out by Downing et al). These changes do not appear to be related to the number of stations in the series (one only — Machakos — until 1903, two until 1956; six until 1962; and seven until 1988). It should be noted that this procedure uses averages for periods that are not identical.
4 The data used in the experiment were obtained from Kirinyaga, Embu and Machakos Districts. A similar attempt was made by Potter (1988) to relate precipitation to livestock production. This is more difficult, given a larger number of variables and two stages in the food chain. Rainfall was related to total annual production of Napier grass forage and its conversion by stock to milk, at Katumani and Makindu, assuming certain farm sizes, forage areas and stocking rates. Notwithstanding its theoretical value, the assumptions of the model (and lack of on-farm trials) do not recommend its use as an indicator of actual livestock production in the District during droughts recorded in the past.

4

Population

MR THIAKA'S STORY

Machakos District follows the Kenyan pattern of high population growth rates; since 1948 it has accounted for some 6−7% of the total population of Kenya. The District's population increased more than fivefold between 1930 and 1989, when it reached 1 393 000. After the devastating famine of 1898−1899 in which, in some areas, 50−75% of the population died (Lindblom, 1920), the population was estimated at only about 102 000. Some eight famines/droughts are recollected in the 19th century (Silberfein, 1989: 50, 31). In the 20th century there have been no such severe checks on population growth; although droughts have entailed food shortages and cattle losses, sufficient food has been transported in to prevent widespread loss of life. A society which drew its norms from a pattern of small, scattered settlements has had to adapt rapidly to land scarcity and also to incorporation into the world economy.

The rapidity of change can be epitomised in one man's experience. Mr Joel Thiaka of Muisuni, Kangundo, told us that his father had arrived there from Lower Mbooni, a few years before he was born in 1906. The area was then empty; a few people had made bush farms there, but they lived elsewhere because of the danger from wild animals. In 1896 a mission had been established and the missionaries began shooting the animals. Consequently, people began to move their homes to the area, clearing the bush by burning and slashing it with locally-smelted *pangas*. (This account confirms the similar story given by one of the missionaries in question (Kenya Land Commission, 1934: Vol.3, Evidence) and with Barnes' account (KNA Barnes, 1937).) Around the 1920s the original practice of shifting cultivation ceased. Mr Thiaka hired his first plough in 1929, when he married and, like others, increased his cultivated land to begin sales to Indian traders. By 1938, he told us, 'this place was becoming a desert' as a result of continuous cultivation and the increase of herds, and he himself worked temporarily in Mombasa. The enclosure of private grazing land began a trend towards improvement. As a Councillor in the 1940s, he was active in agitating for the right to grow coffee, which was secured in the 1950s. In 1990, the population density in Muisuni was 518/km². Leaders were worried by the tiny farms which children were inheriting and by increasing joblessness amongst the young, despite huge parental investments in school fees. Figures 4.1 and 4.2 show areas near Muisuni in 1937 and 1990.

FIGURE 4.1. 'Looking north from below Muisuni trig point to Tala and the Matungulu slopes, possibly the finest stretch of agricultural land in Kenya, producing with Kangundo 5/6 of the maize and beans exported from the Ukamba reserve.' (KNA: R. O. Barnes, 1937, photo 21. Reproduced by permission of Kenya National Archives.)

FIGURE 4.2. Cultivation of coffee and other crops on the terraced slopes of Muisuni in 1990, near the site of Barnes' photo 21 (his exact standpoint could not be identified). (Photo: M. Mortimore)

CENSUS DATA AND BOUNDARIES

The first reliable census, based on house calls by trained enumerators, took place in 1948. Earlier counts were made by low-level officials for taxation purposes. We have used as our baseline the 1932 count of 240 000, which was undertaken with some care to provide evidence to the Kenya Land Commission. However, the true population may have been nearer 260 000. There is no reason to think there was substantial undercounting in the censuses of 1948, 1962, 1969 or 1979. The 1989 census totals for Districts and urban areas were not published till 1991 (Kenya, CBS, 1991).[1]

Our analysis of census data is based on the 1979 boundaries of both the District, and its subdivision, the Location,[2] as shown in Figure 1.1, with one important exception. Between 1969 and 1979 the area under the jurisdiction of the Machakos Municipal Council was enlarged to take in parts of all the neighbouring Locations, and the 'town' grew from 19 km^2 to 323 km^2. Areas such as the Mua Hills where the main occupation was farming were included in the municipal boundaries. In order not to exaggerate the degree of urban growth, we defined as urban only those sub-locations adjacent to 'Machakos Old Town' which had densities over 600/km^2. We refer to these as Machakos Town. The rest, for the purposes of our analysis, were reallocated to their original Location. As far as possible, we did the same with the 1989 data.[3] Locations were grouped into three classes according to predominant AEZs as explained in Chapter 2.

CHANGES IN POPULATION STRUCTURE, 1932–1989

Table 4.1 summarises District data for the period 1932–1989, and compares the figures with Kenya averages. Population growth between 1932 and 1948 was between 2% and 2.5% per annum, depending on the degree of undercounting in 1932. Since 1948, the District growth rates have been over 3% per annum. Up to 1979 they were slightly below the national average; in 1979 they slightly exceeded it (Table 4.1, section 2). Growth rates were as high as 3.76% per annum in the period 1969–1979 but fell back to 3.1% in the period 1979–1989. There is no evidence of much immigration by non-indigenous people, and the population remained predominantly Akamba (Table 4.1, section 5).

Section 3 of Table 4.1 shows that the proportion of males to females was below the Kenya average, particularly at the earlier censuses. The proportion of male to female children has always been comparable to the Kenyan average (see Tiffen, 1991: Table 3). The difference is in the over-15 age group, where the proportion of males has been below the national average due to out-migration by males of working age.[4] Table 4.1 shows that out-migration appears to have fallen steadily since 1948. High fertility, comparable to the Kenyan average, led to a high proportion of the population being aged less than 15 years throughout the period. There appears to be a falling trend from the 54% in 1962 to 50% in 1979, at which time the national figure was 48% (Table 4.1, section 4). A demographic turning point towards smaller families was being reached in Kenya in the 1980s (Kelley and Nobbe, 1990), and it is likely that this was also true in Machakos, but the data to prove it are not yet available from the 1989 census.

TABLE 4.1. Machakos District population, totals, growth rates, age group, sex and tribe, 1932–1989

		1989	1979	1969	1962	1948	1932
1.	Totals						
	1979 boundaries	1 393 000	1 022 522	707 214	566 463	366 199	na
	1948 boundaries				550 779	357 802	238 910
2.	Annual growth rate since previous census	3.09	3.76	3.22	3.17	2.68	na
	(Kenya average)	(3.34)	(3.42)	(3.44)	(3.48)	(na)	
3.	Males/100 females	na	93	92	90	87	73
	(Kenya average)		(98)	(99.6)	(98.1)	(97.5)	(na)
	Males/100 females >15	na	86	82	74	71	51
	(Kenya average)		(96)	(97)	(89)	(88)	(na)
	% Males over 15 apparently absent[1]	na	10	15	17	20	na
4.	Percentage of population <15[2]	na	50	53	54	50	53
	(Kenya average)		(48)	(50.5)	(51)	(48)	(na)
5.	Akamba %[2]	na	96.6	97.6	98.2	98	na

[1]See text, footnote 4, for method of calculation
[2]Using boundaries in operation at the time of census
Sources: Censuses for 1948, 1962, 1969 and 1979; Kenya, CBS (1991) for 1989; Kenya Land Commission (1934: vol.3, Evidence) for 1932; and ODI calculations. The Annual Report, Machakos District, 1932, gives 1220 Europeans and Indians, who have not been included. The 1948 figure includes both African and non-African totals, which were separately counted, to ensure comparability with later censuses.

POPULATION MOVEMENTS IN MACHAKOS, 1932–1989

Interpretations of population movements

Population movements are commonly analysed through typologies of rural–urban and rural–rural movements. This is not very helpful in the case of Machakos since it does not make the distinction between temporary and long-term movements. We preferred therefore to use the distinction between *migration* proper, involving a change in the location of the home, and generally involving a whole family, and *circulation*, or temporary movements for particular purposes, such as herding, wage labour, trade or study, with an intention to return home (therefore circular). Circulation frequently involves an adult male not accompanied by his family. (This typology is based on Clyde Mitchell and developed by Chapman and Prothero (1985).)

Population movement in Machakos has been explained in terms of core–periphery theories. It is suggested that the penetration of capitalism disrupted traditional methods of coping with a variable climate, and gave the capitalists at the core such an unfair share of the rewards of economic activity that African peasants at the periphery were marginalised and labour was pushed into migration or exploitation of the less viable lands (Wisner, 1977; Silberfein, 1989). African farmers were the helpless victims of change. Such views take little note of the natural consequences of population growth, and regard the food shortages of the 1970s as man-made rather than as part of climatic cycles, which include the known droughts of the 19th century.

It is indisputable that colonial policy constrained the Machakos population within boundaries that were fixed at a time when the population was at a low point due to the 1899 famine; that about 2000 Akamba (2% of the population — less than the annual increment) lost some of their better land in the Mua Hills in the period 1908–1910 as well as a small grazing area near Machakos Town; and that extensive bush areas previously used occasionally (often in dispute with the Maasai) became European ranchland or Crown Land (see Figure 1.1). These land losses and the banning of settlement outside the Reserve boundaries prevented the traditional response to population growth, or to falling fertility in land, that had been used for many years, namely, out-migration to farm lower-potential areas (option B, Figure 2.5). Such movements had led to the outward spread of the Akamba from their original settlements in the Mbooni Hills in the 18th century. After 1960, the Akamba recovered almost all the disputed land for settlement. (The exception was the European ranchland, which was the least attractive part of the district for settlement by small farmers.) While a hectare of land in AEZs 2 and 3 will produce more than land in AEZs 4, 5 or 6, given the same crops and technologies, land was more easily available or cheaper in the lower-potential areas, at least up to 1979, with the result that average farm size could be larger. Thus, it was for a long time advantageous for those who inherited only a small farm in a high-potential area to consider a move to lower-potential land where they could establish a larger farm.

The Akamba have always coped with the erratic rains by supplementing agriculture with other means of livelihood. Temporary migrations to work for the Kikuyu or to engage in trade are recorded in the 19th century. At any given time, according to circumstances and their own social needs, individuals and families may choose temporary emigration to earn additional income or to accumulate capital, migration to new land, or intensification of activities on land already farmed (as illustrated in Figure 2.5). The colonial regime temporarily frustrated the movement to new land and this drove larger numbers to temporary emigration during the period 1930–1960, which we show in Chapter 10 to have been more remunerative than crop farming. The Akamba were active problem solvers, rather than passive victims.

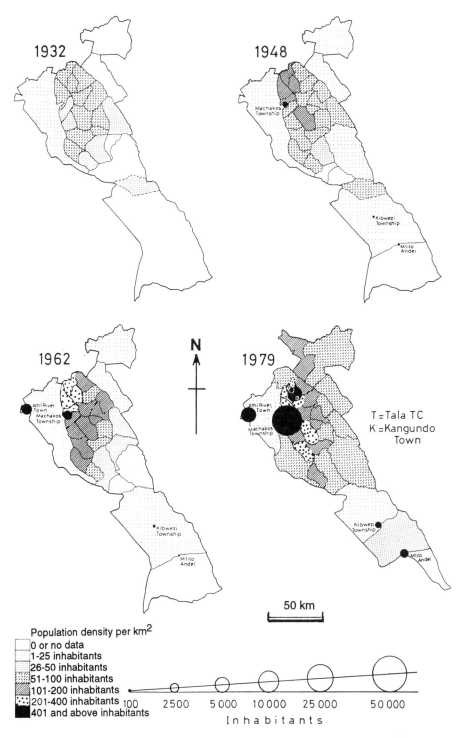

FIGURE 4.3. Population density by Location, 1932, 1948, 1962 and 1979

TABLE 4.2. Population annual growth rates by AEZ or urban area, 1932–1989

	1932–1948	1948–1962	1962–1969	1969–1979	1979–1989
AEZs 2 and 3	2.72	2.14	1.62	1.38	2.98
AEZ 4	2.09	2.64	2.02	2.13	2.67
AEZs 5 and 6	5.16	6.69	7.42	6.38	3.45
Urban areas	na	11.05	5.54	16.10	4.91
District	2.68	3.17	3.22	3.76	3.09

Sources: As for Table 4.1

The surge into AEZs 5 and 6 is shown by the maps of population density in 1948 and 1979 (see Figure 4.3). By 1979, density had reached more than 50/km^2 in the more favoured AEZs 5 and 6 Locations, with only the Settled Area Location, the former white ranching area, remaining comparatively empty. Figure 4.4(a) shows the changed distribution of population over time, with 36% of the population in AEZs 5 and 6 by 1989, compared to 9% in 1932. Changes in density are shown in Figure 4.4(b), with population densities rising from an average of 82 to 383 per km^2 in AEZs 2 and 3, from 56 to 143 in AEZ 4 and from 9 to 36 in AEZs 5 and 6. Because of changes in area, this does not reflect the differences in population growth rates accurately, and these are shown separately in Table 4.2. It will be seen that in AEZs 2, 3 and 4 growth rates have always been below 3%, and were considerably below in the period 1962–1979 when the main movement into AEZs 5 and 6 was taking place (full details, Location by Location, 1932–1979, are given in Tiffen, 1991: Table 6).

Reactions to land scarcity up to 1960

As a result of the combination of population growth, restrictions on movement to new areas, and the introduction of new technologies such as the iron hoe and the plough, practically all the *weu* (unclaimed land) in the Reserve had been claimed by 1937, except for tsetse-infested areas and Crown Land (KNA: Barnes, 1937; Munro, 1975). In the absence of means and incentives to restore fertility, this led to increasing land degradation, and to various rehabilitation measures on the part of the authorities culminating in forcible destocking in 1938.

The Akamba themselves increasingly resented the land losses of the 1908–1910 period. During the session of the Kenya Land Commission at Machakos in 1932, they marshalled 187 complainants to testify to their losses at that time of farms and also of cattle. The Commission was unwilling to displace any white farmers, but, as compensation, agreed to add to the Reserve the Yatta Plateau in the north-east, Makueni in the south-east and some smaller areas around Emali near the railway (Mbitini Location) and north of Kikumbulyu (Kenya Land Commission, 1934). This had the advantage of joining the Akamba settlements in Kikumbulyu to the main Reserve area. However, it did not immediately increase the area available for new farms. The Yattas remained strictly controlled for grazing, and the other areas were tsetse-infested. The recovery of the land on the northern border became the primary motivation behind the formation of the Ukamba Members Association which was linked to the Kikuyu Central Association, and which successfully fought the destocking campaign in 1938 (Newman, 1974). Newman quoted one of his informants as saying:

After our cattle were returned the only thing we wanted back was our land which had been taken by

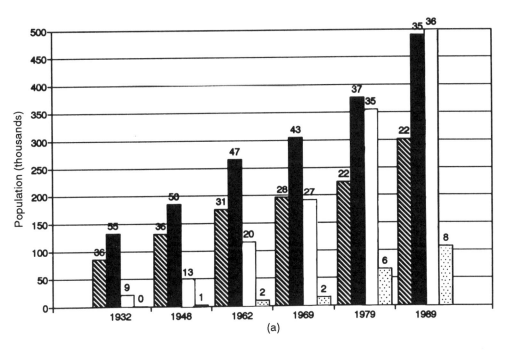

(a)

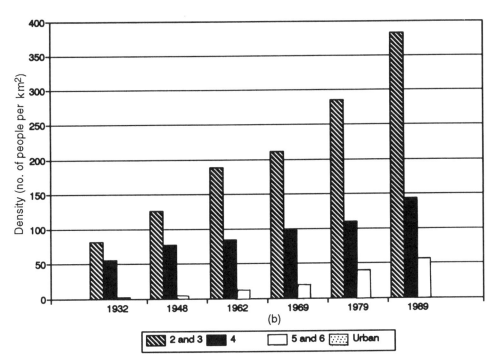

(b)

FIGURE 4.4. Population distribution and density by AEZ and urban area, 1932–1989. (a) Population totals, 1932–1989 (interior figures show the percentage in each zone). (b) Density by AEZ, 1932–1989

the government and for our cattle not to be taken again. Our lands round Mua, Lukwena, and that area up to [Ol Doinyo Sabuk] had been taken . . .[5] When the cattle were returned people still wanted a strong committee to go claiming for the land. (Newman, 1974: 35. Reproduced by permission of Transafrica Press.)

One response of those without adequate land was to take up the option of 'squatting' on European farms. In return for his labour, the squatter was given land and grazing rights for a limited number of cattle. For example, one prominent settler, Major Joyce, had 1350 Akamba on his farm, with 660 cattle, for whom 600 acres of terraced arable land and 5000 acres of grazing were provided (Pereira and Beckley, 1952). The Akamba were driven to squatting later than the Kikuyu, who had lost more land. However, some 2700 families had taken up the squatting option by 1927, and in 1932 it was reported that there were 10 000 squatters on European lands within Machakos District. The number was similar in 1948 as young adults were forced to leave if not required as workers. Evicted young adults constituted part of the 'numerous landless class' noted in 1938 (Munro, 1975: 238, quoting a District report). Other Akamba were on European farms in the Ol Doinyo Sabuk area, then in Thika District, where 560 were said to have signed squatter contracts in 1929 (Munro, 1975: 194–197). The Kenya Land Commission referred to 2000 Machakos Akamba and 6000 Kitui Akamba residing in Thika and 'other areas outside their home districts' (Kenya Land Commission, 1934). The Akamba recovered the Thika area at Independence. The attraction of squatting was the acquisition of grazing rights for cattle (Owako, 1969), but the risk lay in the difficulty in re-establishing rights to family land in the Reserve.

A second response was a circulatory movement to seek temporary work. Until the 1920s most Akamba were able to pay their taxes, meet their other cash needs and buy food as necessary from their sales of maize, supplemented by other foodstuffs, beeswax, hides and skins, and very occasionally, livestock (Peberdy, 1958, based on District reports). Only 7–8% of able-bodied adult males were in employment before and immediately after World War I, but this figure had risen to 15% by 1923 — compared to 55% from the Kikuyu Districts (Stichter, 1982). The Akamba male preferred not to take up agricultural work unless it also gave him grazing rights, as in squatting. Many became drivers, or went into the army, where they often learnt further skills, or the police force, or the railways. The administration had taken the unusual step of establishing an industrial school at Machakos in 1914 (Munro, 1975: 88). The Post Office's telegraph apprentices were all Akamba (Stichter, 1982: 119–120). In 1929 and 1930 there were about 8000 in work, perhaps 18–19% of the able-bodied labour force (Stichter, 1982). This increase may be associated with poor rainfall and locust invasions in the period 1928–1931. Numbers dropped below 5000 in 1932 but rose again to around 9500 in 1937 (Munro, 1975: 209).

The temporary drop in employment in the early 1930s can be attributed to a general shift in the balance of advantage between going out to earn and male participation in farming at home (Kitching, 1980; Stichter, 1982, Chapter 4). The drought of 1928–1929, the falling demand for workers in the slump of 1929–1933, the accompanying fall in the price of livestock and the improvement in roads and marketing led to an expansion of the area under cultivation (Gupta, 1973: 68), which increased the pressure on the farming system. Associated with an apparent expansion in arable production were the beginnings of African commercial businesses within the Reserve (Munro, 1975).

During the 1940s, the balance of advantage swung sharply back to wage labour. Real wages rose, but life within the Reserve was hard, and there was frequently need for famine relief.

In 1944 about 15 000 Machakos Akamba were in formal sector employment, another 11 000 in the armed services, and 1800 had been conscripted as labourers (KNA:MKS/DC/1/8/1, 1945). These amounted to over 35% of the able-bodied men, and this must have depressed agricultural production.

The 1948 census showed about 20% of adult males absent from the District (Table 4.1), but for many the post-war return to the District was only temporary. By the 1950s demand for labour was high as the national economy expanded and as Kikuyu labour was withdrawn during the Mau Mau period. In 1953, 60% of the adult males were thought to be outside the District. In the mid-1950s there were still 43 000 (about 40%) working outside (Peberdy, 1958: 102), with about another 4000 who were employed within the District. Numbers working outside fell after 1956, as Kikuyu and others returned to the labour market (Peberdy, 1961; Gupta, 1973: 70).

The 1948 census also showed the whereabouts of these workers. In the Thika District there were 21 000 Machakos Akamba, a high proportion of whom were women, indicating the presence of squatter families as well as male workers (adult male/female ratios for each Location, 1948, 1962 and 1969, are shown in Tiffen, 1991: Table 7). There were 17 000 in other parts of Kenya, including 7800 in Nairobi District, of whom 6700 were men, most of them circulatory workers. (The Akamba in Mombasa were said to be from Kitui.) There were 2200 Akamba in Kwale District, with equal numbers of men and women, and therefore most probably agricultural settlers. Some Akamba had already settled there in the early years of the century (Lindblom, 1920). The only other District with substantial numbers of Machakos Akamba was Kajiado, with 1000, almost all of them men likely to have been herders, who had temporarily taken cattle into this Maasai pastoral area.

The official response to land scarcity and degradation was a growing conviction that the Reserve was overpopulated. This led to the decision in 1946 to open up the Makueni area for controlled settlement, to be farmed according to strict rules which would prevent degradation (see Chapter 10). The District Officer recommended attractive terms and considerable help for settlers in order to overcome Akamba suspicion that the colonial authorities only wanted to rehabilitate the land prior to taking it over (RH: Brown, 1945; de Wilde, 1967). (The successful Akamba demonstration against destocking in 1938 was still much in the mind of administrators.) The recruitment of settlers proved difficult; by the end of 1948 only 85 families had been attracted. After 1949 applicants came forward in greater numbers largely in response to the appointment of an Akamba, Onesmus Musyoki, as one of the Agricultural Officers and his campaigns to convince people about the settlement, often also using the churches (O. Musyoki, pers. comm., 1990). By 1960 the settlement was said to be 'completely full, having 2187 registered settlers' (Kenya, ALDEV, 1961). This figure represents 12 000–16 000 people, settled at a cost equivalent in 1990 terms to Ksh 101 million (see Chapter 15). At this point the Government lost control of the settlement process; enforcement of the rules lapsed, and funding ceased. However, immigrants continue to flow in; by the 1962 census, there were 20 000 people in the area, and by 1969, 54 000.

Land for the taking, 1960–1979

By 1960 the colonial regime was no longer able to prevent the Akamba from establishing farms in the lands to which they thought themselves entitled. The surge into the former Crown Lands can be clearly seen in Figure 4.1. Some AEZ 5 and 6 Locations experienced growth rates of 10–30% per annum between the censuses of 1962 and 1969 (for further details see Tiffen, 1992).

In the Yattas growth began in the late 1950s, and in Kikumbulyu and the south in the late 1960s.

This unofficial settlement was opposed by both the colonial authorities and the newly independent Government, which wanted an orderly sale of large white-settler farms to Africans on credit terms and continued control of Crown Land. The aim was to establish new settlements with regulated plot sizes, cropping patterns, and communal facilities for marketing, etc. The 'Million-Acre Scheme' for settlement on white farms affected only small areas of Machakos District, but included the land the Akamba had long wanted to recover: the Mua hills near Machakos Town and parts of Thika District. The Mua Hills settlement went according to plan. In the Thika area the Government would have preferred a co-operative to take over the estates, and soldiers expelled 'squatters' in 1963–1965. In one case some 800 co-operative members had created individual farms by 1972, despite military raids (Mbithi and Barnes, 1975). The Government eventually recognised the status quo.

In the Crown Land, colonial policy had been to try to retain North Yatta (later named Masinga) as a possible area for Kikuyu settlement, although the Kikuyu were put off by its arid nature. The Yatta Plateau area was regarded as an overspill area for controlled grazing for the Machakos Akamba. Only a few permanent settlements were allowed between 1952 and 1957; but new areas were opened up for grazing by the construction of dams and the Yatta furrow (see Chapter 12). The settlement controls failed in the run-up to Independence, and the new water supply facilitated the uncontrolled settlement that followed. The attempts to extend controlled grazing from Yatta Plateau to North Yatta led to 'the bitterest of opposition from local people, supported by Akamba politicians' (Kenya, ALDEV, 1961). In the early 1960s many independent settlers arrived (de Wilde, 1967; Neunhauser et al, 1983). In the 1962 census the populations of North Yatta and Yatta Plateau were each 11 000 (from 4500 and 457 in 1948), but by 1969 they had risen to 23 000 and 29 000, respectively. The southern Crown Lands filled up a little later. Would-be settlers were militarily expelled from the Chyulu Hills in Kibwezi Division in 1962 and those going to Ngwata Location suffered intermittent harassment up to 1969, when it had 14 000 people; by 1979 this figure had increased to 57 000.

Since 1979 there has been little land on which people can settle without payment. Village informants in Ngwata in 1989 told us that newcomers would have to buy land, since all land was now owned and demarcated. The closure of the frontier is shown clearly by the fall in the annual growth rate of population in AEZs 5 and 6 to a near normal 3.45% over the period 1979–1989 (Table 4.2).

A study carried out in 1973–1974 surveyed a sample of farmers in three Locations which people were leaving (Kangundo, Masii and Mwala) and in two Locations which were receiving migrants (Yatta and Makueni). Matingu (1974) found that most people had moved because of a felt land shortage. The immigrants to Yatta and Makueni had had smaller than average holdings in their home area, or were landless (land had been taken by relatives, lost on return from squatting, sold by their father, or lost on divorce in the case of women). Similarly, amongst those interviewed who had stayed in their home area, the main reason given for not wishing to move was that the respondent felt he/she had enough productive land, or, that even if the plot was small, it was capable of yielding a good cash income from coffee, fruit, etc. Thus, a move was seen as an opportunity to do better, and the main reason given for choosing a new area was news of large harvests and large holdings. The great majority of migrants went with the intention of farming as well as herding.

In order to acquire the new land settlers had risked and endured great hardships — particularly lack of food in the first seasons, lack of water before tanks or dams could be built, illness,

FIGURE 4.5. This new settler's home in Kikumbulyu in the 1960s illustrates both the hardship of new settlement and the methods of clearance and farming that were alarming conservationists at the time. (Photo: F. N. Owako, 1969. Reproduced with permission.)

FIGURE 4.6. Many such areas are now examples of excellent cultivation and cropping systems to maximise rainfall infiltration, with useful trees conserved in farm boundaries. This farm is near Kambu, Ngwata Location, 1990. (Photo: D. B. Thomas. Reproduced with permission.)

especially malaria, and danger from wild animals such as rhinos and elephants. They cleared the land by traditional slash and burn methods (Figure 4.5). Many had lost cattle in the trek or because of tsetse in the new area. They could only gradually convert it into well conserved farmland (Figure 4.6 and Chapter 10). Some migrants returned to their home areas because of these setbacks. However, it was generally recognised that those who survived the early difficulties were doing better than they would have done if they had stayed in their home areas. For example, the Makueni migrants who had farmed before their move reported an average increase in the number of bags of maize they could produce from 5.5 to 24.5 (Matingu, 1974: 114). The sex ratios in the censuses show that both men and women took part in the move; the men had their traditional role in clearing new land. Settlers chose their destinations carefully. They went first to the Yattas, then to the south. The former European ranch zone was their last choice; however, it is not clear if this was due to its land tenure status, or because its clay soils make it less attractive for mixed farming than the preferred parts of AEZs 5 and 6.

Urban out-migration after 1960

Census data suggests a slowing down of out-migration from the District after 1962. In that year 86.4% of those born in Machakos District were also registered there; 13.6% were registered elsewhere. In 1979, 90.2% of those born in Machakos were also registered there; only 9.8% were registered elsewhere. Amongst the 110 000 people born in Machakos who were counted in another District in the 1979 census, 58 668 were in Nairobi and 11 528 were in Mombasa (Oucho, 1988). Two of the three main rural destinations were areas of settlement: Kwale (12 260) and Embu (5696). Those who went to Kiambu (5317) may have been aiming either for settlement or for work. This suggests strongly that urban work was still preferred to rural work unless the latter involved farming on their own account.

From the 1950s women as well as men migrated, to join their husbands, or for work or study. In the 1962 census the predominant age groups amongst Akamba females in Nairobi municipality was 0−4 and 20−24, where they outnumbered men; in all other age groups there was a distinct male preponderance (Ominde, 1968: Figure 7.21). By 1969 females formed about one-third of the Nairobi Akamba population. The change in the nature of the Nairobi Akamba, and their growth in numbers, are shown in Table 4.3.

The growth rate of the Akamba population in Nairobi[6] was 8% per annum between 1948 and 1962 (13.8% for women only). It surged in the immediate post-independence years to 14% (15.7% for women), and dropped back to 5% per annum (6.4% for women) in the 1969−1979 period. Part of this growth was due to a natural increase in the resident Akamba population. By 1979 about 22% of the Akamba population of Nairobi had been born there. Some had become more

TABLE 4.3. Akamba population of Nairobi District, 1948−1979

	Total	Female	Female %	Total Nairobi population
1948	7 829	1 142	15	118 976
1962	23 864	6 999	29	266 794
1969	60 716	19 469	32	509 286
1979	103 185	36 246	35	827 775

Source: Censuses of 1948, 1962, 1969 and 1979

or less permanent urban residents; most, however, retained close ties with relatives and with land in their own district. The preponderance of males even in 1979 showed that many still regarded themselves as only temporary urban residents.

While migration and circulation are distinct activities, there is an overlap. A man may migrate to an urban occupation with the intention of returning, but the return may be postponed, although it frequently takes place eventually at retirement. If it is postponed indefinitely, the visits to the original home, the despatch home of remittances and the receipt from home of farm produce, etc., may become more and more intermittent, till it can be said that the migrant has established a new home base to which his children feel their primary loyalty. For most Akamba, however, urban life is not an ideal. Even in 1978, nearly 80% said that they accepted temporary migration as a response to drought but that they would not move to a town, and 90% would not contemplate taking their family (Consortium, Report 6, 1978: 79). This reaction is shown clearly by the sex ratios in Table 4.3. Even in Machakos Town there were four adult males to every female in 1948, though the ratio had fallen to 1.7 in 1969 (see Tiffen, 1991: Table 7). And conversation of workers in Machakos Town constantly reverted to their village and its land (Lang, 1974).

URBAN AND INDUSTRIAL GROWTH

Local urban growth

The colonial diagnosis that the District could not support its current agricultural population led to some attempts to encourage industry. The more successful industries were set up just outside the Reserve, in places with transport facilities. Kenya Orchards had a canning factory in the Mua Hills and there was another canner in Thika; both continue to buy in northern Machakos today. Government assistance was given to Liebigs to set up a meat factory in Athi River in 1938, in association with the 1938 destocking campaign. The Akamba were generally able to get better prices for their cattle elsewhere. Within the Reserve an Indian firm set up a wattle-chopping plant alongside a cotton ginnery in Nzaui, in 1938. The ginnery collapsed when cotton failed after four years. The District Commissioner put pressure on the County Council to invest in a sisal factory in the 1950s; when sisal prices collapsed, the Council finances were left in a parlous state.

Urban population still only amounted to about 8% of the total population of the District in 1989. The urban area of Machakos Municipality had only about 58 000 inhabitants. Athi River, the second largest town in the District, with 23 000 people, has developed as a suburb of Nairobi, which is only 35 km distant. It is cut off from the rest of the District by a large, scantily populated ranching area, and has little commercial impact on the rest of the District. All the other towns are small. Tala/Kangundo Town Council, covering two adjacent areas in northern Machakos, had grown to 12 500 people by 1989 (Kenya, CBS, 1991). The next largest town was probably Mtito Andei in the south, with about 8000 people. Amongst other towns surveyed in 1987 only two, Sultan Hamud and Kibwezi, had populations over 2000, and only four were between 1000 and 2000 (Kenya, Ministry of Planning, 1988).

Industrial and urban growth in Machakos has always been hampered by poor transport, and by lack of urban water and electricity supplies. In 1970, Machakos Town had only one small sawmill; employment was mainly in administration, in the main District hospital, in secondary and technical schools, and in commercial shops, two banks, several garages and a few warehouses (Lang, 1974). During the 1970s a Rural Industrial Development Centre was established; by

1978—1979 it had created 177 jobs in 29 projects, not all of which would have been new jobs (Livingstone, 1986: 111—112). The greater part of the town's expansion in the 1970s and 1980s was due to commerce and services. During MIDP Phase 1, 1978—1982, plans were made to build six small industrial estates in rural centres; these were not well conceived, creating few new jobs at very high cost (ODI, 1982). Two were abandoned as electricity was not available. The recent explosive growth of Matuu in northern Machakos, thought to have nearly 2000 people in 1987, is associated with the tarring of the Nairobi—Thika—Garissa road and with the electricity supply (Kenya, Ministry of Planning, 1988).

The development of commercial centres has also been impeded by poor roads. Northern Machakos has been relatively well served by roads. An improved road from Nairobi to a ranch near the District boundary in the 1950s assisted the development of Kangundo town and nearby Tala, both of them servicing coffee and fruit and vegetable growing areas. The coffee areas attracted shopkeepers, labourers and servants from other parts of Machakos District. There seems to have been a fall in the influx and even a reverse movement between 1979 and 1980, with the fall in the coffee price (van Ginneken et al, 1986). Urban growth resumed in the 1980s although hampered by the increasingly bad state of repair of the short road to Nairobi, such that a great deal of traffic preferred the longer route via Machakos Town. Nevertheless, Kangundo/Tala, which obtained electricity in 1990, has numerous small shops and workshops, a bank, Post Office, etc., and the kind of mutually reinforcing symbiotic relationship with its hinterland that has recently been described for another small Kenyan town (Evans, 1992). The same can be said for Matuu in North Yatta Location.

Wote, the administrative centre for the now prosperous Makueni area, had no tarred roads in 1990 and its electricity supply depended on diesel generators. Its ginnery had closed with the second collapse of cotton in the mid-1980s, and when we visited, its co-operative dairy had lost outlying farmer members because of the high costs of transport. In 1992 it became the capital of the new Makueni District and, as such, may acquire some of the necessary infrastructure.

Early development of transport aimed primarily at servicing the export capacity of the white farming areas. Kibwezi, Emali and Mtito Andei, all on the Mombasa highway (and the railway) serviced the ranching areas and enabled farmers like Major Joyce to transport milk by train to Nairobi. However, the depots were unable to develop as commercial centres, since the low population density meant that there were few buyers in their hinterlands. Mtito Andei had only 202 inhabitants in 1948. As settlers came into Ngwata in the 1970s traders in Mtito Andei were able to buy and sell from them. An urban census showed that the population had grown from 2067 in 1979 to 3840 in 1987, when Mtito Andei was also providing services to travellers and tourists as the half-way stage between Nairobi and Mombasa (Kenya, Ministry of Planning, 1988?).

The recently tarred roads in Machakos are those which connect administrative centres, such as the Machakos—Kitui road, and the Nairobi—Garissa road, tarred in 1984—1988, which passes Matuu. It is fortuitous if these roads cross densely settled and productive regions. The Machakos—Kitui road, tarred since 1988, has probably helped the carving village of Wamunyu to expand, but in general it traverses a fairly lightly populated AEZ 5 area.

Urban growth in Kenya, 1948—1979

Machakos farmers have been affected more by the growth of urban population outside the District than within it. In 1948 the urban population of Kenya was only 276 000; over 80% of these were in Nairobi and Mombasa. Urban growth averaged 6.6% to 1962, and accelerated to 7.9% between the 1969 and 1979 censuses. The urban population was calculated as 2 240 000 in 1979, and 3 735 900 in 1989, representing about 16% and 17% of the total population respectively. ('Urban' centres are defined as centres with a population of over 2000 in 1979 and by status (including some small trading centres) in 1989. The urban population is somewhat exaggerated by the inclusion of rural areas in some towns.) Machakos District lies between the two largest urban agglomerations, Nairobi (1989 population: 1 346 000) and Mombasa (1989 population: 465 000). The growth of these two centres has had a substantial effect on the District, by providing an ever-growing market for meat, fruits and vegetables, and other foodstuffs, building materials, especially sand and timber, and charcoal. The increased urban demand for agricultural products seems, in the Machakos case, to be one of the factors leading to a deceleration of migration out of the District.

OCCUPATIONS

Education and dependency

The growth of population did not lead to a great increase in the ratio of agricultural labour to land, although it did lead to a considerable increase in the number of people to be fed, and therefore the local market for food. Many of the additional adults were engaged in education or other non-farming occupations.

By 1979 Machakos had a better educated population than the average in Kenya. Education has a dual effect on development; while it improves the quality of the labour force, it also means that young adults remain dependent on their families for a longer period, thus reducing available labour. Schooling expanded rapidly after 1945 (see Chapter 9). By 1979 children helped on the farm in the holidays and before and after school and at weekends, particularly at peak times, but they could not be considered part of the regular labour force. Of the 15−19 age group, 74% (80% of males, 67% of females) were in school (Table 4.4) in 1979, and of the 20−24 age group, 23% of males and 7% of females were still at school. The continuance of schooling into this age is associated with a late start; Table 4.4 shows that 49% of the children aged 5−9 were not yet in school, while education was almost universal for those aged 10−14. Judging by a study in Kitui District, this late start is due to the difficulties parents have in finding money for school fees, which leads them to postpone schooling for some children (O'Leary, 1984). Table 4.4 shows that Machakos District is comparable to the rest of Kenya in the late start, but that parents were managing to keep their children at school for longer than average. Taking into account the older students and half the age group 55+, the true dependency ratio in 1979 was 65%.

TABLE 4.4. Proportion (as a percentage) of children in school, Machakos and Kenya, 1979

	Age group			
	5−9 years	10−14 years	15−19 years	20−24 years
Machakos	51.4	93.6	74.0	14.4
Kenya	49.9	83.4	55.5	9.7

Source: Calculated from Kenya Population Census 1979, Table 4

Occupations and land—labour relationships

We can only estimate the occupations of those aged over 15 in 1979 (this information was requested in the 1989 census but is not yet published). The Statistical Abstract series shows that formal sector employment within the District rose after independence. Much of this was in the service sector (schools, government services, etc.).

	Machakos employees	% of Kenyan formal employment
1963—1970	15 000—17 400	5—6
1972—1975	19 500—26 750	3
1980—1988	32 300—44 100	3

It is more difficult to estimate the non-formal occupations. There were 7000 licensed business premises in the District in 1987 (Kenya, Ministry of Planning, 1988). A survey in Central Province found 1.6 employees per informal enterprise (Livingstone, 1986: 55, quoting Norcliffe and Freeman, 1979). A similar ratio in Machakos would therefore suggest that owners and employees might total about 18 000 people. We can probably also estimate another 5000 people operating without a licence or in occupations that require no licence such as carving. We have used information from Peberdy (1958) to estimate the number of people in formal employment or having shops in the mid-1950s, and have applied these to 1948. The results are shown in Table 4.5.

It has to be emphasised that Table 4.5 is only a rough estimate; however, it tallies with farm surveys conducted around 1979 (see Chapter 10) which usually reported four adults per household, of whom one was in a non-farm occupation (and one, according to census data, was still at

TABLE 4.5. Growth of the labour force, 1948—1979

		Number 1948	%(A)	Number 1962	%(A)	Number 1979	%(A)
1.	Resident adult population[1]						
	Males	73 530	42	106 934	42	210 389	46
	Females	103 240	58	145 315	58	244 638	54
	Total	176 770	100	252 249	100	455 027	100
2.	Adults in school[2]	0		8 400	3	100 000	22
	Sick, incapable[3]	8 839	5	12 612	5	22 751	5
3.	Labour force	167 932	95	231 237	92	332 276	73
	Formal employment[4]	5 900	3	9 675	4	32 000	7
	Informal businesses, etc.[5]	2 260	1	7 687	3	23 000	5
	Agricultural labour[6]	159 772	90	213 875	85	277 276	61

[1]Census data. Males 16+ and females 14+ in 1948 and 1962. Both sexes 15+ in 1979
[2]1948: assumed none. 1962: estimate: one-third of those with 5+ years of schooling, in census. 1979: census data
[3]Estimated at 5% throughout
[4]1962: employees in District (estimated from Peberdy, 1961) plus those on white farms (agricultural censuses). 1979: Kenya. CBS, *Statistical Abstract*
[5]1948 and 1962: roughly estimated from trends in taxes and licence income (Peberdy, 1961), round a central figure based on number of shops in 1957 (Peberdy, 1958) doubled to allow for other activities
[6]Residual

school). The table shows that the agricultural labour force had grown 1.8 times larger between 1948 and 1979, while the total population had grown 2.8 times. The size of the District had also grown, and, as we shall show in the next chapter, the cropped area had approximately trebled (Table 5.5). The consequences are shown in Table 4.6.

Demand for food in the District increased in proportion to the total population. Table 4.6 shows that cropped hectares per person largely tracked population growth (Chapter 6 shows that most land is still under food crops). Cropped hectares per person engaged in agricultural labour increased slightly in the period 1932−1962, showing an intensification of labour. Although our figures are no more than rough estimates, we know that the proportion of land being fallowed was falling in this period (Table 5.5), which is one sign of intensification. Between 1962 and 1979 cropped hectares per labourer almost doubled, as additional land was being cultivated often by extensive methods (Chapter 10). Labour intensification resumed after 1979 as there was no more land to open up. These are, of course, *district* figures; in each AEZ average land/labour ratios were different.

Our village interviews suggest that farm sizes have recently begun shrinking rapidly, due to subdivision, as it is impossible to find unoccupied farm land. This trend is confirmed by the increase in the 1980s in land under field dividers (see Table 5.4). Everywhere people talked of the burden of school fees, and the difficulty in finding jobs even for children for whose education much had been sacrificed. This was leading some community leaders to favour the teaching of family planning. As they said, it was too late for those who already had their families; the teaching had to start in standard 6 of primary school.[7]

Unfortunately, because of the existing shape of the population pyramid, even if those currently adolescent adopt family planning, population growth in Kenya will only slowly be checked. However, it seems that Kenya has reached the demographic turning point, due in part to the increased costs of rearing children, with an increased proportion of schooling costs now being borne by parents (Kelley and Nobbe, 1990: 14). Preliminary figures for 1989 show a fall in national population growth rates (Table 4.1).

TABLE 4.6. Land/labour relationships

	1932	1948	1962	1979	1989
Total available ha ('000)[1]	636	692	782	1360	1360
Cropped ha ('000)[1]	56	90	126	291	323
Cropped ha (%)	9	13	16	21	24
Agricultural labour ('000)[2]	112	160	214	277	378
as % of population	47	45	38	27	27
Total population ('000)[3]	239	358	566	1023	1400
Cropped ha/labour	0.50	0.56	0.59	1.05	0.85
Cropped ha/person	0.23	0.25	0.22	0.28	0.23
Total ha/labour	5.68	4.33	3.66	4.90	3.60
Total ha/person	2.66	1.93	1.38	1.33	0.97

Sources: Derived from Tables 4.5, 5.1 and 5.5
[1]See Table 5.5 for 1932 and 1961. 1948 figures are based on the 1945 estimate in KNA: MKS/DC/1/8/1. This gives arable as 112 000 ha. Fallow is assumed to be 20%, roughly half-way between the 1932 figure of 33% and the 1961 figure of 5%
[2]See Table 4.5. In the absence of detailed data from the 1989 census, the 1989 figure is assumed to be the same % of the total population as in 1979
[3]See Table 4.1

SUMMARY AND CONCLUSIONS

The population increased at a rate of about 2.5% per annum up to 1948, accelerating afterwards and peaking at over 3.7% during the period 1969–79. There are now signs of a small decline in these high growth rates which have caused a more than fivefold increase in population over the period 1930–1990.

The population was at first compressed within the Reserve boundaries. Population increase without the market incentives to develop and apply more intensive technologies contributed to land degradation. In the absence of market incentives, the natural desire was to provide for the enlarged population by continuing with existing extensive techniques on vacant land. Since this was politically disallowed until about 1960, people resorted instead to temporary out-migration for work. From about 1960 the population pressure was relieved by permanent migration to underdeveloped land within the District, the bulk of it unaided and unsubsidised. Wherever government investments in transport and water facilities have occurred, they have given a greater stimulus to new settlements than have intensive investments in localised settlement schemes. As a consequence of population growth and movement, 35% of the population were living in the dry AEZs 5 and 6 in 1979, as compared with only 9% in these areas in 1932.

Most Akamba do not wish to settle permanently in towns. Within the District, the urban population still formed only 8% of the total in 1989. There has been some permanent out-migration to towns like Nairobi but in 1979 only 6% of the total Akamba population of Kenya was either temporarily or permanently resident in Nairobi District, and 90% of those born in Machakos District were still resident there. The major influence of the growth of large towns such as Nairobi and Mombasa has been to increase the profitability of farming.

Rapid population growth has resulted in a population structure in which 50% of the population is aged under 16. Dependency rates are even higher than this suggests, because a large proportion of 16- to 20-year olds are still at school. The typical farm is short of labour, having only 1.5 adults whose principal occupation is farm work.

We shall see that, in consequence of population pressure and thus more people to feed, investments have been made in farm improvements. There is now no free land for occupation. As farm sizes fall, the urgency of enabling children to qualify for a non-farm job increases, and high educational costs are forcing people to think of family limitation. In the complete absence of free land for development, one of the traditional Akamba options has been eliminated. Income generation must now come from still greater intensification on an already small farm in a difficult farming environment, or the development of new occupations in the processing and servicing sectors of the economy.

NOTES

1 Possible undercounting in 1932 is discussed in Tiffen (1991). It was widely felt there was overcounting in 1989 due to complex questions on family size and a prolonged period of data collection. We were given unofficial 1989 Location totals but have used these only to estimate population in the different AEZs.
2 In some earlier censuses, the 1979 locations were subdivisions of a larger Location. In our tables, the figures relate to the named location and its area at the time of the census in question.
3 The rapidity of urbanisation in Kenya after 1969 can be overstated, since similar expansion of municipal boundaries occurred elsewhere.
4 Establishing the percentage of adult males who are missing is not straightforward. The 1948, 1962 and 1969 censuses classified people simply as adult and child. Females were considered adult at 14

and males at 16, so considerably more females were enumerated as adult. In 1979 ages were recorded but there was a continuing tendency to count some females aged less than 15 as over 15. Using the Kenyan adult sex ratio as the norm, we calculated the number of males that were to be expected in the >15 age group. By expressing the actual number of males as a percentage of the expected, we obtained the percentage of adult males who were apparently out of the District.

5 Areas in the north or near Machakos Town.
6 In 1948 they were all said to be Machakos Akamba. The 1962 and later censuses do not distinguish between the Machakos and Kitui Akamba.
7 As many children do not start primary school until aged 7 or 8, this is at age 13 or 14.

5

Land Use and Tenure[1]

In this chapter we trace the history of land tenure during the period 1930—1990 and analyse the available data on the change in land use. Our expectation, in accordance with the terms of the agricultural intensification thesis, was that we would find indicators of a strengthening of private rights in land, and evidence of the conversion of uncultivated land to arable use and of increasing investments in arable land. This expectation was confirmed. However, customary tenure already recognised private rights, particularly in cultivated land, by 1930. Statutory changes in land tenure — legal demarcation and registration — were, therefore, less important in Machakos than elsewhere. We note that the conversion of grazing land to arable use, and investment in terracing, proceeded more rapidly after 1961 than before.

LAND TENURE

Customary land tenure

Akamba customary rights in cultivated land, as recorded in this century (KNA: Lambert, 1945; Penwill, 1951), were akin to private ownership. They distinguished between unsettled land, *weu*, which was available for communal grazing or for the establishment of new farms, and land which had been cleared and cultivated, which became a family farm or *ng'undu*. The first person to clear a farm could sell it, give it away, or leave it to his sons, without reference to others. The cultivation did not need to be continuous to maintain his rights. A man could even allow others to graze on fallowed land, thus establishing a temporary grazing ground, but such a tenant had to leave when the owner required the land back (according to Akamba representatives on the Reconditioning Committee in 1935 (KNA: DC/MKS/12/2/2)). Sales of cultivated land might be outright or redeemable. This led to disputes, as land became scarcer.[2] Sales were relatively rare when land was plentiful, but Penwill notes that they took place even in the early days of the British administration, usually for a goat or two (Penwill, 1951: 38). Two respondents in Kangundo in 1990 testified to such a sale in about 1920. Sales were sufficiently common for Barnes (KNA: Barnes, 1937) to be able to record the effect that soil erosion had on land prices; they were said to have fallen from £3 to £1 per acre (1 acre = 0.4 ha) in Matungulu, and from Ksh 15 to Ksh 2 per acre in Muputi.[3] Lambert (KNA: Lambert, 1945) reported that the outright sale of land was always customary.

Rights in grazing land were less firm, however. A *kisesi* was a grazing area to which one family claimed exclusive rights, by establishing a cattle post (*syengo*) and marking the surrounding trees. Private grazing rights lasted only while the area was actually used; if the cattle post was abandoned the area reverted to *weu*. However, if part of the *kisesi* was cultivated, it became *ng'undu*. If sons continued to use it for grazing, they inherited it.

Grazing areas and some cultivated fields might be relatively distant from the home base. As the family grew, young men who herded together might locate the site of a new settlement (*utui*) in the *weu*, bringing their wives to cultivate new *ng'undu*. In this way, the *weu* was converted to private, heritable land.

Women acquired rights to land through marriage.[4] Sons were entitled to inherit equal shares in their mother's portion. In practice, while land was plentiful, the older sons would usually establish their own farms in the *weu*, leaving the youngest to take over the old farm and to care for his mother in her old age. A widow kept her cultivation rights till her death. The rights of older sons who had moved away permanently lapsed after a period of time, and the rights of the youngest became absolute. This could lead to disputes, not only between brothers but between nephews and uncles.[5]

Private appropriation of land led to the virtual disappearance of the *weu* in Iveti, near Machakos Town, by 1930 and in the northern half of the Reserve by 1940 (Munro, 1975: 200−201, citing several District files). This led to an increase in land disputes, and in tenancies, since those shifting cultivation and moving house periodically became reluctant to allow their rights in previous holdings to lapse. Those who took up tenancies included an increasing number who had been unable to find new land, or who had inherited, after division, a small farm; 655 holdings of an uneconomic size were reported in the north in 1939 (Munro, 1975: 203). The landless who began to be mentioned in official reports included the sons of squatters on European farms, who had increasing problems in establishing claim to land that their fathers had left inside the Reserve.

Government interventions in custom

As part of efforts to prevent land degradation, the Local Native Council (LNC) passed a resolution in 1938 requiring people to fence or hedge both their arable holding and their *kisesi*. This reinforced a practice that was already occurring in the more crowded areas (see Figure 1.4). Hedges made the *kisesi* permanent. In less crowded areas, such as Masii, leaders told us that grazing was still mainly communal in 1960, but that by 1990 it had all become private.

Many administrators and agriculturalists considered divisible inheritance and fragmentation to be serious obstacles to sound farming, but there was a division of opinion in the Department of Agriculture in the 1940s about the remedy. Some thought that tribal ownership should be revived as a basis for co-operative conservation effort and group farming (Ruthenberg, 1966: 7; Brown, 1968: 39; Throup, 1987: 72).[6] The Swynnerton Plan (Swynnerton, 1954) reversed this view in favour of those in the Department who saw individual security of tenure as essential to progress. It aimed to revolutionise African agriculture through consolidation, the registration of individual titles, and the cultivation, under supervision, of profitable export crops which had been prohibited up till then.

Land consolidation was opposed in Machakos District because farmers valued having land in different ecological niches (de Wilde, 1967, vol.2: 117). Machakos District was declared for registration only in 1965, after insistence on consolidation had been dropped. It got its own adjudication officer in 1968. Most farmers we interviewed regarded registration as valuable, first, for preventing disputes over ownership and, second, for improving access to credit.

TABLE 5.1. Land registration, 1977 and 1992 (% of sub-locations)

	Fully registered	In process	Undeclared
1977	24	26	50
1992	35	45	20

Source for 1977: Consortium, Report 6, (1978: 54); for 1992: calculated from information given by Lands Officer, Machakos District

However, it can take six or seven years to complete registration in a sub-location, since the procedure involves establishing and mapping boundaries (demarcation), and resolving all disputes. Only when all appeals have been heard are certificates issued against payment of a fee. Full land registration had been completed for only 35% of sub-locations by the end of 1991 (Table 5.1).[7]

Farmers are particularly keen to secure registration in the former Crown Lands. Those settling there established rights in their own eyes in the traditional manner by cultivation, and in Ngwata they had these farms demarcated by elders or political leaders (Mbithi and Barnes, 1975; local informants, 1990). However, there have been disputes with large-scale farmers or institutions which have received grants of land from the Government.

Government rulings to regulate sales and to ensure that farmers do not deprive children of their land rights have created some uncertainties, but they have not stopped sales. Some provision is now made for unmarried daughters to inherit plots, but otherwise, according to elderly men and women leaders, the rights of men and women in land remain the same as before.

LAND DISTRIBUTION AND PRICES

There is an active land market. In 1964, 28% of farmers in Kangundo had purchased one or more of their plots, but only 17% of those in Iveti and Masii and less than 10% in Mbooni and Nzaui (Owako, 1969: Appendix 4). Except in Kangundo and Iveti, *weu* was still available. During 1979−1980, Meyers (1982) found that, in older settled areas of AEZ 4, 21% of farmers had purchased some land in the previous five years, and 15% had sold. Renting appears to have been uncommon. In 1986−1987, 97% of Machakos farmers said they were not renting, compared with a national average of 90% (Kenya, CBS, 1989: 29).

Families have never been equal in their access to land. The plough reinforced the inequality, as it enabled its owners to cultivate more than they could with the hoe. Owako found a skewed distribution of land in AEZs 2 and 3 in 1964, with the majority having holdings smaller than 3.6 ha (see Table 5.2). In AEZ 4, by contrast, a majority had holdings larger than this; by 1977, however, the distribution was already shifting in favour of smaller holdings. But in the 1960s and 1970s, many smaller farmers in the older settled areas sold up to finance their move to, and development of, farms in the areas of new settlement (Matingu, 1974).

We do not know the extent of landlessness at any time. Collier and Lal (1980: 25−26) estimated that during 1975−1976 7% of rural households in Eastern Province were landless and without good alternative sources of income. Landlessness may have increased since then, for population growth has cut the inherited share of some to a house-sized plot, and new farm land is unavailable.

In 1990, community leaders estimated that average prices for terraced arable land ranged from Ksh 80 000/acre (with coffee) or Ksh 40 000/acre (without coffee) in Kangundo to Ksh 10 000/acre

TABLE 5.2. Percentage of farmers by land ownership category

1964 Survey			1977 Survey	
Land owned (ha)	AEZ 2/3[1]	AEZ 4[2]	Land owned (ha)	AEZ 4[3]
0−0.4	3.1	0.0	0−0.4	1.2
0.4−1.2	19.4	5.4	0.4−1.2	18.0
1.2−3.6	51.5	35.8	1.6−4.0	46.5
3.6−12	22.1	39.1 .	4.4−12.0	34.3
Over 12	3.9	19.7	Over 12	0.0
Total	100.0	100.0	Total	100.0

[1] Iveti, Kangundo, Mbooni Locations
[2] Masii, Nzaui Locations
[3] Machakos and Kitui Districts
Source for 1964: Owako (1969, Table 10), and our calculations; for 1977: Consortium, Report 3 (1978: Table 2)

in Masii and less than Ksh 5000/acre in Ngwata. We can establish some markers for the price of land in the Kangundo−Matungulu area. In the 1920s, Mr Thiaka's father acquired a plot in exchange for a goat, valued at Ksh 350 in 1990. The price per acre mentioned by Barnes looks to be the equivalent of a cow, valued at Ksh 1800 in 1990. From the 1930s to 1990, the population density had increased fivefold, but the price of land had increased twenty-fold in this part of the District, a sure indication of increasing land scarcity, as well as increased land productivity.

MEASURING LAND-USE CHANGE

These trends in the tenure, distribution and prices of land suggest that land use during the period 1930−1990 has been subject to change on a large scale with, in particular, (a) the extension of cultivated land at the expense of rangelands and woodland, and (b) the terracing of arable land. Objective verification is now sought, using (i) conventional vertical black-and-white air photography (AP); (ii) systematic reconnaissance flight (SRF) low-level air photography, and (iii) official statistics.

Since conventional AP is available for several different years, it offers the possibility of generating compatible data for different points in time. Sequential AP interpretation is potentially a powerful method of evaluating environmental change; subject to satisfactory interpretation, it can generate accurate land-use statistics.[8] The earliest photography of Machakos took place in 1948, but the latest available was in 1978; the data series cannot, therefore, be extended to the present. In 1981 and 1985, SRF surveys were carried out over the whole District, generating large-scale colour slide photographs according to a discontinuous, systematic sampling procedure (Ecosystems, 1982; 1985/6). The large scale and high resolution of the photographs, together with the District-wide sample, provide more detailed and comprehensive land-use data than the conventional air photography. Against this advantage must be counted two disadvantages: the shallow time-depth of the comparison (less than five years), and difficulties of compatibility with the earlier air photography.[9] The methods used with both types of photography are described fully in Rostom and Mortimore (1991).[10]

Agricultural statistics are not immediately compatible with land-use data until allowance has

TABLE 5.3. Areas of the land use classes, 1948–1978 (per cent)

Study area	Size (hectares)	1948			1961			1978		
		C	B	F	C	B	F	C	B	F
Kangundo/Matungulu/Mbiuni	18 000	35.3	61.8	2.9	35.4	62.3	2.3	80.7	13.2	6.1
Kalama/Mbooni	23 000	13.6	85.1	1.3	14.2	82.1	3.7	54.2	40.9	4.9
Masii	16 050	23.4	72.5	4.1	27.6	69.7	2.7	50.9	46.5	2.6
Makueni	13 800	1.2	78.6	20.2	8.0	92.0	0.0	30.1	50.7	19.2
Ngwata	13 200	—[1]	—[1]	—[1]	0	52.2	47.8	19.8	62.3	17.9

Note: C = cultivation, B = bush/scrub/grazing land, F = forest
[1]Ngwata study area was virtually unoccupied in 1948
Source: air-photo interpretation (by courtesy of the Survey of Kenya)

been made for the fact that much land under food crops is cultivated twice a year, and estimated areas therefore need to be halved. There are no data on the proportion of the land which was double-cropped. Assumptions must therefore be made. Crop area figures were estimated by agricultural officers in the field, and they may not be up to date on new settlements. Notwithstanding these disadvantages, Ministry of Agriculture estimates give a guide to land use as far back as 1930.

LAND-USE CHANGE, 1948–1978

Table 5.3 shows the change in land use in five study areas whose Locations are shown in Figure 1.1. They represent a continuum in ecology and population density, from AEZ 2/3 to AEZ 5, and from densities over 200/km^2 (in 1979) to areas below 25/km^2. The last two areas are the most recently settled (Makueni from the 1940s and Ngwata from the 1960s).

Of particular interest is the relationship between population density, the area under cultivation, and the proportion of cultivated land that was terraced in some form (Figure 5.1).[11] The data show that, with the exception of study area 2 (in 1948 and 1961), both the percentage cultivated and the percentage of cultivated land terraced increased with density — whether between study areas in the same year, or between years in the same study area. This strong relationship accords with our theoretical expectations. The extension of both the cultivated area and the proportion terraced fell behind population density during 1948–1961, but recovered later. This lapse corresponded to a fall-back in conservation efforts in the years preceding Independence (see Chapter 11). (The smaller scale, greater amount of cloud cover, and inferior contrast of the 1960–1961 photographs makes them less reliable than those of either 1948 or 1978. For this reason, undue weight should not be put on the 1961 data.)

Figures 5.2 and 5.3 present the results of interpretation of air photography at the beginning and end of the period, for two of the study areas, and we discuss land use in a third. (The full set for all five study areas is available in Rostom and Mortimore (1991).)

Study area 1 (Kangundo, Matungulu and Mbiuni Locations)

This study area includes parts of three Locations, the first two in AEZ 2/3 on the west side of the Kanzalu Range of hills, and the third — much drier, and less densely populated — extending into AEZ 4 on the eastern side. Kangundo and Matungulu were notable for rapid population

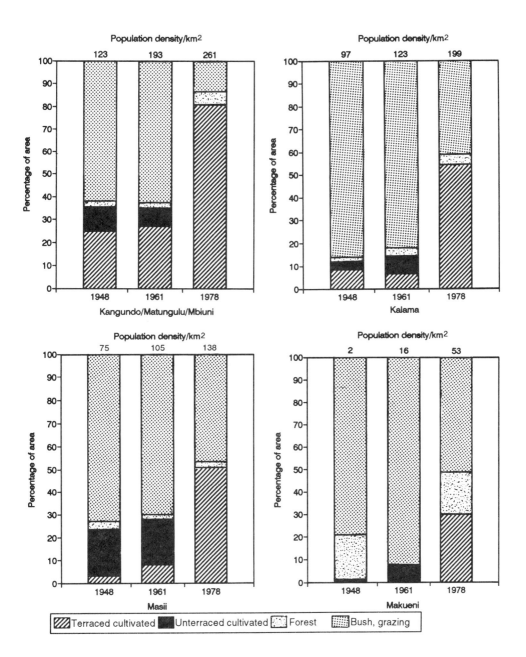

FIGURE 5.1. Uncultivated, cultivated and terraced land in four study areas

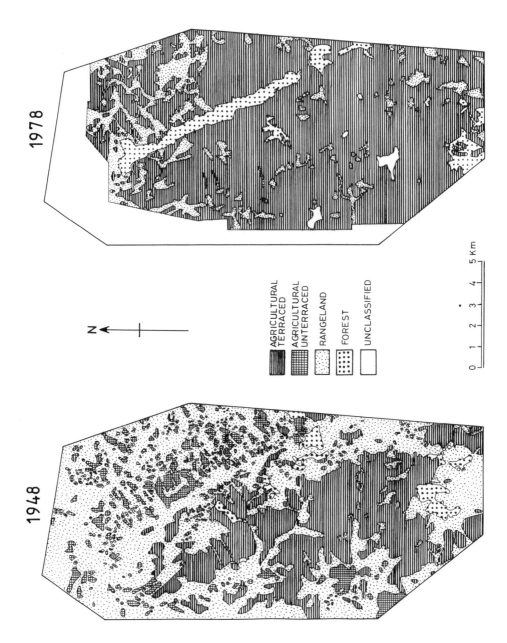

FIGURE 5.2. Land use in Kangundo/Matungulu/Mbiuni study area, 1948 and 1978

1978

1948

N

AGRICULTURAL
TERRACED

AGRICULTURAL
UNTERRACED

RANGELAND

FOREST

UNCLASSIFIED

0 1 2 3 4 5 Km

71

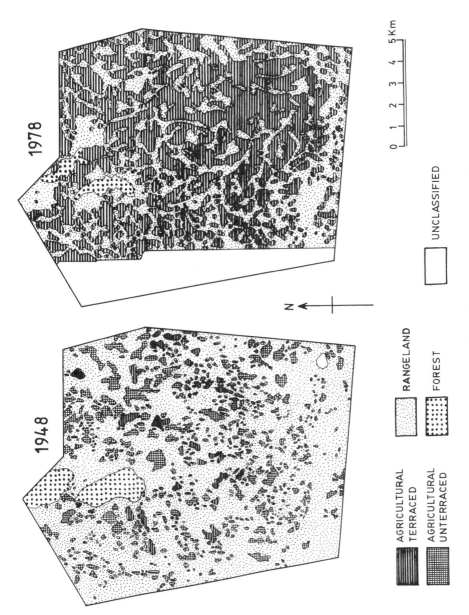

1978

1948

0 1 2 3 4 5 Km

N

AGRICULTURAL
TERRACED

AGRICULTURAL
UNTERRACED

RANGELAND

FOREST

UNCLASSIFIED

FIGURE 5.3. Land use in Masii study area, 1948 and 1978

growth very early in the present century, owing to in-migration from further south. They were also known for their high levels of market participation and farm capitalisation.

Cultivated land increased by 128% between 1948 and 1978, from 35% to over 80% of the study area. Virtually all this increase appears to have occurred after 1961. The area of bushland decreased accordingly, to less than 15%. Forest (with woodland) declined by 21% between 1948 and 1961 but increased by 165% between then and 1978. The total forest area involved is small (less than 1000 ha), and reflects the reclassification of protected woodland on the Kanzalu Range, from bushland on the 1961 photographs to forest on those of 1978. The effect of the Range on spatial patterns of land use and conservation is noticeable. In 1948 cultivation was concentrated to the west of the Range, and up till 1961, terraced cultivation was exclusively distributed on that side. By 1978, cultivation had increased markedly on the eastern side of the Range, and terracing had been extended to all the cultivated blocks. However, taken as a whole, this study area is remarkable for the fact that 70% of its cultivated land was already terraced in some form or other in 1948.

Study area 3 (Masii Location)

This study area is in AEZ 4 and contains no significant hill masses. Its steeply dissected plains were settled early, however, by in-migrants from the hills. A less pronounced acceleration in the extension of cultivated land (compared with study area 1) took place in Masii. Although the proportion more than doubled between 1948 and 1978, the percentage under cultivation only exceeded 50% by 1978. Consequently, the decline in bushland was less dramatic (from 72% to 46%) and reflects a lower intensity of farming, throughout the period, than in study area 1. This reflects poorer farming conditions and a greater emphasis on livestock. Forest and woodland declined steadily to 360 ha; there is no evidence of a reversal of this decline, like that observed in study area 1. Masii made spectacular progress in terracing after 1961; the percentage of cultivated land showing evidence of terraces increased from less than 30% in 1961 to 100% in 1978.

Study area 4 (Makueni Location)

In this study area, in AEZ 4/5, conditions are drier, average altitudes lower, and temperatures higher. The area lay on the fringes of the Reserve and was virtually uninhabited until 1946. Dense thorn bush, wild animals (notably rhinoceros), tsetse fly and water problems discouraged farmers and graziers alike. The area typifies the newer settled lands of the east and south of the District. The amount of cultivated land was negligible (160 ha) in 1948, when the Makueni Resettlement Scheme had only just begun. Thereafter, cultivated land increased rapidly to 8% in 1961, and 30% in 1978, and bushland declined accordingly to about 50% in 1978 (Figure 5.1 and Table 5.3). Forest was not identified on the 1961 photographs, but it is possible that the percentage (20% in 1948 and 19% in 1978) was constant throughout the period, and that the poorer quality and smaller scale of the 1961 photographs are to blame. Initially, farm land was not terraced at Makueni but, notwithstanding the gentleness of many of its slopes, all cultivated land had been terraced by 1978. Conservation was promoted on the settlement scheme in the early years, and later became widely accepted outside the area of the former settlement.

Overall

Analysis of the land-use data generated from the air photographs of 1948, 1960–1961 and 1978[12] suggests the following conclusions:

(1) A gradient of land-use intensity, expressed in the relative percentages of cultivated land and bushland, follows population density in time and in space.
(2) A second marker in this gradient is the chronology of terracing on farmlands. Area 1 had terraced 70% of its farmland in some form by 1948. Area 3 had terraced only 29% by 1961, and Area 4 virtually none. All these areas reached 100% by 1978 (though this does not mean that no further need for conservation existed) but Area 5, settled during the 1960s and 1970s, had terraced only 27% by 1978.
(3) Table 5.3 and Figure 5.1 suggest a sharp acceleration, after 1961, in *both* farmland extension *and* soil conservation on farms, along with a real improvement in the small areas of forest.[13] Negative or ambivalent signals from the period 1948–1961 imply that this was a watershed in the history of land use in the District. It is known that terrace construction stagnated or declined during the later part of that period (see Chapter 11).

LAND-USE CHANGE, 1981–1985

Although separated by only 4.5 years, the two Ecosystems SRF surveys of 1981 and 1985 picked up statistically significant changes in a number of land-use variables (Ecosystems, 1985/6: Vol.4). Unlike the results of the AP interpretation, the data refer to the whole District (Table 5.4).

TABLE 5.4. Changes in land use, 1981–1985 (after Ecosystems, 1985/6: Vol. 4)

Land use	1981	1985	% change/year
	(% of District)		1981–1985
Arable land	20.9	21.9	1.06
1. Cultivated land	17.7	18.2	0.70 ns
2. Seasonal fallows and bare fields	1.0	1.5	9.03
3. Field dividers	1.3	1.7	7.55
4. Estate cash crops	0.9	1.0	0.70 ns
5. Smallholder cash crops	1.0	1.9	14.32
6. Smallholder staple crops	16.8	16.7	−0.05
7. Horticulture	0.1	0.5	31.19
Natural and managed vegetation	75.7	74.7	−0.32 ns
1. Natural forest	2.8	1.2	−17.43
2. Bushland	39.3	19.6	−14.32
3. Woodland	5.7	15.7	25.17
4. Grassland	18.6	28.6	10.05
5. Plantation forest	0.2	0.2	3.5
6. Woodlots	0.3	0.2	4.5

ns = Not significant at $P = 0.050$

Arable and cultivated land

Total arable land (including both cultivated land and fallows) increased at the rate of only 1% per year in the District as a whole, notwithstanding the fact that, under the classification employed, it occupied only 22% of the total area. The average field size decreased by 30% from 0.24 ha to 0.17 ha, and the area under field dividers (hedgerows, fences, etc.) increased significantly. Cultivated land (land under crops) did not change significantly. These facts point to an intensification of farming on existing cultivated land, and there is no evidence of a large-scale extension of the cultivated area.

Natural vegetation

The total area of natural and managed vegetation remained quite stable between 1981 and 1985 (Table 5.4). A decrease was recorded in natural forest, but this was confined to Kibwezi Division, where the forested Chyulu Hills were being rapidly cleared for farming. All other Divisions with any forest showed a significant increase. The bushlands decreased in all eight Divisions reflecting the conversion of this vegetation class into open woodland or grassland, both of which increased significantly in area. It is interesting to note that the diminution in the area of bushland was largely unrelated to the expansion of agriculture. Only 1775 ha/year out of 62 000 ha/year were added to the cultivated area. The diminution of bushland was related to the smallholder livestock sector (see Chapter 7).

  The SRF data show that the rapid changes in land use revealed by AP interpretation between 1961 and 1978 had largely worked themselves out by the mid-1980s, and that the intensification of arable farming and the management of natural vegetation were continuing.

LAND-USE CHANGE, 1930–1962

Using a variety of official or semi-official estimates, Table 5.5 sets out the growth of the cultivated area from 1930 to the 1980s. These estimates are derived from agricultural officers' field observations. Though not easily compatible with the other data sets, they provide a longer series.

  In 1930 the cultivated percentage in the Reserve was between 9 and 13, depending on whether fallows are included and on the assumed size of the Reserve area.[14] However, after 1960–1962, the estimates are only available for the whole District; the inclusion of large areas of uninhabited or sparsely settled bush means that although cultivated area increased, its percentage started climbing only in the 1970s. The average figures reported in the 1970s and 1980s indicate a strong upward movement more recently.

CONCLUSION

This chapter has set out the changes that occurred in land tenure, through both government interventions and the autonomous evolution of custom, and in the distribution and price of land, and has measured changes in land use and conservation investment (terraces) using three incomplete but complementary data sets. These changes are fully consistent with expectations based on our intensification hypothesis, even though their measurement presents some problems of compatibility.

  According to the Department of Agriculture's estimates, the cultivated area grew from

TABLE 5.5. Cultivated areas, 1930s–1980s (according to Department of Agriculture estimates)

Year	Source	Cultivated area '000 ha	per cent	Available area '000 ha	
1930	Land Commission, (1933)[1]	56[1]	9	636	(1)
1957	Peberdy (1958)	101	14	706	(2)
1960–1962	Agricultural Sample Census (1960) (Reserve)	120[1]	15	782	(3)
	Above plus Scheduled Areas (Kenya Agricultural Census, 1962)	137	14	982	(4)
1970–1979	MoA crop area reports (average)	187[2]	14	1370	(5)
1981–1988	MoA crop area reports (average)	313[2]	23	1370	(5)

[1]Cultivated area defined as temporary plus permanent crops. Inclusion of 'temporary fallows' raises the total to 84 000 ha (13%) in 1930 and 126 000 ha (16%) in 1960–62

[2]Assumes that all land under cereal crops is cropped twice yearly, and other cropland twice

(1) Includes temporary grazing in Yatta Plateau

(2) Assumed to include some of Makueni (newly settled), and temporary grazing on Yatta Plateau and Simba Ranch

(3) District (1500) less game park (229), Scheduled Areas (226) and half of Kikumbulyu (150), after Morgan and Shaffer (1966)

(4) Morgan's figures give 982 if Scheduled Areas are added to the total given in Row 3

(5) Census figure for District less game park (1969 and 1979)

56 000 ha in 1930 to 313 000 ha (23% of the District) in the 1980s: a rate of growth closely comparable to that of the population. The SRF data indicate 311 000 ha (22%) in 1985, a closely comparable figure. The much larger cultivated percentages measured in our study areas (Table 5.3) are not compatible. Our sample did not reflect the large geographical area covered by AEZs 5 and 6, where population densities remain low.

NOTES

1 This chapter has been developed from initial research by R. S. Rostom (on land use) and Judith Mbula Bahemuka (on land tenure); see ODI Working Papers 58 and 62 respectively.

2 About 1937 the District Commissioner called a meeting of elders from all locations, who decided that if a consideration of reasonable value had been given, the presumption was for an outright sale (Penwill, 1951: 49).

3 Other factors besides soil erosion may have been at work in lowering prices; the Depression had brought a fall in agricultural prices.

4 Their husband showed them an area to cultivate, and a direction in which to go (the word used for the wife's portion, *mbee*, literally means 'in front' (Penwill, 1951).

5 In such cases the elders would look to see if the youngest had really stayed with his mother, and if she had said that all the land would be his. If the land was divided amongst brothers, each could sell, but the inheritor, unlike the first clearer, was obliged first to offer it to his relatives. In 1946 the LNC formalised this by stating that sales must have the consent of the elders who had customary control, owing, Penwill says, to the prevalence of sons selling off, with the minimum of advertisement, not only their own portion but that of their brothers as well. However, a registration book in the DC's office was not much used (Penwill, 1951: 41).

6 The Machakos Agricultural Officer, M. H. Grieves, designed the projected Makueni settlement on the basis of collective farms, for the Russian model was not then out of fashion. But the LNC successfully insisted on individual titles.

7 Official demarcation of clear boundaries is regarded by many farmers as the most important step, since formal title deeds are only necessary for certain purposes such as loans. Some farmers do not pay the fee to collect title deeds even when registered (Kenya, Ministry of Planning, 1988).

8   Its limitations, however, should be borne in mind. Earlier photographs usually have inferior resolution, and the scope for interpretation error increases with older photographs as ground reference becomes impossible. Differences in scale between one set of photography and another create compatibility problems. Cloud cover and shadows occasionally obscure part of the surface; so quite small areas of cloud, appearing on several sets of photography, can have a damaging effect on sequential analyses which depend on study areas being standardised. Scale distortion on individual photographs (which occur more in hilly areas) must be compensated for. Finally, and most important for sequential analyses of environmental change, the months (seasons) in which the photographs were taken may not be identical from one set to another, and even if they are, inter-annual variability in rainfall distribution affects the images produced, and creates difficulties for the interpretation of change during the intervening years.

9   The issue of compatibility was investigated thoroughly, and it was concluded that this data set could not be used in conjunction with the 1978 photography (Ecosystems, 1985/6: Vol. 4).

10   Earth satellite data are technically available for many points in time from the 1970s to the present, and their use for monitoring environmental change in Africa has been frequently and forcefully advocated. Constraints of time, cost, and the technical facilities available restricted us to a limited methodological experiment on locally available, low-cost Landsat TM false colour imagery, using a visual interpretation method. The data produced are not consistent with those obtained from conventional air photography. It is concluded that the false colour imagery is incapable of harmonisation by visual interpretation with the land-use classes identified on air photographs.

11   Land under cultivation was subdivided into (a) non-terraced and (b) terraced land. Each block was assigned to its class according to whether terrace structures are identified on the photographs assisted by stereoscopic viewing. Terrace maintenance could not be assessed, nor the adequacy of the structures or design.

12   Use of spatially continuous sample blocks, which is necessary for the methodology, does not permit randomisation of the sample population. The blocks were selected to represent a *range* of ecological and demographic conditions, however, and this range is representative of the District, though its *average* may not be. While the internal compatibility of data sets, generated by standard methods of interpretation from black-and-white photography, is greater than that of data sets generated from different types of remotely sensed media, it is not perfect.

13   There was a significant turnaround in the percentage of forest and woodland in some areas, beginning after 1948 in Area 1 and after 1961 in Area 2. It seems that in Makueni, the percentage was relatively stable. This implies that forest reserves were being successfully established. The indicators are negative, however, for Masii (continuing decline of a very small forest area) and Ngwata (showing woodland degradation to bushland).

14   Maher (RH: Maher, 1937) used higher estimates which imply 19% cultivated, a figure higher than that derived from Peberdy's estimate of 1957 and the government's estimates for 1960−1962. It seems probable that Maher's estimates were too high, even allowing that he may have counted in fallow, and excluded the Yatta grazing area from his Reserve Area.

6

Crop and Livestock Production[1]

AIMS AND DATA

Agricultural output per person is an important measure of welfare in any economy where agriculture is the main occupation and where locally grown food is the main basis of family nutrition. It is frequently feared that, where population is growing rapidly, the value of output per person will drop. Output per hectare is an important indicator of productivity, and also of sustainability, since falling output might indicate a deterioration in the resource base. The purpose of this chapter is to chart total agricultural production on a District basis since 1930 in so far as the data allow. It does this by examining in turn the main contributors to farm income — food and non-food crops, and livestock. (The way households in particular AEZ have combined these elements in a farm and income system is examined in Chapter 10.) Tree products are examined separately in Chapter 13. Finally, all products are converted into their value in maize, to provide a common measure over time. District production is then examined on a per head and per hectare basis, as measures of welfare and productivity which take into account the growth of population and the increase in District area in Figures 6.4 and 6.5. We find substantial increases in both. This chapter therefore provides our main evidence for an increase in agricultural productivity which has substantially outpaced population growth. Our figures, admittedly based on crude data, are more likely to understate output in the 1970s and 1980s than to overstate them. Although the general trend is upwards, the constituents of output have varied over time, and have sometimes fallen. The chapter describes the major economic and environmental influences which have affected the nature and quantity of output.

The quality of the data, and gaps in it, make the task of measurement difficult. Only sales out of the District were recorded up to 1969, ignoring the bulk of production which was consumed locally. We then have a new series from 1974, in which total production is estimated.[2] For production data prior to 1974 we have occasional estimates and agricultural 'censuses'.[3] We have used as the baseline the *Agricultural Census 1930* (Kenya, DoA, 1930) without, however, putting too much trust in it. (The data for Kitui and Machakos in the printed version seem to have been transposed; as Machakos is the larger district we always took the larger of the figures given for the two Districts.) For 1957 we have a detailed estimate of cropped areas and total production, with price data (Peberdy, 1958). We have used this as a central element in our graphs of production. However, 1957 was an exceptionally good year. The 1960–1961 agricultural census was the first to sample the whole District. Unfortunately, it took place in a year with two droughts, so production was unusually low. Average production at this time was probably

TABLE 6.1. Crop hectares, output and yields, 1930–1961

	Hectares	Total output (tons)	Yield (kg/ha)
1930			
Maize	9 753	5 016	514
Pulses	19 668	15 011	763
Sorghum and millets	17 937	13 515	753
Roots	12 222	24 545	2 008
Bananas	99	611	na
Vegetables	102	127	1 236
Sugar	284	35 050	na
Others	75	na	na
1957			
Maize	137 632	69 388	504
Beans	109 312	61 224	560
Pigeon peas	8 097	4 535	560
Cowpeas	6 073	2 041	336
Sorghum	810	408	504
Millet	6 883	3 469	504
Arrowroot, cassava	8 097	na	na
Castor oil	6 478	88	14
Sisal	40 486	84	2
Wattle	4 858	1 894	390
Fruits	3 239	7 256	2 240
Bananas	4 059	24 943	6 145
Vegetables	4 858	10 190	2 098
Grams	648	367	567
Others	910	na	na
1960/61			
Maize	190 045	38 049	200
Pulses	161 918	36 656	226
Sorghum	14 164	2 341	165
Millet	28 531	4 783	168
Arrowroot, cassava	22 218	na	na
Sisal	3 278	5 000	1 525
Wattle	1 497	1 650	1 102
Fruits	405	319	788
Bananas	3 399	20 952	6 163
Vegetables	567	1 086	1 917
Grams	na	415	na
Coffee	526	161	306

Note: Hectares add up to more than the total area under crops (Table 5.5) because of double counting of mixed crops.
    Hectares and production for the two seasons have been added
Source: Kenya, DoA (1930); Peberdy (1958) for 1957; Kenya, MoA (1962a) for 1960/61

between these two points, deduced from Peberdy (1961), who charts maize export production and estimated subsistence production from 1943 to 1961. In both 1957 and 1960/1961, fields with mixed crops were double-counted, and the hectares are for two seasons. Table 6.1 compares the data for 1930, 1957 and 1960/1961.

Production data from 1974 have been taken from the Annual Reports of the District Agricultural

Officers. The methods used are probably fairly reliable in respect of trends in average yields, and their variation from year to year due to climatic factors. There may be more of a lag in regard to areas planted, and therefore, total production.[4] Total production of coffee and cotton is available over a longer period of time and is relatively accurate as these products are sold to official monopolies.

While the general accuracy of production data is not high, it should give information on major trends. The data generally show coincidence with what we should expect in relation to the impact of droughts, or price changes. However, several factors influence crop production in any given year. The most important are:

- the amount and distribution of rainfall and the degree to which water conservation is practised;
- the price to be obtained for the output relative to other feasible crops;
- the varieties of seed used and their availability (in the case of annual crops);
- the age of the crop (in the case of tree crops);
- the activities of the extension services;
- the price and availability of fertilisers and other chemical inputs.

Although our study aims to cover six decades, most of the data series are for shorter periods, and this makes the account unavoidably fragmentary. Livestock data are even more crude than crop data.[5]

STAPLE FOOD PRODUCTION

Trends in local food production and requirements

The Kenyan Government and its colonial predecessor have regarded not only national but also District self-sufficiency in staple food as important, because of the cost of food relief (see Chapter 15). From the viewpoint of the household, self-sufficiency is less important than its entitlement to food, whether grown on its own land or earned by sales or off-farm income. Climatic and price variability is such that most farm families continue to aim at feeding themselves, and, in some parts of the District, also at having a surplus for local sales.

The percentage of land under staple crops, defined as grains, roots and pulses, has always been high in Machakos. During 1964–1965 it was about 90%. Owako (1969) shows that cash crops occupied 20–25% of the land in AEZ 2 and 3 locations, and 2–11% in AEZ 4 ones. (AEZ 5, which at the time was only beginning to be settled, was not represented.) In 1985, maize, beans and peas still occupied about 76% of the cultivated land area (see Table 5.4).

Due to the nature of the climate, agricultural officers have generally encouraged the growing of sorghum, millet and cassava in AEZs 4 and 5, but maize has become the preferred food and the preferred crop, particularly since most children are no longer available for bird-scaring. According to the 1930 census, sorghum and millet then occupied nearly twice the area under maize (Table 6.1). Table 6.1 shows the considerable fall in their production according to the 1957 and 1961 figures. By the 1970s they occupied less than 1% of the total area; there was a slight rise in 1988 but much sorghum was then produced for sale, owing to a price rise. Roots were also proportionately less important in the 1950s than in 1930. Some of the preferred roots, such as arrowroot, occupied valley bottom land that by the 1950s was being used for bananas and vegetables. By the 1980s, with the spread of population into the drier areas, cassava and sweet potatoes had become the main reported roots, occupying about 1% of the land in 1977 and 6% in 1987. The continued predominance of maize in the period 1974–1988, is important, since increased production of less demanding crops can be regarded as a sign of impoverishment of both the land and people. (Output of maize was estimated at 111 000 tons in 1988, compared with 6000 tons of sorghum and millet (Mbogoh, 1991: Table A.5).) Despite the larger proportion of the population in AEZs 5 and 6 in the 1980s, compared to 1962, they were not being forced to cultivate less preferred foods.

Food imports remain necessary in years affected by bad droughts. Total maize production in relation to rainfall during 1974–1988 is shown in Figure 6.1. On the whole, the figure shows a relationship between the drought index (measuring the degree of rainfall variation from the average) and production.[6] It suggests that farmers pursue strategies which maintain production in somewhat below-average years, with production only falling severely in very bad years. Figure 6.2 shows the imports of food grains on a per capita basis, including both famine relief and purchases, and the exports of maize, between 1942 and 1962, and 1974 and 1985, years for which data are available. The correlation with rainfall is very good, allowing for some lag effect. For example, output in 1984 was low because of a medium drought in the short rains of 1983 and a severe drought in the long rains of 1984, the latter being the third successive drought season. Output in 1985 was high because of exceptionally good short rains in the latter part of 1984. However, the harvest was not available till March, and in the first quarter of the year substantial imports and famine relief were required.

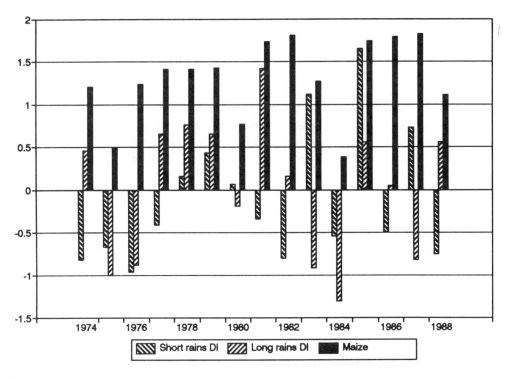

FIGURE 6.1. Maize production and drought, 1974–1988. DI = drought index, short rains previous year plus long rains current year; Maize = maize production in 100 000 tons

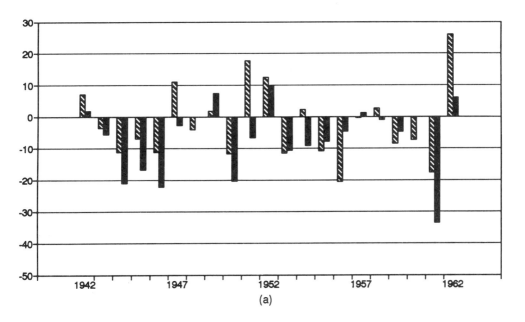

(a)

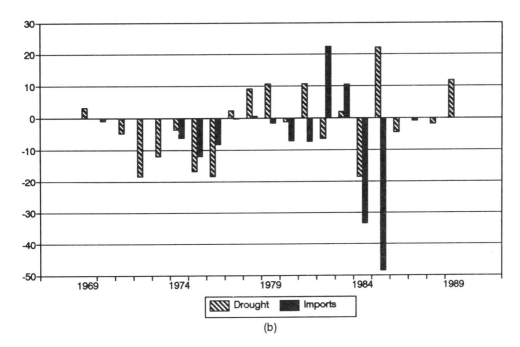

(b)

FIGURE 6.2. Net maize imports/exports per capita: (a) 1942–1962; (b) 1974–1985. Drought = drought index for short rains previous year plus long rains current year, multiplied by 10 (see Chapter 3). Imports = maize imports plus famine relief minus exports (positive values show net exports). Source: 1942–1962: Peberdy (1958) and Owako (1969); 1974–1985: Kliest (1985) and ADEC (1986)

What is remarkable is that in the first series, 1942–1962, net imports averaged 17.4 kg per capita. In the period 1974–1985 they averaged 7.6 kg per capita, despite the substantial growth of total population and the proportions living in AEZs 5 and 6 and in towns (see Chapter 4). Substantial amounts of food were imported via unofficial channels in both periods. The figures relate to net exports and imports of the National Crop Production Board (NCPB) and its predecessor, plus famine relief. The NCPB is the residual buyer and seller for maize, dealing in what farmers cannot sell or obtain locally. The difference between the 1942–1962 and 1974–1985 figures is sufficiently great to allow us to conclude that, despite the large increase in population, food production in relation to District requirements in the 1980s was better than it was in the period 1942–1962.

The data above relate mainly to maize imports, though some pulses are included in the 1981–1985 totals. ADEC (1986) made an estimate of food requirements, 1980–1981 to 1985–1986, and found that although the District usually had a deficit in maize and sorghum, it normally had a surplus of pulses, except in severe drought conditions.

Yield trends

Yields vary erratically according to weather conditions. The 15 years of relatively reliable data from 1974 to 1988 do not complete a drought cycle of 20–22 years. The average for the whole period is a low 850 kg/ha for maize and 550 kg/ha for beans. However, if we take averages for each 5-year period since 1974, yields were apparently higher during 1979–1983, than either before or afterwards. This confirms the necessity, in areas like Machakos, of taking a long view of trends if we are not to be deceived by short-term weather variations.

It is unfortunate that we have no good data on maize yields for the 1960s and 1950s, in order to see if Katumani varieties introduced since about 1966 have had an impact (see Chapter 14). Yields in the early 1960s were said to vary from 220 kg/ha in a bad season to over 1100 kg/ha in a good one (de Wilde, 1967). On this basis the 500 kg reported in the 1957 and 1930 estimates looks about an average figure (Table 6.1). The impact to be expected from Katumani would be a reduction in the depression of yields by bad rainfall, rather than an increase in good years, since Katumani was bred as a drought-evader rather than for yield increase. Increased use of drought-evading types should therefore result in a higher average over a period of years. The average yield of 850 kg/ha for 1974–1988 suggests that maize yields, while still low, were substantially above those of the early 1960s, despite more use of AEZs 5 and 6. (Yield rises are confirmed by farm survey data — see Chapter 10.) Pulse yields, which according to Peberdy (1961) ranged between 200 and 450 kg/ha, appear to have risen to 550 kg/ha during 1974–1988. Chemical fertiliser does not account for the difference, since it was not much used on food crops in the 1980s (Mbogoh, 1991).

The effects of erratic supplies and marketing controls on food prices

The frequent droughts mean that in some years many farmers are food purchasers. However, many have a surplus for the market following good rainfall seasons, and some achieve a surplus in most seasons. This background explains why Eastern Province, of which Machakos District is part, experiences large fluctuations in staple food prices. Due to lack of data this is illustrated in Table 6.2 only for the years 1985–1988. The fluctuations in the levels of prices are both seasonal within the year, and cyclic, between years, reflecting the incidence of droughts. Farmers'

TABLE 6.2. Rural market prices for maize, beans and potatoes in Eastern Province, 1985—1988 (Ksh per kg)

	1985		1986		1987		1988	
	March	Sept.	March	Sept.	March	Sept.	March	Sept.
Maize	3.03	2.27	2.9	2.86	2.43	2.54	2.93	2.74
Beans	9.97	5.70	4.66	4.12	3.96	4.35	6.97	5.55
Potatoes	3.00	2.83	2.57	2.55	2.41	2.18	4.34	3.67

Source: Mbogoh (1991: Table A.22)

purchases are concentrated in the times when prices are highest, when most of them have had a poor season. Table 6.2 suggests that bean prices fluctuate more than maize prices. Local prices vary even more than the table indicates. In Yatta during 1980—1981 farmers reported prices of Ksh 5—8 per kg for maize, compared with Ksh 1—2 when it was in local surplus (Neunhauser et al, 1983: 77). This leads to hardship, loss of savings, and sales of assets.

The Government has continuously tried to regulate the grain trade through what is now the National Cereals and Produce Board (NCPB) and to control grain movements. Between 1943 and 1991 legal trade entailed additional costs in securing a permit from Machakos Town, while illegal trafficking had its own costs; both were at the expense of farmers as producers and consumers. A study in Yatta showed that the NCPB policies meant that farmers who had to buy back maize later in the season paid 146% above the original farm-gate price. Neunhauser et al (1983) note that farmers in Machakos District therefore have to put most land to food crops in order to avoid the necessity of food purchases, but production of food surpluses is not necessarily profitable.

Price trends and comparative advantage

An analysis of price trends in maize would be useful to demonstrate either a continuously rising trend which might show increasing scarcity in the face of continuously rising demand, or the alternatives to which farmers might profitably switch, if they were to pursue a policy of buying some of their food requirements and producing those products for which they had a comparative advantage. However, analysis of long-term price trends in maize is made difficult by the difference in price in different localities. District prices can be reported differently even within the same report (Mbogoh, 1991). For the few years for which data are available (1983—1988), Machakos maize prices were about 60% above the national producer price.

Assuming that there is some relationship between national and local prices, we examined national maize prices deflated by the Nairobi consumer index for the period 1965—1988. These showed high maize prices in 1965—1966 and 1975—1977, but otherwise, a fair degree of stability (Mbogoh, 1991: Figure A4). Farmers can react to a change in the purchasing power of one commodity by switching to some feasible alternative. For all Machakos farmers, beans and livestock represent one such alternative; for some, coffee, horticultural crops or cotton are alternatives, depending on local water supplies and AEZ. The number of kilogrammes of maize required to obtain a kilogramme of an alternative in 1957, 1977 and 1987 is shown in Table 6.3. This shows a rise in the price of livestock products, particularly milk, but also beef, but that maize had appreciated relative to coffee between 1977 and 1987 but had fallen in relation

TABLE 6.3. Maize terms of trade[1] relative to other commodities in Machakos District, 1957, 1977 and 1987

Commodity	Terms of Trade with Maize		
	1957	1977	1987
Clean coffee (kg)	28.1	29.5	10.3
Cotton (kg	na	2.0	1.5
Sorghum (kg)	1.6	na	2.0
Mixed beans (kg)	1.5	2.7	2.3
Tomatoes (kg)	2.4	1.9	1.0
Oranges (kg)	2.8	na	1.7
Beef (meat, kg)	na	4.2	11.7
Cattle, head	470.2	583.1	717.7
Milk (litre)	1.6	1.5	3.1

[1]In terms of the kg of maize required in exchange of specified unit of the other commodities
na = Not available
Source: Mbogoh (1991: Table A.23)

to tomatoes and oranges. (A more detailed examination shows considerable fluctuations, but these three points give a fair idea of trends.) Nevertheless, there had been a move towards increasing production of coffee and horticultural crops and a reduction in the importance of livestock. The explanation lies partly in the increasing scarcity of land which made it important to raise the value of output per hectare; although 1 kg of tomatoes cost 2.4 kg maize in 1957 and only 1 kg maize in 1987, yields of tomatoes are some 25 tons/ha, compared with 1 ton/ha for maize. For the same reason of increasing land scarcity and higher value of output/hectare, farmers are putting proportionately more land into crops than into livestock rearing, though the rising price of milk in the 1980s was one of the reasons behind a move towards keeping fewer but higher grade cows. Although it would make economic sense for farmers who are short of land to put resources into the production of commodities that yield the highest revenue per hectare, and, if necessary, buy food, the risks of such a policy remain high, given the imperfections of the grain marketing system, and the high costs and low quality of the transport system, which leads to local prices behaving differently from national prices.

Machakos has no natural advantage in maize production; the Rift Valley area has far higher yields. Because the national market still does not function efficiently, due to the Board's policies and the high price of transport over bad roads, farmers cannot risk specialisation. Food production has been maintained at a level which normally meets most of local needs at about 200 kg/head, keeping track of population growth, but not moving ahead of it (see Figure 6.4). There has been a recent indication of increasing production of pulses at the expense of maize, but trends are not clear.

NON-FOOD AND HORTICULTURAL CROPS

One of the main responses to increasing population density and to land shortage can be an increase in the proportion of land given to high value crops for sale, in order to achieve a rise in the value of output per worker and per hectare. However, the ability to do this will depend on access to markets and the state of transport, with the higher value and more perishable crops necessitating the best transport facilities. During the early part of the colonial period Africans were prevented from cultivating some profitable crops, including coffee. Therefore, the first cash crop in AEZs 2 and 3 was the less profitable wattle bark (a tanning ingredient), first grown in the 1930s. It was only sporadically mentioned in DAO reports in the 1970s and 1980s, and does not therefore feature in our assessment of current income from cash crops. Some of the farmers we interviewed mentioned wattle bark sales, and sales of wattle trees as firewood — another indication that our revenue assessments are more likely to be understated than overstated. In AEZ 4 sisal from hedges provided cash to buy food in drought years in the 1950s, and most of the 1960−1961 cash crop was sisal (Table 6.1). The price, never attractive when food crops were good, collapsed soon afterwards and it became unimportant. Major non-food crops since 1960 have been coffee in the high potential areas, and cotton in the low potential areas.

Table 6.1 shows that fruit and vegetables began to be important in the 1950s. Together with coffee, they have been the major factor in the growing value of crop production, often grown on land once used for sugar-cane, for local beer-making. Sugar was important in 1930. In Figures 6.4 and 6.5 it has been classified as a cash crop.

Coffee

Coffee planting in the Reserve area began in 1954 under strict Coffee Rules and was permitted to increase only slowly (Mortimore and Wellard, 1991). There were 'illegal' plantings during 1962−1964, but expansion was halted in 1964, two years before Kenya acceded formally to the 1962 International Coffee Agreement, which imposed country quotas. National policy, in the face of a weaker market and increases in the cost of production due to the necessity of spraying against coffee berry disease, was to raise yields per hectare, but to decrease area. Production was controlled by limiting the output of government coffee nurseries. This accounts for the static area in the period 1964−1973, shown in Figure 6.3(a) (Kenya, MoA, 1969). Government policies in relation to prices and co-operatives are discussed in Chapter 15. It is important, however, to note that Kenya generally receives a price above the world average for its coffee, as most of it is high quality Arabica, and that, by African standards, farm-gate prices have been a high percentage of world prices, although taxes and deductions increased markedly in the 1980s.

Coffee was from the outset a profitable crop in the areas to which it was suited, and although Machakos was a marginal area in terms of yields, quality was high and farmers often obtained a grade premium. Revenue was estimated at Ksh 850 per acre, compared with Ksh 150 for food crops, during 1962−1964 (see Mortimore and Wellard (1991: 15) for a discussion). The control on coffee areas broke down during the boom in the mid-1970s. Higher prices led to a great increase in planting, necessitating heavy investment in land preparation, etc. By 1977 this was being reflected in increased production. However, Figure 6.3(a) shows that farmers also responded by securing a large increase in yields. By this date they were using fertiliser as well as sprays on coffee, but we have no detailed information about their techniques. One may suspect that the true increase in area was concealed and that yields are therefore exaggerated. Nevertheless, it is credible that yields rise when prices make extra effort and extra inputs worthwhile. Figure 6.3(a) shows yields in relation to the national price deflated by the national maize price. Coffee production is less affected by drought than maize; if we compare Figures 6.1 and 6.3(a) we see no fall in coffee production in 1975 and 1976, and an increase in production in 1984, when maize was badly affected by drought. Local maize prices were double the national price in 1984. Coffee farmers probably respond to price changes by producing more when the price is attractive,

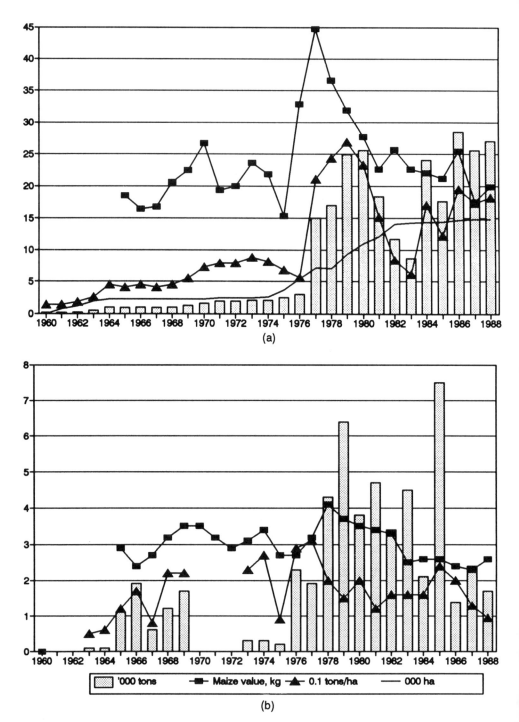

FIGURE 6.3. Output, value, yield and area of coffee and cotton, 1960–1988: (a) coffee; (b) cotton. Note: area data not given for cotton as it distorts the scale; scale refers to units given in the key; value is national price deflated by national maize price.

and also, if possible, when maize prices rise and their need for money is most urgent. The lesser effect of drought may be due to the somewhat better rains in highland areas (see Figure 3.1) and/or to more intensive terracing and water conservation.

Output is also affected by the price and availability of chemical fertiliser. Coffee farmers have always been the most important users of fertiliser in the District; it appears that in 1988 about 138 kg/ha was applied to coffee, and 1.6 kg/ha to food and horticultural crops (Mbogoh, 1991). Coffee farmers can obtain credit and supplies easily through their co-operatives. However, inputs are also bought through commercial channels for cash and Onchere (1976) noted a fall in fertiliser purchases in 1975 compared to 1974 following a poor maize harvest which reduced farmers' cash reserves. According to the General Manager of the Machakos District Co-operative Union, there was a substantial increase in the use of fertiliser in coffee and maize production in Machakos District in the 1980s, especially after 1984 when the Union obtained government approval to import fertilisers directly (pers. comm., 1991), but there was also a sharp drop in sales after a steep price rise in 1989 (Mbogoh, 1991: Tables A16 and A17).

In 1990 farmers in AEZs 2 and 3 remained committed to coffee as one of their most important earners (see Table 10.1). However, it was not as profitable as it had been, due to the combination of falling world prices, rising input prices, higher taxes, and growing inefficiency and delayed payments by the Board to the co-operative societies. The more marginal producers (and during the boom some coffee had been planted in AEZ 4) would have done well to uproot, but this was illegal. Figure 6.3(a) shows that farmers' yields dropped after the coffee boom years. In 1990 coffee was visibly being interplanted with other crops. There is scope for greatly increased production if a price incentive returns. Price is partly dependent on the world market, but also on the internal Kenyan policies, as discussed in Chapter 15.

Cotton

Cotton was introduced by government officers, using semi-compulsory methods, in Nzaui Location in the late 1930s but failed. It was reintroduced in the 1960s, again with semi-compulsory tactics in some Locations (Mortimore and Wellard, 1991), but also with free seed. Production fell after the pressure relented, and when free seed distribution ceased in 1970–1971 (Kenya, MoA, 1971). Heyer (1966) showed that, under most circumstances, cotton in AEZ 4 in the early 1960s was no more attractive than maize, which was itself of low profitability. Given the response to price amongst Machakos farmers which we have demonstrated in the case of coffee, this sufficiently explains the low production in the early 1970s shown in Figure 6.3(b).

Cotton and sunflower were both promoted in 1976, in connection with a credit and extension package introduced through a national donor-assisted programme, but sunflower never overcame marketing problems. Cotton at first seemed set to become the widespread cash crop of AEZs 4 and 5, as agriculturalists had long hoped. Credit was expanded under the Machakos Integrated Development Project (MIDP), which began in 1978. More importantly, MIDP improved the availability of inputs and the efficiency of marketing through its assistance to the Machakos Co-operative Union (see Chapter 15). Many farmers took up the crop; loans for cotton were popular and were repaid in the period 1981–1982 (ODI, 1982). However, there were problems with repayments beginning with the drought of 1983–1984 (ADEC, 1986). Production dropped from 1986 onwards, for which farmers blamed the delays in payment more than the price fall (Figure 6.3(b)). Cotton requires heavy expenditures on spraying and hired labour. Cotton production, while more vulnerable than coffee to climatic factors, could be expanded again given a good marketing environment.

Horticultural crops

Machakos farmers have recently tried to compensate for the falling attraction of coffee and cotton by increasing the production of fruits and vegetables. Their introduction is described in Chapter 14. Horticultural area estimates are particularly difficult to make, with many small plots and individual trees. Table 6.1 shows an estimated 12 000 ha under bananas and other fruits and vegetables in 1957, but there were only 5000 ha according to the estimates of the 1960/1961 census. Both figures are probably exaggerated by the methodology used, which involved double or treble counting of plots with mixed crops. At this time new roads were improving the connections between northern Machakos and Nairobi, and the canning plants in the Mua Hills and at Thika were encouraging production in the Reserve. Fruit and vegetable production became very profitable at the time, and was one of the reasons for the adoption of terracing (see Chapter 11).

With fewer agricultural officers in the 1960s, the recording of horticultural crops became sporadic. They have never been an important part of the messages of agricultural extension. When DOA records resumed about 1974, they showed a lower hectarage than in the 1950s, although descriptions of an active market in fruit and vegetables in the late 1960s make a real fall unlikely (Bottrall, 1969). Steady increases in areas under fruit are recorded from 1974 until about 1983, with a jump in vegetable production after 1979. The increase in fruit production in the late 1970s in AEZ 4 was attested by a survey in Masii (Hayes, 1986) while our own informants implied a more continuous and rapid switch into vegetables in the late 1980s than the DOA figures show. Although one aspect of MIDP programmes in the period 1978−1988 was the encouragement of tree nurseries, they otherwise had 'very little to do in terms of horticultural development' (Mwenge, 1988: 14). The increase in production has been led by increased market demand, from Kenyan towns and from export markets, transmitted by private traders (see Chapter 14).

Fruit trees are grown all over the District. Citrus, pawpaw and mangoes are important in AEZ 4 and even in 5. Vegetables are grown mainly in the better-watered highlands and/or where irrigation is available. Much of the irrigation is very small scale and is managed by individuals or groups (see Chapter 12), but there are also small schemes on the Yatta Furrow and at Kibwezi and Kiboko, both in Kibwezi Division (Mwenge, 1988: 14). According to DOA records, the biggest item in vegetable production is tomatoes, followed jointly by cabbages and kale, and Asian vegetables. Tomatoes, cabbages and kale are grown mainly for the internal market, but the Asian vegetables are also exported to the Indian communities in the United Kingdom. The crop most frequently mentioned to us in the highlands in 1990 was fine French beans (see Table 10.1). All these are high value crops which make very important contributions to the District's agricultural income, as shown by Figures 6.4 and 6.5.

LIVESTOCK

Numbers

In the first half of the study period both cattle and goats had a social value as bride price, and farmers were alleged to keep large numbers of unproductive beasts. However, the animals also had value as an investment that could be sold in times of hardship. They were the chief cash earners, particularly in locations badly served by roads (see Table 10.1). As farming became

TABLE 6.4. Livestock distribution, 1944, 1956 and 1981, by AEZ

Location	SU 1944	SU 1956	ha/SU 1944	SU 1981	ha/SU 1981
AEZs 2 and 3	49 200	79 425	2.11	12 477	6.06
(%)	*23*	*22*		*4*	
AEZ 4	151 400	143 190	1.56	125 073	3.13
(%)	*71*	*40*		*37*	
AEZs 5 and 6	13 450	133 513	3.18	196 324	4.30
(%)	*6*	*37*		*59*	
TOTAL	214 050	356 128	1.79	333 874	4.38

Source: Silberfein (1989: Table 4) for 1944; Peberdy (1958) for 1956; Ecosystems (1982: 1B) for 1981
Note: SU, Stock unit = 1 cow or 5 shoats

more intensive and more crop-oriented, cattle acquired additional value for manure and draught power. By 1990 considerations of utility and profit appeared to dominate in people's livestock decisions, but actual stocks at any given time are much affected by drought and disease.

The main livestock in Machakos are cattle and goats, with smaller numbers of sheep; goat is the preferred meat. In official reports, five sheep or goats (shoats) have been taken as the equivalent of one zebu cow, which we have termed a Stock Unit (SU) to distinguish it from the more scientific Livestock Unit (LU; which takes into account the breed, age, sex, etc.).

In 1930 there were 248 800 cattle in the Reserve and 21 000 in the European ranch area, total 269 800. With 312 500 shoats, the total SUs in the Reserve were then 311 300. In 1944, there were only an estimated 214 000 SUs (see Table 6.4). The one record of sales shows only 2531 cattle sold in the period July 1942 — November 1945, or less than 800 a year, but shoat sales seem to have been maintained at the level of the 1930s. While there was probably some concealment of cattle and illegal trade, it does seem probable that the 1940s saw a fall in the number of cattle, which may have begun in the late 1930s (KNA: DC/MKS Annual Report, 1940). This was only to a minor degree due to the (unsuccessful) destocking attempt of 1938. Droughts, degrading pastures and the difficulties of keeping cattle when large areas were being closed to grazing as part of the rehabilitation measures, all probably played a role. Table 6.4 shows some recovery by 1956, but this was due to more goats rather than more cattle. In 1960 estimates show 222 000 cattle in the Reserve and 50 000 on European land; the only increase in cattle numbers since 1930 appears to have been on the European ranches. (During the 1930s many European farmers in Machakos gave up trying to grow maize and increasingly turned to ranching (Miss Anne Joyce, pers. comm., 1991).

Cattle numbers reported since Independence include both the Reserve and the former ranching areas. They fluctuate very much from year to year, with substantial falls after the droughts of 1975 and 1983–1984. Table 6.5 shows averages for cattle, goats and sheep for available years since 1974. On the basis of these figures, total livestock production has increased since 1960, despite the increasing amount of land put to crops. However, the number of cattle per person declined considerably due to the increase in population, from something like 1 cow per head in 1930 to 0.3 per head by the 1980s. In interviews, farmers reported a fall in the numbers of cattle kept, combined often with a move to improved breeds.

Statistics on goats and sheep are even less reliable than those on cattle. Available figures suggest the shoat/cattle ratio was generally between 1.2 and 1.7. However, more detailed surveys at

TABLE 6.5. Average recorded livestock holdings, 1974–1989

Year	Cattle	Goats	Sheep
1974–1977	465 600	326 600	140 000
1979–1984	388 000	426 500	170 000
1985–1989	402 500	295 000	109 000

Source: Ackello-Ogutu (1991: Tables BB1 and BB2)

Location or household level frequently show higher ratios. The numbers of shoats in relation to cattle are highest in those locations with most emphasis on livestock, and least in those where agriculture is more intensive (Ackello-Ogutu, 1991: Table B.5). This is also the picture which emerges from Owako's observations in the mid 1960s (Owako, 1969). A fall in shoats appears to have occurred after the 1984 drought according to Table 6.5. Our own interviews strongly suggested that farmers had reduced the number of goats kept, especially if they had begun fruit tree farming (this is also in accordance with the data showing falling skins sales: Table 6.6).

Livestock products and sales

We have reports of hides and skins sales, and livestock sold out of the District; figures for the latter are available only up to 1977. Available figures have been averaged for five year periods in Table 6.6. They appear to confirm low numbers of cattle and a large proportion of shoats in the 1950s as compared to the 1930s. Averages give a picture of trends; there is huge year to year variation because of enforced sales, usually due to droughts and occasionally to other causes. Thus, in 1938, the year of destocking, 29 748 cattle were sold, against an average for the decade of 12 000. Sales were again abnormally high in 1951, 1961 and 1967. Numbers are also affected by disease; farmers we interviewed referred to high cattle losses in 1989. Huge numbers of shoats were sold in the 1951 and 1975 drought years. Sales figures are only erratically available in the 1980s.

TABLE 6.6. Average recorded sales, livestock and livestock products

	Cattle sales	Shoat sales	Hides	Skins
1930s	12 227	45 752	25 828	36 371
1940s	na	na	na	na
1950–1954	14 305	58 731	25 076	116 115
1955–1959	11 728	8 469	30 816	114 462
1960–1965	13 228	18 310	23 502	80 572
1965–1969	23 754	14 540	25 033	105 761
1971–1977[1]	18 590	57 524	na	—
1970–1974	na	—	na	170 241
1975–1979	na	na	72 179	277 932
1980–1989	na	na	84 563	206 466

[1]Cattle and shoat sales records stop after 1977. Hides data are missing for 1972–1974 and look incredible in 1971. Skins sales are missing 1972–1973
Source: Ackello-Ogutu (1991: Tables BB4 and BB5). Averages are for periods when at least three figures are available. Full details are given in the original tables

TABLE 6.7. Commercial off-take

Year	Cattle sales as % of total cattle	Hides as % of total cattle	Combined %
1957	5.1	11.5	16.6
1960	5.3	13.9	19.2
1975	–	29.9	29.9
1976	5.5	28.9	33.4
1985	–	19.7	19.7
1986	–	23.0	23.7
1988	–	20.3	20.3
1989	–	15.6	15.6

Note: Sales outside the District. Hides reflect numbers consumed and sold internally
Source: Calculated from Ackello-Ogutu (1991: Tables BB.1, BB.2, BB.4 and BB.5)

Cattle products include meat, hides, milk, milk products, draught power and manure. Commercial off-take can be judged by the combined figures of live cattle sales and hide sales, as a percentage of total cattle. This is given in Table 6.7 for the years in which figures are available.[7] For the purposes of estimating livestock output in Figures 6.4 and 6.5 we have assumed an off-take of 17% up to 1960–1961 (when there was no dipping), 18% in the 1970s and 20% in the 1980s;[8] as shoat data are even more deficient than cattle data, we have simply assumed an off-take of 25% throughout. Assuming hides and skins represent meat locally consumed, meat consumption was about 0.64 SU per head in the 1930s, fell to 0.45 in the 1950s, was around 0.67 in the late 1970s and down to 0.51 in the 1980s. This tends to confirm a fall in local purchasing power in the 1980s compared to the 1970s, to be discussed later.

The official beef cattle price, deflated by the Nairobi consumer index, has shown a fair degree of stability since 1962, with a slightly lower price in the 1980s. Shoat prices showed a slight rising trend from 1962 to 1977, when they boomed alongside coffee (presumably because of high demand for meat), followed by a fall, and then a rather higher level after 1984 (Ackello-Ogutu, 1991: Figures B1 and B2.). The latter suggests that supply may not be meeting demand, now that shoat numbers have fallen (Table 6.5).

Milk is a valued element in the Akamba diet and was always short of demand in the 1950s (Peberdy, 1961). There are few figures on milk output, and most milk has always been consumed by the farm family. Recorded sales show a considerable increase from 1985. Milk prices rose sharply after the 1984 drought (Ackello-Ogutu, 1991, Figure B.3). For lack of data milk is not included in the estimates shown in Figures 6.4 and 6.5. In 1962 there were only 60 European-type cattle in the Reserve area; the rest were the East African zebu, which is not a good milk producer. Better yields are obtained from crosses, and rising demand has led to investment in these. According to the 1983 Ministry of Agriculture and Livestock Development (MALD) census, there were then 57 590 exotic cattle and crosses, known locally as grade cattle. They fell to 23 000 according to MALD's 1984 figures, due to the drought. Since then, most of the increase in cattle numbers has been in these grade dairy cattle, which formed 9% of the herd in 1987 (Kenya, Ministry of Planning, 1988?: 74). A swing to grade cattle was confirmed by our own village interviews in 1990, showing that price responsiveness is active in livestock as well as crop production. Grade cattle are also said locally to produce more manure, but to be heavier feeders and to need more water and care. They thus require both an initial investment to obtain them (many seem to have been purchased rather than bred through the rather erratic artificial insemination service run by the MALD), and continuing inputs of effort.

Draught power and manure are both valued and saleable outputs, which we have not attempted to price. They are increasingly the reason why farmers still continue to keep livestock. In 1940, cows and heifers accounted for 60% of the herd in Nzaui Location, and bulls, steers and oxen for 12%. A survey in the same location in 1980 showed that cows had fallen to 45% and bulls and oxen had increased to 33% (Ackello-Ogutu, 1991: Table B.8). This demonstrates that the productivity of livestock should not be judged solely in terms of meat and milk.

Geographical distribution

Table 6.4 shows livestock distribution in 1944, 1956 and 1981, together with the number of hectares per stock unit (total area divided by SUs). In the 1940s, 23% were recorded in AEZs 2 and 3, and 71% in AEZ 4. (European-owned cattle on the AEZs 5 and 6 ranchlands are not included in the 1944 counts.) By 1956 the shift of cattle population to AEZs 5 and 6 had begun, with new settlements in Makueni and Kikumbulyu. (The shift between 1944 and 1956 is exaggerated by the figures, as the 1956 estimate shows livestock during their seasonal move to Yatta.)

The only available location figures for the 1980s are those derived from the aerial count made by Ecosystems in 1981 (Ecosystems, 1982: Vol. 1). Their figures are much lower than those of the MALD, especially in regard to the highland areas and Kibwezi.[9] However, the scale of the differences from the situation in the 1940s is such that we can say with certainty that the numbers in AEZs 2 and 3 have fallen very substantially. This statement would still hold good even if Ecosystems had missed half the livestock units. In consequence, there is now less pressure on highland fodder resources, but also substantially less manure to apply to highland fields.

The number of stock kept in AEZ 4 has changed less. The expansion has been in AEZs 5 and 6, which now contain at least 60% of the District's livestock — more if MALD is correct on the Kibwezi figure. These animals are supported on about 4.5 ha per stock unit, according to Ecosystems, or about 2 ha if one relies on MALD's figures. This compares with the 3−4 ha the white settlers estimated as needed (possibly for larger beasts), although Akamba farmers use a higher proportion of their land for crops. The ranches in 1989 had about 5.3 ha per SU (Ackello-Ogutu, 1991: Table B.14).

Both the Ecosystems and the MALD data show a considerable fall in the density of livestock per hectare in the older settled areas compared with the position in the 1940s. The larger livestock population is now spread over a much greater area, due to the spread of settlement and the retreat of tsetse. The hectare figure includes cropped and other land in the administrative unit concerned. The proportion of land under crops has increased, but cropped land provides fodder resources (Figure 10.1(b)). Changes in the management of livestock are discussed in Chapters 10 and 14.

TOTAL OUTPUT, PER HEAD AND PER HECTARE, 1930−1990

We are now in a position to compare the value of output per head and per hectare over time. This has been done by converting all production to its 1957 value in maize. Population data have been taken from the nearest census, with adjustment for the appropriate annual growth rate. Land available is as shown in Table 5.5 and increases from 6360 km^2 in 1930 to 13 627 km^2 after 1963.

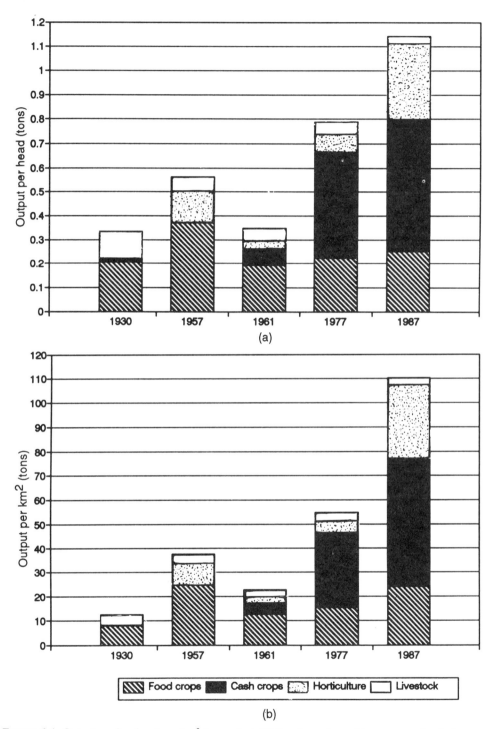

FIGURE 6.4. Output per head and per km² in constant 1957 maize values: (a) output per head; (b) output per km²

Before 1974 we have to select the years for which data are available. 1930 seems to have been an average year. We have data for 1957 and 1960/1961 and give both, but for reasons already discussed average production in the late 1950s should be taken as falling between these two points. For the period after 1974 we selected 1977 and 1987, as average years with one good and one bad season (see Figure 6.1).

Figure 6.4 shows output on a per head and per km^2 basis, at the constant 1957 exchange value with maize. On a per capita basis, it shows grain and pulse production rising from about 200 kg in 1930 to 250 kg in 1987. Livestock output per head declined from a high in 1930 equivalent to over 100 kg of maize, to about one-third of that in 1987 (for, of course, five times as many people). The increase in the value of output has come almost entirely from the huge increases in the volume of horticultural and non-food cash crops, with horticultural growth starting in the 1950s, but most of the expansion having been after 1961. Total value of output per head in maize terms increased more than threefold, from about 300 kg in 1930 to 1150 kg in 1987.

On a per km^2 basis, the value of output in 1957 maize terms has increased tenfold, from about 12 tons in 1930 to 110 tons in 1987. This is despite an increase in area, with almost all the addition being AEZs 5 and 6 land. In volume terms, there is no sign of diminishing returns during recent population increases: indeed, the steepest increase in volume per km^2 has occurred in the period since 1977, when population density was increasing at its fastest rate, with no new land available.

In Figure 6.5 output per head and per km^2 is measured at 1957 prices up to 1961, since we have no current prices for 1930 and 1960/1961. However, the current 1977 and 1987 exchange ratios between maize and other crops are used to value 1977 and 1987 production. This shows a smaller fall in the value of livestock output per head and per km^2, due to the increased maize value of livestock, but a severe fall in the value of non-food cash crops, due to the fall in the price of coffee and cotton, for which increased production of coffee and horticultural crops had been unable to compensate. This could indicate that population density is reaching another danger point at which diminishing returns are being felt. However, this is by no means certain. Some of the fall in the value of output per head, which meant lower purchasing power in the 1980s, was the reflection of poor policies, such as the ban on coffee uprooting, the increased proportion of the coffee price taken by Government, the gross inefficiencies of the Cotton Marketing Board, etc. (see Chapter 15). It is, therefore, quite possible that growth might resume under the influence of reformed policies. Value of output per km^2 was still increasing during the period 1977—1987, but it had not kept up with population growth. People in 1990 complained of feeling poorer, and Figure 6.5 provides an explanation.

Value of agricultural production, as shown in these figures, is not equivalent to total District income. As will be shown in Chapter 10, the increase in the proportion of marketable output, and the increased consumer demand on the part of the farmers, have led to an increase in non-farm income, such that farm income during 1981—1982 amounted to only half total rural income. In 1930 farm output was almost the only income. Naturally also, farmers in different AEZs produce different combinations of output, with some coffee farmers, for example, regularly purchasing food crops from farmers who have no non-food output. Chapter 10 examines changes in farming and income systems.

Just in case we were taking untypical years in 1977 and 1987 we ran a further test by valuing output during the severe 1984 drought seasons and comparing this with the 1960/1961 output. Staple food crop output in 1984 was slightly above 1960/1961 levels; cash crop, horticultural and livestock outputs were substantially above 1960/61 levels. In consequence, output per head

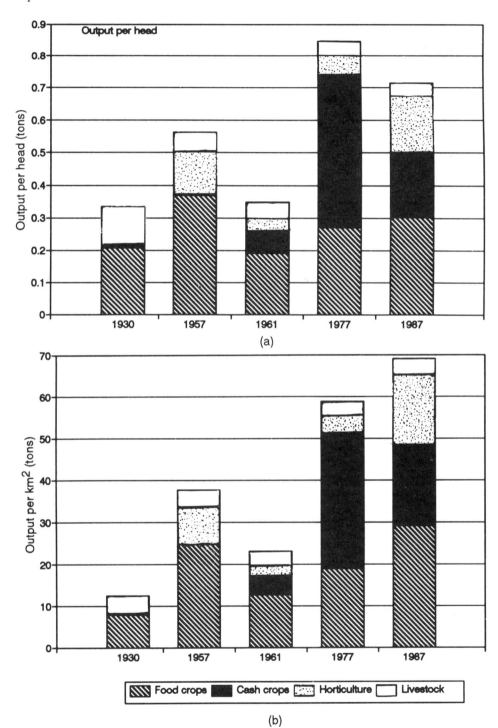

FIGURE 6.5. Output per head and per km^2, maize at 1957, 1977 and 1987 values: (a) output per head; (b) output per km^2

was double the 1960/1961 output, at 1957 exchange ratios. The deviations from average rainfall in the relevant seasons were −0.31 and −0.74 in 1960/1961 and −0.54 and −1.31 in 1984. We conclude that Machakos farmers had also become better able to withstand droughts, which is not to deny that the substantial fall in production in 1984 caused suffering and made imports and food relief necessary.

CONCLUSION

On a District basis, the volume of output has increased greatly. The increase in value of output per hectare has been particularly marked, whether measured by constant or relative prices. Although our statistical basis is shaky, the magnitude of the productivity per hectare change is such that a substantial increase cannot be doubted, and is in any case confirmed by a glance at the contrast between the landscape of 1937 and 1990, shown in Figures 1.2−1.11. This rise is despite the large-scale population movement into areas having less natural potential. On a per head basis, the value of staple food production has kept pace with population growth. The total value of production per head increased substantially between 1960 and 1987, through an increase in the output of non-food and horticultural crops. Changes in relative prices led to a fall in the value of production per head between 1977 and 1987 even though volume increased. However, values in 1987 remained substantially higher than those in the late 1950s. The fall in purchasing power since 1977 was due both to unfavourable world prices and internal policies. Farmers partly mitigated these effects by their move into horticulture. Just as there has been a trend to increase production of crops with a higher value output per hectare, so there has been a trend to increase crop output at the expense of livestock output, which characteristically has a lower output per hectare. Our definition of intensification includes the increase in the value of output per hectare, and these figures leave no doubt that intensification has successfully taken place.

Machakos farmers are shown to face high climatic risks, but to be very responsive to market and price changes, whether in crops or in livestock products. The higher value crops grown mainly for sale on a relatively small area of the District have been vital in increasing the total value of output, but have not reduced the output of staple food. Vulnerability to drought and drastic food shortages has been reduced, but not eliminated. This chapter deals in averages; it is not implied that all families have shared equally in increases of output and income.

NOTES

1 This chapter has been developed from initial research by S. G. Mbogoh and C. Ackello-Ogutu; see ODI Working Paper 55.
2 Data from 1969−1973 are missing or confused, possibly because of the change to recording total production, combined with a change in the way the large areas with more than one crop in the field were counted. In the earlier period, one hectare of maize and beans was recorded as 1 hectare of maize and 1 hectare of beans (see Mbogoh, 1991).
3 All European farmers had to send in annual returns, but the censuses for African areas are never more than incomplete surveys or guestimates. The best, the 1960/1961 census, used observations along transects, or, in two areas, a sample survey.
4 Location staff measure yields on their demonstration plots. The demonstration yield is adjusted to an average yield taking into account the average performance of local farmers. They assess how much land the average farmer puts to each crop, and the number of farmers for whom they are responsible. They also have to send monthly returns to monitor the amount being planted. Planted area plus yield

gives the production. Senior staff monitor the credibility of returns. During the early 1970s, staff numbers were low and the increase in cropping in newly settled districts may have been picked up only after a time lag of some years. We noted various anomalies in the data, which are listed and discussed in detail in Mbogoh (1991). The only cross-check on cultivated area comes from the aerial surveys for 1981 and 1985 (Ecosystems, 1985/6: Vol. 4, Table 2.4). These showed 258 500 ha under cultivation in 1985, and 250 500 ha in 1981. At first sight, this looks substantially below the DAO estimates of cultivated area for the same years — 368 000 ha and 474 000 ha respectively. However, the DAO figures are for two seasons (i.e. the hectares of long and short rains plantings are added) and the Ecosystems for one only. Assuming food crops are cultivated twice, and the main cash crops, cotton and coffee, occupy the land in both seasons, DAO estimates are equivalent to about 211 000 ha in 1981, and about 255 000 ha in 1985. On this assumption, DAO underestimated the cultivated area by about 25% in 1981, and 10% in 1985. This suggests that production in the late 1970s and 1980s may be underestimated.

5 Unusually, the 1930 livestock data are probably of a higher quality than later data, since there was a Veterinary Officer with a brief to obtain livestock numbers, and successful anti-rinderpest campaigns were carried out in the 1920s. Livestock data were for a long time obtained by applying a multiplying factor to the rinderpest vaccination figure. They are currently based on dipping statistics. Sales of hides and skins provide a check. In the 1980s there were some aerial livestock counts and sample surveys; each method gives different results (Ackello-Ogutu, 1991).

6 We are not able to say if anomalies are due to poor distribution of rainfall within a season, or to inaccuracy in the recorded data. One must suspect production was not well estimated in 1976, when we know food was imported (Figure 6.2, and Kliest, 1985).

7 It appears to be quite high, but we have no figures for livestock purchased in. In some years, Machakos farmers will have rebuilt their herds, particularly their plough oxen, by purchase as well as by rearing.

8 An average off-take figure is preferred as an output indicator, since in some years sales are more than the natural increase, and represent loss of capital; in other years sales are less than natural increase when capital is being rebuilt. The maize value is taken as the appropriate percentage of cattle value.

9 Ecosystems (1982: Vol. 1) figures differ substantially from those of the MALD ground-level census conducted in 1983 through chiefs and sub-chiefs as recorded in ADEC, 1986: 6−9 (Ackello-Ogutu, 1991: Table B.3). The MALD figures are probably more sound (because aerial survey methods miss substantial numbers of shoats and stall fed cattle, especially in highland areas,) but they are unfortunately only available on a divisional basis. Surprisingly, the greatest discrepancy in cattle numbers between the two surveys is in Kibwezi Division, where most animals are grazed. Here, MALD found 145 000 cattle, compared with 37 000 in the nearly coincident Makindu Division in Ecosystems (1982: Vol. 1, Table 10E). Household surveys suggest herds are larger in this area than in other parts of Machakos. The MALD data may be exaggerated, but the Ecosystems data seem, on the basis of household evidence, to be an undercount. Dr Norton-Griffiths, formerly Managing Director of Ecosystems, said he thought their methods had led to undercounting (pers. comm., 1992).

7

Soils[1]

INTRODUCTION

The history of soil erosion is reconstructed from the data, descriptions, and studies available. It shows a major turn-around between the 1930s–1940s and the 1970s, and provides a context for recent estimates of the rates of erosion. The status of erosion in 1990 was assessed during field visits by Thomas and Gichuki. It is shown that erosion is no longer associated in general with cultivation, but predominantly with grazing land, where there are recent signs of improved conservation. Changes in the chemical and physical properties of cultivated soils are inferred from selective sampling in the field, and laboratory analyses. The results from a longitudinal comparison of sites over a period of 13 years are inconclusive, but a spatial analogue method shows very low fertility levels on sites with a long history of cultivation without organic or inorganic fertiliser inputs, compared with uncultivated sites protected from grazing. (The management of erosion is described in Chapter 11, together with the political circumstances which helped give rise to the spate of reports in the 1930s.)

FORMS AND CAUSES OF SOIL EROSION

Soil erosion by water is the most conspicuous form of land degradation in Machakos District; wind erosion damage is insignificant. The main forms of water erosion are inter-rill, rill or gully erosion. In inter-rill erosion, the soil is detached by raindrop splash and transported very slowly in overland flow. In rill erosion, soil is detached mainly by scouring and is transported by run-off concentrated in rills. Sheet erosion is the combined effect of inter-rill and rill erosion. Gully erosion is an advanced form of rill erosion, in which intermittent water, draining small catchments, results in 'water fall' erosion at the gully head, and deepening and widening of the gully below. Gully formation is an extension of the natural drainage network.

Less common erosion processes occur locally, such as tunnel erosion, mass movement and watercourse erosion. Mass movement, involving land slipping or slumping, has been reported on steep land in the more humid areas of Kangundo, Mbooni and the Kilome area of Mukaa Location after periods of heavy rainfall.

Erosion in cropland is commonly associated with lack of cover. Where annual crops are grown there is normally little ground cover for the first month after planting and this is generally the time at which the heaviest rains can be expected (Fisher, 1978). Erosion on crop land is therefore associated mainly with annual crops, with perennial crops during the early years of establishment, with sloping land that lacks effective conservation measures, and with terraces that are incorrectly laid out, poorly constructed or not stabilised with grass.

After virgin land is cleared for cultivation, the organic matter levels can be expected to decline and if farmers fail to install effective conservation measures, the risk of erosion is high, especially on sloping land. Erosion might not become apparent till rills have appeared and damage has already been done. Once rills have developed, it is more difficult to make effective conservation structures owing to the concentration of run-off.

Erosion of grazing land in Machakos District has been noted since the early years of the century and has been one of the hardest problems to deal with (Pole-Evans, 1939; Pereira and Beckley, 1952; Peberdy, 1958). Early incidences of erosion were attributed to increased livestock numbers as a result of improved veterinary services, protection from theft, and reduced grazing area. The natural vegetation of the District is characterised by tufted and patchy perennial grasses which, when grazed down, expose the intermittent bare soil to erosion and compaction by rain drops. Such bare patches can be seen clearly in Figure 1.2. Erosion removes the humus in the topsoil, and compaction impedes the infiltration of rainwater and the germination or growth of grasses and herbs (KNA: Cowley, 1947/8). Intensified grazing of the better pastures during periods of drought would have worsened the problem, and at such times, the activities of termites became more noticeable than usual. Pole-Evans (1939) noted that 'they were attacking living thorn trees in the absence of any other material'. Areas of bare or nearly bare ground expanded and coalesced in the manner of a skin disease. These bare lands with capped soils became known as *mangalata*, or 'bad lands', as shown in Figure 7.1.

FIGURE 7.1. 'Typical eroded bare ground covering hundreds of square miles.' (KNA: R. O. Barnes, 1937: photo 14). Barnes notes that the area had been closed to grazing 'a short time' and moisture-holding silt was collecting against the grass at the edge, where seed could take hold. To hasten this process, he advocated artificial barriers to hold silt (Reproduced by permission of Kenya National Archives)

One factor which influences the rate of erosion on grazing land is the presence of a quartz layer on the surface. A quartz horizon 1−2 m below the surface is a common feature of soils derived from metamorphic rocks. Where there is quartz at the surface, it is commonly an indication that the upper soil horizons have been stripped off by erosion (Leslie and Mitchell, 1979).

> The greater portion of the 'bad lands' consist of a red loam, overlying gneisses and schists which occasionally break the surface. There is frequently a horizon of loose quartz conglomerate occurring in the profile, which does not run parallel to the soil surface and is exposed on certain hillsides; the extent of exposure depends on the obliquity of the horizon with the soil surface and the degree of slope. This may give an impression of gravel conditions, but generally there is a good depth of homogenous soil either above or below this horizon, certain gully profiles giving depths up to 30 ft. There is no evidence that this red loam is inherently infertile. (KNA: Cowley, 1947/8. Reproduced by permission of Kenya National Archives.)

A surface layer of quartz decreases the erosion rate in a number of ways. In the first place, stones intercept raindrop energy and run-off scour forces; secondly, they retard run-off and allow more time for infiltration; and thirdly, they facilitate the establishment and survival of grasses and other plants which are less easily grazed down to the roots or trampled out of existence (Thomas and Barber, 1983).

Farmers interviewed in 1990 confirmed that most gullies were started by insignificant water flows in a footpath or stock track. They are particularly noticeable around watering points. However, once a gully has started it can grow rapidly by headward extension, scouring of the bed, and collapse of the walls.

Most *streams* and *rivers* are ephemeral, except for those which derive their flow from underground sources, such as the Kibwezi and Kambu rivers. Those arising directly from the basement land surface receive the biggest proportion of flow from surface run-off. In the past, many of these watercourses had been choked with sand, and water can usually be found in the dry season by digging below the surface. The growing demand for sand for building construction has led to a rate of extraction which exceeds the rate of renewal in stretches of certain rivers. This has in some places resulted in a decrease in water stored in the dry river beds and in an increase in river bank erosion, due to a lowering of the level where run-off joins the river, and to lorries creating tracks that have led to the formation of gullies (Mburu, 1990).

EARLY OBSERVATIONS OF SOIL EROSION

Reconstruction of soil erosion history is handicapped by a lack of baseline data of a quantitative nature for the beginning of the period of study. This reconstruction, therefore, brings together descriptive assessments, photographs and inferences from the early period with the results of field measurements, air surveys, systematic interviewing and observations from the last two decades.

Before the 1930s

At the end of the 19th century, the Akamba were mostly concentrated in the hills. In his description of the vegetation in about 1910, Lindblom (1920: 25−26) made no mention of erosion features, though he observed that hillslopes had been cleared for farming, and that the grass on the plains grew 'in patches, between which the soil is bare'. Barnes (KNA: Barnes, 1937: 1−2) interviewed

Wakamba elders, European settlers and the missionary, Dr Boedaker, in order to reconstruct the soil conditions of the country around the time of the British occupation. He describes bushland and grassland on the hills, absorbent topsoils and an absence of storm runoff; on the flatter country there was dense high grass, trees and a rich topsoil. The larger streams were perennial. Forest patches were rare. However, it is significant that on the hills 'there were some gulleys [sic] but they were covered with vegetation', and that 'there were a few stony patches in the Mbuti area where grass was poor'. This area, Muputi, near Machakos Town, was densely populated by the standards of the time, but 'glowing reports are found [in travellers' accounts] of the wonderful grass to be seen on the caravan route' (Peberdy, 1958: 2).

Soil degradation became a serious concern in the 1920s. Peberdy (1958) quotes the District Commissioner, Machakos, writing in 1927:

> Since 1917 the reserve has become desiccated beyond all knowledge. Large areas which were good pasture land, and in some cases thick bush, are now only tracts of bare soil.

The Agricultural Commission (Kenya, Hall, 1929) reported that

> A journey through the area east and south of Machakos reveals that over large stretches of hillsides vegetation has been almost wholly removed. The soil has been eroded down to the subsoil and its removal will continue at an ever increasing rate. On less steep slopes and on better land, vegetation persists and though Wakamba are primarily a pastoral tribe patches of cultivation are in evidence. But even there, the grazing has been so persistent that the ground is all beaten down into little stock paths and has in turn become open to erosion.

It also reported (para. 121) that 'It is not too much to say that a desert has already been created.'

1930–1947

The situation deteriorated between 1931 and 1936 when there were six moderate or severe droughts in ten seasons (see Table 3.3). Beckley (1935) reported that, in the Reserve, only areas with a high prevalence of tsetse fly were free from severe erosion, hills once forested were denuded and formerly perennial streams had become seasonal sand rivers.

In 1937, Maher reported on the denudation of the Reserve in vivid terms that have already been quoted (Chapter 1). He noted that a considerable portion had lost both top and subsoil and attributed this to the following factors (in descending order of importance): deforestation, overstocking, cultivation of slopes, over-cultivation, ploughing, increases in the cultivated area, road drainage, and livestock damage. The rivers, once perennial, were now but seasonal, liable to 'come down in spate, carrying tons of the soil of the Reserve towards the Indian Ocean' and drying again after a few hours. Maher identified the goat as the greatest single cause of damage, without adducing evidence. Stockdale concurred (Pole-Evans, 1939).

Barnes (KNA: Barnes, 1937) underwrote Maher's assessment, illustrating his report with photographs (see Chapter 1).

> I can say that there is really no part of the inhabited reserve that is free from erosion. Probably 75% suffers from severe erosion in various forms, parts of this almost amounting to complete destruction, 20% with less serious erosion and there may be 5% that is protected by trees or natural conditions. (KNA: Barnes, 1937: 6. Reproduced by permission of Kenya National Archives.).

He offers a more detailed account of the Matungulu–Kangundo area (shown in Figures 4.1,

7.2 and 7.5(a)),

...which must have been one of the finest stretches of agricultural land in Kenya ... local natives say the land was not worked extensively until the War of 1914–1918. Prior to the War the slopes were covered with thick Bush Type Forest and had very fertile soil. One native told me that when he left to go to the War as a porter there was only isolated cultivation ... [Now] In some parts cultivation is continuous for almost a square mile in a block, and there are only odd trees left all over the area.

Now the whole area is suffering from erosion, natives will show you gulleys up to 30 feet deep with vertical sides that used to be paths through the bush. They say that many of these gulleys have increased from small watercourses to their present depth of over 20 feet in 10 or 20 years and two up to 18 feet deep in the last three years [shown in Figure 7.2]. The largest of these gullies are about a mile long. There is sheet erosion over the area and it is very severe to the north of Matungulu Government school.

The reason they give for these gulleys is that the cover is now off the hills above but they do not realise that the enormously increased run-off is also due to the drop in humus content of these huge expanses of cultivation. They do attribute small washouts and gulleys to their own practice of marking out their plots with drains, which catch and concentrate the water [shown in Figure 7.2].

All natives agree that greatly increased areas are responsible for accelerated erosion on cultivated land. They rightly blame the use of ploughs without sufficient care and knowledge, many used to plough up and down hill. They also blame the use of cultivators with oxen. (KNA: Barnes, 1937: 4. Reproduced by permission of Kenya National Archives.)

The Agricultural Officer Hobbs' estimates of the proportion of uncultivated land subject to erosion (quoted in RH: Maher, 1937) range from 13% to 76% in different locations, and were generally lower for the hilly than for the lower locations. (These estimates are reproduced in Thomas, 1991, Table B.1; they were approximate and subjective.)

FIGURE 7.2. 'Showing erosion in the rich Matungulu area, starting from paths and boundary trenches' (KNA: R. O. Barnes, 1937: photo 25). This illustrates why observers were worried by cultivation on the hills. See also Figure 1.4, where Barnes notes numerous small gullies starting out of 'abandoned or closed native shambas' above the road (Reproduced by permission of Kenya National Archives)

Notwithstanding a government reconditioning programme, from which a District Commissioner reported, in 1940, 'many grounds for encouragement' (KNA: DC/MKS, Annual Report 1940), in 1946 erosion was again causing official concern. The British Under Secretary of State for the Colonies visited Machakos District in August 1946, and the *East African Standard* reported that

> He has now seen the worst eroded parts of Kenya. In a tour through the Kamba reserve on Monday he drove mile after mile through hillsides and plains swept bare in many places to the solid rock, through areas where there was hardly a vestige of grass, through acre after acre of dead and wilted maize. (Peberdy, 1958.)

He saw it after two successive severe droughts in the long rains, with an intervening light drought in the short rains (Table 3.3). At that time Cowley (KNA: Cowley, 1947/8) wrote of the area east of Kiima Kimwe as far as the Reserve boundary 'which has deteriorated completely and is generally spoken of as the Machakos "Bad Lands". It covers several hundred square miles of country.' This appears to have been Machakos at its nadir.

EVIDENCE FOR A TURN-AROUND

1948–1978

Aerial photographs (February, 1948, of scale 1:25 000, and January, 1972, of scale 1:12 500) were used by Thomas (1974) to assess erosion trends in the Wamui River basin (1.73 km²) in Kalama Location. Of 29 sites, 10 showed no change in the extent of erosion, 5 showed a decrease and 14 an increase. The percentage of the area showing erosion is shown in Table 7.1. This study drew attention to a fundamental divergence between the impact of grazing and that of cultivation on erosion.

> There is no evidence to show that the increase in the area of erosion is a direct result of increased cultivation. The increase in the area of cultivated land reduces the land available for grazing. As the flatter land is taken for crops, livestock are concentrated on the steeper and more fragile slopes. An increase in the length of contour banks reveals a substantial input of time and effort into soil conservation. Although there is more cultivated land in 1972 than in 1948 it is also very much better protected against erosion. (Thomas, 1974: 61–62. Reproduced by permission of D. B. Thomas.)

TABLE 7.1. Soil erosion and land use in a sub-catchment of the Wamui River Basin, Kalama, 1948–1972

Feature	1948	1972	Change
Non-arable land:			
Moderate erosion %	22	26	+4
Severe erosion %	26	37	+11
Total erosion %	48	63	+15
Cultivated land %	*18*	*26*	+8
Contour banks (m/ha cultivated)	195	667	+472
Sisal rows (m/ha total area)	16	122	+106

Source: Thomas (1974) (Reproduced by permission of D. B. Thomas)

Gully formation is an extension of the natural drainage network, and often occurs in cycles set off by natural or manmade events. The Kalama study showed that the main extension in channel length was completed by 1948, though the 1972 photographs indicated continuing widening, and ground surveys showed some deepening. Evidence obtained from informants who could remember the histories of gullies, together with an absence of any mention of them by travellers who passed through the area in the 1890s (Lugard, quoted in Perham, 1959; Gregory, 1896), led to the conclusion that peak rates of deterioration were in the 1930s and 1940s. During these decades the incidence of drought was high. Figure 7.3 and 7.4 shows a gully visited by D. B. Thomas in 1974 and 1990. The central gully was one of the few formed after 1948, believed to have been initiated by a failed cut-off drain circa 1950. Between 1974 and 1990 there is evidence of only minor expansion, with vegetation beginning on the gully floor (Figure 7.4b). In the Matungulu area gullies which probably formed in the late 1920s or early 1930s were nearly completely vegetated in 1990 (Figures 7.5(a) and (b)). The hills above were protected by conservation works during the period 1939−1950 (Chapter 11).

Thomas (1977) surveyed 121 randomly selected farms in May 1977, in five locations in AEZ 4. He noted that rainfall in April 1977 had been much above average, so that erosion problems showed up clearly. He found:

(1) Most of the farms which appeared to need cut-offs actually had cut-offs. Of 52 cut-offs examined, 42% were completely adequate. Amongst the remainder inadequacy was due to: poor alignment (17%), bank too low (7%), channel silted up (43%) and channel overgrown with bush and weeds (10%). Approximately 48% of the cut-off drains discharged into a grassed area, 31% into bare ground and 14% into stock tracks or footpaths.
(2) Only two of the farms were without terraces. Of the 745 terraces examined, 95% were of the bench type. One-third had inadequate lips.
(3) Much grazing land was bare. This he blamed on droughts, overgrazing, and termite damage. He noted some efforts at improvement through the digging of cut-offs, and a number of farms on which protected grazing provided a contrast to their neighbours (Thomas, 1978).

Zöbisch (1986) studied four catchments, varying in size from 166 to 307 ha, using air photography for 1948, 1967 and 1978. The results for two catchments (Table 7.2) show that between 1948 and 1978 an increase in the area of land under cultivation was accompanied by a marked increase in that protected by conservation measures. During the same period the total area of bush/grazing land declined, and the percentage with good cover, which was already low, dropped even further. Erosion on the cultivated land was reduced owing to the installation of conservation measures, but it increased on the grazing land owing to concentration of livestock on a smaller area.

1978−1990

In 1981 an assessment of soil erosion in the District was carried out using low-level colour air photographs taken in a reconnaissance sample frame (Ecosystems, 1982, vol.3). The relative soil loss from sheetwash and rill erosion on different types of land use was estimated using the Universal Soil Loss Equation (USLE) (Figure 7.6). The results show the relative importance of erosion on grazing land. A second set of low-level photographs were taken four and a half years later, in 1985 (Ecosystems, 1985/6, Vol. 4). Between the two surveys, there were three successive drought seasons: in the long rains of 1983 (a severe drought), the following short rains (a moderate drought), and the long rains of 1984 (severe).

(a)

(b)

FIGURE 7.3. Gullies in Kalama photographed in (a) 1974 (Thomas, 1974) and (b) 1990. The centre gully, which started forming circa 1950, is about 12 m deep. In 1974 it was still widening. In 1990 it was relatively stable. Note the increase in trees. A woman farmer interviewed had planted trees near the gully edge to try to prevent it expanding. (Photos: D. B. Thomas. Reproduced with permission.)

(a)

FIGURE 7.4. (a) Bottom of the central gully in Figure 7.3, in 1972, when major slumping was still occurring (Thomas, 1974). (b) In 1990, vegetation was taking hold at the same spot. (Photos: D. B. Thomas. Reproduced with permission.)

(b)

(a)

FIGURE 7.5. (a) Gully in Matungulu in 1937, said to have expanded from a small water course that could be stepped over 10 years previously, due to run-off from the cultivated fields above (KNA: R. O. Barnes, 1937, photo 29. Reproduced by permission of Kenya National Archives)

(b)

FIGURE 7.5 (*cont.*) (b) The same gully in 1990, wider, but largely revegetated. (Photo: D. B. Thomas.)
The site is near the spot photographed by Barnes, but the exact location of this cannot be identified. Note
terracing and additional tree cover on the hill above (Reproduced with permission)

TABLE 7.2. Land-use change in two catchments, 1948–1978

	Study catchment					
	Kalusi (238 ha)			Makulani (166 ha)		
	1948 (%)	1967 (% change)	1978 (% change)	1948 (%)	1967 (% change)	1978 (% change)
1 Arable areas with soil conservation	9	44	46	1	12	31
2 Arable areas without soil conservation	22	15	3	16	13	7
3 Bush and grazing land, good cover (>50%)	14	5	6	8	9	3
4 Bush and grazing land, poor cover (<50%)	53	33	45	75	66	60
5 Woodland and forest	1	2	1	0	0	0
6 Others	1	1	0	0	0	0
7 Soil conserving land use (1 + 3 + 5)	25	51	52	9	21	33

Note: Column totals may not add up to 100 owing to rounding
Source: Zöbisch (1986: 102) (Reproduced by permission of M. Zöbisch)

TABLE 7.3. Erosion indices and AEZs 1981–1985

AEZ	Average erosion index		
	1981	1985	Change (%)
2/3 (average of 8 locations)	2.9	3.2	10
4 (average of 15 locations)	4.2	5.4	29
5/6 (average of 14 locations)	3.7	6.8	84

Based on Ecosystems (1985/6, Vol. 2, Table 3.33; Vol.3, Table 2.26) (Reproduced by permission of Ecosystems Ltd, Nairobi)

The indices (Table 7.3) show an increase in the extent of erosion between 1981 and 1985. This was a temporary setback in an otherwise declining long-term trend. The changes show a clear relationship with ecology. The locational boundaries fit clumsily into agro-ecological zones, but when the locations are so allocated, it appears that the average erosion indices for 1985 were lowest in AEZ 2/3 and highest in AEZ 5/6, and the percentage changes in the average erosion indices vary in the same way. If we accept that the deterioration during the period was mainly due to drought, this table demonstrates the susceptibility of the drier areas to drought-induced degradation.

Zöbisch (1986) measured erosion on grazing land sites with good, medium and poor vegetative cover. The slope lengths varied from 9 to 15 m and the slope was in the range 14–42%. Results showed that soil loss was closely correlated with ground cover and that an increase in cover from 20 to 40% led to a major reduction in soil loss (Figure 7.7). This emphasises the importance of a management strategy that permits an adequate degree of vegetative cover to be maintained.

Attempts to quantify the rate and distribution of soil erosion began in the 1970s (Barber et al, 1979; Edwards, 1979; Moore et al, 1979; Thomas et al, 1981; Styczen, 1983; Ulsaker and Kilewe, 1983; Wain, 1983; Kilewe, 1987; Muya, 1990). The results of one study are shown in Table 7.4.[2] In such studies, it is important to note that high rates of erosion occur locally where ground is severely denuded, especially if it is sloping. However, within any catchment there are some areas that are well vegetated and conserved, and there are areas of deposition as well as erosion. Overall rates of erosion are therefore much less than soil loss at source from denuded ground.

TABLE 7.4. Estimated soil loss from the Iiuni catchment

Land use	Per cent of area	Soil loss (tons/ha/year)
Degraded grazing land	37	53.3
Cultivated land	43	16.0
Good grazing/bush/woodland	20	1.1
Weighted mean soil loss at source		26.8
Catchment soil loss		5.4

Source: Thomas et al (1981) (Reproduced by permission of D. B. Thomas)

111

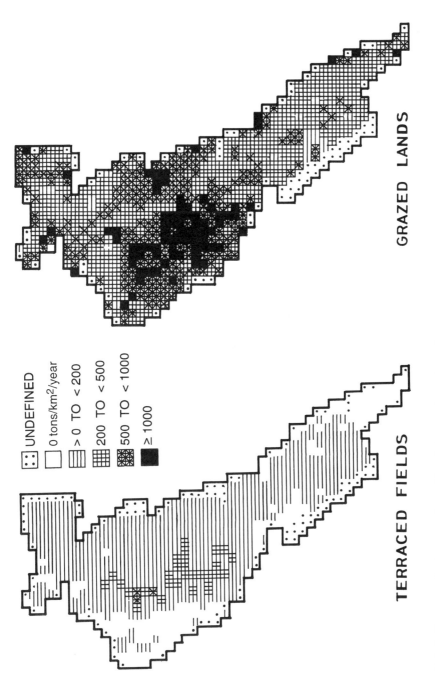

FIGURE 7.6. Sediment production rates from rill and sheetwash erosion (after Reid, 1982). (Reproduced by permission of Ecosystems Ltd., Nairobi)

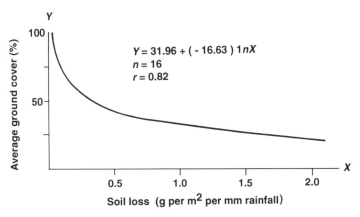

FIGURE 7.7. Influence of vegetative cover on soil loss (after Zöbisch, 1986)

OBSERVATIONS OF EROSION IN 1990

Field observations may suggest the recent history of erosion on cultivated land. For example, near Mavindini in Kathonzweni Location (formerly the southern part of Makueni Location), which is an area of recent settlement, the aerial photos of 1978 showed many of the fields having rills running from the upper to the lower part of the slope, and crossing the conservation structures. In some fields the upper part, nearer the homestead, appeared to have better terraces and few, if any, rills. A visit to the site in 1990 showed that soil is continuing to move. It can be postulated that when the area was settled in the late 1950s or early 1960s, and land was cleared from tall *Acacia/Commiphora* bushland, cultivation began with little attention to conservation structures. After some years and probably some heavy storms, rills began to appear and sooner or later most farmers started to make terraces or leave narrow strips of grass on the contour. Terracing generally starts near the homestead and, when resources of labour are available, is continued to the lower slopes. For the farmer with limited resources this process may take years, during which time erosion continues, and the lower slopes become progressively more dissected. In certain circumstances where erosion is severe, soils are shallow, and nutrient status is low, cultivation has to be abandoned because of a serious decline in productivity. Evidence from the Kambu area near Kibwezi suggests that this can happen within 20–30 years of settlement. Lack of title to land may be responsible for delay in undertaking conservation work. In several cases where denuded land was noticed, there was a land dispute.

Farmers are now well aware of the erosion hazard, the need to control it and the ways in which this can be done. They are also well aware that free land is no longer available. They are therefore putting much more effort into soil conservation than in the past. The time lag between clearing new land for cultivation and installing suitable conservation measures is much less now than in the past (as in areas of Ngwata settled in the 1970s). It can be assumed that the rate of erosion on crop land is being reduced.

On grazing land, there are still patches of bare land scattered throughout the District, and a study of aerial photos indicates that some of them have been bare for a very long time. An example is the denuded land at Kamweleni, about 10 km south-east of Machakos Town, which is bare now and was bare in 1948. The presence of quartz gravel on the surface, as has been noted, decreases erosion. In certain areas it was still noticeable in 1990 that there were patches

FIGURE 7.8. Denuded grazing land in 1990 near Mavindini, Makueni Location, in the left foreground, separated from excellent cover in the right background which is protected by a hedge of thorn branches, demonstrating the effects of different individual management. (Photo: D. B. Thomas. Reproduced with permission.)

of ground where the soil surface was sealed and bare, adjacent to quartz-covered land which was well vegetated. It is possible therefore that the rate of erosion on grazing land has decreased not only because of better management, but also because of the removal of the most easily eroded material.

Although the problem of grazing land management appeared for a long time to be almost insoluble, it is clear that changes have been taking place and the situation is now much more hopeful than in the past. One major reason for this is that most land has been demarcated and registered. Boundaries are now generally recognised and respected and it is not uncommon to find one farm with well managed grazing land separated only by a sisal hedge from another with poor cover, as in Figure 7.8. Improvements in grazing management have been associated with changes in the functions of livestock and in the methods of feeding them (see Chapter 10). The trend towards fodder growing and stall feeding, on certain farms and especially in AEZs 2, 3 and 4, has to some extent reduced the pressure on natural pasture and the hazard of erosion.

An improvement in the general condition of grazing land up to 1991 is also attributable to better rainfall, and there will no doubt be a deterioration in cover when the next sequence of dry years occurs. There are certain areas near water supplies where livestock are concentrated that continue to degrade, due to the combined effects of grazing pressure and livestock tracking and trampling (Muya, 1990).

SOIL FERTILITY IN LONGITUDINAL PERSPECTIVE

It is now recognised that the fertility losses caused by erosion are as important as the physical removal of soil, and need to be addressed by conservation strategies (Stocking, 1984; Stocking and Peake, 1985; Young, 1989). The monitoring of soil properties over time is not normally included in the mandates of soil survey organisations, and few systematic attempts have been made to do it (Young, 1991). Methods for assessing soil degradation at the world scale are at an early stage of development (FAO, 1979), and have rather limited practical value at the local scale (Stocking, 1986).

Using a longitudinal method, soils are monitored at a number of controlled sites over a period of time. This requires baseline samples and analytical results of at least a decade ago, if significant changes are to be detected.

The recorded analytical data from surveys conducted in 1977 (Van de Weg and Mbuvi, 1975; Sketchley et al, 1979; Muchena et al, in prep.) were used in this study as a baseline. Fresh composite samples of topsoil from the vicinity of each pit of the 1977 soil survey were analysed, using identical procedures. Of the 30 soil pits located, 26 were in the Makueni area and only four in the northern Machakos area.[3] In 1977, all sites were uncultivated. In 1990, some of them had been under cultivation for two seasons, so their results are shown in a separate column (Table 7.5).

Readily available plant nutrients are for the greater part stored in the soil organic matter. The soils under investigation contain as a whole very little organic matter. Percentage carbon varies from 0.2 to 1.5; the majority contain less than 1.0%, implying that they are low on organic matter. Again, the soils are low on nitrogen, as all except one contain less than 0.2%.

TABLE 7.5. Soil properties, 1977 and 1990

| | Makueni area | | | | Northern Machakos area | |
| | Uncultivated (19 sites) | | Cultivated (7 sites) | | Uncultivated (4 sites) | |
	1977	1990(%)	1977	1990(%)	1977	1990(%)
Chemical property						
Carbon (%)	0.88	−23	0.86	−13	0.96	−25
Nitrogen (%)	0.11	−10	0.09	+10	0.09	0
Phosphorus (ppm)	23.0	−0.5	17.0	−47	5.0	+40
Calcium (me%)	3.5	+0.5	4.1	+15	1.5	+2.5
Potassium (me%)	0.56	−21	0.53	−19	0.48	−19
Magnesium (me%)	1.8	+0.5	2.1	−9.5	1.5	+27
Soil pH (H$_2$O)	5.4	+0.5	5.9	0	6.2	−9.7
Physical property						
Sand (%)	59	+8	65	+0.5	57	+10
Silt (%)	10	−10	10	−3	12	−25
Clay (%)	30	−10	25	0	30	−7

me: millequivalents
1990(%): per cent change, 1977−90
Uncultivated: woodland and bushland under grazing

A majority (22 of 30 sites) declined in carbon percentage during the period, and the trend in both cultivated and uncultivated land, in both areas, was downwards. But in nitrogen, there was no significant general trend.

Available phosphorus figures are generally low; 18 profiles have less than 20 ppm, indicating a rather acute deficiency in both 1977 and 1990. Of 20 profiles which were deficient in available phosphorus in 1977, 8 showed some gains in 1990, while the remaining 12 showed losses, as high as 67%. Significant losses of phosphorus only occurred on cultivated sites, where they were noticeable, notwithstanding their short history of cultivation (two seasons). There was a small increase in calcium and a small decrease in potassium in all three groups, and no general trend in magnesium. Exchangeable acidity (pH) is not a major problem in the area. There was no clear trend in soil pH during the period.

The textural characteristics show a trend towards more sand, at the expense of the silt and clay fractions, though clay held up on the cultivated sites. The measured changes are, however, small.

THE SPATIAL ANALOGUE METHOD

The longitudinal study failed to demonstrate clear overall trends in soil fertility owing to the small number of sites sampled, the predominance of uncultivated sites, and the variability between profiles. The alternative is a spatial analogue method whereby samples are analysed from sites with known management regimes (cultivation, grazing) and compared with samples from control sites under natural vegetation. The nature of changes through time are inferred from the differences.

The choice of sites

Twenty-seven samples were collected from Kilungu Location. The samples were collected from three categories of site, representing different land uses.

Group 1 are sites which have not been cultivated for over 60 years and are under natural vegetation. Ground cover is 100% including much litter. Slopes are 5−35°. The vegetation consists of large and small trees, shrubs, herbs and some grasses. Soils are dark brown with a good crumb structure and little mineral content is visible. The only management is occasional removal of litter as field manure and perhaps fuel cutting.

Group 2 are sites which have been fallow for 20 years or more and are currently used as grazing land. Ground cover is 60−90% and the slopes 10−40°. The vegetation is lightly wooded shrubland with herbs, sometimes cut to encourage the growth of the grasses. The soils are reddish brown with quartz or mica fragments sometimes visible.

Group 3 are sites which have been under annual cultivation for 40−60 years or more without any known additions of fertiliser and little manuring. In one area, site 3 was on a terrace; in the other two areas, it had not benefited from any land improvement. Ground cover (during the dry season) is 20−50%, including weeds and some standing crops. The slopes are 15−20° (unterraced, and 10−15° on the terrace. The soils are light in colour and sandy, with quartz fragments on the surface and sometimes larger stones a little deeper in the profile. These sites represent the low end of the fertility range on cultivated land, cropped with maize and beans (also cassava and bananas in one area) year after year, with low yields.

TABLE 7.6. Chemical properties of Kilungu soils, 1990

Property	Average values		
	1 Uncultivated sites (*N*=9)	2 Grazing land sites (*N*=9)	3 Cultivated sites (*N*=9)
Soil pH (water)	5.5	5.4	5.0
Potassium (me%)	0.56	0.40	0.29
Calcium (me%)	8.7	2.4	1.1
Magnesium (me%)	3.4	1.4	0.9
Phosphorus (ppm)	23.0	14.0	13.0
Nitrogen (%)	0.35	0.18	0.11
Carbon (%)	2.49	1.25	0.74

RESULTS

The analyses show a definite trend of decline at every site from 1 to 3 (Table 7.6). The only exception to this trend is found in available phosphorus. This nutrient is deficient at all three types of site (uncultivated, grazing and cultivated). Available bases at Group 1 sites range from moderately adequate to rich, except for phosphorus which is low. At Group 2 sites, the range is from moderately adequate to low. At Group 3 sites, all the bases are low, except for potassium which is still moderately adequate.

Of particular significance from the point of view of agriculture is the sharp fall in the nitrogen and carbon content to very low levels relative to those of uncultivated soils. Even long-term fallow, under some grazing, which carries some woody vegetation, is closer on the average to cultivated than to uncultivated land in respect of nitrogen and carbon.

DISCUSSION

A profile of fertility under grazing

Since all the sites sampled for the longitudinal analysis were uncultivated in 1977, and 23 of them remained so in 1990, the analysis offers little guidance on the impact of cultivation (Table 7.5), but does suggest a picture of trends on grazing land, with the proviso that the findings are limited by the sample distribution to the southern part of the District, and may not be applicable in full to the northern hilly areas. They suggest that soils, generally low in organic matter, carbon and nitrogen, and phosphorus, have tended to decline further in carbon content. No clear trend in nitrogen has been shown. Exchangeable bases have shown small changes (positive for calcium and negative for potassium), or no change (magnesium), with the exception of sodium, which appears to have increased noticeably. Phosphorus has remained stable except under cultivation, where it declined. Infiltration and run-off have brought about a small increase in the sand fraction of the soils. However, there is a high degree of variation between sites, as would be expected.

A profile of soil fertility under cultivation

If the Kilungu soils are representative, as they are thought to be, of the hill masses in the long and densely settled areas of the District, they give a graphic picture of the impact of permanent cultivation (without compensating inputs) on the natural soils of the area. A comparison of the analytical results from Group 1 and 3 sites, averaged for the three areas, shows falls in carbon (by a factor of about 3.5), nitrogen (3.0), phosphorus (0.5), calcium (8.0), magnesium (3.5) and potassium (0.5). Soils have also become somewhat more acid.

Inspection of the soils reveals that the dark brown surface horizon of the naturally wooded sites gives way to lighter coloured, sandy soils with quartz fragments noticeable at the surface, an accompanying deterioration of structure and a diminution of plant remains in the surface layers. The evidence is consistent with the view expressed in the 1930s (KNA: Barnes, 1937; RH: Maher, 1937) that the topsoil was being removed by erosion over extensive areas.

Given that the cultivated soils sampled represent the bottom of a range (no fertility inputs, and in two sites, no terracing), it can be concluded that soil properties on better managed land must improve according to the management. They are highly variable. Variation is caused by site factors. In addition, soil properties vary over very small distances according to position relative to terrace structures and ditches, maintenance, crop residue management, and manure or fertiliser placement in preceding seasons. A very large sample would be required to assess average soil properties in these circumstances, and this was beyond the scope of the study.

On the supposition that Group 2 soils were first cleared for cultivation, before reverting to fallow or grazing, the data show that long-term closure to cultivation may not be sufficient to restore the nutrient status of soils to their former levels. Carbon, nitrogen and exchangeable bases have improved relative to the cultivated soils, but by factors of less than 1.0 (with the exception of calcium); and phosphorus is unchanged.

The chemical properties of the uncultivated soils sampled for the longitudinal study in 1990 are expected to resemble those of sites 1 or 2. A comparison (Tables 7.5 and 7.6) shows that this is so for phosphorus and soil pH (Group 1 sites), and exchangeable bases (Group 2 sites). But in nitrogen and carbon content, they resemble Group 3 sites soils, even though there is no history of long-term cultivation. This may reflect the drier ecology of the Makueni area.

Response to declining fertility

Declining soil fertility was identified as the main technical problem confronting the Department of Agriculture in 1932. The Department embarked on a campaign to demonstrate, by its model smallholding, the advantages derived from mixed farming and by propaganda, the importance of farm yard manure, rotation, use of compost and planting of old farms with grass rather than allowing reversion through the cycle of weeds to a poor quality bush (Kenya, DoA, 1932). To increase the supply of manure, night enclosure of livestock was advocated (Kenya, DoA, 1940). In Chapters 10 and 14 we demonstrate the increasing acceptance of manure, which is now in short supply. Chemical fertiliser is relatively little used, except in AEZs 2 and 3, due to the risks incurred through erratic rainfall.

CONCLUSIONS

A reconstruction of the history of erosion in Machakos District has shown that erosion has been reduced since the 1930s and 1940s but has by no means ceased. Its intensity is highly variable over the District. Field measurements of the rate of erosion suggest rates in the range 5−15 tons/ha/year for whole catchments, but much higher figures have been obtained from badly eroding sites.

The greater proportion of soil loss continues to occur on grazing land but the relative contribution from cultivated land varies according to the quality and maintenance of the terraces. Erosion on crop land has been reduced as a result of improvements in terracing rather than changes to the cropping system. Greater awareness appears to have shortened the time lag between opening new land for cultivation and installing terraces to control erosion. Erosion on grazing land has been reduced by land demarcation and registration, as a result of which boundaries are respected and communal grazing has almost disappeared. These management changes will be examined in Chapter 11.

The rainfall record, taken in conjunction with the evidence on soil erosion, and the observations made at the time, suggests a strong link between periods of drought, denudation of grazing lands, and intensified erosion. Erosion from gullies, other than those caused by road drainage, has been reduced partly because many of the older gullies, extremely active 50–60 years ago, have now become stabilised.

Areas which have been maintained under natural vegetation with minimal disturbance are still fertile, well supplied with the necessary plant nutrients. Areas which were cultivated and have been fallowed for a long time, or which have experienced bush clearance and extensive grazing, but are still under a reasonable ground cover which prevents the soil from being eroded away, have a moderate to low supply of plant nutrients. Areas which are under long-term continuous cultivation without inputs, or intensive grazing pressure, have a low supply of plant nutrients. This may be as a result of the removal of the top horizon by erosion.

The fertility of cultivated soils depends on their management. Although terrace construction is often believed to be associated with improved yields, Holmgren and Johansson (1987) found little statistical evidence to support this. The reason is that fertility enhancement through manuring and other improved practices is the major contributor to higher yields on (some) terraced land.

NOTES

1   This chapter has been developed from initial research by D. B. Thomas (erosion) and J. P. Mbuvi (soil fertility), reported in ODI Working Paper 53.

2   Wain (1983) calculated the average annual sediment yield for the Thwake river basin at 12.7 ton/ha/year and compared this with an estimate of 15.0 ton/ha/year for the Maruba river made by Edwards (1979). He concluded that the figure of 5.4 ton/h/year for the Iiuni catchment, which is within the Thwake river basin, was below the average. Styczen (1983) obtained soil losses of 20–30 ton/ha/year from small plots of rangeland with low cover, and showed that if cover exceeds 30%, losses are much reduced.

3   The Kenya Agricultural Research Institute and its predecessors did not maintain archives of soil sample materials. The data files for samples collected in the Kangundo and Wamunyu areas, and most of those collected in the Machakos area, could not be found, and some analytical work was still uncompleted in 1990.

8

Vegetation[1]

PARADIGMS OF GRAZING MANAGEMENT

The nature of the interaction between herbivory by domestic livestock and vegetational change is presently the subject of a major paradigmatic shift (Ellis and Swift, 1988). Moreover the nature and usefulness of some concepts central to sustainable management of the communal rangelands in arid and semi-arid sub-Saharan Africa (for example, carrying capacity and grazing-induced land degradation) are being questioned increasingly by ecologists and development specialists (Warren and Agnew, 1988; Mortimore, 1989b; De Leeuw and Tothill, 1990; Perrier, 1990; Mace, 1991).

The results of this study are in complete disagreement with the widely held belief, based on extant literature, that the semiarid grazing lands of Machakos District are characterised by land degradation (in the forms of soil erosion and surface sealing), caused by overstocking and overgrazing. Our definition of degradation has already been discussed in Chapter 2. It is now generally accepted to mean the stage at which an ecosystem loses its resilience (Hollings, 1973; Walker et al, 1981; Walker and Noy-Meyer, 1982; Harrington et al, 1984) thus resulting in a permanent decline in productive capacity (Abel and Blaikie, 1990).

The yardstick used to judge that stocking rates exceed carrying capacity is normally based on a beef ranch model. Such an approach is totally inappropriate for smallholder livestock production systems in Machakos. As an example, a causal relationship between overstocking, overgrazing, and soil erosion, and by extension land degradation, was reported by Hussain et al (1982) for Makueni Division. They argued that poor livestock management (e.g. retaining 30% males in shoats) and traditional noncommercial attitudes towards livestock development, resulted in overstocking and soil erosion. They reported that 60% of all farmers interviewed overstocked their grazing land. In arriving at this conclusion, they relied on a comparison between recommended stocking rates for poor and good rangelands and actual stocking rates. The assumptions that underlaid the derivation of these recommended stocking rates were based on a commercial beef ranch production system, where economic objectives emphasise such parameters as weight gain, weaning weight, and offtake. Under these circumstances, the tendency will be to maximize production per head. Small farmers and agro-pastoralists, because they have multiple uses for cattle (e.g. meat, milk, manure, draught), tend to maximize production on a per area basis (Cossins 1984, 1985; Behnke, 1985; Coppock et al, 1985; Scoones, 1989). High stocking rates in the semiarid grazing lands of Machakos are rational to the extent that their production goal transcends that of beef production.

This chapter evaluates changes in the natural vegetation resources of Machakos District. It is assumed, on the basis of the evidence presented in Chapter 3, that vegetational change is attributable to management and not to climatic change. The chapter traces the impact of grazing management on natural woodland (settled during the 1950s and 1960s) using standard ecological survey and air-photo interpretation techniques. There is no evidence of irreversible land degradation, though bush encroachment threatens to reduce the value of the grazing for cattle. A study of two selected sites with a longer history of grazing indicates that, at these, woodland communities are being managed sustainably for grazing and other purposes.

HISTORICAL BACKGROUND

In the 1930s, it was believed that 'The chief cause of erosion in Machakos and Kitui is overstocking ... The only solution is to reduce the number of stock to the capacity of the country' (Annual Report, Ukamba Province, 1933; quoted in Otieno, 1984: 64). This was repeated in numerous other reports in the 1930s and 1940s. The vegetation of Machakos was also affected by cultivation and woodcutting, but grazing management (or mismanagement) has dominated the literature. More recently, Ottley et al allude to overstocking and grazing induced soil erosion in the semiarid grazing lands of Machakos thus:

> ... for the most part pasture land is extremely overgrazed, even with heavy death losses incurred in recent drought years. Improved pasture must be a prerequisite to any worthwhile livestock industry and this can be done only when livestock numbers and production capacity of the land are brought into proper balance. It must be further understood that soil erosion will continue to be a major problem until this is done. (Consortium, Report 8, 1978).

The inhabited area of the Reserve was mainly covered by managed rather than natural vegetation at the beginning of our study period. (For Trapnell's classification of ecological zones in northern Machakos, see Farah (1991).) The Crown Land in the Yattas, and some other areas on the fringes of the inhabited area were subject to management by the Veterinary Department, the Akamba being allowed to take fixed numbers of cattle there on payment of licence fees. The Reconditioning Committee in 1935 accepted the recommendation of Edwards, the Grassland Improvement Officer, that the Yatta Plateau should be managed as a pasture area only, with no settlement and no goats. By 1950, five blocks, each with four sections for rotational grazing, had been delimited, and during the early war years and under ALDEV, new watering points were developed. The aim was 'the conversion of a piece of raw Africa into a well managed grazing area in which the number of stock is related to the carrying capacity of the land', maintaining adequate cover and preventing 'desert creep' and 'ever-increasing bush' by means of controlled rotational grazing (Kenya, MoA, 1962b: 277).[2] Despite, or because of controls, a survey in 1957 found the Yatta Plateau heavily encroached by *Acacia pennata, A. Mellifera*, and *Commiphora—Combretum* bush. Annual grasses predominated on overgrazed areas, where 75% of the cover was *Aristida* spp. The causes were said to be illegal overstocking, failure to burn, overestimation of carrying capacity, and the complete breakdown of rotational grazing. In 1959 the Veterinary Department admitted its failure to control North Yatta, and handed over 74 000 ha of grazing and 20 000 ha of tsetse-infested bush to the Agricultural Department (Kenya, Ministry of Animal Husbandry and Water Resources, 1959). There was throughout 'the bitterest of opposition from local people supported by the Kamba politicians to the institution of any grazing scheme' and by 1962 ALDEV had to admit that control everywhere had effectively lapsed (Kenya, MoA, 1962b: 40, 287). The areas were taken over for free settlement (Chapter 4). There was a conflict between the Department's view that the 'correct and, indeed only method of land usage [in these areas] is the ranching of stock' (Kenya, MoA, 1962b: 276), and the Akamba view that they should be used for the usual combination of arable and livestock activities.

Thus, the vegetation of both the Reserve area and the Yattas had been subject to management interventions before 1960. Study sites in the southern, recently settled part of the District, which had not been subject to controls, were therefore chosen to test hypotheses on the impact of grazing on natural vegetation. The investigation aimed to determine changes in the vegetation structure that have occurred in natural grazing lands since available baseline surveys, to evaluate the extent and direction of change in the woody component of the vegetation and to assess the extent to which changes in plant community structure can be related to grazing management.

STUDY SITES

Two Locations, Kathonzweni (formerly the southern part of Makueni Location) and Ngwata were selected. Both sites occur in AEZ 5, and support natural vegetation which is predominantly used for livestock production on an extensive basis under free-ranging conditions, though on private land. They represent areas of recent human settlement (the 1950s for Kathonzweni and the 1960s for Ngwata) and, therefore, can serve to bring out the impact of human activities on vegetation over time. Land use is mainly agro-pastoralism. Average land per household is approximately 20 ha, of which 6 ha are cultivated, and the rest is used for livestock production. Natural vegetation varies from place to place, but mostly ranges from shrubland to dense wooded shrubland, with some areas supporting sufficient perennial grasses to qualify as grassed shrubland.

Two methods were used to analyse the issues (for a full description of the methods used, see Farah, 1991). Black and white aerial photographs (1961 and 1978) were used as benchmarks for evaluating physiognomic changes in vegetation and a field inventory of the vegetation was undertaken in August/September 1990.

In the field inventory sampling plots were located in 5 km transects. In each one, several vegetation parameters were surveyed:

(a) species inventory;
(b) per cent cover of each species by life form;
(c) density and heights of a *selected* woody species having economic value.

The choice of *Acacia tortilis* was based on its multiple values in semi-arid rangelands of Machakos. As a legume, it fixes nitrogen and thus increases or at least helps to maintain soil fertility. This is important in the face of declining soil fertility reported for cultivated portions of southern Machakos (Hussain et al, 1982). It is a source of feed for both cattle and small ruminants, and provides high quality charcoal and shade. In addition, *Combretum exalatum* and *Commiphora schimperii* were selected for Ngwata and Kathonzweni respectively, as woody species which are ecologically significant in these habitats but are nevertheless not under much utilisation pressure from man and livestock, compared with *A. tortilis*.

To interpret the physiognomy of the vegetation from the aerial photos, it was necessary to locate the transects on them. An overall determination of the physiognomic class was based on dominant lifeforms and classification (e.g. grassed shrubland) following Pratt and Gwynne (1977), as modified by Pomery and Service (1986).

Field analysis showed that the vegetations of Kathonzweni and Ngwata Locations are physiognomically similar and can be described as dense wooded shrubland, although the per cent cover of woody species is much greater in Ngwata. There is, however, some difference in the floristic composition of the vegetation at the two locations. At Kathonzweni, the dominant woody species are *Acacia mellifera* and *Commiphora schimperii* while at Ngwata they are *Acacia tortilis* and *Combretum exalatum*. *Eragrostis superba* and *Aristida kiniensis* are the dominant grasses at Kathonzweni, whereas *Chloris roxburghiana* and *Aristida kiniensis* are dominant at Ngwata.

VEGETATIONAL CHANGE IN SOUTHERN MACHAKOS

There was a marked increase of the woody component of the vegetation in both Locations between 1960 and 1990 (Table 8.1), which changed physiognomically from grassed shrubland to dense wooded shrubland. It is significant that Ngwata's vegetation had become dense wooded shrubland by 1978, whereas Kathonzweni remained a grassed shrubland until after 1978. Clemensian climax theory would suggest that the semiarid grazing lands of Machakos District are improving, because vegetation is progressing towards a higher successional status. But, because these grazing lands primarily support cattle, increased shrubs or woodland mean a lowered economic capacity.

Lightly and heavily grazed portions of the two study areas show a marked difference in vegetation structure and composition (Table 8.2), suggesting that grazing plays an important role in structuring the vegetation. These results — an increase in the woody and shrub component at the expense of grasses — are in agreement with established principles of range management and most community ecology literature regarding the impact of herbivory on plant community structure (Heady, 1975; Stoddart et al, 1975; McNaughton, 1979; Crawley, 1983; Harrington et al, 1984).

In both Makueni and Kibwezi Divisions, the principal domestic livestock are cattle. Cattle are graziers and their grazing on a continuous basis usually shifts vegetation composition towards woody types. This occurs with greater likelihood when utilisation intensity on the grasses is relatively high. Evidence of high intensity ($>60\%$) on perennial grasses was seen in many areas. In heavily grazed areas, 'increaser' species (e.g. *Solanum incanum*) further support the inference that cattle grazing is contributing to a change in vegetation structure towards woody species.

TABLE 8.1. Changes in the vegetation structure of Kathonzweni and Ngwata between 1960 and 1990

Year	Life form (% cover)			Physiognomic classification
	Trees	Shrubs	Grasses and forbs	
Kathonzweni				
1960	2	39	59	GS
1978	9	35	51	GS
1990	15	38	29	WSD
Ngwata				
1960	1	37	62	GS
1978	6	45	19	WSD
1990	11	62	18	WSD

GS: Grassed shrubland; WSD: dense wooded shrubland

It can thus be stated that with respect only to cattle production, the vegetation of both Kathonzweni and Ngwata is degrading in the sense that grazing capacity is on the decline.

It is probable that increasing woodiness may also be explained in part by a lack of fire. Fire is an ecological factor that tends to kill woody vegetation selectively and promote graminoid species, mainly because the perennating organs of the former are above the ground and hence are killed. In the management of rangelands, burning is used, *inter alia*, for regulating the relative proportions of woody and grass species (Stoddart et al, 1975; Heady, 1975; Pratt and Gwynne, 1977: 132; Valentine, 1981; Harrington et al, 1984). Both in colonial Kenya and after independence, the authorities proscribed burning (especially on State and Trust lands). However, early vegetation descriptions identified fire as one of the determinants maintaining some vegetation types, for example the 'savanna' or 'orchard' type of woodland of Makueni (KNA: Parsons, 1952; KNA: Trapnell, 1958). An interaction of grazing pressure with fire control and an episodic and fluctuating rainfall regime has probably led to increased woodiness. About 1944, Gerald Hopkins (then District Commissioner) noted that burning was discouraged 'with the utmost ferocity', leading to grazing on the same sites all year round. He thought that overgrazing during the previous 20 years had weakened the grass far more seriously than burning did and had enabled thorn bush to re-establish itself. This brought in its train the tsetse fly, dangerous game, and a retreat of cattle grazing from areas in the south (KNA: Hopkins, 1943). By 1958 some agriculturalists were convinced a *hot* burn was necessary to control bush regeneration, and recommended a rest (i.e. no grazing) for two rains, followed by a burn (Peberdy, 1958: 128). However, soon afterwards, the colonial authorities lost control of the Crown Lands, which were then settled (Chapter 4).

Figure 8.1 shows evidence of degradation in the economic sense. At Ngwata, 87% of the *Acacia tortilis* individuals sampled had a height of less than 2 m, and at Kathonzweni, 81% of sampled individuals were less than 4 m in height, suggesting that most of the mature plants had been removed by selective cutting. On the other hand, two ecologically dominant woody species, *Commiphora schimperii* in Kathonzweni, and *Combretum exalatum* in Ngwata, which possess much less range value than *A. tortilis*, displayed an unskewed size class structure.

A very important question that needs to be addressed is whether stocking rates maintained by the agro-pastoralists of Machakos are ecologically sustainable. Evidence against this must ultimately come in the form of irreversible grazing-induced land degradation. The results given above indicate that this has not yet occurred in southern Machakos. Ottley et al (Consortium, Report 8, 1978), while drawing attention to grazing-induced land degradation in the form of soil loss (a widely held belief among conservationists and development planners), admit that

TABLE 8.2. Vegetation composition under lightly and heavily grazing management (per cent cover)

Study location	Life form	Light grazing	Heavy grazing
Kathonzweni	Trees	4	18
	Shrubs	26	50
	Herb grasses	54	18
Ngwata	Trees	7	15
	Shrubs	35	48
	Forbs	9	14
	Grasses	22	19

Determination of grazing intensity was based on field indicators

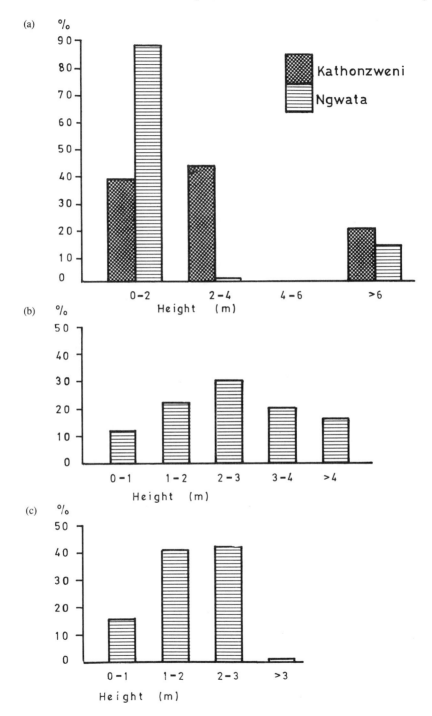

FIGURE 8.1. Height class distribution of selected woody species: (a) *Acacia tortilis* at Kathonzweni and Ngwata; (b) *Commiphora schimperii* at Kathonzweni; (c) *Combretum exalatum* at Ngwata

in the semi-arid grazing lands of Machakos, it takes only two years to regain the productive potential of the land.

VEGETATIONAL CHANGE IN NORTHERN MACHAKOS

In northern Machakos there is a longer history of grazing management, and it was here that the linkage with land degradation was first suggested. According to Lindblom (1920) and Barnes' (KNA: Barnes, 1937) reconstruction from interviews, the Reserve was much more wooded at the turn of the century. (Lindblom's field work was carried out during 1911—1912; see also Chapter 7.) However, all sources agree that most of the forests had been removed from the settled hills before the end of the 19th century, except for the sanctified 'podo' patches.

> The flatter country surrounding the hills and in the Mabuti—Kiteta areas was [at the time of the British occupation] practically uninhabited, it was covered with dense high grass and bush trees, and also had rich top soil. (KNA: Barnes, 1937: 1. Reproduced by permission of Kenya National Archives.)

These areas were

> . . . often of the savanna type, but usually overgrown with a more or less dense bush which, with its thorns of all shapes and sizes, is a plague to travellers . . . Large trees are seldom to be seen; only those of medium height and under. They do not grow close together, but scattered about; a coarse kind of grass grows between them though not, as in northern Europe, in continuous sward, but in patches, between which the soil is bare. Different species of acacia and mimosa are predominant among the trees. Typical of the drier bush are varieties of the genus *Sansevieria* . . . further up on the hillsides grow species of *Euphorbia* . . . around the villages, and as weeds in the fields, grow *Rhinus communis* in abundance, often attaining the height of a small tree. (Lindblom, 1920: 24—26.)

Deforestation was indicated by solitary trees and immense stumps on some of the hillsides (taken over for cultivation), and in one area,

> A small, thickly populated district close to Machakos is called *mutituni* ('in the forest') and the old people say that it was once entirely overgrown with forest and the haunt of elephants. Now the district is almost entirely devoid of even fuel, to procure which women have laboriously to dig up the remains of trees long since dead. (Lindblom, 1920: 24—26.)

These accounts, and descriptions provided later by Edwards (1940) and Trapnell (KNA: Trapnell, 1958), lead to the conclusion that, at one time, northern Machakos was as wooded as southern Machakos was when it was settled in the 1950s and 1960s, and that the vegetation communities, below the hills, were similar.

Since the results reported above show that the effect of continuous grazing by cattle is to increase the woody component of the vegetation, an explanation has to be sought for its reduction — nearly to vanishing point — in large areas of northern Machakos, before our period began. There can be little doubt that the chief agent of this reduction was fire. Lindblom's description, quoted above, implies the existence of areas of 'savanna type' woodland or 'orchard' (KNA: Parsons, 1982), whose development and maintenance are furthered by fire. When the livestock owners moved from the hills to the lower country.

> The areas which are now devastated [in 1937] were long grass and bush and stock owners burned the grass frequently to get short grass for their stock . . . Bush trees they say were destroyed and many cut to make bomas and for firewood . . . (KNA: Barnes, 1937: 2. Reproduced by permission of Kenya National Archives.)

The clearance of woodland from the hillslopes (as in Mutituni, described above) had already created a fuelwood shortage. As the population increased and shifted downslope, the remaining trees, never large or abundant (according to Lindblom) would have come under exponential pressure. The photographs taken by Barnes in 1937 (Chapter 1), when tree cover was perhaps at its nadir, show that some natural regeneration of woody plants occurred nearly everywhere. But where individuals can be discerned, they are sparse, small, illformed and heavily cut. This was still so in the early 1950s (Figure 12.2a).

Hopkins (KNA, Hopkins, 1943) reported that bush encroachment led to the abandonment of some newly settled places in the south-east. (Hopkins noted that in the less populated south and the Yattas, the bush easily regenerated, by seed blown down wind from the 'bush belts which are ever pressing in along the east and south boundaries'.) This again raises the intriguing possibility that economic degradation accompanied, in some areas, the proscription of fire, which was intended to protect the natural resource. Increasingly deprived of browse, the rapidly growing livestock population became dependent almost entirely on grasses and forbs which are prone to fail in drought. Tufted grasses leave much ground bare, which was noticed by Lindblom in the first decade of the century. Such bare patches, enlarged during drought, would be prone to surface sealing on the resumption of rainfall, preventing seed regeneration, and increasing run-off and sheetwash. Areas of *mangalata* with stony surfaces were noticed in Maputi early in the century. The presence of woody canopies, on the other hand, protects the surface from rainsplash, enriches the soil with leaf litter, prevents sealing and obstructs run-off.

The demarcation of private rights to land, including the *kisese* or grazing land, was encouraged by the administration from the 1930s onwards. The enclosure of *kisese* permitted it to be managed as an integrated grazing, fuelwood, charcoal and beekeeping resource, as well as permitting produce to be harvested from multi-purpose trees (Gielen, 1982: 47). Increasing woodiness of grazing lands in northern Machakos (shown in Figure 12.2b) is not, however, due to shrub regrowth under heavy cattle grazing but to the managed regeneration of canopied trees.

Evidence in support of this hypothesis was provided at two sites on managed grazing land in Masii Location in August 1990 (Table 8.3: see Farah, 1991). Site 1 corresponds to 'dry Combretum' vegetation on the sandy soils characteristic of this area, dominated by *Combretum zeyheri* and *Terminalia kilimendscherica* (its management history is reported in Farah, 1991). Site 2 corresponds to *Acacia tortilis* woodland, on red soils, and dominated by *Acacia* and *Commiphora* spp. The management histories of the two sites are notable for careful control of stocking levels, protection of woody species, use of goats to control bush regrowth, restricted offtake for fuel wood, and the conscious management of natural succession, on land which is

TABLE 8.3. Vetegation at two sites on managed grazing land in Masii Location (per cent cover)

Life form	Site 1	Site 2
Trees	0	21
Shrubs	65	34
Grasses	51	49
Litter	40	38

The data were obtained from four randomly selected plots of 20×20 m at each site. Canopy and ground cover were measured using the methods described earlier

subject to secure family tenure. The need to maintain viable grazing land for later inheritance is influential. Site 2 is summarised as follows:

The land was purchased in 1950 in a badly denuded condition (described as *mangalata*), thought to be due to overgrazing, with sheet and rill erosion. The trees included *Acacia tortilis, A. mellifera* (very common), *Commiphora schimperii, C. Campestris,* a few *Combretum* and *Terminalia; Acacia brevispica* grew by the stream courses. The site was closed to grazing for 10 years after purchase (the owner had alternative grazing for his livestock). He tried planting star grass (*Cynodon plectostachyus*), collected from the riverside. He is aware of a natural succession: *Aristida kiniensis, A. adscensioni* were followed by the perennial grasses including *Chloris roxburghiana, Latipes senegalensis, Enteropogon macrostachys* (common under trees), *Heteropogon* which grows on sandy pockets associated with *Eragrostis superba, E.caesipitasa* and *Themeda triandra* which is now disappearing. Where the ground cover is incomplete, *Microchloa kunthii* characterises the succession. With regard to shrubs, *Griidia latifolia* was the indicator species of denuded land in 1950. *Lantana camara* was introduced to the area in the 1970s, as a plant for live hedges, and is now being spread by birds, suppressing the pasture grasses in places. However, in colonising denuded land, it protects the surface from run-off and helps restore fertility, being replaced by other woody plants in time. Goats are used to control thick bush.

Grazing was resumed in the 1960s, but the owner's livestock were decimated by the droughts of the 1970s (from 18 cattle to 6, with 7 dying and 5 being sold). Although the land deteriorated, it was better than when he bought it. His cattle herd recovered to 12, but he lost animals again during 1983–1984. He now owns 8, including a grade animal, and would prefer more grade animals to a larger herd. His goats have decreased through sales. By the 1980s he was grazing the site on a seasonal rotation though he cannot afford to make paddocks. There is no burning. Charcoal burning (for sale to Machakos Town) was the primary factor that prevented regeneration from taking place before the land was bought, but now that it is under the owner's control, offtake is limited, though both fuelwood and charcoal are still obtained from it. The owner's management objective is to undergraze the land so that it can be subdivided on inheritance by his two sons in viable condition. He has never received technical advice and has no off-farm income now.

CONCLUSION

If these sites are representative, it can be concluded that grazing areas in northern Machakos are coming under increasingly conservationary management. They are important as fuel resources. Increasing woodiness is not here an unwanted byproduct of cattle grazing but the result of protecting trees. Bush control may even benefit from browsing by the maligned 'ruin bringing goat' (RH: Maher, 1937).

This admits the possibility of an earlier decline in pasture productivity, but shows that it is perceived to be reversible. Soil degradation of an irreversible kind is restricted to gullies and severely denuded sites, although there is still some evidence (reported in Chapter 7) of high rates of soil loss on some grazing land. Such rates, if continued indefinitely, threaten a loss of pasture productivity and ultimately irreversible land degradation. On the other hand, the examples of management given above show the possibilities for maintaining or improving productivity.

We conclude that present grazing management is neither irrational nor inherently degradational in its impact on the natural vegetation. In recently settled areas of southern Machakos, while heavy grazing causes changes which may reduce the cattle-carrying capacity, such changes are not degradational in an ecological sense. In northern Machakos, conservationary attitudes to the management of private grazing lands are almost certainly widespread.

NOTES

1 This chapter has been developed from research by Kassim O. Farah; see ODI Working Paper 53.
2 The chapter from which this quotation is taken was written by R.O. Hennings, Deputy Chief Secretary in Kenya.

PART III

MANAGEMENT AND MANAGERS

9

Akamba Social Institutions[1]

AIMS AND METHODOLOGY

The importance of knowledge and human capital in economic growth has recently been re-emphasised. Improved capabilities come not only from formal education, but importantly, from family and village institutions, which can be assisted by a deliberate community development approach. This chapter traces change in the basic Akamba institutions of family, mutual help groups, markets and local community leadership, which since 1930 have been challenged by major crises and new opportunities, and have interacted with introduced institutions such as the missions, Government, or commercial organisations. The new and the old are now interwoven as society has become more complex, with new specialised institutions to facilitate the processing of knowledge, the adoption of innovations, and the ease of transactions.[2,3] Knowledge is only effective if implemented, and this requires the ability to raise capital and organise labour at the level of the family enterprise and its community environment. However, success may also require complementary facilities which only governments can easily provide, or it may require a change in government policy. A study of farming and economic change must also, therefore, be concerned with institutions which develop leadership and organisational skills at the village level, and with villages' links to higher authority at the District and national level.

Mbithi (1971b: 171) showed the close association between increases in the number of specialised institutions in a village (primary schools, tea houses, shops of different types, co-operatives, churches, dips, agricultural extension, banks, etc), and firstly, its physical links by roads and paths to other centres and, secondly, increasing or high rates of change in farming (see Mbula Bahemuka and Tiffen, 1992: Table 1). The village facilities are provided in part by individuals (shops, etc.), in part by community effort and self-help, and in part by government action. Villages with good communications hear what is going on elsewhere, getting both knowledge and inspiration to create facilities themselves. Economic development therefore reflects not merely what is happening to the average farmer, but also growth in the capacity of social institutions.

Our database was provided by a review of literature and archival materials, interviews with key informants, and group interviews with elderly men and women leaders. The latter, which took place in five selected sub-locations, proved a valuable method of tapping oral history and social responses unrecorded in files. It focused on three easily identifiable epochs: the present (1990); the years immediately preceding independence (1960–1963), and 1945, when many Akamba soldiers returned from the war. (Mbula Bahemuka and Tiffen (1992) contains further details and the open-ended questionnaire used.) H. E. Lambert's interviews with the elders of the reserve in 1945 provided another baseline for identifying change.

THE FAMILY

The family circa 1930–1945

The family has always been the basic Akamba economic unit for production, consumption, investment and insurance. The ideal in the 1930s was an extended family based on polygyny, including adult children, with large herds and cultivable land for each wife. It was well adapted to the colonisation and clearing of new land in circumstances where the population was scattered and each family had to supply almost all its own needs and do what it could to modify the risks to which it was subject. The extended family was part of a more diffuse clan, which provided mutual support during times of disaster or conflict. Every Mukamba belonged to one of 25 patrilineal clans, and marriage was with a member of a different clan.

The larger the extended family, the greater a man's social prestige and territorial sphere of influence, through clan and kinship mechanisms, as his older sons settled elsewhere. Although only the rich could afford polygyny, it was the general aspiration and the norm on which the rules of inheritance were based (Chapter 5 has discussed land tenure). The nuclear, monogamous family was seen as a stage in the family developmental cycle or as temporarily necessary through economic circumstances. Bride price was paid mainly in cattle and goats, so a family's livestock were intimately bound up with its past and future. Even those without livestock opposed the idea of any limitation on herds (KNA: Lambert, 1945: 114). Livestock could be devastated by bad management, drought and disease, and some families became much more wealthy and influential than others. A man with much livestock was able to marry more than one wife, have many children, and provide wives for his sons, thus increasing his agricultural labour force, his farm size, and the geographic spread of the family land and livestock holdings, and thus reduce risk (Ndeti, 1972; Mbula, 1974, 1977). In the 1930s there was still fairly strict division of labour by age and sex. Breaking new ground for planting was done by men, while weeding was done by women and children. Bird-scaring and livestock care was the work of young boys. Younger family men and boys might spend part of the year at a distance, at a cattle post.

Although each of the sub-units consisting of a wife and her children were largely independent of each other (KNA: Lambert, 1945: 140), there was also a strong feeling of mutual support. Older married sons, who departed to form new households on previously uncultivated land, retained a feeling of responsibility towards the family head and those remaining in his household. This was true also of those who left home to work. If either the family head or his unmarried adult children were away from home earning, as became increasingly common in the period 1930–1960, they usually contributed part of their earnings to the support of those at home.

The family was also the educational unit. Parents and grandparents were responsible for passing on not only the knowledge necessary for managing household, agricultural and pastoral activities, but also important social values such as egalitarianism, reciprocity and mutual responsibility. The latter two provide some security against disaster; the larger a person's social networks and the more people that are indebted to him or her, the more he or she can rely on help in time of need. Egalitarianism requires more explanation. Several scholars have emphasised the value that the Akamba put on the individual, and relate this to their disinclination to invest any single person or group with too much power, which meant that there was almost no permanent leadership structure above the associations of neighbouring villages. However, equality was within categories and certain categories ranked above others. The oldest men in the *utui* (village) constituted the senior age-grade, and formed the village council of elders. The male family head controlled all other family members. Men as a category ranked higher than women, although there was said to be 'an amazing equality (relative to other African societies), for although the man is the overt leader, the mutual obligations between men and women are highly reciprocal and in courtship it is the girl who chooses the boy' (Nida, 1962, quoted by Consortium, Report 6, 1978: 44). Nevertheless, women generally were expected to behave with respect towards men and to obey their lead. Within each category social equality was accompanied by respect for the wealthy, successful individual and achievement was desired and emulated.

Changes within the family, 1930–1990

Akamba society has long been noted for its fluidity and openness to change[4] and by 1990 the family had different functions, structures and ideals (Mbula, 1974; 1977). Wealth and prestige are no longer measured by the number of wives and the size of the herd. Education, clothing, medication and household effects, once supplied by family labour, are now acquired through money. The pressure for a minimum cash income contributed to rural–urban migration. At first this was almost exclusively by men (see Chapter 4) and at times over 40% of families in rural Machakos had absentee male adults. Women were compelled to take on male roles and tasks — such as house repairs, breaking ground for planting, using the plough and determining family policy on youth education. This led to an increasing economically imposed maternal dominance. Marriage break-down and divorce, once frowned on, became more common. Male migration, absenteeism and, more importantly, the frequent inability of the male to obtain gainful employment and exert his role in supporting his family could lead to male alienation and alcoholism, frequently noted by observers in the 1960s (Mbula, 1974, 1986; P. M. Mbithi, pers. comm.). (Drunkenness, on which DCs frequently commented in colonial times, was a notable social phenomenon according to Owako, a friendly observer in the 1960s (F. N. Owako, pers. comm. 1990); it was not a noticeable feature to us in 1990.)

However, many families have successfully surmounted these strains, and evolved a new marital relationship based on shared decision-making, and shared work roles on the ever smaller farms (see Figure 9.1). In a Kenya-wide study, in 1986, men reported that husbands made the major household decisions in 65% of cases, the wife in 6% and both together in 20%. (Women respondents tended to report rather higher numbers for decision-making by the wife or jointly.) As far as day-to-day farming decisions were concerned, the husband was said to make them in 44% of cases, the wife in 21% and they were made jointly by 28% (percentages exclude households where a female head had no husband) (Mbula Bahemuka, 1986). In Machakos, the importance of female decision-making within the household is likely to be above average, due to the higher than average status of Akamba women within society, and the continued absence of some men. In a 1980 survey in AEZ 4, 82% of the households were headed by males, but 29% of household heads resided away from home (Meyers, 1981: 87). This suggests day-to-day decision-making was in nearly half the cases in female hands.

By the late 1970s the nuclear family had become the social norm in older settled areas. The same survey found only 6% of households were polygamous. Although 32% of households had two or more sub-units, these included not only second wives, but also households with married sons or, in 10% of the cases, married brothers (Meyers, 1981: 87). The change to a nuclear unit as an ideal was encouraged by Christianity and western education. Christian values emphasised the marital bond and the 'unity of body' (Mbula, 1977). They also raised the status of women.

However, the extended family may still have economic functions. These take, however, two

FIGURE 9.1. A young woman takes a moment off to attend to her children while she works with her husband at planting onions. This was just before nightfall: it typifies the longer inputs of labour that intensive farming requires. (Photo: M. Mortimore)

different forms. In the older-settled areas the inheritance of smaller farms, and the lack of new land to settle, means that brothers sometimes farm the land they inherit jointly. In more newly settled zones, where land was available to those who could cultivate it till the 1970s, polygyny remained common, for additional wives gave control over additional farm land. Village leaders said that most men in Ngwata were polygynous in 1990 — and this was confirmed by a survey in the Kibwezi area (CARE, 1991).

A positive aspect of the change to nuclear families is that men no longer confine themselves to clearing land for new farms and caring for livestock, but, if their main role is farming, like the women they may contribute to all stages of crop production (see Figure 9.1). One woman leader in Mbooni told us that men have now become more helpful. The farm labour force has become more flexible. It is, however, reduced in size, on average older, and predominantly female, since more men than women have off-farm jobs. The expanding local off-farm sector has provided men with new local roles in trade, transport, building, etc. (see Chapter 10). (Women predominate in retail markets and basket making (both are combined with farming) and are important in the professions, particularly in education, health, community development, and agricultural extension.) With young people going to school or working off-farm, parents or hired labour have taken over most of the activities traditionally performed by children. If the father is away or in a local non-farm occupation, these additional tasks add to the daily load on women. However, many of the off-farm workers, male and female, swell the work force at peak periods.

Feelings of obligation towards the head of the family remain strong and family resource pooling is still important, not only in labour but also through remittances and gifts. Although land ownership remains an essential expression of the Akamba psyche,[5] the family now spreads its risks by having several occupations, rather than farms and herds in different areas. As a corollary, livestock are a minor aspect of family investment in the long-settled areas.[6] The dominating ambition now is to give children the best possible education, through which they will have access to a diversity of occupations. They are expected to make a return in information and capital to improve the family farm. If they earn locally and live at home, they normally contribute to some farm activities and would be counted by the head of the household as part of the farm unit. If they have established a new household based on a non-rural occupation, they may continue to make regular or emergency contributions to their parent's general welfare, or special contributions to the improvement of the farm which lies at the heart not only of the family economy but also of family affections.

The socialisation and education of the young, once completely in the hands of parents and grandparents, has been taken on by churches, schools, peer groups and other organisations like youth clubs. Between 1930 and 1960, most Akamba parents felt insecure because they were less educated in book knowledge than their children. Wanting to retain the respect and esteem of their children, they tended to defer to the knowledge of the young people, who became a channel for innovation (Mbula, 1977; P. M. Mbithi, pers. comm. 1990).

In the interviews with community leaders it was apparent that one of the chief causes in 1990 of stress and poverty was the closing of job opportunities for the young. Despite ever greater sacrifices to extend their children's education and their qualifications, young people may not get a job, and there is no longer new land to clear. For their part, the less successful young become frustrated. They may fall into crime as an alternative to a rural life they have come to dislike. In some villages these stresses led leaders on to discuss the importance of family planning knowledge. It is beginning to be seen as desirable to have a smaller family than heretofore.

MUTUAL HELP GROUPS

Traditional mutual help

As in many parts of Africa, mutual assistance groups had a long history. According both to our informants and to Mutiso (1975) three types were common before 1945:

- *Mwilaso*: a small group of friends and neighbours, traditionally either all boys or all girls, who worked on each other's farms on a strictly rotational basis. This still continues in the 1990s, but nowadays the participants are often older. The main purpose was and is to make routine farm work, cutting of firewood, etc., easier, pleasanter and more productive. However, it could by agreement be used for other purposes.
- *Mwethya*: called by an individual who needed assistance with a definite, short-term task. It was composed of relatives, friends and neighbours. *Mwethya* was an *utui* organisation. The host would (usually) cook a meal. It was not rotational, but people who participated in *mwethya* could expect *mwethya* help from others when they needed it. Such work might be either for normal farm operations, or for farm improvements.
- *Vuli*: if the task was too large to be handled by the *utui*, elders or friends from different villages could arrange for several *mwethya* groups to join in a *vuli*. The caller would slaughter a bull and brew beer. It was used by comparatively rich persons for projects such as building a house, or opening a new field. Its purpose was essentially to create a new capital asset.

Community development, self-help and politics

The colonial authorities tried to use the elders and the *mwethya* to create community improvements by compulsory labour. To an extent this was accepted for desirable community assets. One DC remarked that the Akamba were always willing to turn out for schools or roads (RH: Penwill, 1953). They were also used in the compulsory reconditioning programme, as will be described in Chapter 11. In 1946 four Kamba Chiefs were sent to Fort Hall (Muranga District) to observe what was then considered a successful terracing programme, where the elders of each village were responsible for managing communal labour twice a week. The system was then adopted in Machakos. It differed fundamentally from *mwethya*; it was compulsory, it was for a long continuing activity rather than a special day-long project, it was instigated by government officers and led, not by an individual host who wanted the project, but the chief, government officials or those whom the Government regarded as elders. People were taken to court and fined if they did not turn up. It was not, therefore, a voluntary response to 'felt needs'. Informants in several villages in 1990 agreed that compulsion helped to kill (their word) traditional *mwethya* at this time (except for *mwilaso*), although the absence of men on migratory labour contributed by dislocating mechanisms for handing on the custom.

This damage was unwitting. Colonial policy at the time aimed to promote self-help and local organisations. In 1948 the Colonial Secretary issued a *Despatch on Community Development*. In Kenya what was variously known as the Community Development (CD) or Mass Education Department was established (which later became part of the Ministry of Social Services). Jeanes Schools[7] (later the Institute of Administration) were established to train workers and leaders. Machakos was given a Social Welfare Officer in 1948 who began recruiting local staff and trying to interest communities in building meeting halls, adult literacy and educational films, women's clubs, and improved farming, nutrition and family management. Given the Colonial Secretary's interest, the SWO's reports were attached in full to the District Officer's Annual Report for the next two years. The SWO was not replaced but an African assistant continued the programme. In 1949 there were reported to be no indigenous women's organisations in the District (*mwilaso* and *mwethya* obviously not being counted) but in 1955 the DC reported 125 *Maendeleo* clubs, to which some European wives gave talks. He approved of their political and social value in preventing a gap between the men who had surged ahead and the women who had been left behind, but, as we shall see, they later developed a more threatening aspect to the authorities. They were also supported by the churches. Women CD leaders were recruited and trained (KNA: 2/DC/MKS/8/6).

In 1953 the District Commissioner requested a Jeanes School team to improve agricultural methods and promote farm consolidation and registration of tenure (RH: Penwill, 1953). John Malinda, a local man, became African District Assistant, responsible for CD work, and he diverted it into the strengthening of the soil conservation groups, while trying to make more use of the traditional *mwethya* ethic. The groups still did communal work as previously, but under locally elected committees, who decided where to work, and used their own methods of ensuring compliance, rather than relying on the chief's sanctions. In addition to terracing, they undertook the making of boundaries for newly demarcated land, constructed dams, made roads, and built new houses (interview recorded by Hill, 1991: 32). Betterment teams to encourage community work were formed in most locations, with Malinda responsible for those in the north, and using the clan-based *mwethya*, while those in the south under Jonathan Nzioka continued on the communal work system (Peberdy, 1958: 26). By 1958–1960, the Kenya Community Development Commissioner was referring to Machakos as a model.

In the meantime the returning soldiers had revivified the clans as a means of continuing their association on a District-wide basis and of raising funds to send students to high schools, Makerere College and overseas universities.[8] The authorities watched suspiciously but could not object to welfare activities. The DC noted: 'All the principal Kamba clans now have their Clan Society with prominent elders as their officers, and many have large sums in the Post Office Savings Bank' (KNA: DC/MKS/ Annual Report 1948).

The ex-soldiers regarded it as beneath their dignity to participate in communal soil conservation labour. The *mwethya* groups therefore tended to be dominated by women, initially as rhythm leaders, but increasingly they took the lead in general organisation and they had representatives at the Location and Divisional level for conservation and other projects such as schools and health centres (Peter Muasya, pers. comm. 1991).

In 1961 Paul Ngei, the grandson of an outstanding Akamba leader, Masaku, and an ex-soldier who had been arrested with Kenyatta for political activities, was released. This resulted in a contest for the Machakos constituency in 1963 between Ngei and Mulli, the previous MP and a member of the dominant political party KANU (Kenyan African National Union). Ngei saw the political potential of the women's clan organisations, and invited their leaders to organise his support. A powerful women's organisation emerged, the *Mbai sya eitu*, particularly in northern Machakos. Many of its leaders were the wives of World War II soldiers. They had a president for each clan (one of the most important being Ngei's mother), and sergeants and corporals responsible for organising women at the sub-location and below (Mutiso, 1975: 264–267). They remained involved in self-help. Competitive fund-raising meetings were attended by local dignitaries and accompanied by speech-making and celebratory dancing (Mbithi, 1972: 161–162). After the leaders had taken their cut (the women expected their leaders to become wealthy, as did men leaders), the money might be passed on to favoured political leaders, or used to finance and organise a self-help project in a particular Location. At the inaugural meeting for the project the men would be instigated by songs and dances into increasing their financial contribution (Mutiso, 1975). The President represented the District at national meetings, and found that 'we can whistle from Lake Victoria to the Indian Ocean' (Peter Muasya, pers. comm. 1990). Women had acquired a national network.

In 1963 President Kenyatta made *harambee* ('pulling together in self-help') a national development mode. The Community Development Department of the Ministry of Cooperatives and Social Services was put in charge of monitoring the *harambee* activities, through the Community Development Assistants (CDAs) who worked for the County Councils. In the Northern Division of Machakos in which *Mbai sya eitu* was active, projects worth Ksh 3 197 966 were carried out between 1965 and 1970. Of this, Central Government contributed Ksh 44 000 and the County Council Ksh 8300, while the people contributed over Ksh 3 million — Ksh 1 million in cash and Ksh 2 million as labour (Mutiso, 1975: 276–277). One sub-location of 1500 households, Karaba, during 1962–1968 constructed four dams, two local roads, a secondary school, and a nursery school, and cleared bush for cotton. Mbithi contrasted the enthusiastic competitive spirit which spurred activity for the community's own chosen objective and which utilised traditional kinship and organisational patterns with the comparative failure of governmental campaigns for forced communal dam-making, communal terrace making, compost making, etc (Mbithi, 1971b: 183–186).

However, by 1969 struggles within the dominant national political party, KANU, meant that the clan-based *Mbai sya eitu* was seen as an undesirable political organisation. The Community Development Department was told to register groups only for particular projects, rather than as clans carrying out a series of projects (Peter Muasya, 1991, pers. comm.). Project-based groups, however, elect sub-location committees, and upwards to District level, as shown in Figure 9.2. At the Divisional and District level the Government's Social Development Department keeps an eye on the groups politically as well as assisting them through the Community Development Assistants to plan new projects. The Maendeleo clubs for women were incorporated into KANU (KANU *Maendeleo ya Wanawake*). Other women's groups register because this gives them access to funding through the Women's Bureau of the Ministry of Social Services (Consortium, Report 7, 1978: 177). They are not distinctive in their function from the self-help groups which contain members of both sexes, and some contain male members. Figure 9.2 shows how the women's and other self-help groups fit into the formal and informal leadership structure.

Modern self-help and women's groups

In 1990 the role of clan elders and presidents was recollected as a feature of community leadership in the period 1945−1963 (Table 9.1) but they were no longer felt to be important. Informants insisted that the current self-help group and women's groups also differed fundamentally from the older *mwethya*. The new type, they said, evolved in the late 1960s.[9] Their distinguishing characteristics are long-term objectives and a programme to achieve them, elected officers, legal recognition and registration with the Ministry of Social Services so that they can operate bank accounts, etc, and the contribution of money as well as work towards the objective in hand. The objectives are agreed by the group, and may range from the provision of a community amenity (a school, dip, dam, etc), to the establishment of an income-earning activity (tailoring business, poultry rearing, building houses for rent, establishing a nursery for sale of planting material, etc.), to mutual assistance (turn-by-turn weeding or terracing of members' farms, improvement of members' kitchens, etc.). They are therefore very important mechanisms for social and family capital accumulation, interacting with other new institutions such as banks, and strengthened by the spread of literacy through schooling and adult education. Although people outside Kenya tend to associate them with soil conservation, this is only one of their activities. A survey in 1987 found that for every group involved in an 'ecological' activity such as terracing or tree-planting, three were engaged in an income-generating activity including farming (Ondiege, 1992). The *mwilaso* type of group continues for recurrent farming activities such as weeding.

Unlike many other government junior staff, the CDAs continued to be employed by the County Council. This meant that they were local people. Their length of service, age and the emphasis their training gave to interaction and communication, made them more respected and effective than the average government agricultural and veterinary assistant (Mbindyo, 1974). In the 1980s the Machakos Integrated Development Plan provided some additional funds for training and for 'topping up' community efforts in self-help projects, and later bicycles to help the CDAs get around. During 1980−1982 Locational CDAs ran 65 courses for 7500 self-help group leaders and 30 courses for 2600 women's group leaders. An annual seminar for CDAs from all Locations increased information flows. In 1981, the resources available to self-help projects were recorded as nearly Ksh 27 million. Of this, just over Ksh 24 million represented CDAs' estimates of local contributions in cash, kind and labour (likely to be understated) and Ksh 2.7 million represented grants from the Government, NGOs or aid agencies (ODI, 1982). The groups have a very wide membership; in a Yatta sample 90% of families had a *mwethya* member (generally a woman) (Neunhauser et al, 1983: 95). Elsewhere, lower but still substantial family representation was found, of the order of 50−60% of families. Groups generally meet once

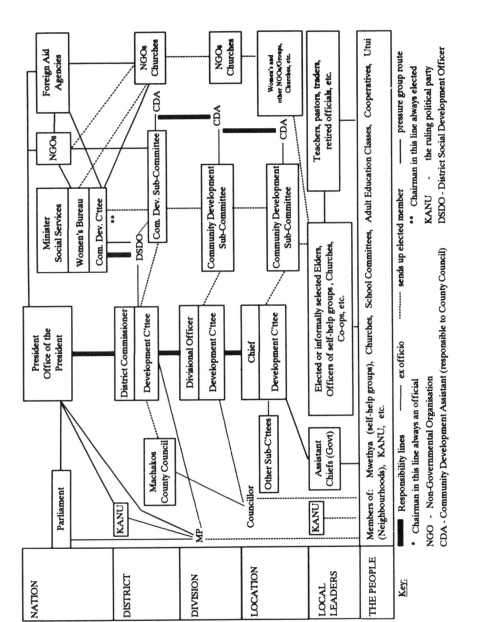

FIGURE 9.2. People, leaders and government, 1990

or twice a week for work on their project or on each others' farms. Poorer women are least able to join, as they are unable to afford membership fees or hospitality.

The food shortages of the 1970s and early 1980s increased the activity of NGOs, often working with church organisations. The groups can therefore obtain advice and monetary resources both within and outside Kenya, if their leaders are skilful in using their hierarchical and political connections shown in Figure 9.2. The variety of aid available can be illustrated in four locations around Kibwezi, where the local Catholic missions were looking in the late 1970s for means to assist the impoverished new settlers. They approached the Council for Human Ecology — Kenya (CHEK), through a former pupil of one of their schools. After a series of meetings between the CHEK vice-chairman, the Catholic sisters and the leaders of 81 women's groups, several programmes were formulated including bee-keeping, brick-making, goat-breeding and basket-exporting. CHEK secured technical advice from the Ministry of Livestock Development, the Ministry of Social Services, Peace Corps volunteers, and Action AID craftsmen, and small grants from CARE, USAID, the Gesellschaft für Technische Zusammenarbeit, the Canadian Presbyterian Church, Oxfam, the UK Beatrice Laing Trust, the FAO, African Development Foundation, and the Chicago branch of the United Nations Association. CHEK also pressured the local Member of Parliament to get a land registration team for the area. By 1989 most of the projects were said to be self-supporting and sustainable, although some of the brick-making groups were stagnant or had changed direction, and the honey refinery, originally intended to be collectively owned by the groups, seems to have become government-operated. The group activities were said to have contributed to a considerable development of business activities in Kibwezi Town, an expansion in formal education services, the opening of a bank and the expansion of the Post Office (United Nations Centre for Human Settlements, 1990).

The original principle of CD work was that the groups should raise 90% of the cost of a project before getting a topping up from government sources — for example, raising a school to ceiling height and getting help with the roofing materials (Peter Muasya, pers. comm. to Mary Tiffen, 1982). One of the dangers of the quantity of resources now available is that commitment and self-reliance may be sapped. People realise that forming groups is attractive to donors, but resources alone cannot guarantee success. It was found in 1982 that many groups which had received USAID funding for poultry enterprises had failed because they did not have the necessary technical knowledge, whereas more spontaneously formed groups making school uniforms, who had the basic necessary skill, succeeded (ODI, 1982). The agenda of outside agencies may be accepted for the sake of the rewards; one NGO, for example, pays groups for their surviving indigenous tree seedlings, although people buy and care for exotic trees without such an incentive (Kaluli, 1992).

LOCAL LEADERSHIP, LOCAL POLITICS AND LOCAL GOVERNMENT

The colonial period to 1945

Before the colonial period, leadership was firmly in the hands of the senior age grade male family heads of the *utui* (village). These elders had a special meeting place where they settled disputes, arrived at community decisions, etc. They increased their solidarity by drinking beer together (forbidden to women and young men). Each *utui* selected one or two elders to represent them in the *kivalo* — a group of neighbouring *utui* which habitually co-operated and between whom there were links of kinship and marriage, corresponding roughly to the present day sub-location.

There were also religious people who were respected and provided leadership during times of crisis, such as rain-makers and prophets. The *utui* elders were supported by clan elders who were leaders of kinship groups based on the male line. In the older settlements all the households might belong to a single clan, but in the newer ones several clans would be represented. The clan provided a unitary thread between people in different *utui*, and a basis for co-operation at crisis points, since there was a spiritual loyalty to the parent clan and its totem. The clan collected compensation payments for accidental killings by one of its members. However, its functions were limited by the dispersion of its members throughout Ukambani and there was little organisation above the *kivalo* (Morgan, 1967; Mutiso, 1975). Association was occasional, through particularly successful and wealthy individuals, who might host dances for a wide area, or respected judges called in by relatively distant *utui*. Masaku, after whom the District takes its name, was one of these widely respected leaders (KNA: Lambert, 1945: 14).

The Colonial Government imposed a geographically based hierarchy on these dispersed groupings of neighbours and kin. Leadership at the District level was provided by the District Commissioner. Government-appointed chiefs were placed in charge of Locations, with Headmen at the level of the *kivalo*. These were assisted by *asili* in the *utui* who were to a certain extent assimilated with the elders. Native tribunals were constituted from the elders to decide cases at the Location level. Chiefs were sometimes from prominent families and sometimes from a new elite known as *asomi* — those who had moved outside tradition by acquiring some education, and who perhaps had had a job away from the District. The chiefs' power came from the colonial authorities, backed if necessary by the police. They were chosen for their willingness to carry out government policies and were frequently able to use their position to acquire land, livestock or other forms of wealth.

The expatriate members of the administration came and went, relatively few having time to develop a deep knowledge of the District, or to appreciate what was already known. There were eight District Commissioners between May 1944 and 1953 (though one served twice) (Throup, 1987). As one wrote, 'so many officers arrive at Machakos, have a fit at what they see, and make another plan starting from scratch . . .' (KNA: DC/MKS/Handing over notes, 1951). Local people knew the fad of one officer would be forgotten by his successor. Cowley's Makaveti research was, for example, ignored by his successor, Hughes Rice, who thought he knew what to do already (J. R. Peberdy, pers. comm. 1992).

Local Native Councils (LNCs) were set up in most Districts in 1925 and 1926 to provide the District Commissioner with advice at the level of the District (Kitching, 1980: 188). There was an elected element but chiefs and other appointed *asomi* were in the majority. The Councils were given limited responsibility for raising additional taxation and deciding its allocation, authorising communal labour and administering the rudimentary initial health and education services. Councillors were not entirely separated from the concerns of the majority, and as noted in Chapter 4, at the time of the Carter Commission they organised a vigorous defence of Akamba interests. They opposed certain administrative decisions, registering opposition to the compulsory sale of cattle, but did not organise the 1938 demonstration against destocking. However, the Council was not seen by ordinary people as a means through which they could influence government policy. Our informants were surprisingly agreed that as late as 1945 the people who took the decisions and had influence were the District Commissioner, the chief, and perhaps, the elders on local matters (see Table 9.1). Government was an alien institution over which people had no control, in which they did not participate, and which they deeply distrusted. Chapter 11 will show that Akamba representation in the design of the reconditioning programme was

TABLE 9.1. **Leadership patterns**

Locations	Period		
	About 1945	1960–1963	Since 1990
Kangundo	District officers Church leaders	District officers Chiefs Political leaders Church leaders Presidents of clan committees Self-help leaders	Chiefs Political leaders Volunteers Church leaders Men and women self-help leaders
Mbooni	Colonial government administration *Utui* elders Clan elders	District officers Chiefs Elders Assistant chiefs	Assistant chiefs Pastors KANU leaders Members of parliament Councillor Community development assistants Women's group leaders Elders
Masii	Clan elders Headmen and chiefs	Chief and sub-chief Clan leaders Headmen Political leaders after independence Councillors	Party leaders Councillor Clan elders
Makueni	Settlement area from 1946 Sub-chief Village elders	Chief (appointed in 1951) DOs, Agricultural Officers Village elders Councillor Party leaders	Church and school leaders 'Mwethya' group leaders Chiefs Assistant chiefs Provincial administration
Ngwata	Not settled	(Settlement in the 1960s) Chief and Colonial administrators Member of parliament Councillor Clan leaders Cattle rustler leader Judicial elders	Church leaders Party leaders Village elders Provincial Administrators Councillors Men and women group leaders Chief KANU leaders and MPs Elders Church leaders

Source: Key informants and village leaders questionnaire

steadily reduced over the period 1932–1954, and that actions which the Government thought it was taking for the good of the people (such as providing labour teams and mechanised equipment for terracing) were in consequence misinterpreted and fiercely opposed. Lambert (KNA: Lambert, 1945: 13) agreed that, at that time, neither the chiefs nor the Local Native Council were seen as truly local institutions.

Local leadership, central government and politics since 1945

A dramatic change to a more politicised leadership, effective at District level and with national links, was signalised by elections to the LNC in 1947:

> Only three of the former members were re-elected. New members included six ex-askaris [soldiers], all young and all traders, one African Inland Mission teacher and the rest traders with an educational bias of one sort or another. In short, few of the traditional tribal elders were chosen, and no Chiefs, apart from those officially nominated ... It was not uncommon to hear the provisions of the Atlantic Charter[10] bandied about and the compulsory labour for Makueni came in for much criticism. (KNA: DC/MKS Annual Report 1947. Reproduced by permission of Kenya National Archives.)

The same report refers to the Councillors' visit to Makueni, where Jomo Kenyatta spoke strongly against the settlement rules on which the administration was insisting (see Chapter 10). The *asomi* had, with the return of the soldiers, begun to replace or at least to supplement, the traditional patriarchal elders. They had political connections with the coming leadership of independent Kenya. The new Council was seen as one of the vehicles by which local people could influence policy: Mr Thiaka (see Chapter 4) was asked by two teachers who had been in Kikuyu country to raise the question of coffee growing with the Council in 1947, and as Councillor he opposed the DC's ban on his Location's profitable bean exports in 1949.

The LNC became the African District Council (ADC) and then the Masaku County Council. Its revenue raising powers were increased, enforcing more dialogue between the new leaders and the District Commissioner. This gradually led to improved acceptance of the reconditioning programme (Chapter 11) and of local afforestation (Chapter 13). By 1957 the ADC consisted of 22 elected members, one from each Location, and 10 nominated members; the District Commissioner was President, but there was an elected Vice-President. In 1957 the first African chairmen for its standing committees (Finance, Trade and Markets, Natural Resources, Health, Public Works, Education) were elected (Peberdy, 1958). Its status was recognised by the opening of its new buildings in 1958, which are still more impressive than most Government offices.

The Council's finance originally came from its share of the General Rate paid by all householders (Ksh 13 in 1956). To this was added a Ksh 2 educational building rate, and a Ksh 1 rate for Locational projects, and small imposed cesses on the growing trade in fruits, vegetables, coriander, beans and hides and skins. The Council also obtained revenue from licensing of carts, bicycles and certain occupations, and market plot fees, which expanded with economic growth in the 1950s. Until 1956–1957 it seems to have received a government subvention for education, but in 1958 it became responsible for all educational expenditure which substantially increased its outgoings from K£19,000 in 1956–1957 to K£110,000 in 1958. It was responsible for roads inside the Reserve, receiving a 100% grant for the 84 miles (1 mile = 1.609 km) of secondary road, but paying 75% of the costs for the 482 miles classified as minor, its expenditure amounting to K£7430 in 1957 (Peberdy, 1958).

The improvement and extension of roads seems to have been a feature of 1953–1954, with the introduction of road-making machinery, the construction of the Machakos–Kitui road, and various link roads (Kenya, Agricultural Department, Southern Province, 1953, 1954) (see Figure 2.4). Such untarred roads depend on maintenance for continuing efficiency, and apparently in 1957 the majority of main roads were passable by car in wet weather. There were also 358 miles of Administrative Tracks. The Council's contribution to agricultural betterment was normally of the order of K£2000–3000 per annum up to 1956, when it rose to K£6000–7000 (Peberdy, 1958).

In the run up to independence, one way of demonstrating opposition was refusal to pay tax. Peberdy (1961) notes increased difficulty in raising the general rate, although people continued to pay for education. As Peberdy demonstrates, there were also genuine difficulties with paying taxes in years of poor harvests.

Centralised and devolved political systems

The formation of new political structures had as its background the struggle, which takes place in many countries, between centralising and devolutionary tendencies, and between theory and practice (discussed in more detail in Mbula Bahemuka and Tiffen, 1992). The theoretical advantage of a good centralised government in environmental management is that it can employ experts to manage, conserve and allocate national resources efficiently and equitably. This concept has obvious attractions for both politicians and experts operating at the centre. Chapter 11 will show the central government operating to impose techniques of soil conservation since farmers were believed incapable of perceiving their long-term interests correctly. In practice central governments, even unelected ones, are subject to internal pressure groups which, if sufficiently powerful and organised, secure for at least some of the time favourable policies or allocations of resources. In the colonial period these were, as the Akamba knew, the white farmers, who used the Government's fears of soil degradation to oppose any grants of new land for the Akamba to settle. Central governments are also subject to external pressures, such as those coming in the colonial period from the Colonial Office in London and UK public opinion, and since Independence from aid agencies and public opinion in donor countries.

A devolutionary system has strong local governments reflecting local priorities, with a wide range of functions including the raising and allocation of local revenues. This was the political objective of the Colonial Office after 1945, and it put pressure on all colonies to increase the elective element in local councils[11] prior to the (distant) granting of independence. Between 1920 and 1960 the LNC/ADC spent 78% of development funds (defined as non-salary expenditure), since most central government revenue went on salaries (Consortium, Report 7, 1978: 220). The Council also paid the salaries of low-level staff, such as market staff, CDAs, some teachers, etc. Although it had to oversee the great expansion in education and other services demanded by its electorate, it was also persuaded by the DC to operate business ventures such as a sisal factory and a ranch for fattening cattle (part of the Government's plan for encouraging destocking by facilitating sales). Neither was very successful and the former proved particularly disastrous after sisal prices collapsed. The Council's finances never really recovered. This hampered its ability to support health, education, roads and veterinary services, etc., and laid it and other Councils in Kenya open to attack after Independence. Politicians, bureaucrats and experts, for good reasons as well as self-interested ones, prefer to amass control and patronage at the centre. The centralising force was already reflected in the colonial period by special programmes and a proliferation of Boards and parastatals for controlling the growing and marketing of most crops, as will be discussed in Chapter 15.

Central government since independence

Independent Kenya evolved in the direction of a powerful central government, with elections in a one-party framework (till 1992). In 1967 the Government rejected the Hardacre Report which suggested that committees of the County Councils should replace the advisory District Development Committee which consisted mainly of officials. In 1969 three important functions of County Councils — primary education, health and most roads — and their major revenue source, the Graduated Personal Tax, were transferred to the centre. Without major funds apart from some produce cesses (in the case of Machakos mainly from coffee and sand), Councils found it difficult to carry out their remaining duties in respect of markets, community development services, and minor roads (Wallis, 1990). Thus, after 1969 there virtually ceased to be a bottom-up political input into the formation of agricultural policy. Fortunately for Kenya, large African farmers replaced large white farmers as an effective political lobby for high farm-gate prices (Bates, 1989). This has maintained incentives for on-farm investment.

The interweaving of politics and patronage has led to the proliferation of government departments, noticeable by 1972 and continuing unabated since:

> Where development is implemented 'from above', each agency begins its work by strengthening its central office in Nairobi, a tendency exacerbated by the shortages of suitable housing in the rural areas and by the desire of both technical assistance staff and their Kenyan counterparts to keep near the centre of power and innovation in Nairobi itself.

Governmental organisation resembles not a narrowing pyramid, but a tree:

> . . . the Nairobi agencies constituting the sunlit leaves and interlocked branches at the top; the provincial organization being the solid trunk; and the local sub-district organizations forming roots of unknown depth and strength, invisible in the muck beneath . . . The structure encourages an intense but distinctive type of politicization, wherein local clients line up beneath their national patrons. From the simplistic vantage point of a local man looking upwards, the main feature about national level administration is that it appears to afford almost unlimited access to influence and privilege. (Moris, 1972: 144. Reproduced by permission of The African Review.)

Central planning decisions are therefore subject to modification by local manipulation, through the routes illustrated in Figure 9.2, which tries to show the view of the villager looking up. String-pulling through local leaders, a class of persons frequently mentioned in Machakos conversations, secures resources that are not available through official plans and normal government services. Local leaders include those who have good connections with the politicians (MPs, KANU members, Councillors) or with the hierarchy which leads directly from the Chief to the Office of the President (Figure 9.2 and Table 9.1). They do not include the Government's technical officers who come and go at the level of the Division and District, although these may be a resource that can be used by the influential. Under the District Focus programme inaugurated by President Moi in 1983, which in Machakos was preceded by the Machakos Integrated Development Plan in 1978 (see Chapter 15), there is supposed to be a hierarchy of District Development Committees (DDC) (Figure 9.2), but at the Divisional level upwards they are constituted predominantly by officials of the various government departments.

Government revenue is absorbed mainly by salaries, leaving comparatively little for operational resources, unless there is some special programme supported by foreign funding. Therefore, as one perceptive group of local leaders commented, there have always been two sorts of development; from the Church and from the Government. The Church figures prominently in local descriptions of development leadership (Table 9.1). It also provides a range of contacts nationally and internationally (Figure 9.2).

Shortage of funds (more limited in the case of Kenya than for some other African governments because over-taxation of the farmer has not been a political option) means that the Government has to depend on self-help activities and earning political support by assistance to the local *harambee* effort. Active local groups with good connections pre-empt government planning; government services, as in the case of Kibwezi illustrated earlier, follow to such areas, particularly if they are supported by the local MP.

Thus, by 1990 there were neither centrally planned services with adequate revenues for their operations, nor local elective bodies with powers to raise substantial revenues and decide priorities on a District basis. Roads have particularly suffered from this situation, since group activity here and there cannot maintain those that carry heavy traffic.

THE MISSIONS AND CHURCHES

The first missions were established in the 1890s, the most important being the African Inland Mission, with stations at Nzaui (1895), Kangundo (1896), Mumbuni (1902), and Mbooni (1909). The Catholic Church established a mission in Kabaa in Mwala Location in 1912 and, from this station, moved on to establish missions in Kilungu, Mbitini and Kangundo. This was accompanied by the opening of schools, which taught not only literacy and the Bible, but also new methods of farming, house construction, carpentry and general hygiene (Philp, 1936). To the *asomi*, those who could read, who emerged from these schools, a new range of jobs was open. They were at first a suspect minority, often drawn from those who were outsiders or unfortunates in traditional society, and respectable elders did not emulate their innovations. However, from about 1935 conversion proceeded more rapidly, and especially after the return of soldiers from the war, when many had accepted Christian teaching in the army. There was also an increase in the number of white missionaries after the war, who met the insistent demand for schools, and whose pupils accepted Christianity. The new converts themselves became evangelists (Mbiti, 1971: 15–23). By 1962, 60% of the population reported themselves as Christian in the census, although Mbiti (1971) estimated churchgoers as only one-third; 11% claimed to be Roman Catholic and 50% Protestant.

At the same time there was a reaction against the continued dominance of white missionaries, particularly in the African Inland Mission, and local leadership of the churches developed. In 1945 the first independent church, the Akamba Brotherhood Church, was founded and grew rapidly. The Akamba Christian elite mobilised local people to work toward independence, one aspect of which was independent churches (Mbula, 1974). After independence the religious denominations co-operated in development, particularly by building new churches and *harambee* schools (see Table 9.2), and this led to the emergence of new types of leaders, men and women, distinct from the traditional elders, as church officers, project leaders and school committee members. Most of the churches (e.g. the Catholic and Church of the Province of Kenya Dioceses) developed a hierarchical organisational structure, which provided an alternative framework to the clans and the Government for contact, information flows and co-operation at District level, and these, in turn, were linked into national and international networks. Church-led community projects, especially in health care, famine relief, food production, food storage, domestic water and irrigation, were able to unite local resources and enterprise with additional support derived from national and international NGOs. Amongst the largest in 1990 was the Machakos Catholic

FIGURE 9.3. The Iiani women's group of the Catholic diocese run a tree nursery as their main activity but also do gully protection (on which their male members were engaged the day we visited). (Photo: M. Mortimore)

Diocese, with 973 development staff for 80 projects (this seems to have included teachers for church-supported schools and adult education classes; Mutiso Consultants, 1986; Kaluli, 1992).

John Mbiti credits the churches with effecting a major change in philosophical attitude (Mbiti, 1971). They taught a society which had been oriented towards the immediate past, and in which grandfathers set the rules, to govern its actions by contemplation of the future and the Second Coming. It is quite possible that the new orientations of Christianity undermined traditional constraints, and made the acceptance of change and of planning for the future socially easier.

EDUCATION

The development of the education system in Machakos is the result of the concerted efforts of the Government, the local Council, the churches and parents. It is notable for its emphasis on primary and technical education; secondary education has been a comparative laggard. The LNC did not wish to rely on the missions for education and by 1930 had established a school teaching literacy in most of the Locations. Initially, people had to be encouraged to attend by gifts of clothing, sugar and salt. However, there were already those who saw technical education as a means of transforming their own economy and society. A government technical school had been established in Machakos Town in 1914. The colonial authorities were frequently disappointed that graduates dispersed to the villages and set up their own businesses rather than joining government services, but in so doing they provided vital repair and support services for the development of the agricultural economy (Munro, 1975). In 1951 there was also an Artisans' Training School, described as 'entirely self-supporting and entirely African run ... an enthusiastic effort at imaginative self-help', and the government Rural Industries Officer moved his headquarters to Machakos for the express purpose of building it up (KNA: DC/MKS/Annual Report 1950).

During World War II Akamba soldiers overseas were made aware of the importance of education, as well as benefiting from the Army Educational Corps (Shorter, 1974: 121). Annual Reports of the District Commissioners from the period 1946–1953 carry frequent mention of returning men's drive for new schools, including schools for girls,[12] and of oversubscription for Jeanes school courses. The DC at first attempted to limit schools in the interests of quality, but reported that the 'Wakamba prefer to be taught badly than not at all' — a reference to an 'illegal' African Brotherhood Church school in the 1946 Annual Report. By the 1962 census, 20% of men over the age of 15 and 10% of women, had had 1–4 years of education. There were still only two Akamba graduates (Dr Owako, pers. comm., 1990), but from then on there were increasing numbers, some of whom reached high positions in Government, where they were able to influence the flow of funds towards their home District (as officials from other Districts were also doing). It was at this time that the effort to provide secondary education, through government or *harambee* schools, took hold.

Table 9.2 shows the progress of education between 1958 and 1987 in terms of the number of schools available, and the role of self-help in their provision. In 1958 parents had to pay fees for all types of schooling. By 1987 only secondary schools charged fees but, in practice, sending a child to primary school involves costs in contributing to the building fund, buying educational materials, uniforms, etc. In the 1962 census, 64% of males and 85% of females aged over 15 had had no education; by the 1979 census the proportions had fallen to 30% and 47% respectively. Literacy was above the national average (see Table 10.7). However, the quality of education in secondary schools remained poor, with 60% of their teachers untrained.

Partly because of the failings of the secondary sector, and partly through the traditional interest in technical skills, Machakos District has been a leader in the construction and maintenance of Village (since renamed Youth) Polytechnics. These schools aim not only to train primary school leavers, but also to introduce new intermediate technology products and services which local people need. The community provides the land, money, supplies, labour, trainees, people to serve on the management committee, contracts for the trainees, the market for the trainee products as well as money-making opportunities. The teachers are paid partly by the Government and partly by parents. Machakos acquired its first government-aided Polytechnics in 1972. Five years later there were 18, of which 7 were government-aided, 5 were self-help and 6 were church-aided (Consortium, Report 7, 1978). By 1987 there were 44, of which 18 were government-assisted and 26 were operated by NGOs (Kenya, Ministry of Planning, 1988?). A sample survey showed that 56% of their graduates found work as employees, 27% were self-employed, and 17% were unemployed (Mbula Bahemuka and Tiffen, 1992: 30, citing Nzioka, 1986).

Older people have taken advantage of adult education classes so that they can participate more fully in self-help groups, use banks, and acquire information more easily. Adult literacy classes began in 1948, but in 1977 there were only 456 students (Consortium, Report 7, 1978: 170). There was then a new national drive. The MIDP provided additional funds, and the District was regarded as a pilot area for new methodologies. In 1982 there were nearly 35 000 women and 4000 men in classes, with 140 full-time and 380 part-time teachers provided through the Government and a further 575 teachers spponsored by the churches or self-help (ODI, 1982).

TABLE 9.2. School infrastructure, 1958 and 1987

Year		Total	Goverment	Church	
1958	Primary	264	112	152	
1987	Primary	1287	na	na	
1958	Intermediate	44	20	24	
1987	Intermediate	—	—	—	
				Harambee	Private
1958	Secondary	3	na	na	na
1987	Secondary	218	40	150[1]	28

[1]Categorised as 96 assisted Harambee, 54 pure Harambee. These include church-linked schools
na = not available
Source: Peberdy (1958) and Kenya, Ministry of Planning, (1988)

The effect of education on farming has been largely indirect. The main objective has been to fit young people for a non-farm job. However, a study in the 1960s demonstrated the strong connection of non-farm jobs and agricultural innovation, and of education with non-farm jobs (Mbithi, 1971c: 114). A similar finding was made through a Kenya-wide analysis of smallholder incomes in 1974−1975: 'Education has a strong and significant effect on incomes from regular employment. Such income has a strong and significant impact upon agricultural innovation. Agricultural innovation has a strong and significant impact on farm income' (Bigsten and Collier, 1980: 13. Reproduced by permission of the authors).

TRAVEL, MARKETS AND BUSINESSES

Marketing is important for the encouragement it gives to specialisation and economies of scale, for the incentives it provides for investment in land improvement, and for the signals it gives about changes in products or technology. The British and Indians who arrived in Kenya had developed institutions which reduce the costs of transactions by such means as grading standards, legal rules affecting the behaviour of merchants, accountancy, money transfer mechanisms, land registration, etc. These had replaced more costly transacting mechanisms, which work well enough in local markets where reputations are known, or where goods can be personally inspected, but which are inefficient over a distance (North, 1990). Colonial officials and British and Indian traders brought these institutions to Kenya as part of their intellectual baggage, and were at first rather scornful of Kenyans entering the modernised trading sector. However, the latter proved able to adapt relatively quickly to the new situation.

In 1945 the market was an 'institution of considerable continuity and permanence . . . In normal times, it was regularly attended by the people, especially women, living over a much wider area . . . It was essentially a place where commodities could be obtained and family shortages made up in exchange for family surpluses (KNA: Lambert, 1945: 12). As such, they continue today (Figure 9.4), but those well sited in relation to roads are also visited by traders who feed the urban and export markets. They are also supplemented by shops.

The long-distance caravan trade had been a mainly male occupation, and it was this that was transformed by new institutions and technologies. As feeder roads to the railway developed, ox carts, lorries and bicycles appeared on the scene. One of our respondents told us that, by

FIGURE 9.4. Women weave baskets, some of which will be exported, while waiting for local customers for their cabbages in Masii market place (on a non-market day). (Photo: Mary Tiffen)

1924, the AIM missionaries had constructed a road system connecting Kangundo, Machakos Town, Mbooni and Mukaa (Aaron Kasyoki, pers. comm., 1990). This helped to make Kangundo the leader in agricultural development (as Barnes observed in 1937; see quotation in Chapter 7). By 1932 there were more than 200 Indian trading families in the District (KNA: MKS AR 1932).

During the 1930s, despite hampering restrictions, new shops and transport businesses were established throughout the District, usually by returning migrants. Newman quotes a former worker turned entrepreneur who by 1938 reported, 'I had many helpers: some to push carts, others to assist in the shops, and when I bought a vehicle I hired a driver and with him a turnboy ... I had a large farm and two ploughs and harrows' (Newman, 1974: 13). The DC recorded in 1946 'an avalanche of applications for trade plots and lorries' to be funded from soldiers' savings and gratuities (KNA: DC/MKS Annual Report 1946).

The increase in number shown in Table 9.3 indicates the increase in commercialisation. Village leaders in Kangundo credited Indians with the increased production of grams, coriander and Indian vegetables in the 1940s. The long-standing connections continue today, particularly through the export of what are known as 'Asian vegetables' to the Indian communities now living in the United Kingdom (see Chapter 14). Indian traders aroused jealousy and after Independence they were banned from rural areas. However, by then the development of African trade meant that there was generally a competitive situation. A survey in 1957 recorded an average of 75 shops per Location (Peberdy, 1958); most were described as 'general goods' (which would still be true today), but butcheries, hotels and hide dealers formed other large categories.

TABLE 9.3. Commercial development

	1929	1936	1957	1987
Markets	11	28	101	700
Licensed shops and kiosks	85	na	1600	8000

na = not available
Source: For 1929 and 1936: Munro (1975). Kamba-owned shops only
For 1957: Peberdy (1958). Excludes shops in Machakos and railway townships
For 1987: Kenya, Ministry of Planning (1988)

Trade in cattle was often restricted by quarantines, and the Government's concern to protect the European dairy and export industry. There were quality controls on hides and skins to facilitate exports. The Meat Livestock Board has always had trouble in competing with butchers and other traders offering 'inflated prices' in the rural areas.[13] The higher value of cattle on the local market than for the export market or meat processing industry was one of the reasons for the intense Akamba bitterness at forced sales to the Liebig plant in 1938.

A typical administrative view of African traders was that they were idle cheats who should be regulated, confined to supervised market places and licensed. Licences also provided revenue for local government. In 1951 the District Commissioner, Machakos, wrote:

We have had a campaign against the illegal isolated coffee shops which spring up along the roadside, but there are still far too many. They should all normally be within markets (ADC byelaws). Within or without, they are dens of idle loafers and sisal spivs[14] who make the maximum of money with the minimum of work. (KNA: J. W. Howard 2/DC/MKS, Handing Over Notes, May 1951. Reproduced by permission of Kenya National Archives.)

Akamba traders mainly operate in small informal groups or as individuals. The groups were active in fruit and vegetable marketing in Mbooni and Tala in 1969. In Tala they were associated with coffee co-operatives, often using their buildings for meetings but having separate officers and separate accounts; they had contracts with Thika Canners but, in some cases, also sold direct to the wholesale market in Nairobi. The groups hired a lorry; an official of the group recorded members' produce and its weight; one member accompanied the lorry to Nairobi and recorded prices and, after paying transport costs, distributed payments to the farmers immediately upon his return. In Mbooni there were similar groups but, since trade was long-distance, they consisted more of specialist traders than of farmer producers. Here, the groups seem to have grown out of a co-operative founded in 1956/1957 but which collapsed in 1962. They saw no need to revive it (Bottrall, 1969). Some women's groups are known to invest in shops, and some have federated to acquire transport and technical assistance for marketing (Ondiege, 1992). Individual traders are probably more common, although less frequently described in the literature.

Restrictions on grain movement originated in 1936, and were reinforced during the war. They have always been evaded, but add to trading costs.

A large, regular and quite uncontrollable black market trade took place . . . between the fertile districts of Embu and Meru . . . and the impoverished arid districts of Kitui and Machakos . . . In the case of maize district officials even connived at such trade . . . because of the high price differential between producer and consumer through the official control. (Brown, 1968: 73. Reproduced by permission of the Food Research Institute.)

During the 1975 shortages, 'traders handled large volumes of maize and beans from "Kikuyu"' (Onchere, 1976: 132). In 1977, about 30% of the marketed food produce in Machakos District was being channelled through the informal sector, while the rest went through the Co-operative Societies (30%), and agents of the Board (40%) (Consortium, Report 3, 1978: 42). The latter are often shop-owners in the local market centres. In Mbooni between 18 and 23% of maize and bean production in 1978 was sold in local markets, compared with none to 12% being sold to the Marketing Board. In Masii the respective figures were 24–36% sold locally and 10–13% sold to the Board, the rest being consumed (Jaetzold and Schmidt, 1983: Table 13a). In 1982–1983 it was estimated that 60% of the grain trade was outside the formal network (Musyoki, 1986: 178). Private traders usually resell to areas of shortage within the District, but also sell outside.

The Akamba have a saying, '*Tuma itho, kutu kwi mbitya*' (use your eye, the ear is deceptive). Trade means travel, and travel brings observations and innovations. The most famous example is the Akamba porter who observed during World War I that the Makonde carvers of Tanzania were doing good business with European settlers. He learnt the trade and brought it back to his village, Wamunyu (Elkan, 1958), where about 2000 people earned some part of their income from it in the mid 1980s (Ondiege, 1992). Soldiers serving in India in World War II got the idea of running teashops and bakeries, which are now found in most Akamba villages. The war as a source of new ideas was often mentioned to us by older leaders. The deliberate use of observation is illustrated by a man who retired from carving in Mombasa and devoted every Saturday to bicycle trips throughout the District so that he could observe and discuss the practices of good farming before building up his own dairy farm (G. Mutiso, pers. comm.).

Although Table 9.3 shows the substantial increase in marketing facilities since the 1950s, these facilities are still very defective. While the Government has theoretical plans for the development of first, second and third order commercial centres well spaced around the District, an analysis of market importance carried out in 1987 showed that Machakos Town was the only first-order centre, and that Tala and Matuu, both in the north, were the only second-order centres. The rest of the District had 19 third-order centres and 24 fourth-order centres. The fourth-level markets meet weekly and serve mainly local needs. Musyoki describes the District as having such a poorly developed marketing system such that long-distance wholesalers, who use lorries, and who need to collect large volumes, reside principally in Machakos Town. Most small traders and small markets are oriented to the nearest bigger centre, moving goods by head load or *matatu*. Musyoki blamed the poor competitive situation on poor roads, with only two major all-weather trunk roads connecting the District with the rest of the country, and internal roads impassable in the rains (Musyoki, 1987).

There have been few studies of Kenyan trade, and we know little about the methods used to raise capital, or the interconnections between trade, education and politics. Heyer noted already in 1962 that Masii people were taking shares in transport ventures and ranches. Government promotion of co-operatives and their role will be examined in Chapter 15. It was beyond the scope of the present study to examine the mechanisms of rural trade, which we nevertheless signal as important.

CONCLUSION

Characteristic of the period under review is an expansion in the number and complexity of institutions which convey and process knowledge or capital, or which allow manipulation of the changing economic and political situation, through a broadening of the leadership base at village level. The pool of talent in a society once dominated by male patriarchs has been enlarged by bringing women, younger educated people, traders and retired workers into positions of influence. Government is now felt to be part of society, and people understand how to communicate with it. As a consequence, they feel somewhat more in control of their lives; they still have to contend with an uncontrollable and uncertain environment, and have only limited means to affect general government policies, but, as compared with the colonial period, they are more able to pool knowledge, capital and labour for private and community projects and to achieve improvements at the farm and village level. There are also alternative means of drawing in resources and obtaining experience in planning and management, through the churches, co-operatives and NGOs; these channels have become more necessary as the Government becomes more constrained by the imbalance between staffing costs and operational resources. However, they are not able to compensate for the lack of resources for the types of services that must necessarily be planned, operated and maintained at the District level or above, prime examples of which are roads and some types of water resource development (Tiffen, 1985).

The family remains an important economic unit, through which knowledge and capital flow between those engaged in farm, non-farm and educational activities. Education and conversion to Christianity have helped to change the family, which suffered stress due to male out-migration, but which has proved in most cases sufficiently flexible to survive. Within the family, women are now playing a greater role in decision-making, and men are sharing in agricultural activities. Through education, increased trade, and membership of co-operatives and self-help groups farmers have developed contacts with banks, larger firms, etc, and other institutions originally developed to serve European farming.

Self-help groups have developed from the sporadic efforts characteristic of *mwethya* into continuing organisations with a programme, goals, organisation and funds. They have operated both to create community assets and, on a rotational basis, to develop individual members' farms, houses or businesses. They have been particularly important for women, providing them with a means of becoming leaders at village level, positions from which they were previously excluded. Machakos (and, indeed, other parts of Kenya) has been fortunate in the way in which the traditional mutual-assistance groups have survived to take new forms. Professional assistance has been steered towards them through community development training and adult education, and, latterly, through NGOs.

NOTES

1   This chapter has been developed from initial research by Judith Mbula Bahemuka and J. W. Kaluli; see ODI Working Paper 62.
2   Currently, many sociologists are pre-occupied with the 'empowerment' of under-privileged groups to enable them to make better use of their own assets and social and political institutions. This, however, is only one possible consequence of the diffusion of knowledge. We prefer therefore to take as a key social variable the mechanisms which facilitate knowledge flows. This was first applied to East African communities, including samples from Machakos by Mbithi (1971b). His theoretical approach is derived from Young and Young (1963).
3   Another recent element in the understanding of social and economic interrelationships is the inclusion of transaction costs (the costs of defining, protecting and monitoring rights, qualities, etc.) in the costs of production (North, 1990: 28). These become more important with the growth of specialisation and exchange, and depend on knowledge.
4   Oliver (1965: 426) quotes comments by early missionaries, officials and anthropologists.

5   Akamba colleagues in the University of Nairobi half-laughingly acknowledge they cannot help but spend time and money on the family farm.
6   However, in southern Machakos, where grazing land is still plentiful, leaders equated the two types of investment. Women leaders said 'A home with cattle is the same as having a person with a degree' (Muthingiini Sub-location, Ngwata Location, 1990).
7   Jeanes schools originated in the southern United States. They trained teachers to take a wider developmental role in the community. They were introduced into Zambia, Malawi and Kenya as part of the community development movement, running short intensive courses for local community leaders.
8   The authorities feared that demobilised soldiers might become an uncomfortable pressure group, and kept a close eye on possibly 'illegal' or politically motivated associations. Many soldiers felt that they had been deliberately demobilised rapidly and dispersed back to their villages and they wanted to keep in touch with former comrades and to pursue jointly the new ambitions which they had formed in the army.
9   Political considerations would have given leaders an incentive to emphasise the break with the past. However, there is no doubt that the self-help groups are differently structured now, and that clans, as one informant said, no longer have importance to anyone aged under 40.
10 The Atlantic Charter was signed by Churchill and Roosevelt in 1941, very much at the latter's wish, as a statement of war aims that would accommodate anti-colonialism in America. It included their agreement to 'respect the right of all people to choose the form of government under which they will live ... [and] the object of securing for all improved labour standards' (Churchill, 1950; Chester Wilmott, 1952).
11 Creech Jones, Colonial Secretary, in his 1947 *Despatch to African Governors* stated that the key to success in programmes of political, social and economic development lay in the development of an *efficient* and *democratic* system of *local* government (his italics) (Hicks, 1961: 4).
12 A handing-over note in 1949 noted that the Akamba appeared to appreciate the importance of girls' education and were enthusiastic about the opening of the first all-girls government school in Kenya in Machakos.
13 The description given in an official report on the African Livestock Marketing Organisation which had been set up in 1952 (Jones, 1959: 43). Veterinary officers saw markets as a means to destocking, but they nevertheless tended to think that prices above the low export valuation on native cattle were in some way improper.
14 At the time, sisal sales were enabling the Akamba to buy food despite poor harvests.

10

Household Farming and Income Systems

INTRODUCTION

Households use their resources of land, labour and capital to generate income from both farming and non-farming activities (Moock, 1986; Low, 1988: 29). Off-farm work detracts from the labour available for farming activities, but increases the resources for family consumption and investments and their sources of information. It sets the opportunity cost of farm labour.

The household has to react to the consequences of population growth, both within its own unit and in its environment; to changes in the markets for its labour and for the products it can produce; and to the variable, semi-arid climate in which it operates. The last makes it essential to have some insurance against drought, by storing food or money, by supplementing cropping with livestock that can be sold, or by having some family members in a non-farm activity. The last is a common strategy in Kenya. The climate also means that agricultural intensification can only proceed if the best possible use is made of rainfall, as this is the greatest single determinant of productivity.[1]

We begin by describing the main farming and other income-generating activities in the different AEZs over time. Secondly, we examine factor relationships and output in the farm activities, in so far as the data allow. There are no farming systems studies before 1962 and few after 1981; the latter lacuna is unfortunate since in the 1980s there was no new land to settle and average farm size decreased rapidly. For the situation before the 1960s and since 1982 we are mainly dependent on our own interviews with village leaders in five study areas, and with a quick non-random survey of 40 farmers. (See Tiffen (1992) and Mbula Bahemuka and Tiffen (1992) for the farmers' and leaders' schedules respectively.)

The inadequacies of the historical data mean that a classic analysis of farm factor relationships and output over time is not possible. The general trend has been towards intensification, as defined in the Appendix to Chapter 2. It is generally agreed that as population density increases, so does frequency of cultivation. Fallows shorten until there is only a short (grass) fallow. The next stages are annual cultivation, followed by multiple cropping (Boserup, 1965; Ruthenberg, 1980). Barnes (KNA: Barnes, 1937) makes it clear that by the 1930s long fallows had already ceased in most of the Reserve; the most productive area in the north had reached at least the stage of annual cropping, and possibly double cropping,[2] and the rest was at the short grass fallow stage with about one-third of the cultivated area estimated to be under fallow. The transition from ever shorter grass fallows to permanent cropping is identified by Ruthenberg (1980: 101) as being problematic, since increased inputs of labour, organic fertilisers, and capital are necessary to maintain fertility, but the incentives for this are not always present. Alternatives, in terms of our model in Figure 2.5, are out-migration for work or settlement of new land. The latter makes extensive techniques again temporarily appropriate.

Table 10.1 reports the chief cash sources from the farm in 1945, 1960 and 1990. The population density gradient flows from the old settled areas with high densities (Kangundo, Mbooni and Masii) to the area settled in the 1950s (Makueni) and the late 1960s (Ngwata), which have the lowest population densities. Livestock form the chief cash source at low densities, and, as densities rise, sales of surplus food crops are followed by higher value crops such as coffee, fruit and vegetables. A second gradient shows fruit and vegetables appearing first in the higher-potential areas with good access to markets (Kangundo), spreading to high-potential zones further from the markets (Mbooni), and then into lower-potential zones, starting again in those with good market access (Masii) and passing on to less well served areas (Makueni) as population density increases. Thus, increasing crop sales are associated with higher population densities, but market facilities are also important.

At any given time farming systems vary by agro-ecological zone (the main determinant according to those who calculate carrying capacity), but also by market access. In 1961, Porter (1965) sketched three farming systems in Machakos: at Ngelani (AEZ 2/3), well connected to markets, population densities already 600 km^2, with a technology involving terraces, ploughs, manure, insecticides, and Irish potatoes as a cash crop; at Wamunyu (AEZ 4), with some terraces, less manuring, less weeding, food crops only and vulnerable to famine; and at Kikumbulyu[3] (AEZ 5), with very low population densities, shifting cultivation, no ploughing, broadcast seed, almost no manuring and terracing, and heavy reliance on livestock. In each of these places farming has also changed over time, and it is on this dynamic that we concentrate.

The discussion is necessarily in terms of the average or typical family. However, families are not, and never have been, equal in terms of their access to capital, labour and land. The land situation in the 1960s is shown in Table 5.2. The typical, modal farm remained smaller than the arithmetical average in 1980; in AEZ 4 the average holding was then 3.9 ha, but 40% had less than 2 ha (Meyers, 1981: 90). Cattle distribution is also skewed. In the 1930s and 1940s there are frequent references to 'cattle barons' with large herds (KNA: Lambert, 1945: 100; Munro, 1975: 218). About 30% of farmers in the 1960s owned no cattle. In Masii, where there was a high proportion of cattle owners, 74% had 1–10 cattle, 13% had 11–20 and 3% had 20–40 (Owako, 1969). The 1978–1980 differences between large and small farms are shown in Tables 10.4 and 10.6. Farming and income systems therefore vary not only according to time and AEZ, but also according to family assets. Our discussion on the relative scarcity of the factors, land, labour and capital, takes into account their distribution between families, as well as their differing opportunity costs over time.

Thirdly, we look at constraints on farming, as perceived by the farmer, and at achievements, in terms of improved average living standards over time.

THE LIVESTOCK AND OUT-MIGRATION SYSTEM, 1930–1965

During this period almost all families had a small cultivated plot for subsistence grains and pulses. These were not marketable, except in the Kangundo–Matungulu area which had a road system, and which Barnes identified as the source of most grain exports (see Figure 4.1). The only possible source of cash was livestock, which also contributed importantly to subsistence and to insurance against famine. However, average herds were not large; they were estimated at 5 cattle and

TABLE 10.1. Main farm cash income sources, 1945–1990

	1945	1960	1990
Kangundo	Wheat, grams, coriander, sugar, bananas, other food crops, cattle, milk	Fruit, vegetables, coffee	Coffee, French beans
Mbooni			
(men)	Livestock, sugar, bananas	Sugar, English potatoes, wattle, livestock	Coffee, vegetables, trees
(women)	Livestock, food crops	Food crops, livestock	Coffee, vegetables, handicrafts
Masii			
(men)	Cattle, millet	Livestock, millet	Cotton, fruits, pawpaws, tomatoes, beans, maize, livestock
(women)	Ghee, cattle	Goats and cattle	Peas, beans, maize, mangoes
Makueni	—	Goats, peas, beans, maize, grams	Fruits, cotton
Ngwata			
(men)	—	(1965–1970) Charcoal, honey, ivory	Maize, beans, livestock, pigeon peas, cotton, grams
(women)	—	Remittances and help from home	Grams, sorghum, cowpeas, charcoal, livestock

Source: Interviews with village leaders, 1990

6 shoats in 1933 (Kenya Land Commission, 1934). A survey in Nzaui in 1940 found 3 cattle and 10 shoats (Table 10.2). Table 10.1 shows the dominance of cattle as a source of cash in all areas except Kangundo in 1945. Even there, our elderly informants said that their wealth had been in cattle in the 1920s (Asamba and Thomas-Slayter (1991) call their study in a nearby sub-location *'From Cattle to Coffee'*).

Young households preferred to create new farms rather than to take over exhausted parental land, but in the northern areas this was not possible, as all land was claimed by the 1930s. With the deterioration of grazing, out-migration for work or squatting became increasingly attractive relative to livestock rearing and farming (see Chapter 4). This led to a shortage of men in farming which would have further reduced productivity, since traditionally they did the heavy work of periodically opening up new arable land.

Peberdy (1961) estimated District cash income in the years 1954−1961. Wages and remittances usually provided about two-thirds of cash, and in bad years had to make up sizeable food deficits from the family farm. Crop exports came mainly from fruit and vegetables grown in AEZs 2 and 3. Hand-decorticated sisal from the hedges was occasionally important, depending on world prices or the dire necessity of purchasing food (see Figure 6.4 in Chapter 6).

The bind in which a short fallow system finds itself, when fallowing is reduced but there is no financial incentive for increasing labour and capital inputs, can be illustrated by the first farm level analyses in Masii in the early 1960s (Heyer, 1966, 1967 for 1962; Owako, 1969 (for 1964). Although population density was 105/km^2 in 1962, degraded unclaimed communal grazing land was locally available, but was not used to provide fallowing as in a ley system. Many fields had been cultivated for over 25 years. The majority of farmers applied manure in patches on the nearer plots only (Owako, 1969: 222). The main change since 1930 was the enlargement of the cultivated area with the help of the plough, which our Masii informants said had become common after World War II. The average arable area had increased to 4 ha (Table 5.2). The main sign of intensification was in soil conservation works, which Heyer considered to be good in five cases, fair in eight and poor in three. (These would have been compulsory narrow-base terraces; leaders told us that they started making voluntary bench terraces only around 1969−1970.) According to leaders, row planting, which makes weeding easier, began replacing the broadcasting of seed only in the 1960s. (Heyer found row planting on only 12 out of 74 plots.)

One would expect growing population pressure to lead to double cropping. In Masii, because of the small size of the farms, 88% practised what Owako called 'overlapping cropping', or inserting seed amongst the weeds and stubble of the previous harvest, since with long-season maize and sorghum there was little gap between the harvest of the short rains and the onset of the long rains. The effort made in the long rains depended on the short-rains harvest (Owako, 1969: 219−222). Heyer observed an exceptionally good short-rains harvest in 1962−1963, and thought that planting in the long rains was only substantial when the short rains failed (Heyer, 1967: 7). This would make sense if there was no profitable market for surplus grain.

Heyer found that labour was a key constraint at weeding, ploughing and some harvesting times, although, at other times of the year, it was not scarce. The only items of capital considered to limit production were oxen and ploughs, to which some people could not get access at the optimal time. She considered soil conservation works, manure use and row planting as part of the residual management variable, although we would consider the first as land capitalisation. She found that the best managers were able to produce three to four times as much as the worst with any given level of labour and land resources (Heyer, 1967: 69−70). Her observations related

TABLE 10.2. Machakos District, AEZ 4: changes in agricultural characteristics and practices, 1940–1981, Nzaui and Masii Locations

Item	Nzaui 1940[1]	Nzaui 1964[2]	Nzaui 1980–81[3]	Masii 1964[2]	Masii 1978[4]
Farm size (ha)	na	9.4	5.2	9.2	5.6
Arable (%)	na	49	50	44	43
Arable (ha)	2	4.6	2.6	4.1	2.4
Cash crops	Cotton av. 0.04 ha	Cotton: av. 0.015 ha (20% of farmers) Sugar: av. 0.013 ha (20% of farmers)	Cotton (50%) Average 0.6 ha	Av. 0.035 ha cotton (10% of farmers)	Av. 0.1 ha cotton
Food sales	na	na	26% sold maize in short rains 19% sold maize in long rains	na	40–50% of production
Owning plough (%)	0.05	56	62	na	na
Solo crop maize (%)	na	27	56% in Long Rains None in Short Rains	14	31
Use of manure (%)	10% on part of farm	39	46	65% used a little	Av. use on maize: SR: 0.5 tons/ha LR: 0.8 tons/ha
Use of fertilizer (%)	0	0	2	0	Av. use on maize: SR: 2 kg/ha LR: 5 kg/ha
Cattle owned	3.4	9.8	11 (9.5)	7.5	6.5
Shoats	10.1	11.7	26 (21)	8.1	16.2
Stock units	5.4	12.1	16.2 (13.7)	9.1	9.75

Sources and notes

[1] KNA: DC/MKS/Nzaui file. Form for World Agricultural Census, 1940. Population given as 10 396 — assumed as 2000 families. Livestock figures given exactly, cropped estimates mostly rounded to nearest 1000 acres
[2] Owako (1969). Two farmers with more than 80 ha omitted from his Nzaui sample; two farmers with more than 260 ha omitted from his Masii sample
[3] Pollard (1989). First livestock figure as he reported it; second figure is average including those with none of the specified livestock
[4] Jaetzold and Schmidt (1983). Cattle figure amended because original had an obvious typographical error

to a season of very good short rains with relatively high yields and, consequently, low prices, but she also ran her model for average and low rainfall scenarios, and to test the effect of the introduction of cotton and short-season Katumani maize, both of which were just being launched by the Department of Agriculture. She concluded that neither provided good returns: the farmer with average managerial skills could earn Ksh 33, 59 or 75 a month, depending on rainfall conditions. The average wage in Masii for unskilled work was then Ksh 50−70 per month (with few jobs available), and 'anything from Ksh 120 in Kenya's urban areas' (Heyer, 1967: 63). This confirmed local opinion that it was not worth investing in farming. Heyer makes the point that capital was being invested in non-farm enterprises such as bus transport and ranches. In farming, the level of profitability was such that farmers found it difficult even to purchase hoes. In the circumstances, it is not surprising that over 60% of the adult men were absent, working away from the farm.

Masii men and women leaders said that in 1960 almost all families had 10−50 cattle, and very large numbers of goats. Owako's 1964 data (Table 10.2) give rather smaller numbers, but he thought people were understating their livestock holdings (which would be understandable in view of the Government's long efforts to reduce them). Livestock were, the women farmers said, a bank; they provided milk and could be exchanged for other food. Arable farming was not taken seriously. Judging by the recollected importance of livestock, their return to labour, the scarce factor, is likely to have been more attractive than the return to labour in crop production.[4] However, both men and women agreed that over-reliance on livestock had left them very vulnerable to famine and reliant on food relief in the period 1940−1965.

SPECIALISATION AND INCOME DIVERSIFICATION IN AEZS 2 AND 3, 1945−1990

The densely settled hill areas were the leaders in a change to commercially oriented cropping, at first through an expansion in arable areas made feasible by the plough. By 1945 the main cash source in Kangundo was foodstuffs such as beans, grams and coriander seed, sold mainly to Indian traders (Table 10.1). In the 1950s the growth of Nairobi and the construction of new roads (Chapter 9) made vegetable production very profitable. For this, water conservation was essential, and bench terracing suddenly became popular (see Chapter 11). Farmers also secured the right to grow small amounts of coffee. In Mbooni in 1964, 0.2 ha produced Ksh 1400−1800 under tomatoes, compared with Ksh 900−1200 under coffee, and less than Ksh 100 under maize (Owako, 1969: 259).

Increasing population density made farm expansion impossible. By 1964 population densities in Kangundo were 250−270/km^2. Farms were small and predominantly arable, with an average size of 3−3.5 ha, of which 80% was arable and 20% grazing. Livestock ownership averaged only 2.4 cattle (for ploughing) and 1.2 shoats. Farmers ploughed their land early and some already planted ahead of the short rains. What manure there was, was concentrated on coffee. Coffee trees were, according to instruction, planted in prepared pits on bench terraces, and well weeded and mulched, to conserve all possible water. The average amount under coffee was relatively small, between 0.2 and 0.4 ha, although about 40% of farmers had more than this (Owako, 1969).

By 1972−1973 northern highland farmers could take the risk of relying on purchases for some of their subsistence needs. In a year with one good rain and one severe drought, 60% of households did not grow enough to cover their needs of maize and beans. The more prosperous areas, with a farm income of Ksh 1800, derived 45% of their income from coffee; the less

TABLE 10.3. Incomes in Kangundo (AEZs 2 and 3) and two AEZ 4 villages, 1975

	Kangundo		Two AEZ 4 villages	
	Ksh	%	Ksh	%
Farm				
Food crops	197	7	490	18
Cash crops[1]	887	33	99	4
Livestock[1]	548	20	685	26
Subtotal, farm	1632	61	1274	48
Non-farm	1044	39	1386	52
TOTAL	2676	100	2660	100

[1]Milk and vegetables omitted, although both are mentioned in the text as quite important
Source: Onchere (1976: 66)

prosperous area, with a farm income of Ksh 1056, derived 37% from coffee. The latter area produced least food (Tiffen, 1992: Table 4, derived from Kolkena and Pronk, 1975). A study during the drought of 1975 found a variety of fruits and vegetables grown, although coffee was the main earner (Onchere, 1976). Cash crops formed a third of total income, by contrast with neighbouring AEZ 4 farmers who relied more on non-farm income (Table 10.3). Table 10.3 shows that Kangundo farmers had less dependence on non-farm income, although in this drought year it formed 40% of the total. Coffee provided some of the insurance previously derived from cattle or off-farm work, enabling farmers to cut down on food crops in favour of a more profitable crop; as Kangundo leaders told us in 1990, after the expansion of coffee in the coffee boom (Chapter 6), 'Now, coffee is the cow'. Coffee also provided the cash for farm inputs: Onchere found that 67% of farmers in Kangundo purchased fertiliser for their coffee and 40% for their maize. In a neighbouring AEZ 4 area only 17% purchased fertiliser for maize. Thus commercialisation provided the means to invest in fertility restoration and sustainable permanent cropping.

Insurance against bad seasons was also provided by non-farm jobs. One-third of household heads had a *local*, off-farm income and this was associated with the highest family incomes (Ksh 5230 and 3800 in the high- and medium-potential coffee areas, respectively). In second place were those with a family head working away from the farm. Those who relied solely on farming averaged only Ksh 2700 and Ksh 1600 in the high and medium areas respectively. For many people in the less productive area, farming alone would not have secured the minimum reasonable standard of living, estimated at Ksh 1500 for a household of six persons (Kolkena and Pronk, 1975). The important change from the situation earlier, and from the contemporary situation in villages which could not generate cash from farming, was the increase in local jobs. Population densities had risen to levels common in Asia, where there is a more specialised, productive rural economy and mutual stimulation between farm and non-farm sectors (Haggblade et al, 1989). A study of 243 women with pre-school children in Matungulu in 1979 showed that (ignoring the 11% without husbands) only 26% of husbands were farmers only. Amongst the remainder, 16% were unskilled labourers, and the others artisans, skilled workers, or professional people (usually in combination with farming) (Tiffen, 1992: Table 7, derived from Rabeneck, 1982).

TABLE 10.4. Farm strategies by farm size, 1978

	Mbooni		Masii	
	Small farm	Large farm	Small farm	Large farm
Total size (ha)	1.5	10.4	1.3	10.5
Maize, beans, SR	0.6	1.6	0.9	2.2
Maize, beans, LR	0.6	0.9	1.0	1.9
Coffee	0.3	0.3	0	0.1
Citrus	0	0	0	0.1
Others, SR[1]	0	0.5	0	0.7
Cotton	0	0	0.1	0.6
Sunflower, LR	0	0.1	0	0.5
Grazing (ha)	0.4	6.9	0.2	5.9
Grazing, %	27	66	15	56
Cattle, local, LU[2]	2.3	3.2	2.8	4.9
Cattle, grade, LU[2]	0.1	1.5	0.6	1.0
Shoats, LU[2]	0.5	1.0	0.8	2.1
Total LU[2]	2.9	5.7	4.2	8.0
Family adults on farm	2.2	2.8	2.1	2.5
Hired labour	1.1	1.0	0.3	0.7

[1]In Mbooni, others were cabbages, tomatoes, English potatoes, sugar, millet. In Masii they were cowpeas, pigeon peas, sorghum and millet
[2]1 improved cow = 1 LU; 1 zebu = 0.65 LU; 1 shoat = 0.15 LU
Source: Jaetzold and Schmidt (1983: 178–179)

In the Mbooni hills population densities were substantially lower, and in 1978 the average farm size was larger than in Kangundo, with 4.5 ha,[5] of which more (55%) was under pasture, with 28% under annual crops (mainly maize and beans), 8% under coffee (with an average holding of 0.3 ha), and 4% under fodder crops. The average farm had more livestock and less coffee than in Kangundo. Details of farms in the upper and lowest quartile are shown in Table 10.4. The larger farmers also planted sugar, English potatoes, cabbages and tomatoes, with exports of vegetables to Mombasa (Bottrall, 1969).

Between 1979 and 1989 population density rose rapidly from 367 to 518/km² in Kangundo and from 239 to 317/km² in Mbooni, as out-migration to new farms stopped. Leaders in Kangundo in 1990 were desperately worried by the ever smaller size of farms (with young farmers inheriting only about 1.2 ha), the difficulty in finding jobs even for educated young people, and the burden of educational expenditure for longer periods in the desperate hope of fitting children for jobs. Change of crops was hampered by the large areas under coffee, although they had moved into French beans, which provide a very high income from a small area. (One study found the return from a 17 × 10 m plot to be Ksh 300; Ayako et al, 1989.) Few were able to afford grade cattle. People who could afford it purchased manure from the ranch areas, a practice that had begun in the 1950s. Maize residues were used as coffee mulch, since they were not needed for livestock. The leaders felt that further farm intensification would be possible with irrigation, but water rights were unobtainable. Their only hope for the future lay in campaigning for electrification to increase non-farm jobs. Areas like Matuu, where vegetables are irrigated from the Yatta canal, and which has electricity and a tarred road, demonstrated the growth potential of the non-farm informal sector.

Densities in Kangundo may be reaching a point where expansion of the non-farm sector is vital. In Mbooni, where coffee had never been quite so dominant, and where land was slightly more plentiful, the farming system had developed into a combination of dairying, with a crossbred cow kept under zero grazing and with planted fodder on the terrace banks, coffee, a small but productive area of vegetables, and maize and beans. Leaders said that most farmers had acquired a crossbred. In both Mbooni and Kangundo, leaders in 1990 said that smaller farms and a shortage of grazing meant that fewer people kept draft oxen, and more used hand tools. There was a consequent shortage of manure, and problems in maintaining fertility.

COMMERCIALISED FARMING IN AEZ 4, 1965–1990

Farm survey data for AEZ 4 show a reduction in farm size (Table 10.2) and an increase in commercialisation between 1964 and the late 1970s. Maize, beans, cowpeas and pigeon peas remained the main crops, occupying 75–85% of the arable area in 1979. Village leaders interviewed in 1990, agreed that though yields still fell damagingly in bad seasons, the effect of less rain was no longer so drastic as before the 1960s. Women said that efficient double cropping had reduced food shortages since 1960, despite smaller farms, and had resulted in surpluses for sale (Tables 10.1 and 10.2). In 1978 farmers sold 40–50% of their production in both seasons (Jaetzold and Schmidt, 1983). Food purchases still occur on small farms and in bad seasons, particularly when two or more bad seasons follow in sequence.

Improved output per hectare is a result of investment in bench terracing and cut-offs which collect water and bring it to the top of the terrace system. The cut-offs are planted with bananas and other trees (Figure 11.4). Ploughing along the contour and planting in lines have replaced the broadcasting of seed, so that the first weeding can also be done by plough (reinforcing the water-trapping ridges as well as overcoming a previous labour bottleneck in weeding). By 1974 almost 100% of farmers did their first weeding with oxen. Lynam (1978) credits the shorter season Katumani maize with the change to (efficient) double cropping, but it is used in conjunction with farmer-bred varieties (Chapter 14). The new farming system demands, as some farmers put it, that they be better organised. Oxen must be kept in good condition by feeding them with crop residues so that they can dry plough, thus securing early planting. Manure must be collected and applied.

These tactics ensure that normally the first season is harvested sufficiently early to allow the land to be prepared properly for the long-rains crop, thus raising yields. In the long rains of 1978, which were slightly above average, the pure maize yield was 1756 kg/ha, and the yield of maize in a maize–bean mixture was 1093 kg/ha. Just over half the maize was solo-cropped (Jaetzold and Schmidt, 1983). The mixture yield in the altogether exceptionally good short rains of 1962–1963 was 1295 kg/ha (Heyer, 1966).

Cotton was grown only by the larger farmers (Table 10.4), for, as Lynam (1978) showed, smaller farmers had to keep most land under food crops to provide for the risk of bad seasons. In the 1980s farmers turned increasingly to fruit trees, particularly oranges, pawpaws and mangoes which can provide a higher income from a smaller area (Table 10.1 and Chapter 13). The surveys of 1979–1980 list fruit trees as being grown, but say little about sales. Those early into citrus, rather like those early into tomatoes and other vegetables in the 1950s, made good incomes.[6] Planting citrus and other trees in AEZ 4 demands considerable effort in land preparation and manuring (Figure 14.1).

Livestock numbers remained quite large during 1978–1980 (Table 10.2), but were closely integrated with the cropping activities. An important constituent of the herd is the (zebu) plough bulls or oxen, and on small farms these have a higher priority than milk. Surveys showed that circa 1980 between 55 and 75% of AEZ 4 farmers owned ploughs, with use being even higher because of borrowing. Farmers without their own plough oxen are severely handicapped because they cannot plant at the best times. In all five of the villages where we interviewed, the importance of cattle now was for ploughing, manure, cash, food security and milk, roughly in that order. They were no longer important for prestige or bride price.

Cattle are now confined to enclosed permanent grazing land belonging to the farm, or tethered (Figure 10.1(a)). The former communal areas have become new private farms. In the dry season, when grassland shows signs of deterioration, the livestock are kept in the *boma* (enclosure) and fed on crop residues (for which there is a market). The grazing fields are carefully managed so that they also produce an income from charcoal and building timber, and fuel for domestic use (Chapter 8). Livestock-keeping methods vary in intensity according to farm size: in 1978 Masii farmers with 1.8 ha farms had only 0.2 ha under grazing, and yet kept 4.2 livestock units (LUs); farmers with 10.5 ha had 5.9 ha under grazing for 8 LUs (Table 10.4). Leaders said that by 1990 fewer zebu and goats were kept, but some were investing in crossbred cows for milk.

THE FAILURE OF 'SCIENTIFIC' LEY FARMING IN MAKUENI

Agriculturalists in the 1940s were so concerned with the state of farming in the Reserve that they thought the only answer was to move people to a new area and to impose 'scientific' farming, thus bypassing a haphazard and slow process of learning to deal with a new environment (KNA: DC/MKS/1/29). During 1946−1962, government expenditure on the Makueni scheme which lies on the border between AEZs 4 and 5, and which was covered with thick bush which hosted dangerous animals and tsetse fly, was 8% of the African Land Development Board's income for its Kenya-wide projects — £148 for each of the 2187 settler families (Kenya, ALDEV, 1962).[7] These costs covered dam and borehole construction, clearance of the bush to create fly barriers, by bulldozer and semi-compulsory labour,[8] organised shoots of rhino and other wild animals, rations for the settlers prior to the first harvest, assistance to the settlers in initial ploughing and house-building, staff costs, mechanical terracing, etc. In 1954 the Makueni payroll numbered 212 ALDEV employees, and many other settlers were employed by the Agricultural and Veterinary Departments, or by the colonial Administration. Despite this expenditure of money and manpower, the scheme must be considered a relative failure compared with free settlement.

The standard holding varied between 8 and 12−16 ha according to soil potential. The cultivated area was to be just over 2 ha, with the rest providing grazing for the 8 cattle and 16 shoats whose manure would maintain fertility. Under a rotational ley system, in the third year and every year thereafter the farmer was to plant 0.8 ha of arable to grass, and to open up 0.8 ha of the existing uncultivated area. Every year he was to clear and stump 1.6 ha of bush until none remained. Other detailed rules provided for paddocking, a roofed cattle *boma*, silage manufacture, manuring, and specified proportions of arable under maize, sorghum, and cassava.

The ley system proved impossible to maintain, because of its heavy labour requirements, when labour, as Heyer describes, was already short for cropping. The continual risk was the reversion of the area under grass to bush. Brown estimated in 1958 that bush control required 8 man days per 0.4 ha, i.e. 120 days per year on the smaller farms. A 1957 report said that the settlers 'slashed, and the bush came back thicker than ever'. The authorities resorted to mechanical stumping in 1955 and 1956 (MKS/MAKU/1/29).

(a)

(b)

FIGURE 10.1. (a) A tethered cow in a recently settled area, Kambu, Ngwata Location, showing grazing management. (b) Livestock feeding on pigeon pea residues, in the same Location. (Photos: D. B. Thomas. Reproduced with permission.)

Once supervision was removed in 1960, the ley system was abandoned. Farmers said this was because of lack of money, labour or equipment to open up new land (Heyer, 1975). Farmers also increased their livestock holdings. In 1974, the average farmer had about 10 cattle (Heyer, 1975) and three times as many shoats (Kenya, MoA, 1971: 15); goats were a chief source of income in the early 1960s (Table 10.1). Rotational paddocks were abandoned, since, if the grass was rested, bushes grew very fast and destroyed the grazing. The making of silage was not practised in 1990 even by Mr Onesmus Musyoki, a settler who was Assistant Agricultural Officer in Makueni in the 1950s.[9] In 1990 most farmers fed their livestock on their own grazing and crop residues; a few had to buy in grass and a few cultivated fodder. Such a semi-intensive system was probably adequate except in times of drought. (A 1982 investigation found that the poor condition of oxen was delaying planting, but the authors omit to note that there had been a light drought in the short rains of 1980 and a severe drought in those of 1981; Hussain et al, 1982.)

The selection of a cash crop depended on economic calculations. Cotton was grown for a few years till the Ministry stopped free seed distribution in 1970−1971 (Kenya, MoA, 1971: 11). By 1974 the most common cash crop was grams (Heyer, 1975). In 1982 the price and market conditions for cotton had improved (Chapter 6) and the average farm had increased its arable area to 5.2 ha, including about 1 ha of cotton with 10 ha of permanent grazing further out (66% of the farm). Competition between maize and cotton for the available labour and equipment in the short optimum planting season limited the amount of cotton grown and the yields obtained; cotton was given lower priority so that it was generally planted late, and yields were low. Hussain et al (1982) estimated the average return from cotton to be only about Ksh 16 per labour day, compared with the then casual labour rate of about Ksh 15/day. Although these yields and returns apply to a season with a severe drought, they help to explain why many farmers gave the crop up when the price fell and the Cotton Board delayed payments. By 1990 the main sources of cash were oranges and surpluses of maize and pulses (Table 10.1).

The grazing area circa 1982 carried an average of 6.7 cattle and 17.5 shoats — a considerable drop since 1974, suggesting that farmers had not attempted to rebuild their herds to the old levels after the 1974−1975 drought. Hussain et al (1982) considered the numbers large in relation to some theoretical carrying capacity but at over 1 ha per livestock unit this was much less intensive than in most AEZ 4 areas (Table 10.2). Since 1982 those who went into orange trees commercially have reduced their goat holdings. There also appears to have been a move towards keeping fewer, but better grade, cattle. Dairying expansion is limited at present by lack of local demand, with most farmers able to meet their own needs and unable to transport the surplus to urban centres. (A co-operative dairy was established in 1981, reselling to local hotels, etc. It still existed in 1990, but active membership had fallen from a peak of 42 to 30. The manager blamed high transport costs and unreliable transport for outlying farmers.) Sales of live cattle remain important. We were told that there were many cattle traders in the area, and that marketing live animals was no problem. Nevertheless, because of transport costs, prices were about a third of those in Machakos Town. Makueni still suffered from appalling roads.

Makueni illustrates the difficulties in a ley system. The conversion of bush to grazing land is not easy, because of the regeneration problem. Arable areas remain limited if there is no market for crops, but expand if there is a commercial outlet for crops such as cotton, or if rising population density increases the need for food crops. Farmers now terrace to conserve water, which means that rotation between grazing and arable is difficult, but Makueni farming is still less intensive than in areas where new settlement was unregulated, partly because of the initial imposition of large farms.

EXTENSIFICATION AND INTENSIFICATION IN NEW SETTLEMENT AREAS

The Makueni scheme had been opposed by the Local Native Council (KNA: Machakos District, Annual Report, 1946), which wanted free settlement and insisted that the Akamba needed no teaching on how to settle new farms. In the 1970s the Government, and many academics, still feared that free migration by farmers into the drier areas would increase land degradation, vulnerability to famine, and government expenditure on food aid (Mbithi and Wisner, 1972; Lynam, 1978). New settlers were perceived as 'mining' the land — cultivating it briefly before moving on (J. Heyer, 1992, pers. comm.). Observers failed to consider how far the methods of new settlers were necessary adaptations to their factor endowment, which included a severe shortage of liquid capital and livestock, since, unlike the Makueni settlers, they received no food rations in their first year, no assistance with clearing and first ploughing, etc, and little help in developing water resources. Whereas in Makueni roads, schools and a cattle dip were provided by the Government, in Ngwata Location these were provided by self-help groups (Mbithi and Barnes, 1975: 147). The main sources of cash were the products of the bush - honey, ivory and charcoal — or remittances and help from their home areas (Table 10.1). Rapid in-migration has in fact led to the rapid development of land scarcity and the adoption of intensive systems similar to those of AEZ 4.

The Ngwata settlers initially 'simply burn(ed) the bush and weeds and plant(ed) seeds on the hard exposed surfaces' (Mbithi and Barnes, 1975: 171 and Figure 4.5). Settlers reverted to the methods of Mr Thiaka's father (see Chapter 4) for good reason; it was appropriate in the face of land plenty and labour shortage. Land was successively cleared, cropped and allowed to revert to grazing because cultivation secured land rights under Akamba custom (Mr Maithya, who settled in Matuu in the 1960s, pers. comm.). Observers mistakenly thought this was shifting cultivation.[10] Burning was the only practical method of clearing; the Makueni settlers, in contrast, had the help of labour and tractors for the thorough clearance and stumping necessary before the first ploughing of their fields by tractor.

Mbithi and Barnes found that settlers in 1972 used few intensive technologies. However, this was not due to ignorance. Community leaders said that at first they were unable to keep livestock because of tsetse; this explains the lack of ploughs and manuring. Shortage of cash probably impeded purchase of Katumani seed or cotton seed, and this, plus lack of secure legal rights, would make for low investment in fruit trees. In fact, the new settlers, unlike the original Kikumbulyu inhabitants described by Porter (1965), knew the conservation techniques used in their home areas, and in time, as they acquired the means, they put them into practice (see Chapter 11).

Although the aim was a large farm, community leaders said that many settlers sold some of the cleared land at very low prices to newcomers, since they needed the help of more people to keep the game away. This led to much smaller farms than in Makueni. A survey in Kibwezi in 1990 found an average of 2.8 ha cultivated land per household (CARE, 1991). (Our informants thought that most farms were 4—8 ha, with about 40% for crops and 60% for grazing.) Terracing, according to the leaders, was done in the late 1970s and 1980s, with, they insisted, no government help. Instead, they used hired labour or rotational groups. Livestock became important. Almost every farmer kept goats in 1990, the average, according to the men, being 50, and to the women, 5 or 6 (men were probably quoting for the extended family and women for their own unit) (Figure 10.1(b)). Initially, cattle could graze anywhere; now they stay on their own farm or go to another after the agreement of the owner has been negotiated. They are also given crop residues. Numbers were reduced by nearly half in the 1983—1984 droughts, when a survey in neighbouring areas of southern Machakos found the average post-drought holding was 18 cattle, 25 goats and 7 sheep. Losses in the drought were lower and recuperation rates after the drought were higher than on immediately adjacent Maasai ranches, showing the value of the mixed farming system that had been evolved (Mukhebi et al, 1985).

(a)

(b)

FIGURE 10.2. (a) *Acacia tortilis* in the unsettled Yatta Plateau, circa 1969. (Photo: F. N. Owako, 1969). Reproduced with permission. (b) Farmland in the Yatta Plateau, 1990. (Photo: Mary Tiffen)

The retreat of tsetse made ox-ploughing possible. Ngwata people also hire tractors, since about half of them, according to the leaders, still have no cattle, or have lost what they acquired through drought or disease — the 1989 epidemic was again mentioned. Ploughing made possible the type of farming practised in Masii, and assisted terracing. Crops and livestock then became the main sources of income, although, according to the women leaders, charcoal remains important (Table 10.1). Despite the doubts of observers in the early 1970s, Ngwata settlers had adopted a semi-intensive system more rapidly than farmers in the older areas, although population density was still only 50/km² in 1989.

The settlement of the Yattas in the late 1950s was similar. Figure 10.2 shows the conversion of this dry grazing land to terraced farms. By 1981 farms were similar in size and intensification to Masii and Nzaui (Table 10.2), and considerably more intensively cultivated than in Makueni. After the poor short rains of 1981, nearly 40% of the farmers had harvested only 10% of the usually expected maize yield. In consequence, 50% of them had to buy in food, with 36% able to sell a surplus and the remainder just meeting their needs. Of those needing to buy food, most resorted either to livestock sales or to casual labour, with smaller numbers selling charcoal (in the most newly settled area). Neunhauser et al (1983) concluded that the farmers' first aim was to satisfy the subsistence requirements of their families; 94% of the farmers interviewed therefore planted their food crops first, with cash crops and low-preference food crops such as sorghum being planted later. Farmers allocate land to food crops bearing in mind the possibilities of low yields and the need to keep a reserve against a subsequent poor season (cf. Lynam, 1978). In good seasons, they have a surplus for sale. As the condition of livestock deteriorated in bad seasons and there were also losses to disease, Neunhauser et al calculated that livestock production was not particularly profitable, and that the value of livestock lay rather in their use as a capital reserve, and their contributions of milk, manure and draft power (Neunhauser et al, 1983).

DISTRICT INCOME SYSTEMS IN THE 1970S AND 1980S

Peberdy (1961) showed how income and its constituents varied from year to year with rainfall. Relatively few of the several farm surveys made in the period 1978—1981 give adequate rainfall data, so the deviation from the average cannot be estimated. This, together with differences in methods of calculating income and in the use of national or local prices to value subsistence production, means that their results cannot be compared (Tiffen, 1992: 43—48). We rely therefore mainly on two surveys carried out by the Central Bureau of Statistics.

During the 1974—1975 Integrated Rural Survey, Eastern Province was affected by drought. Farm incomes in the zone in which the AEZ 4 areas of Machakos falls were estimated as Ksh 2479 for the year, of which 26% was derived from the farm operating surplus (Table 10.5).[11] Some 60% of smallholders fell below the estimated poverty line of Ksh 2000 compared with 40% nationally (Consortium, Report 3, 1978: 84 and 91). In the coffee zones, incomes were higher, and a larger percentage came from the farms (as confirmed by Table 10.2). In a similar household budget survey in 1981—1982 (Kenya, CBS, 1988) average rural household income in Machakos District was Ksh 864 per month (Ksh 10 368 per annum), more or less in the middle of the national range at District level. This survey found that 50% of income derived from the farm operating surplus, and this may be more reflective of the normal position in a non-drought year than the 1974—1975 survey. The remaining income came from salaries, wages, income from off-farm enterprises and other sources. The best available estimate of non-farm income in 1960 is also shown in Table 10.5. It shows that since 1960, non-farm income has increased

TABLE 10.5. Farm and non-farm income estimates (percentages)

	Farm income	Non-farm business	Wages	Remittances
1960[1]	80	2[2]	6[3]	11[3]
1974–1975				
Coffee[4]	51	5	32	12
Cotton[5]	26	25	31	32
1981–1982[6]	51	17	24[7]	9[7]

Notes and Sources
[1]Peberdy (1961: Table VI)
 (Calculation of Total District Income plus subsistence production). 1960 was a bad year, but slightly better than 1974–1975
[2]Refers to carvings only
[3]Wages: earned in District. Remittances: 20% of wages earned outside District
[4]Kenya, CBS (1977), *Integrated Rural Survey*, 1974–1975: Table 8.7. Incomes for Coffee Zone East of Rift (includes
 Machakos AEZ 2 and 3). Total household income: Ksh 4087
[5]As above. Incomes for Lower Cotton East of Rift (includes Machakos AEZs 4, 5 and 6). Total household income:
 Ksh 2479
[6]Kenya, CBS (1988) Table 3.12. Machakos District. Total household income: Ksh 10 368. 1981 had a severe drought
 in the short rains, affecting the early 1982 harvest, but good long rains
[7]Wages: no information on whether internal or external. No 'Remittance' heading. Remaining heading was 'Other sources'

as a percentage of total income, and more is now generated locally, and less by remittances from absent men.

The comparative wealth coming from specialisation by some farmers on coffee, fruit and vegetables has generated both a wide variety of non-farm jobs, and an internal market for food crops and livestock from AEZs 4, 5 and 6. The diversity of income sources was confirmed by ADEC (1986) which analysed it by AEZ (details in Tiffen, 1992, Table 13; the large number of AEZs used by ADEC were reduced to 3). Everywhere, 40–48% of households had income from wages or salaries and 36–43% from crafts; cash crops (which probably to the farmer include fruits and vegetables when grown for sale, as well as coffee and cotton) were most frequently mentioned in AEZs 2 and 3; income from food crops was more frequently mentioned in AEZs 4, 5 and 6; cattle, goats, hides, skins and charcoal showed the expected increase in AEZs 4, 5 and 6, but not milk or firewood. Sales of chickens (not covered in most farm surveys) are used by most families to meet small expenses. Sisal string baskets provide a small supplementary income to many women, selling both locally and abroad. The other major craft, wood carving, is pursued by men, mainly round Wamunyu village, and provides a fairly substantial income source to a more concentrated group of people (Figure 10.3).[12]

As we have emphasised, non-farm income contributes not merely to current living standards, but is an insurance in emergencies, playing the role formerly fulfilled only by cattle. In 1990 women leaders in Ngwata said, 'A home with cattle is the same as having a person with a degree'.

LAND, LABOUR AND CAPITAL RELATIONSHIPS

Relatively few thorough economic analyses have been performed on the farming systems surveys in the area. Heyer (1966) and Lynam (1978) carried out linear programming on the crop element, and largely ignored the livestock and non-farm element. Heyer incorporated high and low rainfall variants, while Lynam dealt with risk by analysing the farm sizes at which minimum needs and crop diversification could be met. Heyer found that in the farming system practised in Masii

FIGURE 10.3. A co-operative carving workshop, Wamunyu, 1990. The building received funding from MIDP, but the activity goes back to 1917. (Photo: Mary Tiffen)

in the 1960s working capital requirements were very small, and not much of a problem except after famine, when purchases of seed was necessary (Heyer, 1967: 56). She subdivided fixed capital into items that could be acquired through labour and free local materials, such as stores, fencing and soil conservation works, and items requiring cash outlays, such as oxen, ploughs, sprayers, etc By the 1990s this distinction was no longer valid; Chapter 11 shows that many farmers used hired labour to construct or rehabilitate terraces. She found that capital for equipment could be a problem because of the risks involved; people preferred non-farm investments.

By the late 1970s capital was much more important in farming than in 1960. However, the surveys carried out then ignored fixed capital such as terraces, dams, trees, etc, and only one analysis included farm buildings. An economic analysis showing high returns to terracing for maize and beans is quoted in Chapter 11. In AEZs 2 and 3, farmers, through their co-operative societies, have invested in coffee-bean processing plants. Initial capital is also required for a switch to grade cattle, not only for the beast, but also for housing and watering, etc. Many farmers have invested in brick houses, tin roofs, guttering and roof-water catchment tanks, which save labour (see Chapter 12). Orange and other fruit-tree cultivation on a commercial scale requires cash investment for the initial planting material, and, very probably purchases of manure and hired labour to prepare the planting site. The value which farmers put on trees can be seen in the prices they are prepared to pay; in 1990, land in Kangundo with coffee trees cost Ksh 200 000 per ha, compared with Ksh 100 000 without. In Ngwata, unterraced grazing land cost Ksh 5000 per ha, compared with Ksh 12 500 for arable with terraces.

In the AEZs 2 and 3 areas, working capital for fertiliser, hired labour and other inputs is

TABLE 10.6. Farm strategies on large and small farms in Mwala, 1980

	1	2	3	4
Farm size (ha)	1.3	3.24	7.54	17.8
Cropped area (ha)	1.02	1.62	1.92	3.24
Cattle owned	4	5	8	11
Shoats owned	7	12	16	16
Cash expenses (Ksh): labour	287	164	23	1007
Cash expenses (Ksh): other inputs	338	309	320	438
Cash inputs/cultivated ha	331	191	167	135
Return per cultivated ha to inputs	4.89	3.19	1.6	1.14
Total net farm income	2105	1980	2050	2736
Net cash farm income	636	464	803	605
Subsistence farm income	1469	1516	1248	2131
% subsistence in farm income	70	77	61	78
% farm cash from livestock	57	60	78	66
Net farm income/ha	1619	611	272	154
Off-farm income	3529	1503	1811	2628
Per capita income[1]	626	387	429	596

[1]Assumes 9 persons per family in each class. No data given to show if family size varied by farm class
Source: Rukandema et al (1981), and own calculations

clearly needed for coffee and vegetables. In all areas, as the numbers of livestock fall, those farmers with few livestock need to buy in manure or chemical fertiliser for their food crops, and the returns to such expenditures can be high (Table 10.6).

Given the skewed distribution of land holdings, some farmers are short of land and others of labour. Whether they are short of capital will depend in part on their non-farm income. A short study by Rukandema et al (1981) in Mwala, AEZ 4, is useful in illustrating strategies pursued by farmers with different farm sizes, and the importance of taking into account non-farm occupations. It is summarised in Table 10.6. Only 16−18% of farms had permanent labourers, although about 33% made use of casual labour. (Other surveys confirm this level of use of hired labour in the drier areas.) This labour was concentrated on the larger farms, which spent an average of Ksh 1007 — nearly four times as much as any other group. Rukandema ascribed the need for labour to the larger cropped area on the large farms rather than to their larger holdings of cattle, since there are economies of scale in the management of cattle. These large farmers invested only Ksh 135 per cropped hectare in non-labour inputs, and received back only 1.14 times this amount; the return to this expenditure in terms of income per hectare was very poor. Returns to farm labour were still (as in the 1960s) very low, unless labour was adequately combined with working capital. However, the wage expenditure freed some family members for off-farm work; this group had the second highest off-farm income and this gave them the second highest income per capita.

Those with least land earned most off-farm income. They spent Ksh 338/ha on non-labour cash inputs for their farm and obtained a return of Ksh 1619/ha. They also spent Ksh 287/ha on labour. This group with the smallest farms did best on a per capita income basis, through a combination of very high returns per hectare to capital-intensive farming and off-farm income. Half the farmers, forming the two middle groups, required little hired labour for their farms.

However, they also earned relatively small amounts off-farm, spent less on inputs, and obtained less revenue than the smallest farms on a per hectare basis. Compared with the largest and smallest farmers, they had distributed their labour badly, obtaining the least on a per capita basis.[13]

The analysis showed the importance of working capital, and that an important section of the farming community has difficulty in obtaining enough. In an effort to overcome the capital constraint, the Government has from time to time launched credit schemes. Meyers compared farmers taking or not taking MIDP credit, making the assumption that capital, especially capital to hire labour at peak periods, might be limiting crop production.[14] In fact he found that hired labour was not associated with credit, but primarily with what he termed the high-income group, particularly those receiving remittances from absent members, but also those with high non-farm income from local sources, high crop sales and livestock assets. Credit acceptance was linked to cash income from crops (to be expected as it was tied to a cotton or sunflower package). He ended, therefore, by confirming the importance of off-farm income, both in providing farmers with that extra amount of capital which enables crop production to become more profitable (through increased inputs of fertiliser, soil conservation, manuring, timely labour, etc), and for providing the cushion which protects them from overwhelming losses in bad seasons (Meyers, 1982: 148–149).

Another critical capital element is the plough. Onchere (1982) found a significant positive relationship between the ownership and use of oxen and the quantity of food produced and consumed. As many studies note, ownership of a plough is crucial because farmers without ploughs inevitably plant and weed late. (This may not affect very small farms.)

Credit has succeeded in the coffee areas, where it is associated with a profitable crop, and where deductions of credit for inputs can be easily made when the coffee is brought to the co-operative for sale. The problem is how to make farming profitable, which is a prior condition for a successful credit scheme. Farmers seem to have been able to obtain capital from family or other unofficial sources to move into grade cattle and fruit trees.

The flows of capital to and from the farm are illustrated in a recent study of 16 farms, including some in Machakos. This found:

> Five of the participating farmers had invested surplus resources in the ownership or management of a shop in a nearby town. In two other cases, the male head of the farm household had permanent off-farm work. In a further six cases, other members of the farm household had permanent off-farm work, and contributed either to the maintenance of the farm household or to re-investment in the farm . . . In some cases, sons who had received higher education and were employed in well-paid positions . . . re-invested capital in their parents' farm and met the costs of hired labour, thereby effectively replacing their own previous labour input to the farm. On one farm, off-farm earnings were used for establishing citrus terraces and the hiring of tractors to re-develop old terraces for cropping. (Ockwell et al, 1990).

Labour is a limiting factor on some farms, but this is linked to the profitability of the enterprise, since labour can be hired. Lubega carried out a production function analysis on crop production alone in an AEZ 4 area and found that labour inputs had the strongest impact on crop output, followed by equipment, and then land (Lubega, 1987: 56). It seems likely that labour is more limiting in an enterprise consisting of crops alone, than in an enterprise which includes both crops and livestock. The larger farms tend to put a higher proportion to livestock (Tables 10.4 and 10.6).

In Masii, Hayes found that in the 32% of households hiring labour in 1982, three employees were employed on home duties (amongst the five females employed). Of the remaining 37, of whom 35 were male (and of whom 33 were aged less than 25), 14 were employed solely on livestock care, 12 combined livestock care with other duties, 8 were on agricultural work only, and 1 was engaged to dig a dam and fetch wood (Hayes, 1986: 121−122). Hayes' data suggest that in AEZ 4, before the importance of fruit farming, hired labour was strongly associated with livestock, which is confirmed by Meyers (1982: 104). The use of cheap young labour for livestock care releases family labour for more profitable activities. Both surveys find labour hire is associated with the upper category of farmers in terms of general assets (Meyers, 1982: 104; Hayes, 1986: 124).

In the coffee and vegetable areas the returns to labour may be different. These farms employ more labour; in Mbooni, both large and small farms employed in 1978 an average of one hired labourer per household (Table 10.4). This suggests a considerable rise in employment of hired labourers in AEZs 2 and 3 since Owako found less than 10% of Mbooni households employed labour in 1964. The increase in labour hire coincides with the increase in coffee planting. From our own incidental interviews it is clear that labour employment also takes place in vegetable and fruit areas and these have increased since 1980.

CONSTRAINTS ON ENTERPRISE DEVELOPMENT AS PERCEIVED BY THE FARMER

When farmers in Machakos and Kitui were asked in 1977 to rate possible problems from a pre-selected list, drought was rated as severe by the largest number (64.5%), followed by food (49.6%) and water supply (47.5%). Erosion followed at 39%. When farmers were asked to suggest problems that had not been listed, the most frequently mentioned problem was roads (230 mentions), which is probably linked with the 130 mentions of transport. Too few hospitals and schools were mentioned by 129 and 114, respectively (Consortium, Report 6). (The authors note that it is difficult to put comparable percentages on these figures since it was an open-ended question, with non-respondents, invalid replies, and a variety of answers. The sample was just over 2000 farmers.) Ten years later, when ADEC made a similar enquiry to a large sample in Machakos, the main perceived needs were for water supplies, improved roads and transport infrastructure, and enhanced health facilities (ADEC, 1986: 1−15).

Poor infrastructure is thus seen as an important constraint. Farming in a semi-arid area depends fundamentally on water, whether as stored in the land, or as available for domestic and livestock use. Good roads are a necessity for profitable marketing. These factors were also mentioned to us in 1990, when job scarcity and, in highland areas, land scarcity were also mentioned.

We asked farmers to compare their present maize yields with those they had when they started farming. The 38 respondents were strongly biased towards the older farmers, who were regarded as leaders in their community. Sixteen farmers felt that yields were better or had been maintained, and 22 thought they were worse. Amongst the 16 who felt yields were better, 11 ascribed improvements to more use of manure, and 9 credited terraces. Of the 22 thinking that fertility had fallen, 14 mentioned lack of manure, of whom 9 referred to money for manure or fertiliser purchase. Despite the small and imperfect sample, two things are apparent. One is the importance farmers put on manure as a means of combating soil erosion and fertility loss, and the other is their consciousness of the need for capital either to acquire manure if they have not enough animals, or to use fertiliser, build terraces and make other improvements. The capital shortage is likely to be more strongly felt in the farming community as a whole.

STANDARDS OF LIVING

In 1990, both community leaders and individual farmers referred to problems of poverty, and in particular, the burden of school fees. However, two-thirds of our small sample thought themselves better off than their fathers, and one-third worse off. Those who thought life had got worse complained of having to work harder, having smaller farms, and also of inflation. As one woman said: 'My father could sing and dance, but I have no time.' Those who felt better off generally referred to the way they had developed their farms, better organisation of work and greater information.

By 1981–1982 the Machakos farmer, although far from rich, was in the middle of the income range for Kenya,[15] whereas in the 1940s and early 1950s the District was a problem area, needing famine relief in most years. By the first half of the 1980s the assets of the people were above the national average in housing and education (Table 10.7). The main deficiencies they suffer are in physical infrastructure: their lack of transport facilities is confirmed, as are their difficulties with water. The nutrition studies of 1974–1981, despite the droughts of the period, found the habitual diet to be of good quality but somewhat low in quantity compared with recommended intakes.[16] Table 10.7 shows Machakos in line with Kenyan averages.

TABLE 10.7. Social indicators, 1982–1983

	Machakos (%)	Nation (%)
1. *Education*		
Population within 2 km of:		
(a) Primary school	71.3	75.6
(b) Adult education centre	51.4	68.0
% males able to read	68.3	61.1
% females able to read	42.1	38.4
2. *Housing quality*[1]		
% of households with a thatch roof	52.2	56.3
% of households with a mud floor	76.7	84.9
% of households with mud wall	49.4	74.4
% of households with electric lighting	0	0.9
3. *Infrastructure*		
% less than 2 km to:		
water in dry season	83.3	88.1
cattle dip	40.8	53
market	30	41
bus/matatu route	53.5	67.4
maize mill	40.4	58.4
postal service	17.6	21.3
4. *Child health*		
Height for age	94.0	94.2
Weight for height	99.4	100.7

[1]Percentages show those with *low* quality housing — thatch instead of an improved material, mud wall instead of brick, etc.
Sources: Kenya, CBS (1983, 1985)

The rise in the standard of living, despite some indications of increasing poverty in the late 1980s, accords with our findings on increased productivity per person and per hectare (see Chapter 6) and the increasing contribution of non-farm income. More intensive farming systems have generated labour incomes for the poor on the farms, and jobs in supplying inputs, services and consumer goods to more prosperous farmers. As yet, farming systems have fewer backward linkages than in Asia, since they make relatively little use of purchased inputs such as fertiliser, and many of the capital assets have a high labour content, compared with, for example, irrigation systems. Farm and non-farm sectors are closely linked through families who manage flows of income and capital between them.

NOTES

1 Compare with Botswana (Norman and Baker (1986: 49). Unfortunately, none of the existing studies examines farming systems in terms of their return to rainfall or soil moisture. Returns to water have been examined in some irrigation studies, amongst others, Tiffen (1990).
2 There was a debate in the Reconditioning Committee in 1948, when white farmers thought there was an excessive amount of double cropping in the Reserve.
3 Porter writes 'Kilungu', but his map shows clearly he means Kikumbulyu.
4 Heyer gave no information on livestock holdings, but showed that keeping livestock on arable land would give considerably smaller returns than keeping it under crops. However, livestock, as she acknowledged, were generally kept on the poorer land that was not regarded as fit for cropping, and this type of land was still, in the early 1960s, relatively plentiful.
5 Owako reported average farm size as 3.04 ha. The two surveys were in slightly different areas. Conditions can vary considerably within a single location, which might provide an explanation. The level of population growth would have led one to expect a reduction in average farm size.
6 Meyers quotes a rural teacher in his sample with a large orange grove from which he made Ksh 17 000 in 1978 — four times the mean cash crop income (Meyers, 1982: 99).
7 Equivalent in total to about Ksh 101 million in 1988, in terms of the maize purchasing power described in Chapter 6, or Ksh 46 000 per settler family.
8 Elderly leaders in Kangundo said that every young man of 14 and over was forced to go to Makueni and was not paid till the end of a two-year contract.
9 The first African in this post, and later Chairman of Masaku County Council. He said white ants destroyed silage, and in any case, people did not like to cut maize when it was nearly ready for harvesting.
10 Netting has described how the Kofyar tribe in Nigeria, who practised a very intensive system of agriculture on the Jos Figureau, adopted shifting techniques to develop new land in the plains (Netting, 1965). Lower Makueni and Yatta settlers were described as having a slash-and-burn bush-fallowing system around a settled base (Consortium, Report 6, 1978: 68).
11 This takes into account losses of Ksh 1300 in livestock and in stored farm produce, due to drought during the period of observation. Without these losses, which are not taken into account in many other estimates of farm income, total income was Ksh 3790, of which the farm operating surplus contributed 52% (Consortium, Report 3, 1978: 83).
12 Kenya's exports of Akamba wood carvings averaged £1.4 million in 1985—1989; those of sisal baskets averaged £2.9 million (information from the Ministry of Commerce, 1990). Both these figures include the earnings of traders and transporters, but they exclude sales within Kenya to tourists and residents. (They can be compared with the value of Machakos cotton production in 1987 of K£6 million.)
13 Rukandema et al (1981) use the sample average of 9 persons in the household to calculate these per capita figures. If there was any tendency for the larger farms to have larger households, their per capita income would have been even lower. Mukhebi (1981) came to a contrary result to that which we have derived from Rukandema et al, but he disregarded labour engaged in non-farm work and seems to have standardised non-farm income across his three groups. The inconclusive nature of his findings suggests that he had neglected a crucial factor here.

14 His sample consisted of 67 recipients of MIDP credit in four AEZ 4 sub-locations (87% of all such recipients) and a systematic sample of 40 of the remaining households from randomly selected *motui* (villages) in each of the four areas, i.e. 160 households. Results were given separately for each group; we quote here for the non-credit takers unless otherwise stated, since these were the majority. Those taking official credit were on the whole wealthier, better educated, more tied to cash-crop production, and made more use of exchange labour, than non-loanees. They represented a middle level of wealth. Those in the upper level of wealth were characterised by the importance of non-farm earnings, and remittance income from non-farm earning relatives. This group did not find credit worth the trouble. Meyers' model might have had more explanatory power if he had looked at total income rather than cash receipts. He ignored subsistence income, cash expenses in farming, and livestock receipts.

15 Agricultural incomes declined after 1982, due to the fall in the real prices of coffee and cotton (see Chapter 6). However, this would also have affected other agricultural areas, and there is no reason to think that Machakos's place in the rank order would have materially changed.

16 The energy intake was sufficient in women 'to support adequate foetal growth and lactation performance with maintenance of maternal health throughout the reproductive cycle'. Amongst pre-school children severe malnutrition was rare, occurring mainly in socially deprived households. After the age of six months, weight for age and height for age dropped to 83% and 92% respectively of Harvard standards (Kusin and Jansen, 1984: 209−210).

11

Soil Conservation

INTRODUCTION

The prevention of erosion on cultivated land depends essentially on the reduction of soil detachment and the velocity of run-off, and on grazing land on the maintenance of adequate vegetative ground cover. At the beginning of this century, arable land management was through shifting cultivation, and pasture management and bush reduction by burning of grass. As population density increased, new methods of management had to be found. In semi-arid areas important productive gains on arable lands are realised by retaining water so as to encourage infiltration, but the breakdown of the retaining structure has to be avoided, as this leads to gullying and soil loss. In this chapter we consider the use of structures to retain soil and improve water retention.[1] We also consider the management of grazing lands by grass planting, controlled grazing and other techniques.[2]

Conservation history in Machakos District is divided into four periods: 1930–1945, 1946–1962, 1962–1978 and 1978–1990. In each period, we consider both the diagnosis, and the remedies proposed and undertaken, on the one hand, by the Government, and on the other, by individual households and communities. We conclude with a discussion of why the early strategy of controlled resettlement, communal grazing and grass planting, and compulsory, communally-constructed narrow base terraces, was only partially successful; and why farmers have preferred individually managed farms, spontaneous settlement, private grazing areas and the bench terrace. There have been areas of ignorance on the part of both the government and farmers, the greatest lacuna on the official side being the management of water. Increasingly, as land became scarce, the aim of farmers has been to conserve not only their soil, but also the rainfall, which, as shown in Chapter 3, is erratic, often insufficient, and closely related to yields.

FROM PERSUASION TO COMPULSION, 1931–1945

Political background

Anderson (1984) has described the mounting international concern about soil erosion in the 1930s, which led to a policy of direct intervention in African farming practices, and an increasingly high political profile for conservation matters. A unifying force in British colonial territories was provided by Sir Frank Stockdale, the Colonial Office Agricultural Adviser, who visited the Ukamba Reserve in 1931 and again in 1937 (Pole-Evans, 1939). In 1938 the Colonial Secretary committed colonial development funds to anti-erosion measures in East Africa. The Colonial Office began demanding an annual account of conservation work from all colonies, and a special session of the Governors' conference for East Africa was devoted to conservation policies. In Kenya, the ecological crisis was particularly evident in the semi-arid Districts, Machakos, Kitui and Baringo, and in the more densely populated Kikuyu Districts (Throup, 1987). The Governor of Kenya, Mitchell, visited Machakos shortly after taking office in December 1944. Creech Jones, the Colonial Secretary, toured the District in 1946.

Anderson identifies the chief influences on Kenyan conservation policies. The first was the alarm generated by the Dust Bowl in the United States which reached its height in 1935. Literature began to arrive in Kenya in the late 1920s. The USA and South Africa (with which Kenyan settlers and officials had strong links) provided examples of state enforcement of soil conservation. In Kenya, Colin Maher was a graduate of the Imperial College of Tropical Agriculture in Trinidad, opened in 1922, which had spread professional interest in conservation; he was very influential through his enthusiastic reports and writings. Technical understanding was initially poor; as the Americans were most active in trying to do something, most of the experiments originated there. Attempts were made to estimate the human and livestock carrying capacity of African reserves: work in Northern Rhodesia in 1937 (Allan, 1965) was followed by studies by Humphrey and Hughes Rice in Kikuyu country in 1944. Hughes Rice became Agricultural Officer in Machakos in 1951–1953 (Throup, 1987).

The second influence was the noticeable increase in the African population from the mid 1920s, which put pressure on reserves originally deemed more or less adequate for much smaller numbers. The Akamba always disputed the boundaries imposed by the Government, claiming that pastures that were scheduled for white settlement or designated as Crown Land were necessary to sustain their livestock, especially in dry years. But pressure to extend the Reserve or grazing access was resisted by the Government on political grounds. (This thesis has been developed by (among others) Kimambo (1970), Leys (1975), Wisner (1977) and Otieno (1984), who quotes Provincial and District annual reports.)

Thirdly, the economic consequences of the Depression made the Kenyan Government anxious to increase its revenues from Africans as well as from Europeans, and to avoid the expenses of famine relief. The threat that the Government might put more resources into developing African agriculture, and less into assistance to Europeans, led to European anxiety. They argued that any additional land given to Africans would rapidly be degraded.

Finally, there was anxiety about an apparently increasing incidence of droughts. In Kenya there had been droughts in 1928 and 1929, followed by a sequence of bad seasons in 1933–1936 (see Chapter 3).

The period 1930–1945 was therefore one of steadily increasing official concern about erosion. Forceful intervention came to prevail over persuasion, external funding over local resources, and external advice over consultation with local people.

The diagnosis

The succession of reports on erosion in Machakos in the 1930s have already been described (see Chapter 7). The Carter Commission in 1933 had established that the Akamba did not have more livestock than they needed for subsistence. Therefore the problem was perceived as too many people, ignorant of scientific farming, and unable to adapt to the shorter fallows, and pressure on grazing land caused by population growth. Increasingly, the answer seemed to be destocking, resettlement of at least part of the surplus population, and the development of off-farm work, since the slow spread of new knowledge and techniques seemed inadequate. The expansion of cultivation, at the expense of grazing, was seen as a danger rather than a remedy, since a high ratio of stock (which required extensive grazing) to cultivated area was deemed a necessity to provide manure. Indeed, Pole-Evans held the Department of Agriculture responsible for the degradation, by 'encouraging the Wakamba to break their land for cash crops and to adopt intensive methods of agriculture, when their country was largely unsuited to such a procedure' (Pole-Evans, 1939: 6).

Rehabilitation of grazing lands

The focus was first on the grazing lands. The Government posted the first District Agricultural Officer, a Mr Leckie, to Machakos District, for a survey in 1931, and permanently in 1932. He worked with a reconditioning sub-committee of the Local Native Council (LNC), consisting of five African members under the Chairmanship of the District Commissioner (Peberdy, 1958). The programme, with a European supervisor funded from LNC revenues, started in Mbooni, after much consultation with the elders, on 80 ha of steep, badly eroded land which was contour-trenched. Mauritius beans were sown along the trench banks. Cattle were kept off the area which was planted with indigenous grass (particularly *Cynodon romi* noted for its fast spreading and drought-resistant habits) and exotic drought-resistant forage plants. Gullies were supplied with wash-stops. This was intended to serve as a demonstration; the reclamation of larger areas was to be left to the people. A nursery was set up to supply fodder plants, trees, and wash-stop grasses. The main species were Mexican daisy, spineless cactus, napier, woolly-finger, Bermuda and crested wheat grass, Kudzu vine, black Mauritius bean, and drought-resistant fodder trees and shrubs (Kenya, DoA, 1932).

Reconditioning work by the Akamba themselves started at Kiteta. In September 1934, the LNC empowered the Headmen of Kiteta and Masii Locations to restrict or prohibit grazing in areas set apart for reconditioning and planting of fodder-producing plants and grasses. The experimental area was destocked and three trials were set up to assess the economics of reconditioning; these were destocking alone, destocking with contour trenching, and with contour trenching and planting with indigenous grasses (*Cynodon romi*). The last treatment proved to be the most successful (Kenya, DoA, 1934). Farmers started to fence and make contour trenches in small areas. Persuasion by the Administration improved the adoption rate. These efforts were complemented by a regular supply of prisoners' labour for reconditioning work, because, although the Akamba volunteers were said to be committed, they could only work spasmodically and they had inefficient tools for trench digging (Kenya, DoA, 1934). The focus on persuasion was deliberate. The DC in 1932 deplored the other proposed remedy of a meat factory to convert culled cattle into fertiliser, mainly because culling involved compulsion, when cattle were the Akamba's main asset. He recommended persuading the Akamba to sell some cattle to buy the carts necessary for the transport of manure. (KNA:DC/MKS/8/4; undated note, assumed by the DC, headed *Propaganda*, written a few days after the first Agricultural Officer took up post).

In 1935 the Department of Agriculture produced a bulletin on 'Soil Erosion' emphasising its dangers and techniques of control. In December 1935, Leckie, now Provincial Agricultural Officer, reported to a new Machakos Reconditioning Committee his dissatisfaction with progress. He said that various officers had tried out their own ideas; there had been no coordinated effort and some mistakes (KNA: DC/MKS/12/2, Reconditioning Committee). (Peberdy (1958) refers to damage caused by the ploughing of 200 acres of eroded land, and changes of stance on trash lines, first recommended, then condemned because they harboured pests.) The new Committee consisted of staff of the Agriculture, Veterinary and Forestry Departments, some white settlers, and the District Commissioner but only two African members of the LNC. It began by classifying the district into areas:

(i) Pasture:
     (a) very eroded
     (b) semi-eroded
     (c) not eroded, but needing protection
(ii) arable.

For the very eroded pasture areas, the Committee recommended the use of contour trenching, planting napier grass, water improvements, destocking and planning of stock routes, rotational grazing and demarcation of holdings with sisal boundaries, to be carried out by the owner of the land or the people communally in communal areas. The Committee took information on grazing rights from its native members, and hoped that by improving security of tenure, the owner would feel responsible for reconditioning his own land (Kenya, DoA, 1935; KNA: DC/MKS/12/2/2). Stagger trenching had to be abandoned because of the high labour requirements.

For semi-eroded pasture areas, rotational grazing was recommended, with grass fires heavily punished. The Committee was also anxious to reduce stock numbers and, after receiving a memo from Maher, came to the conclusion that compulsory control would be necessary (native members dissenting). In 1937 the Committee held its last recorded meeting, at which the gist of Maher's report was explained to the native members. The minutes say that the European members endorsed it completely. They also proposed an experimental settlement at Makueni, and noted a grant of £5000 from the Colonial Development Fund for water development, which seems to have been the first instance of external assistance.

Between 1935 and 1936, the reconditioning campaign had closed off approximately 8000 ha of land, marked out 50 farms near Makaveti for napier grass planting, and established 7500 compost pits in the Iveti, Kangundo and Matungulu area. By 1937, 10 000 ha were temporarily closed to stock under organised schemes of rotational grazing, which was said to have resulted in remarkable regeneration of natural grass and bush (Kenya, DoA, 1937). But Maher (RH: Maher, 1937) estimated that, at such a rate, 32 years would be needed to close off all the badly eroded areas, and that the amount of contour trenching so far achieved was negligible. He wanted 40 000 ha per year closed (which was never achieved — see Table 11.1), the temporary removal of the population, the culling of cattle 'to accord with the true carrying capacity of the Reserve', and the elimination of all goats. In 1938, he became head of the new Soil Conservation Service within the DoA, with R. O. Barnes as the Soil Engineer. Barnes agreed that work up to 1937 'had been useful as propaganda, but has produced no appreciable results on the reserve's condition . . . There is no hope of improved conditions without a vast expansion of effort' (KNA: Barnes, 1937: 8). While working through and with 'the natives themselves, even using local committees' would be an ideal, the situation demanded more drastic action, including moving cultivators off the steeper areas, use of tractors for terracing and greatly increased agricultural supervision.

In 1938 the Government embarked on compulsory destocking, discussed at intervals since

TABLE 11.1. Reconditioning in the late 1930s and early 1940s

Year	Area closed (ha)	Grass planted (ha)	Terracing (ha)	Land demarcation (ha)
1937	10 121	na	—	na
1938	na	na	127	na
1939	13 283	460	—	164 991
1940	6 579	3230	35 769	1 300
1941	10 407	1360	6 975	17 761
1942	7 822	1864	5 453	7 817
1943	7 609	620	656[1]	na
1944	10 574	1986	477[1]	na

na = not available
[1]Figures are for km
Sources: Kenya, DoA Reports (1937–1944). Peberdy (1958) for terracing

the Hall Commission in 1929.[3] Officers allocated quotas to every livestock owner. 'Surplus' cattle were requisitioned and sold at nominal prices to the Liebig factory at Athi River. Mr Thiaka (Chapter 4) recalled his family losing seven cattle, leaving two for his father and one for his brother. Discontent mounted; co-operation ceased; 1500 Akamba marched to Nairobi and camped near Government House for six weeks, while those in the Reserve ferried food to them. The order was rescinded and destocking abandoned.[4] In the future more attention was paid to Akamba sensibilities, but for many years all government initiatives were treated with acute suspicion.

While the Government made a tactical retreat from stock culling, it did not abandon its objectives. The LNC passed a resolution in 1938 for enforcing sisal or other hedging on private land and demarcation and fencing went ahead on a very large scale (Table 11.1). The DC in his 1940 Annual Report seemed optimistic about progress; he reported a new system of working in close co-operation with the Chiefs and *asilis*, with the aim of the complete cessation of grass burning. Experimentation continued on 20 ha of badly degraded land at Lower Mbooni, including cutting out thornbush to make stock-proof fences, grass planting, building of contour terraces, gully stopping, and planting trees. Use of crescents for planting grass was found helpful. However, napier grass planted in 1937 had succumbed to the 'unprecedented drought'.[5] Closing areas to grazing and grass planting continued during the war years (Table 11.1). The main grasses recommended were *Panicum makarikariensis, Cynodon plectostachium* and *Eragrostis curvula* (Kenya, DoA, 1947).

The 1938 resolution on hedging aimed at strengthening individuals' incentive to improve their own land. However, Grieves, who became Agriculture Officer in 1936 or 1937, was one of those who thought communal tribal tenure preferable (see Chapter 5). He declared in 1944 that individual tenure had been a failure:

> A very few isolated individuals did begin to take more interest in their land, but there was no mass movement towards better farming. About 90% of the grazing areas in the District were duly demarcated by their owners, and grazing was much more confined by the enclosures. The grazing certainly improved in some areas, but the greatest improvement was brought about by the compulsory closing of areas to stock by the authorities and not by the owners themselves.
>
> It was soon found that little progress could be made by individual effort . . . (Quoted by KNA: Lambert, 1945: 45. Reproduced by permission of Kenya National Archives.)

Backed by the settlers on the Reconditioning Committee, Grieves wanted to bring down the average stock holding to four units (rather than the six that the Carter Commission had reckoned was only just sufficient for needs). Administrative officers, remembering 1938, were equally convinced that compulsory culling was politically impossible. Closing of grazing land continued during the war, with the expelled cattle moved to the Yattas (Table 11.1), although at nothing like the rate which Maher wanted.

Conservation of arable lands

In the hill areas with a higher proportion of arable land the Reconditioning Committee in 1935 recommended the use of manure, rotational grazing, grazing closures, the planting of fodder crops and prohibition of maize growing in some areas (Peberdy, 1958). Barnes, who was placed in technical control of soil conservation work in Machakos District, said that the first terraces were at Muisuni (in Kangundo),[6] Matungulu, and Makaveti (in Kalama), made with ox-graders late in 1937 (KNA: 3/Agri/1/29). Ksh 200 000 was allocated to an experimental 127 ha of mechanical terracing at Matungulu. Barnes was particularly concerned for this rich area, for which he saw no cheap answers. Chief Uku of Matungulu was appointed Soil Conservation Headman. The DC's Annual Report in 1940 referred to blocks of cultivation safeguarded with 'contour ridges and spectacular grassed drainage ways'. Barnes (KNA: Barnes, 1937) shows that he intended these to run parallel to gullies such as that shown in Figure 7.5, in order to prevent the latter expanding. The Matungula/Kangundo strips are probably those photographed in 1952 (shown in Figure 11.1). A grassed drainway still functioning in 1990 is shown in Figure 11.2.

Terracing continued in the early war years (Table 11.1), but funded out of normal Departmental revenue and LNC grants. Each location had two levellers and communal work seems to have been supervised by chiefs and supplemented by famine relief gangs (Peberdy, 1958: 18).

The Akamba response

As we have seen, the LNC initially supported the conservation experiments, as did communities in Mbooni, and individuals. People were, however, conscious that the Agricultural Officers did not necessarily know what they were doing. Some individuals agreed to terracing on their farms by the Government; others carried it out with their own oxen after being lent graders. (The tendency of government officers was to start with large farmers such as chiefs, who were often unpopular and who had resources the normal farmer did not.)

After the failure of compulsory culling in 1938, some Matungulu people took oaths against conservation (Barnes, 1959, in KNA: MKS/3/AGRI/1/29). Lambert (KNA: Lambert, 1945), investigating Akamba attitudes to the Government's plans, found strong opposition to limitations on cattle ownership (see Chapter 9). Fencing grazing lands, however, was in accordance with the evolution of custom (see Chapter 5), and Table 11.1 shows how rapidly it was done. Although Grieves thought there was little improvement, some elderly respondents identify this period as a turning point (see interview with Mr Thiaka, quoted in Chapter 4). Over time people have invested in their grazing land and reduced their stock, but it was not necessarily their first priority. During the war, it was investment in expanding cultivation that brought in profits.

The Akamba elders saw erosion as caused mainly by the Reserve boundaries, which prevented a family from moving to a new site where grazing and cultivation could be combined. For them

(a)

(b)

FIGURE 11.1. Matungulu conservation area, (a) 1952 and (b) 1990. The original 'contour ditches' which 'spill into grassed run-offs' have been converted to benches (Photos: Kenya, ALUS, 1953, Crown Copyright, Reproduced with permission of the Central Office of Information, and D. B. Thomas)

FIGURE 11.2. One of the original waterways in Matungulu, as seen in 1990. (Photo: D. B. Thomas.
Reproduced with permission)

temporary relief grazing on the Yattas was very much a second best, necessitating the transport of food from the home. The desirable areas for settlement and grazing were the lands disputed with the Europeans in the north, or the Yattas, and resentment at land lost was particularly strong in the north (KNA: Lambert, 1945). In 1938 the DC told a meeting in a northern location that they were putting too many cattle on too small a land (comparing this to a bag). One of those attending reported: 'But I said we had a bigger bag on Yatta and Mua Hills where we could take our cattle but the Europeans had made the bag too small . . . the people . . . all raised their hands [in agreement]' (Newman, 1974: 14).

They thought the proposed settlement area at Makueni very unhealthy (KNA: Lambert, 1945). (This was not unreasonable; on lowland irrigation schemes in Kenya there has been considerable mortality from malaria amongst the families of new settlers coming from highland areas.) The majority did indeed see new settlements as the answer, but under their own control and in areas of their own choice.

LARGE-SCALE INVESTMENT WITH LITTLE LOCAL CONSULTATION: 1945–1962

During the period 1945–1962 government policy and people's reactions to the various aspects of a considerable investment programme are examined together. Machakos benefitted from a high proportion of the expenditures made by what became the African Land Development Board (ALDEV — see Chapter 15). The development of the Makueni settlement absorbed much of its resources at first, but an intensive drive for communal compulsory terracing in the populated areas was also important from the start, even in the absence of sound knowledge as to the best technology. Development of agricultural potential began after 1951 and gathered momentum, with much enlarged staff resources, after 1953.

Compulsory terracing

The Akamba knew that many Europeans were claiming that the only solutions to the denudation problem were compulsory destocking and the movement of large numbers of people to the European farms as labourers, and that there were proposals to regard them as tribal tenants, not owners of their land (see Chapter 5). They resolved to oppose any government step that might be preliminary to annexation of their land (interview, 1990, confirmed by references in DC's reports). As cultivation gave ownership rights in custom, in 1946, to the incomprehension of administrators, 'they [the Akamba] refused to allow paid Labour Companies to do soil conservation work on their land even though the results were free' (RH: Penwill, 1953). In 1947, funds were provided for tractors to work in areas with a low population density, but people threw themselves in front of the government machines, which had to be withdrawn (Clayton, 1964). In any case, mechanised terracing cost the Government more, and although used a little between 1952 and 1957 when Akamba hostility lessened, it was then stopped.[7]

The Akamba did accept food for work in famine years, and communal work on their own land. In 1946, the first year of the new programme, 130 km of terraces and 24 km of cut-off drains were laid and constructed. In the same year, Major Joyce, a Machakos rancher who was on the ALDEV board,[8] recommended the Muranga'a system, where labour for terracing was organised by local elders. Chief Uku and four other chiefs visited Muranga'a, and Uku told the Committee that he thought the *utui* elders could organise a similar programme in Machakos. All adults had to turn out for two days a week, but as the men were often away, most of the work fell on the women. A touring note (dated 10 July 1947) says that 'several semi-educated men [in Matungulu] challenged the Government's right to order women to work'. The officer told them all men and women must work.[9] Organisation was left to the Chiefs.[10] The policy was set out by the DC:

> The AI [Agricultural Instructor] in consultation with the Chief should set out the reconditioning programme ... If the people are idle, their *Nzama ya Motui* [headman of the *utui*] should deal with them and only report to the Chief if they persistently disobey. The Chief should hereafter run them before the local tribunal under the Soil Conservation Ordinance, the Local Native Authority Ordinance, or better still, Standing Resolutions of the LNC ... While collective work on block areas is the aim of the *utui* system individual *kisese* holders should at all times be encouraged to safeguard their own holding both from the wider aspect of land preservation and their own self-interest. ... If they do not co-operate they should be told that their stock at present grazing on Machakos B1 Yatta and Emali will be returned and replaced with those from other *utui*. (KNA: DC/MKS/8/5: undated note by D. C. Howes, 1947–1948. Reproduced by permission of Kenya National Archives.)

A minute of the Reconditioning Committee (February 1948) refers to a change of policy, to use Betterment Funds to buy hoes, shovels and a few ploughs for communal work, instead of for paying labour. This made the programmes more effective. Respondents told us that people used to fight to get the tools. However, touring notes show a mixed response, with work going on in some areas on building long terraces which crossed both cultivated land and *mangalata*, while in other areas terracing was neglected except when the administrative officer got the chief to prosecute those who did not turn up.

Unfortunately, there seems to have been no scientific assessment of the impact of the compulsory terracing, closure and grass-planting programmes on the *mangalata*. However, by 1954, the Annual Report, Southern Province reported considerable improvement:

> Four years ago standing on any hill top in Machakos provided a terrible spectacle of bare red land by the thousands of acres. The 'badlands' . . . amounted to two thirds of the total, were a desolation . . . Today a trip through the area presents a remarkable difference. Masii and Kiteta Locations, which were then amongst the worst, are now appreciably grass covered and the old '*Mangalata*' is hardly to be seen. Indeed, the pasture is still not capable of carrying much stock, but it is ground cover again . . . On all sides today bush clearing and paddocking can be seen and river valleys are being stabilised with napier grass. (Kenya, Agricultural Dept, Southern Province, 1954.)

In the period following the Swynnerton Plan, 1954–1962, there were far more agricultural officers and even stricter enforcement of closed grazing areas with cattle confined to roofed sheds. Today these lands have become private farms, part grazed, part cultivated and terraced (see Figure 11.3 and interviews later in this chapter). A 1981 survey in AEZ 4 found that 30%

FIGURE 11.3. Pastor Mutua and his farm, 1990, on land reclaimed from *mangalata* in the 1950s. (Photo: D. B. Thomas. Reproduced with permission)

of farmers claimed to have done some re-seeding of pasture (Meyers, 1981: 95). This suggests adoption of a 1950s technology of scratch ploughing and scattering seed encouraged by Peberdy (1992 pers. comm.).

Terrace technologies

Three types of conservation structure have been important in Machakos. In the story of each we can see government introduction (in at least one case supplemented by farmer introduction), farmer testing and adaptation, and farmer evaluation. The latter led to the selection of the bench terrace as the favourite for cultivated land, initially in the hills, and to the development of cut-off drains as water-harvesting structures.

Cut-off drains and infiltration ditches

Cut-off drains are used to divert excess run-off, and either convey it to a waterway for safe disposal, or encourage infiltration through increased detention time. The soil is thrown downhill to increase the size of the channel, thereby minimising overtopping. The channel should be vegetated (possibly with Star or Kikuyu grass), and the embankment can be planted with fodder grass or trees. Cut-off drains were observed on farms in Mbooni in 1937 (RH: Maher, 1937: 18).

Farmers give three reasons for the poor adoption of cut-off drains in the early days: their high labour requirements; taking land out of production; and the high maintenance cost of de-silting. Initially, cut-off drains were seen as run-off control structures. However, farmers in Masii were planting bananas in pits in such drains in 1948 (KNA: DC/MKS/8/5). Hughes Rice (Agricultural Officer, 1951–1953) subsequently promoted this practice[11] (Figure 11.4). Over time, farmers made more and more use of the cut-off drain for tree crops, as they have high soil fertility, owing to the trapping of nutrients washed from upslope. Farmers also soon realised that they can be used to lead water to the top of terrace systems, and improve water availability (Joseph Mutunga of Kilome, at Machakos workshop, 1991).

Narrow-based terraces

A contemporary sketch of the recommended types of terraces in 1948 is shown in Figure 11.5. Type 1 (shallow narrow-based) was recommended for African farms, while types 2 and 3 were for European farms. Type 4 (bench) was to be used only for high-value crops such as tea, coffee and vegetables on steep slopes, because of its high labour requirement. At the time, coffee and tea were European crops.

The narrow-based terrace has a channel behind the ridge formed by throwing the soil downslope (Figure 11.5), giving them their local name, *fanya chini* ('soil thrown down hill'). The channel could be either graded (to convey run-off at a safe velocity to a natural drain way or to a grassed strip) or level, for retaining water in the field. Although they used only half as much labour in construction as bench terraces, the ditches had to be de-silted prior to each season. The danger, particularly if they were constructed without a grade, as the note accompanying the sketch says was usually the case, was that in a heavy storm they would overtop, breaking the bank, and damaging other terraces below.

Many government officers continued to believe in this technology throughout the 1950s. Peberdy, DAO 1954–1961, was still recommending them in 1961:

(a)

(b)

FIGURE 11.4. Banana trenches, (a) 1952 and (b) 1990. The 1952 caption notes how the trench prevents wash from the road and hill-side destroying the terraced arable. Pastor Mutua's banana trench in 1990 is also trapping water from a small road near the farm; water infiltrating out of it will feed his recently planted coffee, which he is experimenting with although this is AEZ 4. (Photos: Kenya, ALUS, 1953, Crown Copyright, reproduced with permission of the Central Office of Information and D. B. Thomas)

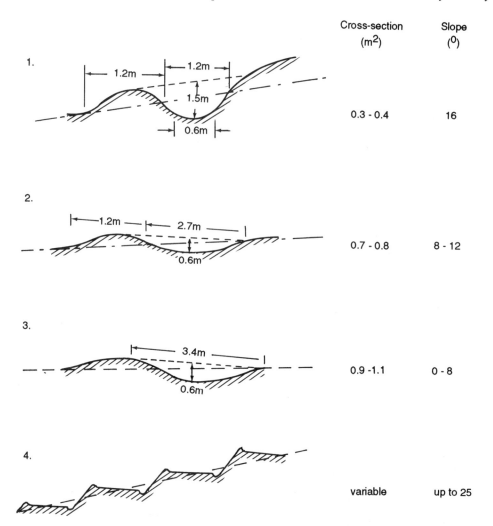

FIGURE 11.5. Types of terraces used in the 1940s. (Source: KNA: DC/MKS/8/5 Reconditioning)

Whilst benching must be the ultimate answer in all cultivated land narrow base is the next best provided they are properly constructed and grassed. In many places there is insufficient land for proper grass strip (i.e. half cultivation, half grass) and cattle would eat all the grass down and they would therefore be valueless during the rains. If sufficient pressure could be brought to get adequate grass strip and closure to grazing then it would be possible to get grassed narrow base terraces which would last and be more valuable. (Peberdy, 1961: 4).

The grass strip was wasted land from the farmer's viewpoint, since, to be effective, it provided no fodder. While the ditches collected and held some water, allowing it to infiltrate the soil, this benefit seems to have been mainly felt in the bank. Cowley noted 'It is commonly observed that plants grown on terrace banks withstand droughts for longer periods than those grown in the terraces' (KNA: Cowley, 1947/8). Farmers therefore did not grass the bank, but cultivated it, which made it easier for water to erode it (J. R. Peberdy, 1992, pers. comm.).

Bench terraces

- *Fanya juu terracing*: Throwing the soil uphill from the contour ditch, Fanya juu terracing has the great advantage of gradually leading to the formation of bench terraces (Type 4 in Figure 11.5). No land is wasted, the bank provides fodder and the rear ditch can be used for tree planting (Figures 11.3 and 11.4). They are also better at water conservation than the narrow-base since the ditch at the rear provides water to the terrace, not the bank. Benches are of three types:
- *Forward sloping terraces*: these reduce the slope, slowing the run-off and therefore the rate of erosion.[12] They are only a partial solution since some erosion between the embankments is likely to occur. With time, soil movement between embankments leads to the development of a level terrace. A terrace lip is required to pond the water, and a channel on the lower side of the embankment to contain any run-off that may over-top it.
- *Backward sloping terraces* accumulate run-off at the rear of the bench, thereby eliminating it completely. They are recommended in areas with deep permeable soil and where moisture conservation rather than water removal is of primary importance.
- *Level bench terraces* are relatively easy to construct where the natural slope is not great, as in the Machakos lowlands. They involve some loss of cultivable land in the highlands with steep slopes, unless the bank can be used for fodder.

From narrow-based to fanya juu terraces

Barnes thought that much of the ground was 'too steep to work without terraces of the true bench type' and that this could not be left to individual natives, since it would have to cover a section of hillside. He also thought 'many natives will not be fit to carry on cultivation on benched areas, and such people will have to be moved to cleared areas' (KNA: Barnes, 1937: 30). He thought narrow-based terraces could be used lower down the hillsides. He made an exception of the area around the Mission at Muisuni where 'the natives are probably the most progressive in the reserve ... of a type who will be able to work Bench terraced areas'. In 1937, Barnes and Maher saw preliminary pegging out of terrace lines in Muisuni and Iveti (KNA: Barnes, 1937: 41; RH: Maher, 1937: 17), supervised by Mr Hobbs, then the Agricultural Officer. Barnes later wrote:

> The first series of '*fanya juu*' were made in 1937 in a Machakos area but owing to the bank or burm not being kept up or maintained at the top of the step, they have not progressed into becoming true benches and in fact to some extent simply continue to erode on the slope and are very little flatter than when made twenty three years ago. (RH: Barnes, 1960: 63. Reproduced by permission of Rhodes House Library, Oxford.)

Mr J. Mwilu of Tala confirmed this when the site was visited in 1990, saying that benches with the soil thrown uphill were started in 1937 under the direction of Chief Uku. Since 1960 the terraces have developed into level benches with embankments 1.2−1.5 m high and a small lip at the top, planted with grass. The terraces were constructed between widely spaced cut-off drains, of which no signs remained in 1990 (Mr Mutunga, Muisuni, 1990, pers. comm.).

Maher had no preference initially as to the type of terrace, but after a visit to the USA in 1940 he made type 1, the shallow narrow-based, also called a contour ditch, the standard technology for compulsory terracing in the African reserves. He thought them most suitable because of the shortage of tools and their low labour requirement compared to bench terraces. Although he would have liked to integrate improved farming techniques into the programme, recognising the importance of promoting biological activity in the soil, in practice hard-pressed agricultural offers could only pursue narrow-based terracing (Throup, 1987).[13]

Officers of the Agricultural Department, including L. R. Brown, always believed the bench terrace was preferable to the narrow-based, but were not sufficiently senior to overrule Maher, who resigned only in 1951 (Throup, 1987). The narrow-based was sometimes queried, including by the Member for Agriculture in 1948.[14] In the same year the Agricultural Officer in Machakos told the Reconditioning Committee that haphazard terracing by untrained people without sufficient technical advice might do more harm than good, but the DC and other members thought that it would be disastrous to stop the communal work.[15] There were certainly problems with washouts in heavy rains.[16] There are references in agricultural files to inadequate terrace maintenance, numerous breaks in banks and silting of ditches. In March 1952, for example, there was 'a further decline in communal effort . . . even cleaning out of terraces preparatory to the Long Rains has been neglected' (KNA: DAO/MKS/1/88). According to our informants in 1990, people did not maintain the terraces because they broke so easily; their labour was wasted.

However, the alternative bench terrace was a technology whose time had come, and its reintroduction may have had more than one source. It was associated with vegetables, and it would seem that the expanding market for these and the attractive profits provided the first incentive, and that it was later also used for staple crops. In 1949, the DC drew attention to some progressive farmers, including: 'Chania of Kalama who has made bench terraces (copying what he saw in India) and grows onions' (KNA: DC/MKS/Annual Report 1949).

Another story in Kangundo is that a farmer misunderstood instructions, threw the soil uphill, and found that he had better results than his neighbours. In February 1952 it was noted that 1425 yards (1 yard = 0.914 m) of bench terraces had been constructed, 'mostly in Mbooni, where this latter method is regarded with growing favour'. In August 'bench terraces were really catching on, especially in Kangundo and Mbooni. News was getting round of big money being made by some Kangundo cultivators. One told the ADC he had sold Ksh 5000 worth of tomatoes from his smallish benched shamba!' (KNA:DAO/MKS/1/88). The DAO then turned paid gangs on to constructing bench terraces in the Iveti hills as demonstrations. He referred to it as the New Method brought from Nyeri (where L. R. Brown was introducing bench terracing).[17] The paid gangs were closed down at the end of 1952, but the DAO reported that 'quite a few ex-gang employees are now making benches for themselves'.

In 1953, 94 km of bench terraces were recorded, still small in comparison with the 4300 km of narrow-base terraces constructed by communal labour in the same year. By 1956 their lengths were nearly equal. In 1958, 4300 km of benches were constructed, compared to 1750 km of narrow-base. By this time, much of the terracing was done by *mwethya* groups (see Chapter 9). These were not directed by chiefs but made their own programmes and were hosted by the farmer on whose field the work was done, who provided food (Kalama informant, 1990). Bench terraces were voluntary, popular, and competitively built by different clans. Informants insisted that this type of terrace was always maintained, whereas official figures show that the number of narrow-based terraces falling into disrepair grew each year, by 1958 being double the number of new constructions. Consequently, the number of adequately protected cultivated farms fell drastically, and within the adequately protected area, the proportion with bench terraces increased, as shown in Figure 11.6.

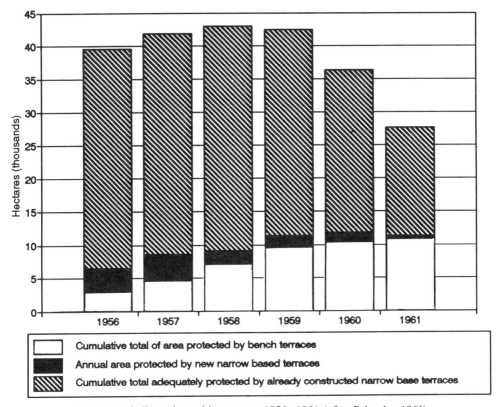

FIGURE 11.6. Terracing achievements, 1956–1961 (after Peberdy, 1961)

The Betterment approach

Hughes Rice developed a new Betterment Plan in 1951 which could be put into operation as new funding became available under the Swynnerton Plan. This financed more staff for closer supervision of the reconditioning programme, and encouragement of increased commercial participation by the African farmer, also closely supervised. The emphasis was on individual farm development and the recognition of individual land rights (see Chapter 5). A model farm was established at Ngelani,[18] which included market gardening and fruit growing. The introduction of coffee in limited areas of the highlands resulted in better soil and water conservation because coffee growers were required to plant in pits on benched land, and because improved returns encouraged and enabled farmer investment. Farmers later adopted these planting techniques for oranges in the dryer areas (Figure 14.1). This period saw the beginning of a true extension system, which expanded as more trained divisional staff became available (see Chapter 15).

In 1957 the ALDEV Annual Report claimed that 'with the already progressive locations forging ahead, and the laggards . . . beginning to show signs of awakening', terracing, manuring, cattle sheds, stall-feeding and paddocking were going ahead and fodder crop production was beginning. Streams flowed for longer than for 15 years previously (1957 had good rains).

From 1959 onwards the interest of the Akamba turned to political activity in the build up to Independence, achieved in 1963. Officials had to reduce their pressure, and were switched into duties such as preparations for elections. They were disheartened by the slackening conservation effort as shown in Figure 11.6, and the lack of 'discipline'. As already noted in Chapter 2, a report in the mid 1960s implied that the programme had only been very partially successful (de Wilde, 1967).

SOIL CONSERVATION BY THE FARMER, 1960–1978

By 1961, the area conserved by both types of terrace had fallen to 27 000 ha, compared with a peak of 42 000 ha in 1958 (Figure 11.6). The cultivated area was about 110 000 ha. In the short rains of 1961, much damage was done by abnormally heavy rainfall. Officially, compulsion was ruled out, with what observers regarded as a devastating effect. Closed grazing areas were re-opened, and red 'sores', the forerunners of serious erosion, began to reappear in 1962–1963 (Heyer, 1966: 25). Figure 11.7 shows deteriorated terracing in Kilungu, circa 1964. (The photograph was taken by Owako to illustrate achievements in terracing under the ALDEV programme).

Agricultural staff were cut back (Mbogoh, 1991). They concentrated on farmer training and extension programmes; and grazing controls, soil and water conservation and controlled settlement largely ceased (Lynam, 1978: 62, writing of 1974). Officials periodically recorded large numbers of narrow-based terraces and grass strips (Gichuki, 1991: 49), but surveys carried out in the 1970s made no mention of them. Our own informants all recollected that benching began again,

FIGURE 11.7. Terracing in Kilungu, 1964. Although this was taken to illustrate 'post World War II achievements in soil conservation', it clearly shows the decay of narrow-based terraces, and other areas where *fanya juu* have been installed. (Photo: F. N. Owako, 1969. Reproduced with permission)

on a voluntary basis, from the mid-1960s, either using hired labour or voluntary *mwethya* groups, mainly on arable land. They agreed that narrow-based terraces were generally abandoned. The activity in terracing is confirmed by air photos (Chapter 5) and by farmers interviewed in 1990.

Examples of such private initiatives in farm conservation follow:[19]

(1) In Kangundo (AEZ 2/3), a coffee farmer said that his original terraces developed between widely spaced cut-off drains on bare *mangalata*. Afterwards, bench terraces were constructed in between them.

(2) Mr Musyoki, in Mbiuni (AEZ 3/4), had constructed and maintained impressive terraces. The terrace banks were stabilised by beating them when wet to compact the soil. They had become very hard like sun-dried bricks. The bank height was about 1.2 m and the bank angle about 75°. There was a sufficient lip to prevent overtopping.

(3) In Kalama (AEZ 4) a large farmer said that his father, who worked for the MOA, settled in the early 1950s, with a farm of 40 ha on east-facing slopes. The denuded grazing land was reclaimed by *fanya juu*, cultivating and reseeding. The terraces were constructed in the 1970s, mainly by hired labour. A neighbour has not reclaimed his east-facing slope, which is still denuded grazing, because he has concentrated resources on improving his west-facing slopes. Here he has his cultivated land where he has converted the narrow-based terraces built in the 1950s to *fanya juu* benches. Farmers know that the western and eastern slopes differ in rainfall and soil.

(4) Pastor Mutua's mother recollected that their farm had been part of a *mangalata* area closed to grazing. A *mwethya* group planted star grass. Later, they terraced it mainly by their own efforts but with some help from *mwethya*. The benches shown in Figure 11.3 had been financed by the sale of goats and sheep. The farm was 3.6 ha, half cultivated and half grazed.

(5) In Makueni (AEZ 4/5), where slopes are more gentle, some farmers still use *fanya chini*. A farmer who arrived in 1960, and bought a 12 ha farm, had hired labour to help his family build *fanya chini* in 1979. A woman farmer with 7 ha still had the *fanya chini* constructed by tractor in colonial times, some of which had developed into grass strips, but maintenance was poor, due to shortage of labour. However, most farmers prefer *fanya juu*. A farmer who settled in 1963, and acquired 30 ha, later hired tractors to make *fanya juu*. Before his area was demarcated in 1980, he said that there was communal grazing, which had led to the depletion of vegetation. Rilling began along farm boundaries, if these were also cattle tracks or roads. He had used check dams of stone and napier grass to control gullies on his own farm.

(6) In Ngwata (AEZ 5) erosion started soon after farmers settled there in the 1960s, especially on grazing land. People from the older areas of Machakos began constructing *fanya chini* with *mwethya* groups. About 1976, they changed to *fanya juu* because of siltation problems. By 1983, most farmers had terraced their farms.

Immigrants brought terracing technology from the hills.[20] Thus, one farmer, who arrived in 1968, had well laid out *fanya juu* and said he learnt from his father at Kimutwa. He was still developing his farm; having planted *Cassia siamea* round his homestead, his next intention was to plant it along his boundaries. Another man acquired a small farm of 2.6 ha as a reward for helping a relative clear land in 1969–1971. Unlike some in the area, he has been able to get extension advice on the layout of his terraces, which were constructed by a *mwethya* group. In November 1989, he laid out a trash line to reduce the terrace width, and this reduced soil loss. He used stone checks, bush cuttings and planted *Eragrostis superba* in one gully and napier grass and sugar cane in a second one. He used *Panicum maximum* to stabilise his banks, and planted *Eragrostis superba, Cenchrus ciliaris* and *Cynodon dactylon* on denuded grazing land.

(7) Mr Kavoi started clearing his farm in Ngwata in 1965. When he began terracing in 1970 he was initially criticised for following colonial practices, but he is now a recognised authority and other people ask his help in laying out terraces. He has 3.3 ha under crops and 1.67 ha under grazing. He finished his well-made terraces in 1978. They have a lip at the front edge, but occasionally, if the rains are heavy, he may make a hole in the embankment to drain out surplus water safely. He has used various grasses to stabilise the embankment, and finds *Makarikari* the least competitive with his crop. He has a small patch of valley bottom land which he irrigates.

During this period, the scale of operation was the individual farm (even when *mwethya* labour was used), in contrast to the schemes imposed on a whole ridge or group of farms in the earlier period. It is clear, both from air photographs and the evidence of interviews, that a remarkable turn-around occurred in the attitudes of farmers to terrace construction during this period, and in their ability to make private investments in conservation. From 1960 to 1975 there were few Department of Agriculture soil and water conservation staff in the District.

GOVERNMENT AND DONOR-SUPPORTED PROGRAMMES, 1978–1990

Government programmes

The drought of 1975 led to renewed awareness of the need to conserve the natural environment, and the Government began to increase the availability of trained manpower, and to seek increased financial support externally. By 1990, the soil and water conservation service in the District was adequately staffed at senior level[21] although sometimes those trained were not in appropriate jobs. During the period 1983–1987, it was necessary to plan catchment conservation to protect new dams, which required high skills. The efforts of the Department of Agriculture were complemented by the Permanent Presidential Commission of Soil Conservation and Afforestation. There are Presidential soil conservation sites scattered throughout the country. In Machakos District the Mwanyani site was started in 1982, Uuni in 1984 and Masinga in 1985. These are demonstration sites of gully control, cut-off drains and terraces, fodder establishment, afforestation and pasture reclamation on badly eroded land.

The Swedish International Development Agency (SIDA) began to support soil and water conservation in the Ministry from 1974, and began field work in Kangundo Division of Machakos in 1978. It supported the construction of cut-off drains and terraces with food for work schemes, and assisted *mwethya* groups through the provision of tools. It concentrated on the AEZ 2 and 3 areas of the Division, where its activities have contributed significantly to the control of soil and run-off losses on farms that had not previously been terraced.[22] SIDA's method is a 'whole farm' approach using voluntary labour, agreed farm plans, and technical assistance.

The Machakos Integrated Development Programme (MIDP), 1978–1988 (Chapter 15), adopted the SIDA 'whole farm' approach whereby unpaid labour was supplied for on-farm work, but hired labour was provided for external works such as gully control and cut-off drains (ODI, 1982: Chapter 9). It was found that paying for cut-off drains led to their being built in an ill-considered way, and that providing training for low level government staff was not having much of a multiplier effect. A community development approach was adopted and worked well in the period 1980−1982 (ODI, 1982). The MIDP employed 40 soil conservation supervisors to train farmers' own leaders in the use of line levels and the layout of structures, aiming to generate self-help. The provision of hand tools made the *mwethya* group activities more effective and were an important incentive.[23] By 1984, the MIDP had also established catchment protection activities in every sub-location of the District, which included the demonstration of pasture rehabilitation, afforestation, gully control, and the promotion of roof water harvesting. There was also a massive campaign aimed at publicising the need for soil and water conservation through the use of films and slide shows, showing various methodologies for achieving it through using the *Leucaena* tree in agroforestry, gully control, and terracing. Some of the farmers interviewed in 1990 recalled the impact that the films had on their perceptions of soil erosion and conservation. Others credited the programme with having enlightened their children.

Non-governmental organisations

NGOs have contributed to soil and water conservation activities, particularly since the drought of 1984. NGOs active in the District include the Catholic Diocese of Machakos, the Institute of Cultural Affairs, the Green Belt Movement, ActionAid, AMREF, World Neighbours, the National Council of Christians of Kenya, and the Kenya Institute of Organic Farming. Their main activities in natural resource management include the promotion of conservation and organic farming, tree nurseries, gully control and water supply. They have supported community mobilisation for self help, and provided financial assistance for minor rehabilitation works and the promotion of better farming (Kaluli, 1992). They work mainly with *mwethya* groups.

Family effort

Despite the extent of governmental, donor-supported and NGO programmes, most farmers we met insisted that their terraces had been built by themselves, often using hired labour, sometimes assisted by a *mwethya* group. We were concentrating on the older farmers, and it could well be that younger and newer farmers needed help in building or renewing terraces in the 1980s, when agricultural prices were more depressed than in the 1970s (see Chapter 6). However, in the period 1981−1985 half the new terraces are likely to have been constructed without external

TABLE 11.2. Conservation works and agency support, representative years 1981−1985 (km)

		Terraces		
	Cut-off drains	Bench or *fanya juu*	Narrow-based	All types
SIDA (1982)	447	1167	379	1546
MIDP (1984)	350			2035
RC Diocese (1985)				1075
Total agencies, per year				4656
Average per year for district, 1981−1985[1]				8500

[1]Ecosystems (1985/1986), Vol. 4, Table 2.15

TABLE 11.3. Progress in soil conservation (%), 1981−1985 (after Ecosystems, 1985/6: Vol. 4, Tables 2.14, 2.15, reproduced by permission of Ecosystems Ltd, Nairobi)

		Slope classes[1]				
	Flat	Gently undulating	Undulating	Rolling	Hilly	All classes
Percentage of arable land with some conservation measures[2]						
in 1981	44	57	78	89	92	69
in 1985	49	84	88	95	97	85
Improvement 1985−1981	11	47	13	7	5	23
Percentage of conservation requirements achieved[3]						
in 1981	22	35	61	38	23	36
in 1985	40	67	83	57	30	54
Increase per annum in terraces and bunds	41.7	27.3	10.4	16.1	10.1	15.0

[1]Defined by the Kenya Soil Survey
[2]Terraces, bunds and other field dividers
[3]Based on Ministry of Agriculture recommendations for arable land of the respective slope classes

assistance. Table 11.2 shows that an average of 8500 km of terraces were constructed per year, of which about 4600 km were constructed with donor or NGO support. This compares with a peak rate of about 5000 km per year in the 1950s.

The most rapid progress was on undulating and quietly undulating land, which includes most of the areas in AEZs 4 and 5/6 which were settled after 1960. But the largest percentage of arable land having some conservation measures was in the older settled rolling and hilly areas. According to a technical measure of conservation requirements, 54% of the District's arable was adequately conserved in 1985, and in undulating areas, no less than 83% (Table 11.3).

The state of conservation in 1990

In 1990, *fanya juu* terrace construction was the most common method. In many areas it had progressed to a forward-sloping, level or backward-sloping terrace. In the relatively flatter semi-arid areas, ridge-and-furrow tillage systems complemented *fanya juu* terraces. Table 11.4, based on our own limited survey and the work done by Muya (1990), shows the dominance of the bench terrace in its various forms. Most of the few narrow-based channel terraces were found on shallow soils with slopes of 5−20%. These terraces showed signs of silting and in some cases of overtopping. Some embankments were protected using sown grass, but most had sparsely populated self-sown grasses and weeds. The owners often expressed interest in changing to *fanya juu*.

There exist many variations of the *fanya juu* structure and the utilisation of land around it, including the grassed or non-grassed embankment, channel on lower side, banana and other fruit tree pits on lower side. Embankment protection is identified by farmers as the main maintenance requirement. The common practice is to build up the embankment to ensure that there is sufficient run-off storage to reduce the risk of overtopping. The condition of terrace embankments varies, but most of them are in fair condition. Maintenance costs, like construction costs, are a function of the height of the terraces. The original cost of a terrace rising 1.5 m from a ditch 80 cm wide and 40 cm deep on its other side was Ksh 20 per metre (financed

TABLE 11.4. Types of terraces, 1980–1990

Terrace type	Number of Terraces			Percentage
	Muya	ODI	Total	
Narrow-based channel	7	5	12	2
Broad-based channel	8	—	8	2
Bench terraces				
Fanya juu	143	24	167	33
Forward sloping	240	20	260	52
Level bench	37	6	43	9
Backward sloping	8	5	13	2
Total	443	60	503	100

Source: Muya (1990); ODI: this study, 1990

by the sale of goats and sheep), and the annual cost of maintenance Ksh 4 per metre (1990 prices). Only well-off farmers using hired labour have an effective maintenance programme, coupled with high value cropping (mangoes, citrus, pawpaws, vegetables, etc). While most of the terraces observed were effective for controlling soil movement and run-off, in a few areas the results are disappointing. Absence of maintenance has led to some rills in terraced land, particularly in the lower benches.

Some cut-off drains are inadequate to handle large storms. Poorly laid or maintained drains lead to gully erosion as a result of poor outlet conditions, low spots within the drain and blockage. Channel silting occurs in some. Cropping in the trenches, although beneficial, seems to reduce the conveyance and storage capacity of the terrace, thereby leaving it susceptible to overflowing through the low and weak spots.

THE ECONOMICS OF TERRACING

SIDA has promoted studies of the economics of *fanya juu* terraces in Kangundo Division. The analysis is not easy because of the difficulties in finding matched pairs of terraced and unterraced fields in the same ecological area. Within each group, yields show a large range, due to the many variants involved, such as type of seed used, manuring or fertilising practice, planting date, use of family labour and management. Further, results vary according to circumstances in each year. In one observed season (1984–5), the short rains were very good, but farmers were extremely short of seed, especially bean seed, and of manure and cash, because of droughts in the previous three seasons. Differences between terraced and unterraced farms were only significant in the drier AEZ 4, where the maize mean yield was 1854 kg/ha on terraced and 1047 kg/ha on unterraced land. In AEZ 2/3, where water was plentiful that season, there was only a small and statistically insignificant increase on terraced land. Effects of manuring were also very noticeable but the sample was too small to produce statistically significant results between terraced and unterraced land, each with or without manure (Figueiredo, 1986). A repeat of the tests in the long rains of 1987, on most of the same farms (some had in the meantime been terraced), in rains which were substantially below average, showed terraced farms gaining an income of Ksh 4050 per ha and non-terraced Ksh 2606. This had no statistical significance, due to the great variations within the groups (Holmgren and Johannson, 1987). Taken together,

TABLE 11.5. Economic value of soil conservation for farmers (Ksh/farm)

	1. Farm without soil conservation	2. Average soil conservation practices	3. Superior soil conservation practices
Total revenue	7 550	12 187	14 732
Variable costs			
Food crops	853	853	853
Soil conservation crops	—	170	230
Total variable costs	853	1 023	1 083
Gross margin	6 697	11 164	13 649
Annualized costs			
Investment in soil conservation	—	165	165
Gross margin minus annualized investment (net return)	6 697	10 999	13 484
Labour requirement (person-days)			
Cultivation	585	636	692
Soil conservation work	—	45	45
Total labour requirement	585	681	737
Net return for person-day of labour	11.44	16.15	18.29

Source: Holmberg (1990) (Reproduced by permission of Earthscan Publications Ltd.)

results suggest large benefits from terracing in dry years in AEZs 2 and 3 and in all years in AEZ 4. Data for a third season, the short rains of 1987–1988, were also collected and the results weighted by the frequency of the rainfall pattern. This gave an average increase of 400 kg/ha for maize and 77 kg/ha for beans in favour of terracing (Lindgren, 1988).

A better study was carried out in the neighbouring Kitui District in an AEZ 4 area with about 65% of its arable on *fanya juu* terraces. The observed seasons were the short rains of 1984 and 1985, whose untypicality has been noted. However, farmers were also questioned to obtain an estimate of more normal production and costs. This is shown in Table 11.5. This study included the annualised costs of the investment in the construction of terraces, and the labour requirement for maintenance. It shows clearly both the higher labour requirements on well conserved farms, and the higher net return per person day, resulting in a much higher annual revenue (Holmberg, 1990). (Due to the great variation in farmer practices the best way to obtain sound data on the benefits of terracing, with and without manure, and on its effect on water available to the crops, would be field trials in a research farm situation. However, most trials of water conservation effects at Katumani experimental station have been done on tillage methods rather than terracing.)

CONCLUSIONS

The degradation problem feared in the 1930s has been reversed. The long history of conservation interventions in the District has created a favourable environment for attaining sustainable agriculture. There has been a long-term political, social, economic and technical commitment to soil and water conservation. The results of this commitment include an impressive increase in conserved land according to several indicators.

Widespread investment in benching was facilitated by its profitability for high value crops, and its demonstrated superiority for maize yields in dry years and dry areas. Food-for-work and tools-for-work have helped poorer farmers achieve terraces through *mwethya* groups, but hired labour has been used by those with the necessary resources, some of which have come from off-farm work or through the sale of livestock. Credit has played very little part in the conservation story.

Soil moisture conditions under conservationary management are under-researched. It is likely that improved soil moisture, especially during growing seasons with below-average rainfall, is mainly responsible for the yield superiority commonly observed on well terraced fields. However, benefits from manure placement will also be superior in such conditions.

Well designed, constructed and maintained terraces can control run-off and soil loss, but, if they are poorly constructed and maintained, run-off passes from one to the next, and embankment breakage and rilling damage increase downslope. Bench terraces cost twice as much to construct as narrow-based terraces. Although they need regular maintenance, they do not need desilting twice a year. It is important to offer farmers a choice of technologies (*fanya juu*, narrow-based, trash lines, etc.) so that they can make a choice, given the great variation in family circumstances and in micro-ecological conditions. Farmers have not made much use of cheaper and easier methods of erosion control such as trash lines or leaving crop residues as a protective mulch, because of the greater value of the materials for livestock feed.

Doubts about security of title in the 1940s impeded acceptance of terracing, and may have delayed it on newly settled Crown Land in the 1960s and 1970s. Public control of communal grazing land was a failure compared with the development of private smallholdings, with a mixture of terraced arable and private grazing.

Farmers in the newly settled areas neglected soil conservation at first, partly because land was plentiful, and partly because they had more urgent investments to make in housing, land clearance, demarcation, purchase of stock, etc. In recent years, the delay between first settlement and the establishment of terraces has shortened and the various programmes promoted by NGOs and MIDP in these areas have probably assisted the poorer farmer. Improved capacity of the technical and community mobilisation staff added impetus to soil and water conservation activities in the 1980s, but in 1990 informants said that soil conservation efforts were slowing down. This was said to be partly due to the fact that the most important works had been done, and partly to the scarcity of tools, a reflection of the economic depression of the time.

NOTES

1 Ploughing, manuring and weeding also improve moisture supply to the crop (see Chapter 3.6). Residue management (e.g. trash lines) protects bare soil, but residues may have greater value for feeding livestock.
2 Literature review, including archival material, was supplemented by traverses of farms in the study areas, and on-farm interviews by Donald Thomas and Francis Gichuki, undertaken between August and December 1990 (see Gichuki, 1991).
3 The Administration's hesitation was eventually overcome by proponents of destocking, supported by Elspeth Huxley (1937) whose furious advocacy included calling out the troops, if necessary.
4 This was partly achieved through successful lobbying at Westminster with the help of an Indian lawyer, and partly because of the Administration's realisation that the discontent might spread to the police and army, in which the Akamba were already numerous (Newman, 1974).
5 Droughts in Machakos are frequently called 'unprecedented'; Table 3.3 shows a severe drought in the short rains of 1939, but not the worst on record.
6 Barnes refers to 'Matingulu'. He includes the Muisuni mission area, which is now in Kangundo Location.

7   Between 1952 and 1957, the mechanical unit had terraced 5595 ha at an expenditure (personal emoluments and running cost) of K£116 740 and a capital cost of K£32 705. This compares with an estimated cost of K£8000 per annum for providing levellers and tools to assist 500 *utuis* (KNA: 3/Agri/1/29: Note on Reconditioning Policy, Machakos District. DC Howard, May, 1949). The DC noted it was cheap because communal labour was free. (While it was free to the Government, it had, of course, an opportunity cost for the people concerned.)

8   Major Joyce started farming in Machakos in 1912 and was distinguished by his early interest in conservation work, and his keen support for good farming in the Reserve. His daughter, Anne Joyce, who continued farming from his death in 1959 till her retirement in 1985, told us he kept in touch with US developments. Barnes noted he had terraced the lands of his squatters in 1939. Miss Joyce died in 1991.

9   This shows that Matungulu people were aware of a campaign by former soldiers in Muranga'a District (the colonial Fort Hall), which began in 1946, and which used the local vernacular press to condemn female communal labour. Kenyatta took up the issue in a speech in Muranga'a on 20 July 1947, leading the following day to a women's strike (Throup, 1987: 151–152). Touring notes are in KNA: DC/MKS/8/5.

10 Throup (1987) noted that chiefs in Kikuyu country were judged by their soil conservation progress, and during the war good performance was rewarded by access to lucrative licences and permits, much resented by the returning soldiers. The same presumably also applied in Machakos.

11 M. Wallis, 1991, pers. comm.; who thought, however, that this was an original idea of Hughes Rice. The archival record shows it to have been already in practice by some farmers.

12 In a 1977 letter to Donald Thomas, Leslie Brown wrote that he thought the fundamental objection to the narrow-base terrace was that it *increases* mean slope, and, hence, velocity of run-off (his underlining).

13 Cowley (KNA: Cowley, 1947/8) explicitly recognised this, stating '. . . no single factor such as relief of population, grass planting or terracing will provide a cure. Fundamentally the biological processes in the soil will have much to do with the success of reconditioning and it is the general interaction of factors which, on balance, promote the suitable conditions for biological activity that is of consequence.'

14 Mitchell created an incipient Ministerial system, with Members of the legislature having special responsibilities. The Member for Agriculture and Natural Resources was Cavendish Bentinck, a leading white settler. His letter has not been found, but was debated by the Reconditioning Committee.

15 He was told that trained African staff were available to give advice. The DC said that it would be disastrous if doubts were now thrown on the value of terracing '. . . the meeting concurred that the communal terracing just established should continue' (KNA: DC/MKS/12/2/1). The terraces were laid out by 19 Agricultural Instructors paid by the African District Council, with the assistance of 116 levellers, but there was at this stage only one Agricultural Officer and one Assistant Soil Conservation Officer.

16 F. D. H. Weldon, in a letter to *African Field and Farm*, 1950, said for this reason reported achievements were greatly exaggerated; Peberdy's later reports, however, give figures for both terraces built and terraces lapsing.

17 In a 1977 letter to Donald Thomas, Brown wrote: '. . . the narrow base terrace was forced down our throats by Colin Maher and enthusiastically supported by e.g. Tom Hughes Rice . . . . It was not until I became P.A.O. in Nyeri in 1953 that I was able to fight Colin Maher successfully on this point; and as you know the bench terrace became the standard form of soil conservation generally thereafter.' His recollection of dates seems faulty.

18 Ngelani was one of the disputed land areas. According to Akamba witnesses to the Carter Commission, they had originally given the land to a mission. The missionary later sold it to a white settler. The Administration hoped to cure the long-running resentment of this by making it a DAO model farm 'for the benefit of the Akamba people'.

19 The sources are interviews conducted in 1990 by D. B. Thomas and F. N. Gichuki.

20 The official fear has always been that immigrants from the hills will bring unsuitable technologies to the semi-arid lowlands.

21 However, Mwenge (1988: 38) reported that sometimes those who had undertaken postgraduate training in soil conservation were assigned to other duties.

22 Harrison (1987) credits SIDA with much of the improvement in Machakos. This does not give the correct credit to what farmers had achieved earlier. Our air-photo evidence shows the amount of terracing accomplished throughout the District by 1978 when the SIDA programme started in one Division (Figure 5.1).

23 The programme was disrupted when the Training and Visit extension system was introduced, as many of the soil conservation supervisors did not qualify to become technical assistants, and were dismissed in 1986 (Mwenge, 1988).

12

Water Conservation[1]

INTRODUCTION

The most limiting resource in Machakos District as a whole always has been, and still is, water. The rainfall is characterised by temporal and spatial variability from season to season and year to year (Chapter 3). There are some perennial rivers including the Athi, Kiboko and others, but most are seasonal. Groundwater is limited in most basins (Kenya, Ministry of Water Development, 1991).

As water is a year-round necessity for people and livestock, its availability influences the nature and extent of human settlement and grazing patterns. Increased population pressure, however, has forced people to settle in the areas where the labour costs of obtaining water in the dry season are high (Figure 12.1(a)). Water developments have opened up new areas, but their high cost and ever increasing demand mean that water is the main constraint not only to agricultural development, but also to rural services and industries. The water requirements of plant production are far higher than those of people and animals, but they are seasonal and largely dependent on rainfall.

IMPROVING WATER AVAILABILITY FOR PLANT PRODUCTION

1930–1960

The total amount and temporal distribution of rainfall determine the sowing period, the periods of sufficient soil moisture and of moisture deficit, crop yields and crop production risk. Water conservation activities aim at increasing water availability and efficiency in its use. Although the political emphasis had at first been solely on soil conservation (Chapter 11), by the 1950s extension officers in Machakos were teaching that terraces conserved water as well as soil (Peberdy, 1961; de Wilde, 1967).[2]

Water conservation was first sought to re-establish cover on the denuded communal grazing areas in the Reserve. The experiments in Mbooni in the early 1930s, using rip-ploughing, accompanied by grass planting or natural regeneration, on land that was closed to grazing, have been described in Chapter 11. Records show 1000–3000 ha planted annually in the period 1940–1944. Pole-Evans (1939) recommended pasture research as a priority in Kenya, and Cowley (KNA: Cowley, 1947/8) was adamant that large-scale work on pasture restoration should not be undertaken without further experimentation on management. This was endorsed in official policy, although in fact terracing and/or scratch-ploughing on pastureland went ahead, with 2000–4500 ha prepared for planting annually, 1949–1957. (The plan to terrace all arable land with communal labour by 1952 and to encourage grass planting on the *mangalata* in the lower areas were therefore described in the DC's 1949 Reconditioning Policy guideline as *palliative* or *salvage* work (to be continued without waiting for research results.)

At the same time, research on methods of pasture management was being carried out on an area known as the Makaveti square mile. This land (63 ha) was loaned[3] to the Department of Agriculture by its owners, in a condition described as badly overgrazed and eroded (Pereira and Beckley, 1952). Notwithstanding two drought years (1949 and 1950), effective grass cover had been achieved by the short rains of 1950 and grazing could recommence. It was shown that the infiltration rate improved when the soil surface crust was broken. The best pastures were obtained by contour ploughing and ridging, with the incorporation of a small dressing of cattle manure. Ploughing and ridging conserve moisture, but deep ripping did not assist in grass establishment under low rainfall conditions. It demonstrated that irrevocable loss of soil fertility had not occurred, and that temporary closure and intensive management could restore a grassland visibly more productive than that outside the fence. After 10 years, however, neither the fertility nor the structure of the soil benefitted significantly from the long grass ley. Such management may not have been an economic option for smallholders. The returns per acre from animal production on the restored grassland were less than half those of crop production (Pereira et al, 1961).

In the meantime, water conservation and pasture rehabilitation were based, as far as we can see, on the earlier experiments and on those made by European settlers on the dry ranchlands. In 1946, Captain Wilson, one of the European settlers, carried out ripping experiments on grassland which shattered the soil to a depth of 50 cm, with the objective of improving water penetration and allowing plant roots to extend to deeper zones. The yield of *Cenchrus ciliaris* was 20 times higher than on untreated land. This method was expensive, and other European farmers had established grass cover using ox-drawn ploughs (KNA: Cowley, 1947/8?). The main method used on the thousands of acres annually prepared for grass replanting seems to have been scratch ploughing (making a shallow furrow without the share) which trapped enough water for seed germination (Brown in a letter to Thomas, 1977; Peberdy, 1992, pers. comm.). Narrow-base terraces were also used. Records are patchy, since pasture management was something of a no-man's land falling between the agricultural and livestock staff.

Fallow ley was being practised by some European farmers in the 1940s as a moisture conservation practice. They also normally planted only in the long rains, to utilise water stored in the soil from the short rains. In the more crowded parts of the Reserve this was already not feasible, and Cowley noted that peasant farmers were unwilling to risk losing what might be a possible crop.

Crop residue management had a positive impact on water conservation through improving infiltration, the water-holding capacity of the soil, and reducing evapotranspiration. This technique was well adapted for high value crops (coffee and vegetables), then grown mainly on European farms, but on small farms residues were already needed for fodder.

1960–1990

Pasture research was included in the mandate of the Katumani experimental station when it was established in 1956, though activity was on a small scale and seems to have been subsidiary to plant breeding and general crop husbandry (Kenya, DoA, 1956; Thomas, 1956). (It was later upgraded to a National Dryland Research Station.) In 1961 the station started trials on soil moisture utilisation by crops under low rainfall conditions. Soil and water conservation research has included work on tillage systems, erosion and control methods and the reclamation of degraded lands. Most research programmes have been confined to the station, but there have also been on-farm trials which aimed at testing techniques under the farmers' operating environment, both to determine their performance and to promote acceptance. In view of the importance of understanding soil moisture regimes under various conservational practices (and especially terracing), it is surprising that little research has been attempted on quantifying the dimensions of these regimes. This lacuna is not confined to Kenya, but is international (Norman Hudson, 1992, pers. comm.).

During this period, water conservation activities extended both in the number of techniques used, and in levels of farmer adoption (see Chapter 10). Improved methods such as dry tillage catch the first rains and store the water; ridge tillage forms furrows that increase surface water retention, thereby reducing run-off, and increasing infiltration; and mulch tillage retains surface vegetative cover, to reduce raindrop impact and evaporation. Figure 7.2 shows some of these in use. The use of farmyard manure as compost improves soil water-holding capacity and soil fertility, and increases water use efficiency. Water harvesting methods capture roadside run-off, and permit the intensive cultivation of cut-off drains and infiltration ditches and use of banana pits (Figure 11.4). Modifications of the cropping system can also increase the efficiency of water use by plants. Such methods include timely planting and optimal planting density, the use of drought-evading and drought-resistant crops, crop rotation and fallowing, intercropping, relay planting and weed control.

Stewart (1980) drew the following lessons from experimental research:

(i) the earlier the onset of the rains, the better the chances of a good rainfall;
(ii) the land should be cultivated and planted as quickly as the rains or soil conditions permit;
(iii) maize should not be planted in the short rains if the onset of rains is after 23 November nor in the long rains if the onset is after 3 April; and
(iv) mid-season adjustments can be made.

He developed recommendations for 'response farming' of maize in the short and long rains. They were not adopted for the following reasons (our interviews, 1992):

(i) complexity in implementing because of lack of rainfall data at farm level, the high requirement of extension input and farmers' views on production risk management;
(ii) farmers' reluctance to change their traditional methods of crop management;
(iii) the recommendations were based on a maize monoculture whereas farmers also practise intercropping;
(iv) mid-season adjustment involves a waste of seed and scarce labour resources.

IMPROVING WATER AVAILABILITY FOR DOMESTIC AND LIVESTOCK USE

Long walking distances to fetch water seriously constrain the productivity of women, who are the major providers of labour for agricultural production (see Figure 12.1). This is particularly

FIGURE 12.1. (a) Carrying water home, near the Kambu river, AEZ 5, August 1990. (b) A hand pump supplied by the African Medical Research Foundation (AMREF) in Kibwezi Division, typical of NGO programmes. (Photos: D. B. Thomas, reproduced with permission)

so during peak demand periods. Reducing walking distances for livestock conserves the energy for meat or milk production. Where watering paths are shortened or eliminated (particularly where there is a danger of gully erosion developing) there is also indirect soil conservation.

Only 65 earth dams are reported to have been constructed by 1940 (KNA, DC/MKS/8/3). This was probably due to the low level of government intervention in water supply which may be attributed to the low demand for urban water, self-sufficiency on European farms, settlement by African farmers close to water sources, and extensive grazing which took livestock closer to water sources. However, the position was obviously unsatisfactory, and partly accounted for pressure on land in the Reserve area. It was estimated in 1945 that 23% of the Reserve area was unusable owing to tsetse fly and lack of water (KNA: MKS/DC/1/8/1).

The first Colonial Development and Welfare Fund grant was for water and dams were built in the early 1940s. Later projects were funded by ALDEV. Water was seen as a prerequisite for the Makueni settlement, and was provided by boreholes and dams. The mechanised unit, which had been unpopular for terracing, constructed the larger dams of the ALDEV period, while the smaller ones were constructed by labour-intensive methods and draft animal power. A summary of accomplishments is presented in Table 12.1. The dams were built both in the Reserve area which was part of the Machakos Betterment programme, and in the areas under the various controlled grazing schemes of the Veterinary Department, including the Yattas. Dams were important in extending the areas that cattle could graze. An important technology introduced in the late 1950s was sub-surface dams in the river-beds; this was started in 1955 and 38 were constructed in 1957 (Peberdy, 1958: 55). Sub-surface dams are generally constructed on a rock foundation at the bottom of a river bed. They are cheap and easy to construct, as they only require an experienced mason to raise the masonry wall by 30 cm each season. Some farmers have constructed their own. The main problem still lies in a conflict of interest with excavators of sand for the Nairobi building market, who pay a tax which forms an important part of County Council revenue.

In the late 1950s water supply projects were partly financed by a water rate of Ksh 2 per capita per annum, which was part of the African District Council rate. The money was mainly used to cover recurrent costs and loan charges, for the small element built with ALDEV loan funds. By 1962 the ADC was reported to be in serious financial difficulties and was expected to be unable to service the outstanding loans for water supplies. Non-payment of the water rate was blamed on hard times brought about by the 1960/1961 drought and 1961 floods and for political reasons (Kenya, MoA, 1962b). As already seen in Chapter 9, the local authority's responsibilities were drastically reduced in 1969 although it was still responsible for some boreholes in 1982 (ODI, 1982).

TABLE 12.1. ALDEV water conservation works

Type	Number
Large surface dams	52
Seasonal dams	269
Rock catchments	3
Subsurface dams	226
Total	550

1970—1990

In 1970 a Water Department was formed within the Ministry of Agriculture to improve rural water supplies. It implemented five reticulated water supply projects in Machakos, serving approximately 10 000 people (Njui and Daines, 1977). A Ministry of Water Development was set up in 1974 and charged with the planning, design and construction of water conservation works, with the target of providing every Kenyan with safe drinking water by the year 2000. The Ministry played a crucial role in implementing rural and urban supplies, but was limited by the degree of availability of donor funding. This resulted in a change in emphasis from large centrally managed water projects to the promotion of community-managed self-help projects with technical advice and with the community providing the labour and part of the finance. By 1977, the 550 dams of the ALDEV period were estimated to have increased to 826 surface dams in Machakos district of which 596 were of less than 5000 m^3 capacity. The rest of the finance was provided either by the District Development Committee out of the Rural Development Fund, or by donations from donors such as CARE, AMREF, etc. Most projects were small, and consisted of sub-surface dams, rock catchments, spring protection and pipes, sub-surface intakes on sandy river bends, and storage tanks.

Water projects for minor urban centres also began in 1974. The most important, the Loolturesh project, implemented in 1989—1992, gets its water from Loolturesh springs in Kajiado District, and supplies Sultan Hamud, Machakos Town, Athi River in Machakos District as well as Kajiado. It should facilitate diversity of employment and urban growth.

The MIDP water sector

The inauguration of the MIDP made more funds available for water development, which initial consultations had shown to be a high priority amongst Machakos people. Its brief included domestic, livestock and minor irrigation needs (ODI, 1982). While MIDP Phase I assisted about 100 small projects, including 76 sub-surface dams, the main effort went into preparing medium technology projects consisting of intakes and dams on the perennial rivers in the higher areas, with piping to convey the water to the lower areas. This technology was adopted because the unit cost of water development directly in the drier areas, with seasonal rivers, low rainfall reliability and high sedimentation rates, would have been very high. In Phase II, support to the smaller projects (totalling 2400) continued, including roof catchments. The main achievements were four medium-sized dams completed with piping systems, and two smaller earth dams; four older dams were desilted. These projects undoubtedly brought considerable benefit to large numbers of people. At first, chiefs were asked to appoint committees to supervise the water installation and undertake operation and maintenance. This method proved unsatisfactory, and they were replaced with elected committees, with the Social Services Department supervising the elections, organising training courses and monitoring performance.

Roof catchments have played a major role recently in providing domestic water and lessening the drudgery of water collection, although they do not generally provide a year round supply. Those who can afford it build brick houses with corrugated iron roofs, as thatched roofs are a much less efficient source of water. In the 1980s many NGOs and the MIDP gave assistance to groups investing in this form of water harvesting (Kaluli, 1992).

CANALS AND IRRIGATION

A major ALDEV project was the construction of the Yatta Furrow (or canal), which was begun in 1953, using the labour of Mau Mau detainees; when these were released in 1957, the Furrow was completed by 1959 with hired labour and the Government's mechanical construction unit. Its main purpose was to provide domestic and stock water to the north Yatta area of Matuu and to part of the Yatta area in Kitui District, including delivery of water to a natural river to provide it with year-round supplies. In addition, it was to provide irrigation water. The Furrow is generally referred to as the 'lifeline' of the Yatta Plateau, and has facilitated settlement of the area. Permitted use in 1983 was 0.283 m^3/s for domestic use, and 1.416 m^3/s for general use including irrigation of 870 ha, mainly used now for the production of fruit and vegetables (see Chapter 14). Two much smaller schemes in the south were also started in the 1950s.

However, much of the irrigation in the District is by small groups or individual households. The number of water permits has risen substantially each decade, with permitted abstraction totalling 8 litres/s at the end of the 1950s and 437 litres/s at the end of the 1970s. Generally more water is abstracted than permitted, and there are many small illegal abstractions. Permitted abstraction for irrigation in the District as a whole reached 4290 litres/s by 1990. However, this reflected plans for some large schemes which had not been implemented. The District's irrigation potential is estimated at 22 000 ha; of this, somewhat under 5000 ha was implemented.

CONCLUSION

Water conservation activities have contributed to resource conservation. They have freed labour from fetching water and facilitated economic diversification in rural areas. Infiltration ditches and cut-off drains have reduced the amount of run-off and the risk of erosion. They have increased the value of land through the provision of water resources, and facilitated settlement in drier areas. Tillage techniques have contributed to the restoration of grazing land as well as increased productivity on arable fields.

Government investment and demonstration of techniques was important in the 1940s, 1950s and 1980s. Many facilities have also been created by self-help. Although provided primarily with the intention of increasing seasonal grazing areas, the additional dams built in the Yattas and southern Machakos in the 1940s and 1950s must have helped the spontaneous settlement that occurred in the 1960s. Demand for irrigation water is constantly increasing, as a means to intensify production and to produce high value crops, but as yet it plays a relatively small role in the agriculture of the District. The demand for irrigation water has to be balanced against the need of communities for more essential purposes. As yet, there has been no assessment of the economic benefits of irrigation.

Additional water has been developed, although more remains to be done. In 1988 an assessment concluded that more than 50% of the population was still supplied with drinking water that needed to be boiled before use and approximately 15% did not have a year-round supply (Mwenge, 1988). Water shortage remained an overriding concern in the villages where we conducted interviews.

Water conservation for plant production has direct benefits to a farmer through increased crop yield, reduced risk of crop failure, cultivation of higher value crops, and reduced erosion risk. Indirect benefits include increased groundwater recharge, dry season river flows and water

(a)

(b)

FIGURE 12.2. (a) A dam built by the mechanical unit of ALDEV, photographed in 1952. It also showed 'the extent to which the terraced badlands have recovered'. (Photo: Kenya, ALUS, 1953. Crown Copyright. Reproduced with permission of the Central Office of Information). (b) In 1990 this land was still used for grazing, with increased tree cover, and the dam was still in use. (Photo: M. Mortimore.)

availability. All these benefits translate into improvements in the productivity of land and labour resources, the standard of living and the commitment to resource conservation.

NOTES

1   This chapter summarises a longer report by Francis Gichuki, which will appear as a future ODI Working Paper.
2   Brown in retrospect felt that the colonial conservation drive should everywhere have stressed water conservation rather than soil alone. He noted that 'water is a thing that everyone needs and wants, whereas everyone thinks that the soil is just there.' (L. Brown in a letter to D. B. Thomas dated 22 July 1977).
3   The DC was adamant the landowners must agree and that the Department must return it at the end of the experimental period. This was done.

13

Tree Management

INTRODUCTION

The purpose of this chapter is to review woodland management during the period 1930—1990. The central paradox confronted in such a review is that while, in the 1930s, the Ukamba Reserve was held to be severely degraded, perhaps irreversibly, and a major aspect of this degradation was the loss of tree cover, now after six decades and a sixfold increase of the population, the position has improved. Encapsulated within this paradox is another: the closely related issue of wood fuel supply and consumption. (In this chapter, the term 'wood fuel' includes both firewood (or fuelwood) and charcoal; it excludes crop residues.) While there has long been a perceived scarcity of wood fuel in the District, the term 'crisis' is a misnomer, and a sustainable wood fuel equation is within reach. The solutions to both these paradoxes lie not in the effectiveness of government initiatives in forest reservation and plantation, but in an autonomous development of smallholder tree management, or indigenous agroforestry. This development, while successfully absorbing extension forestry interventions, has often been a step ahead of the agents of intervention, both in conceptual and practical terms.

GOVERNMENT INTERVENTIONS: FOREST RESERVES AND PLANTATIONS

Rates of afforestation

Afforestation was identified early on as a major part of the Government's response to the 'Machakos problem' of grazing-induced land degradation. One reason for this perception of priorities was the belief that forests bring about improved rainfall (KNA: Bolton, 1953; Leakey, 1955, quoted in Peberdy, 1958: 92). They were also thought to improve perennial stream flow, protect the surface from erosion, and break the force of desiccating winds (Nicholson and Walter, no date). In 1920—1921, therefore, a plan was begun to plant up the Machakos Hills, using paid labour, and assigning the ownership of the trees to individuals. So critical was the afforestation effort believed to be that one District Commissioner tried to remove the control and ownership of nurseries and plantations from the Reserve, and to ban grazing in forest areas. This issue became so contentious that a deputation was sent to the Acting Governor asking for the DC to be removed, and he was replaced in 1927 (Peberdy, 1958: 7—9).

The Crown Lands outside the Reserve were under natural forest. Here the policy was to restrict

TABLE 13.1. Forest reserves, Machakos District (hectares)

Year	Gazetted	Planted	Set aside[1]
1920–1921	985		
1932–1933	4 224[2]		
1947	1 040	985	
1956	1 040	985 <[3]	> 14 000
1962	6 520[4]	na	na
1977	14 502[5]	4 746	1 744
1989	15 394	na	na

[1]Before gazetting, forest land had to be surveyed, set aside by the LNC, and
  demarcated.
[2]In addition, up to 400 ha of LNC plantations existed in 1937 (KNA: Logan, 1948)
[3]Planting in progress
[4]Including 1920 ha in the Scheduled Areas
[5]Includes 5686 ha in the Kibwezi Reserve
na = Data not available
Sources: KNA: Logan (1948); KNA: Bolton (1953); Peberdy (1958); Consortium,
Report 5 (1978); Kenya, Ministry of Planning (1988)

settlement and to regulate grazing (see Chapters 4 and 8). Within the Reserve, legislation provided for gazetted 'native forest reserves' (NFRs) managed by the Forest Department, though the Local Native Council (LNC) was expected to make financial contributions, and to receive any profit from the sale of forest produce. (In addition to the plantations controlled by the Forest Department, there were some very small plantations controlled by the LNC, later African District Council (ADC) and finally Masaku County Council.) The sites, mainly on the hilltops, had first to be set aside by the LNC. Table 13.1 shows progress. According to Logan (KNA: Logan, 1948), the sites 'were dedicated to forestry when pressure on the land was far less acute ... the few people cultivating or grazing in the areas were ordered to move out and the Forest Department commenced afforestation operations'. Extensive planting was undertaken, supported by nurseries on or near the sites, so that some 'native forest reserves' became, in effect, government-run plantations of eucalypts, pine, cypress and other exotic species.

During World War II, the afforestation effort stagnated. During the 10 years ending in 1947, the area of gazetted forest was reduced effectively, on account of cultivation and settlement (KNA: Bolton, 1953; Peberdy, 1958: 92), the most glaring example being the 3200 ha Momandu Reserve in which only 350 ha were effectively controlled by the Forest Department. In 1946 there were only 1045 ha managed by the Forest Department and 325 ha managed by the LNC in numerous small plots. Following the Logan Report in 1948, there was a change of priority, and afforestation resumed a high profile. Most of the new reserves were to be managed by the African District Council (ADC), under the supervision of the Forest Department, in the expectation that the Akamba were not averse to forests as such, provided they owned them. By 1962 about 4000 ha had been included in afforestation schemes and the better land had been almost entirely planted (Kenya, MoA, 1962b: 32). The quickened pace of forest reservation was maintained until the 1970s. By 1977, however, only 32% of the gazetted are of 14 700 ha had been planted. The rate of planting was modest — about 200 ha/year. Such planting was based on species trials which, although begun in the 1930s, were not put on to a fully scientific basis until 1970 (Odera, 1981).

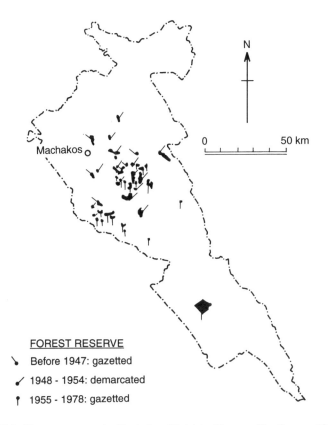

FOREST RESERVE

❧ Before 1947: gazetted

✓ 1948 - 1954: demarcated

❡ 1955 - 1978: gazetted

FIGURE 13.1. Forest reserves in Machakos District. (Source: Mortimore, 1992)

In 1989 the area of gazetted reserves remained substantially the same as in 1977 (Figure 13.1). The slowdown in the acquisition of land for afforestation reflects an increasing scarcity of land in the District. Under the MIDP, targets for 2000 ha of productive timber plantations by 1982, and 600 ha of protective hill plantations, were met only in part — 37% and 62% respectively. In Phase II of the MIDP (1984−1987), the target achievement rate for protective forestry improved to 75%, but average planting rates in plantation forestry were lower than before the MIDP started. Productive forestry was dropped — as an explicit policy objective and as a separate category in the statistics — underlining the modesty of both objectives and achievements. These indicate that serious difficulties stand in the way of large-scale, government-run afforestation. Between 1984 and 1988, planting continued to fall behind targets, with implementation rates of 60% in plantations and 43% on protective sites; low rainfall was blamed for this (Kenya, Ministry of Planning, 1988). Quick-growing exotics were and still are relied on exclusively, with the aim of supplying the timber market, and with fuelwood production only a subsidiary objective. Seedling survival rates can be as low as 10% owing to moisture stress and damage from termites (Mwenge, 1988: 5.4). Indigenous trees, however, are included in plans for future protective hill planting programmes.

Perception of forest reserve benefits

The benefits of forest reservation and plantation were articulated in colonial reports to justify the large gap between departmental revenues and expenditures. These benefits were believed to be: (i) climatic amelioration, (ii) erosion prevention, (iii) the conservation of soil moisture and permanent springs, (iv) employment creation, in the cutting, carting, marketing and processing of timber products, and (v) the provision of fuel and timber. The revenue from selling forest produce (fuel, poles, timber and charcoal) was set against expenditures and profits were to be paid to the LNC. However, the gazetted reserves always ran at a loss (KNA: Logan, 1948; KNA: Bolton, 1953; Leakey, quoted in Peberdy, 1958: 91–92). Forest royalties (or selling prices) were not increased from 1920 to 1953, on the grounds that increases would encourage the cutting of indigenous trees — the very outcome the Forest Department wanted to prevent. In other words, the high costs of forest reservation (which, in Machakos, included extensive planting, maintenance and protection work) were justified in social and environmental, not commercial, terms.

However, the Akamba did not like handing over land for gazetted reserves; they settled and cultivated inside the reserves illegally (which resulted in large 'excisions' having to be made from the gazetted areas), insisted on grazing forest areas wherever possible, lobbied for de-gazetting some reserved areas, and regarded the reserves as belonging to the Government, and not to them. The last point was especially significant, given their sensitivity to land alienation. Forest guards, therefore, were major costs in the Department's budget. The Department had to plant up the reserves without delay. Bolton (KNA: Bolton, 1953) rejected spontaneous regeneration as a lower cost alternative to planting. Unless a reserve was planted, the Akamba 'will believe it is not being put to the use originally stated, and will abuse the land, either by grazing, or, if the area is not continually patrolled, will *return* [emphasis added] and commence cultivating'. Gazetting extinguished all individual rights. 'Legally, therefore, eviction is clearly in order but in practice it presents very considerable difficulties' (KNA: Logan, 1948: 4). He gave two reasons for Akamba disillusionment: 'the people feel that the land and the forests thereon are no longer theirs; they enjoy no rights, privileges or any share on the control thereof and look upon the land as alienated'. Secondly, 'they have as yet had no revenue from any of these forests'.[1]

Fuelwood production was not the primary objective of plantation management because, given the high costs, it was rarely profitable. Yet by 1984, according to an official estimate (Kenya Forest Department, 1984), wood fuel was being consumed at four times the national rate of natural regeneration. Studies carried out in Machakos related consumption levels to population growth, projected an accelerating scarcity into the future, and prescribed extensive fuelwood plantations by the Government, as the solution. A comparison of three estimates shows a rapid escalation in estimated consumption per person and in the amount of planting necessary to meet future demand (KNA: Logan, 1948; Peberdy, 1958; Mung'ala and Openshaw, 1984). The last of these, in projecting demand to the year 2000, concluded that 'an acute shortage of woodfuel is imminent' (p. 117). Planting programmes in hand by the Government, including those financed by the MIDP, promised to deliver only 15% of the anticipated demand. No less than 226 000 ha of plantations would be needed by the year 2000. (A summary and critique of the estimates is provided in Mortimore, 1992.) Such a target was incapable of achievement as long as the existing planting programme, small as it was, fell behind on account of costs.

The high costs of running plantations included nursery maintenance, weeding and cleaning work and road maintenance. Three-quarters of the money spent on forestry 'went on cleaning and removing weeds from existing forests' (KNA: Machakos Reconditioning Committee, 24 February 1953). New planting competed with extension forestry for what was left. Thus in 1953, small (community-accessible) nurseries were closed down to save money for the plantations (KNA: Bolton, 1953). An evaluation carried out in 1977 identified a formidable list of difficulties facing plantation forestry (Consortium, Report 5, 1978), including acquiring land, combating drought, termites, and infertility, and overcoming inadequate labour and nursery provision. The costs of maintaining the plantation forestry sector thus created a powerful inertia against extension or farm forestry.

GOVERNMENT INTERVENTIONS: EXTENSION FORESTRY

Farm tree planting is much cheaper than plantations, raises none of the questions regarding procurement of land, or ownership and control of trees, transfers most of the costs to the farmer, and offers potential marketable and consumable products directly to the household.

Early efforts in afforestation placed much emphasis on tree planting by farmers. In 1930, a tree-planting campaign distributed 415 000 seedlings, and was considered at the time to have been a success (Peberdy, 1958: 94). These early campaigns were not without impact. A thin scatter of exotic trees is a significant feature of photographs taken at several locations in the Reserve by Barnes (see Chapter 1). These appear to have been growing on or near arable land or house sites. There were also some private plantations.

According to Peberdy, however, these efforts were largely unsuccessful, and in 1958, 'despite the fact that tens of thousands of trees have been distributed to farmers since 1921, the beginning of the Swynnerton period [1954] still found Machakos very bare of trees' (Peberdy, 1958: 91). This was attributed to 'the attitude, antipathy, and in some cases, laziness of the people which prevented the proper care of the seedlings after planting.' Logan (KNA: Logan, 1948: 5) considered that 'the principal causes of this are probably lack of advice as to the best species for planting, bad planting, lack of aftercare and unrestricted grazing by goats'. Neither Peberdy nor Logan thought to question the suitability of the species offered by the nurseries, yet 'chiefly Gums and Cypress are raised for this purpose. At present sales do not appear to be brisk and there are considerable surpluses of overgrown seedlings left in the nurseries' (KNA: Logan, 1948: 5). Nor, apparently, was there any attempt to investigate tenurial or other constraints in the farming system that might have affected tree planting. Droughts must also take a share of the blame. In the drier areas, the seasonal rainfall may be quite inadequate for establishment.

By the 1970s a shift in policy towards extension forestry was inevitable in view of the problems being encountered in the plantations, though when it came (in 1971) it was justified mainly for energy and timber production on farm holdings (Kenya Forest Department, 1984). Such a shift called for a significant reorientation away from punitive regulation of the forest resource to new forms of co-operation with local communities (Odera, 1981). The Rural Afforestation Extension Programme (RAES) opened offices in every District, location chiefs were ordered to open nurseries, and the number of seedlings produced for rural planting in all nurseries reached 75 million in 1983 (Kenya Forest Department, 1984).

Under the MIDP, rural afforestation became, in Phase II, the foremost objective of the programme. Target achievement in rural planting was not high — less than 62% in Phase I and only 52% in Phase II — and the targets themselves were very modest. But the MIDP nurseries themselves only achieved 46% of target seedling production in Phase II, and they had to supply protective plantations as well as the farmers, which suggests that the Government's failure to deliver seedlings in adequate quantities may have been a major contributor to underachievement in farm tree planting.

In view of the negative assessments offered, as late as 1958, of the farmers' propensity to plant and protect trees, the change that has occurred subsequently is very remarkable. A comparison of arable landscapes as they appear in 1990 with Barnes' photographs taken in 1937 (see Chapter 1) shows, at every site, a substantial increase in both the density and the average size of farm trees. They occur as woodlots, windbreaks, hedges and in the planting up of gullies that are otherwise unusable land. They are becoming permanent features of the landscape, expanding from the original positions we can trace in the 1937 photographs. They are providing for the increasing demand for building timber with population growth, as well as fuel and amenity shade around houses. This change is so significant in its implications for biomass management that the term 'revolution' is not inappropriate.

However, the Forest Department cannot claim all the credit for the change. Fast-growing exotics were propagated through the Department's nurseries with a view to meeting an assumed demand for timber and fuelwood. Eucalypts and other exotics may be seen on arable lands today, indicating considerable acceptance. Eucalypts provide useful timber, but they are poorly suited for fuelwood and only residues are so used. It is significant that wattle, which does not appear to have been supplied from the Forestry Department's nurseries, was more popular until the 1950s. Wattle bark was, and is, a cash crop but the trees also provide fuel and poles for local use.[2] More recently, it is known that women farmers' tree planting has favoured fruit trees. Fruit trees have been promoted by the Agricultural Department since 1925, but no record of the promotion of wattle has been found (see Peberdy, 1958: 9; 288−289). These anomalies suggest that the choice of species offered may have contributed to the early failure of extension forestry. Fruit trees on arable land increased between 1981 and 1985, according to Ecosystems (1985/6, Vol. 4: 2.15). In the 1980s fruit trees were the most important component of farm tree planting and major contributors to the observed increase in the densities of trees.

SMALLHOLDER TREE MANAGEMENT

It is now clear to the observer that Mung'ala and Openshaw's prognosis that 'at the present consumption rate [1977] all the [wood] stock could be depleted as early as 1986' was not what occurred. Both woodland and bushland (on the one hand) and farm trees (on the other) are visible in all parts of the District. The evident paradox that the District has become more, not less, wooded as its population grew fivefold, has not been addressed by the proponents of plantations.

The air photographic evidence of 1948, 1960−1961, and 1978 (Chapter 5) provides no evidence of woodland degradation in the longer term — though much woodland was converted to cultivation. Surface photography taken in 1937 (KNA: Barnes, 1937), and repeated in 1990, does not indicate any significant reduction in the timber volume of woody vegetation communities. There is some evidence of bush encroachment on grazing lands (see Chapter 8). Although there has been a large-scale transfer of land from woodland and bush to cultivation, this has gone along with a noticeable increase in the density and size of farm trees. Similar developments have occurred in western Kenya (Bradley, 1991).

Trees and shrubs on grazing land

Grazing land is now almost all subject to individual tenure, and in the older settled areas of the former Reserve, nearly all is enclosed by hedges of Euphorbia, Lantana, Cassia and other species which produce fuel, etc. The natural woodland on it is managed for grazing, woodcutting, beekeeping and the collection of wild produce. The proscription of firing, throughout our period of study, gave the competitive advantage to woody species at the expense of grasses under heavy grazing by cattle. (Examples of the species composition of grazed communities in AEZs 4 and 5 are provided in Chapter 5.)

The indigenous trees that grow on grazing land have a variety of uses (Neunhauser et al, 1983). It is noteworthy that several species (*Acacia* spp. and *Terminalia brownii*) that have high use ratings on Yatta farms appear with the greatest frequency, indicating that a large proportion of households consider them important and maintain them for this reason. *Terminalia brownii*, for example, gives termite-resistant timber for the construction of houses, stores, oxen yokes, farm and household tools. The systematic and knowledgeable use of trees and shrubs on grazing land is widely attested (Fliervoet, 1982; Gielen, 1982; Neunhauser et al, 1983; Rocheleau and van den Hoek, 1984).

The management of grazing land includes the clearing of unwanted vegetation (especially the invader, *Lantana camara*), occasional lopping of trees to improve timber growth, and the use of goats to control bush encroachment, as well as the planting of creeping grasses (Gielen, 1982: 53−54). Tree planting is not usually attempted on grazing land; the farmer's task is seen as the selective control of spontaneous regeneration.

Trees on cultivated farmland

When land is cleared for cultivation, the dominant acacias (except for *A. tortilis*) are removed and volunteers controlled, because of their thorny habit and reputation for harbouring crop pests. *Terminalia brownii*, on the other hand, is preserved. The composition of indigenous woody vegetation on farmland shows the extent to which the natural conditions have been modified by management, which includes selective control, protection, and planting. In the Yatta farms, *Terminalia brownii* and *Acacia tortilis* still head the list, but many other species common on the grazing lands (e.g. *Acacia etbaica, A. brevispica, Balanites aegyptiaca, Commiphora africana*) appear much less frequently on farmland, while *Euphorbia terucalli*, the favourite hedging plant, becomes commonplace (Gielen, 1982).

More significant, however, in its impact on the farmland ecosystem, is the planting of exotics, and especially of fruit trees. Surveys conducted during the early 1980s showed a high level of planting activity, whether measured in terms of the incidence of planting households, the diversity of species planted (often five or more per household), or the numbers of individuals planted per household (Table 13.2). Hayes (1986) found that 93% of a sample of 87 Masii families planted trees. Among the fruit trees planted in Mbiuni and Masii, lemon is the most common, but banana, followed by orange, is reported in the largest numbers per household. In drier Yatta, citrus and banana growing households are less frequent, but mango and pawpaw maintain their popularity. Among the other trees planted, *Eucalyptus* spp. is the most common; more than

TABLE 13.2. Tree planting by households (most frequent species, %)

Species	Households			Households growing < 10 individuals > 10 (Masii)	
	Mbiuni (N=56) AEZ 3/4	Masii (N=87) AEZ 4	Yatta (N=61) AEZ 5[1]		
Fruit trees planted					
Lemon	32	70	15 (10)	84	16
Orange	18	59	8 (13)	57	43
Mango	61	57	41 (16)	72	28
Pawpaw	50	55	51 (3)	· 73	27
Banana	68	53	31 (3)	35	65
Guava	32	26	11 (8)	78	22
Other trees planted					
Eucalyptus spp.	13	31	6 (18)	44	56
Croton megalocarpus	23	0	2 (13)	—	—
Jacaranda spp.	7	13	3 (8)	82	18
Cassia siamea	5	9	0 (2)	75	25
Grevillea spp.	4	7	5 (3)	—	—
Leucaena spp.	0	6	0 (0)	—	—
Cypress spp.	1	3	0 (0)	—	—
Azadirachta indica	—	—	na (2)	—	—
Melia azadirach	—	—	na (2)	—	—
Euphorbia terucalli	R	—	R	—	—

[1]Figures in brackets are the percentages of Yatta households planting in the year prior to the survey
— Not reported, or numbers too small to have meaning
R: reported, no numbers
Sources: for Mbiuni, Gielen (1982: 33, 68); for Masii, Hayes (1986: 212–235); for Yatta, Neunhauser et al (1983: 51, 55)

planting households in Masii have more than 10 individuals, in which respect it compares only with banana among the fruit trees. Reported in Mbiuni and Yatta, but not in Masii, is the planting of *Croton megalocarpus*, the only indigenous species listed in Table 13.2. It is valued as fuel (especially) and construction timber. Gielen (1982) also reported the planting of hedgerow trees. Almost all farms have planted rows of *Euphorbia terucalli* (finger euphorbia), and *Commiphora* spp. is also common, especially for fencing cattle bomas. But indigenous multi-purpose trees are slow in growth performance, as a general rule (Jama et al, 1989).

It is important, if possible, to quantify this landscape transformation. Using Gielen's data, Table 13.3 shows the average densities of trees per hectare of cultivated land, by size class of farm holding. The overall densities are impressively high (the locations are in AEZ 3/4), even if bananas are excluded. Nevertheless, the figures understate the total because some less common fruit trees, and all planted non-fruit exotics, are omitted, together with hedgerows, which add significantly to the standing volume of timber.

An equally remarkable feature of Table 13.3 is the gradient in the density of fruit trees from 59/ha on the smallest cultivated holdings to 21/ha on the largest. This provides strong support for a hypothesis relating this form of intensification to land scarcity; and it does not support the hypothesis that the land-poor cannot invest in trees.

This review of trees on cultivated land leads, therefore, to the following conclusions:

TABLE 13.3. Tree densities per hectare in Mbiuni Location

	I	II	III	IV	All
Farm size class (ha)	<0.5	0.51−1.0	1.01−1.5	>1.5	
Average cultivated area (ha)	0.44	0.78	1.32	2.5	1.23
Tree densities/ha:					
banana clumps	45.5	30.8	17.4	13.1	20.3
mango	6.8	3.8	3.0	1.6	3.3
pawpaw	4.5	2.6	4.5	2.0	3.3
lemon	0	6.8	5.1	3.6	4.8
guava	2.3	0	3.0	0.4	1.1
Total fruit trees	59.1	44.0	33.0	20.7	32.8
Indigenous trees	na	na	na	na	1.7[1]
All trees[2]	60.8	45.7	34.7	22.4	34.5
All trees (excl. bananas)	15.3	14.9	17.3	9.3	14.2

[1]Computed from a total of 117 trees at 2.1/household
[2]Data are not given on indigenous trees by farm size class; so the average density has been added to each total for fruit trees
na = not available
Source: Gielen (1982: 17, 33−45)

(1) A managed ecosystem combining crop production with fruit and other trees of economic value is well established on cultivated land in the District.
(2) The species composition of the woody component of this system, owing to protection, control, and planting, represents a major transformation of the woody vegetation, as found under natural conditions, and as still managed on grazing lands.
(3) Planting by smallholders favours fruit trees over other trees.
(4) Amongst the other trees, planting favours exotic over indigenous species, with one major exception (*Croton megalocarpus*).
(5) Diversity is characteristic of the tree population on individual smallholdings.
(6) Tree planting on cultivated land, and especially fruit tree planting, may reach very high densities; there is evidence that this is a form of intensification correlating inversely with the size of cultivated holding.

Tree planting and control

Smallholders do not plant trees in response to a generalised rationale of conservation, still less to theories about the influence of trees on rainfall, but for reasons that are specific to the species in question. Trees are investments of capital and labour and have implications for the management of the smallholding. The early failures of extension forestry suggest that this principle was not adequately grasped.

The decision to plant a tree reflects a gender division of responsibility and rights of access on the farm. Men plant trees for timber, e.g. building poles (*Eucalyptus* spp.); fuel (e.g. *Croton megalocarpus*); windbreaks and hedgerows (e.g. *Euphorbia terucalli*); and for ornamental, shade or amenity purposes (e.g. *Jacaranda* spp., *Grevillea* spp.) (Mbithi and Kayongo-Male, 1978: 128, 721; Gielen, 1982: 69). Women favour fruit trees (Hayes, 1986; Rocheleau, 1991). This is because of their need both for household food supplies and for an independent source of cash, needs that are accentuated by frequent absences of the men. Furthermore, small-scale fruit tree planting requires little start-up capital or special education, and competes minimally with the production of crops, representing an attainable form of intensification as Table 13.3 shows. Men's involvement in planting fruit trees may be necessary for bananas and commercial oranges, which are usually put into deep mulched or fertilised pits (see Figures 11.4 and 14.1). However, fruit trees may be grown on a commercial scale by men or women farmers and Table 13.2 shows that 43% of households in Masii had more than 10 orange trees; we observed the occasional orange or pawpaw orchard.

Fruit tree seedlings are either bought — from local nurseries or markets, or by family members on their travels — or raised from seed in farm nurseries (Hayes, 1986: 215–229). Little management is given to fruit trees, unless in orchards, but some women fertilise or water orange trees, or construct micro-catchments and terraces around them. Rights to produce are exercised exclusively or jointly by the women in the great majority of households, even including bananas. Rights to the produce of other trees are ill-defined, according to Hayes (Hayes, 1986: 230–235), but it can probably be assumed that men normally exercise rights to the timber, while women collect the trimmings and dead wood for fuel.

Early forestry extension programmes failed to 'target' those who today do much of the planting and management of trees (women), and in stressing conservation objectives — to be achieved through quick-growing exotics — they may have under-rated the specific needs of the household for special quality timbers, fodder, food or medicines.

Agroforestry is not new to Machakos, except in the sense of certain formal designs such as alley-cropping. The Kathama study (Hoekstra et al, 1984; Rocheleau, 1985) generated a conception of farmers (men or women) as 'choosing, mixing and matching' from a selection of possible practices (Rocheleau and Malaret, 1987: 16; Rocheleau et al, 1989). Technical innovations, such as species trials and conservation strategies, proposed by the participating scientists were filtered through farmers' own perceptions of rationality.

Woodfuel management

The most popular trees for firewood and charcoal making in the Yatta area are *Acacia mellifera, A. tortilis, A. etbaica* and *Terminalia brownii* (Neunhauser et al, 1983: 56). According to Lubega (1987: 37), the first two are preferred charcoal burners, for their hardness, but scarcity forces other woods, even eucalypts, to be used. Women collect firewood, but men usually make charcoal, or undertake brick-making — a widespread rural industry. The first is a regular harvesting activity, making use of a range of woody resources in the locality. The second is an intermittent industrial operation requiring a substantial bulk of wood, if not entire trees, at the site. The first is directed to the consumption needs of the household; the second (in large part) to the market, a form of income diversification.

Women's collection sites for firewood include: (i) the household's cultivated land (hedgerows, trimming or pollarding of farm trees); (ii) grazing land (dead wood, loppings and, rarely, coppicing of trees and shrubs); (iii) roadsides, pathways and river banks; (iv) other common access woodland, if any; (v) government forests, if within reach; and (vi) the lands of other households, by consent of the owners or, if absent, their wives (Gielen, 1982: 72; Rocheleau and van den Hoek, 1984; Hayes, 1986).

Household sufficiency in firewood is critically important. Of Gielen's 56 households in Mbiuni, 47% supplied themselves from their own lands, but only 37% reported no problems with their supply (Gielen, 1982: 73). Labour constraints (distance and time) were cited most commonly, and lack of enough wood came third. Lubega (1987: 37) found that 50% of a sample of women interviewed ranked firewood collection among the five most time-consuming activities in their work load, though few recognised a present scarcity. Hayes' study classified 87 women householders on a scale of self-sufficiency. Less than half (46%) of the sample perceived a scarcity of wood in their households, and awareness of scarcity was predictably related to self-sufficiency. In time perspective, for some 13% of the sample, wood had become more scarce, but, for a few, an improvement had occurred.

Women who 'borrow' collecting rights are subject to various forms of restriction, as might be expected from what we have already reported on grazing land management (Chapter 7). The most common restrictions are against collecting green wood, fencing material, cut wood or trees, and being limited to places shown, or to wood already on the ground. The costs of such rights of access are various forms of informal payment, such as farm labour and water carrying, which increase their already heavy work load (Hayes, 1986: 195–196). Such 'borrowing', though not articulated in a formal market, incurs a form of social indebtedness (Rocheleau and van den Hoek, 1984: 30), which emphasises inter-household inequalities. Only 12% of Hayes' households sold firewood, and 5% sold whole trees (contingency sales) at the time of the survey; these figures had not changed significantly since 'the past', and men were more often than not the agents (Hayes, 1986: 279–280). Such figures do not make a strong case for the existence of a developed firewood market, especially when the inter-household differentiation, considered above, is taken into account. Rather, inequality in resource endowment is dealt with by the women's negotiation of collecting rights in a framework of reciprocal obligations. (The position is different with charcoal, which, being made intermittently in bulk, is normally bought and sold even in rural areas.)

The critical question concerns scarcity. If, as earlier analyses argued, the wood resources of the District have been and are being over-exploited (i.e. the average annual off-take exceeds the mean annual increment to the standing stock), then degradation of the woody vegetation is a necessary consequence. A reduction of the standing volume means in turn that wood fuel requirements, even if held constant, can only be met by mining the stock at an exponential rate.

Such an argument fails to square unequivocally with the evidence.

(1) No objective photographic or quantitative evidence has been recovered that suggests a general degradation — in terms of timber volume or tree density — in areas of natural woodland.

(2) The two household-level studies reviewed above — in Mbiuni and Masii Locations — found that about half the households were self-sufficient or in surplus (47% in Gielen's and 56% in Hayes'). There is no evidence as to whether the ratio is changing.

(3) The amount of time taken in collecting firewood (though it may be undesirable) is not excessive, given the nature of the work. Mung'ala and Openshaw's survey found that household woodfuel collection in 1977 took 59 man-days per year — or one day in six for one woman per household. Hayes (1986: 174,177,180) and Neunhauser et al (1983: 56) give comparable estimates. There is no evidence as to whether average collecting times are changing.

(4) The firewood market is not strongly developed in the District. Of Mung'ala and Openshaw's households, 74% relied entirely on collected firewood and only 9% depended exclusively on the market. Of Hayes' households, only 6% depended exclusively on the market. The District was only 6% urbanised in 1979. There is little evidence of inter-locational movements of firewood, nor of movements into or out of the District.

(5) Men do not plant trees, on the whole, in order to produce household fuel (with the exception of charcoal), even though common access woodland is scarce and most wood fuel is now obtained from private land (Mbithi and Kayongo-Male, 1978). Eucalyptus, wattle and other trees are grown for sale for building poles or to one of the several small sawmills in the district. And the women prefer to plant fruit trees (Hayes, 1986: 214, 236).

That wood fuel, and firewood in particular, is widely perceived to be scarce is not in doubt (80% of Mung'ala and Openshaw's respondents said that fuelwood was 'scarce' or 'very scarce' in 1977; 88% of Neunhauser et al's women respondents thought it was scarce in 1982). Resources are carefully husbanded at the household level and fuel-efficient stoves are believed to be in widespread use. What evidence there is, however, suggests that this scarcity falls well short of a crisis. (The widespread conception of a fuelwood crisis is based on false premises; see, for example, Cline-Cole et al, 1990, and Dewees, 1989.) This is the opposite of intuitive expectation in a densely populated semi-arid area.

RE-EVALUATING TREE MANAGEMENT

The history of the Government's afforestation efforts, acted out against the backcloth of the Ukamba Reserve's special conservation problem, reveals a tension between centralised (forest reservation and plantation) and decentralised (extension forestry) approaches. The commitment of a large proportion of expenditures to running and extending the Government's forest estate left little over for extension forestry, whose early programmes were thought, despite the photographic evidence to which we have referred, to have had little impact. Still less effort was available for tailoring the services provided to the real needs of the smallholders and addressing the constraints under which the farming systems operated — in particular, tenure, which recent studies of farm forestry have shown to be significant. Policy priorities were corrected with the commencement of the RAES in 1971. But the end of our period of study still finds government nurseries and advice inadequate, species provision often inappropriate, and planting failure rates high (ADEC, 1986). Private nurseries, and farmers themselves, fill this gap. Rather than presiding over the reafforestation of the farmlands, or driving a revolution in the management of the grazing lands, the Forest Department is still heavily committed to running the forest estate — an economic enclave as far as the bulk of the Akamba are concerned.

   With respect to the long-term conservation objectives of government afforestation policy, three comments are in order.

(1) There is no evidence to show any generalised ameliorative impact of plantation forestry on rainfall, whose record (see Chapter 3) shows no correlation either with deforestation in the longer term or with the limited progress made since 1947 in protective afforestation. ('Occult precipitation' that occurs on forested hilltops is due primarily to altitude and is local.)
(2) The area of gazetted forest is just over 1% of the District, and has been achieved at considerable cost over a period of about 70 years. A substantial extension of this area seems impracticable within the foreseeable future. The area should be compared with that occupied by 'field dividers' (including woody hedgerows), which was estimated to be 1.7% in 1985 (Ecosystems, 1985/6, Vol. 4: 2.9). These cost the Government nothing and yield many valuable products, including fuel.
(3) Afforestation of hillsides and dam catchments is beneficial, or may be in future (when new

plantations become established), in reducing erosion and conserving soil moisture locally. However, this benefit has been achieved by removing land from arable or grazing use. As a general strategy, therefore, its scope is increasingly limited by the scarcity of land for farming. There remain many steep and eroded sites, mostly on private land, where afforestation is beneficial and is occurring. But on such sites (see Figures 7.3 and 7.5), establishment costs are higher and expected income lower than on the better sites.

In Phase I of the MIDP, the greater part (64%) of the afforestation budget was allocated to 'productive forest plantation', only 26% to 'rural afforestation' and a mere 10% to 'protective forest plantation'. A proposed forest research station was to cost more than all three combined (ODI, 1982: 10.2). In Phase II, productive plantations were dropped, and rural afforestation was accorded priority, though budget data are not available. This highly significant reversal of priorities was maintained in the ensuing District Development Plan for 1989—1993. Such a shift is strongly supported by the evidence and arguments presented in this chapter. It stands to reason that, with almost 99% of the District outside Forest Department management, and most of it in the hands of smallholders, the farmers themselves must continue to be the main agents of afforestation.

Tree planting, management and control are linked to the gender division of labour and farm responsibilities, but gender roles in farming are less significant that previously. Smallholder tree management has effected a transformation of the natural woodland: 'what has gone on is a process of improvement upon what nature gave in the first place' (Shepherd, 1989: 27,28). The logic of the situation suggests that scarcity will help to drive an intensification of farm forestry, in which fruit trees are gaining over other trees, and useful exotics over indigenous species, though the last still have a role to play.

At the village scale, households regulate access rights to their land. In this area, the securing of individual title has had a profound impact. On the one hand, it weakened shared interests in common access resources, which declined in importance and in extent, while, on the other, it strengthened incentives for individuals to manage, under a sustainable regime, the lands to which they enjoy secure and heritable title. However, individual title does nothing to generate the capital and labour required to institute such regimes. Consequently, the cadastral mosaic of access rights is itself reflected in an uneven quality of management. Population growth and the subdivision of holdings provide incentives for the conversion of more grazing land to arable and more tree planting on this arable. Agroforestry technologies that can improve the efficiency of nutrient cycling on such diminishing holdings are a priority.

To strengthen private tree planting the Government needs to commit more of its resources to the support of the private nurseries which are proliferating in response to the demand for seedlings. Nursery techniques are widely understood, as found in Western Kenya (Bradley, 1991). Seed provision and technical advice can assist farmers to propagate their own plant material.

NOTES

1   In the expansion of afforestation activity that followed the Logan Report in 1948, communal ownership of forests was recommended (KNA: Waterer, 1951). Nevertheless, a recent evaluation (Mwenge, 1988: 51) found 'there is hardly any participation of the local communities in tree planting' at Tulimani.
2   Wattle (*Acacia melasma*) bark exports from the District commenced in 1936 and peaked at 2130 tons in 1954 (Peberdy, 1958: 153, 288—289). Private wattle plantations were so extensive, in some places, that trimmings from these trees undercut the local market for Forest Department produce (KNA: Bolton, 1953). Yet wattle is not mentioned among the seedlings supplied by the nurseries.

14

Technological Change

INTRODUCTION

In less than a century, Akamba farming systems have moved from extensive cattle and goat rearing, accompanied by shifting cultivation with the digging stick, and having little integration of crops and livestock, to permanent terraced fields with ox-ploughing, intensive tree crops and horticulture, and relatively integrated crop and livestock enterprises. The land resource itself has been transformed from an apparently misused and rapidly degrading latent 'desert' into a partially capitalised, still productive, and appreciating asset.

According to Boserup (1965, 1981), endogenous technological change may be driven by population growth. That is to say, even in a system having no significant integration with the market, as the dependent population grows and agricultural land becomes scarce, intensification technologies that are already known tend to be applied on a wider scale, so that average output per hectare increases. Such a view of technological change implies that innovation is an integral part of economic change and can only be understood in an historical context.

According to some modernisation theorists, technological change is exogenous, that is to say, innovations originate from sources external to the system. Farmers are cast in the somewhat passive role of 'adopters' and differentiated by response — early or 'progressive', average, late or 'laggard'. Often, economic or technical incentives are seen as driving forces and socio-cultural factors as barriers or impediments. Therefore promotion or extension is necessary to speed up the rate of adoption. This is implicit in views traditionally held in agricultural research and extension organisations.

Formal theories may not always pay much attention to the observable intricacies of decision-making by small-scale farmers and livestock owners. Recent research, however, has re-emphasised the experimental and adaptive properties of smallholder resource management. There is increasing recognition of the value of their accumulated experience in managing specific agro-ecological environments. The reasons for their sceptical reception of some technologies, energetically promoted by external agents of change, are also better understood.

The sources, promotion and diffusion of innovations are of interest to agencies of intervention, whether government or non-government. To accommodate the observable diversity of sources and modes of diffusion, Biggs (1989) has proposed a multiple source model, which provides an alternative to a centralised and hierarchical view of agricultural transformation as the outcome of government research institutions and extension services. It stresses that 'innovations come from anywhere in geographic space, from any research or extension institution, and from any instant in historical time' (Biggs, 1989: 26). Such a model accommodates the possibility of endogenous change and a more active, even equal, role for the farmer.

The dynamism of its production systems, and the number and diversity of technologies that have been tried (if not always widely adopted), indicate that Machakos provides an innovatory environment suitable for testing theories of technological change. It is implicit in the analysis which follows that the technologies identified were either exogenous (introduced to the District during the period 1930−1990) or endogenous (their adoption has significantly extended in the District during that time, though they were present at the beginning). We do not, however, consider this distinction to be important. Whether a given technology originated inside or outside the District boundary is less important than its subsequent adoption, adaptation, and impact on the system.

The objective of this chapter is to construct a chronological framework of change for selected productive technologies, as far as our incomplete sources of information allow. These are improved maize; horticultural crops; the ox-plough and compost and manure.[1] It is implicit in any evolutionary theory that timing is important. The lessons that can be learnt from each of the technologies selected are related to the driving forces of promotion, farmer experimentation, population growth and market penetration.

KATUMANI COMPOSITE B MAIZE

Maize and food security

The analysis of cropping choices during the period 1930−1990 takes place against the background of a long-term shift from sorghum and millet to maize, among both the Akamba and Kenyans at large. According to Peberdy (1958: 250), maize became popular from the 1920s, when employees on European farms were paid partly in maize or maize flour. It is easy to grow, is less susceptible to disease than sorghum, and requires less labour for bird scaring and threshing. Farmers today confirm that child labour for bird scaring is scarce, given the high priority placed on education. Maize also involves the women in less grinding. Famine relief programmes, and commercial imports in drought years, reinforced the trend to maize (Owako, 1969: 202−203).

In 1930, maize was estimated to occupy 42% of the cropped area, and sorghum and the millets together, only 21% (Table 6.1). The decline of sorghum has been discussed in Chapter 6. The growth in domestic maize production is believed to have come mainly from area expansion. Low producer prices and the variable rainfall provide little incentive for the adoption of purchased inputs; there has been no significant increase in fertiliser consumption over the last decade in Kenya as a whole (Wyckoff, 1989). The low yields and frequent failures encountered in marginal areas worsen food security, both locally and nationally.

Antecedents

Maize was being sold at railway stations in 1902, a year before the arrival of the first European settlers. A few years later, in 1908, the Administration, in an effort to improve seed quality, which was seen, with low rainfall, as a cause of low yields, issued imported maize seed along with beans and groundnuts (Peberdy, 1958: 2). From 1932 onwards, the Agricultural Department carried out trials on 10 or more imported varieties, at least one of which was bulked up for sale in the District, about 10 Kenyan varieties, and hybrids. Only yellow maize offered improvements over local varieties, whose number, according to Peberdy (1958) was 'infinite' owing to importations in famine years and farmers' own selections for hardiness over 10—20 years. It seems certain that this experience of experimenting with new varieties of maize prepared the ground for the reception of the Katumani varieties after 1956.

Breeding the Katumani varieties

In most of Machakos District (the hills excepted), the two main agroclimatic challenges posed to crop husbandry are the shortness of the growing seasons and the frequency of droughts. With regard to the growing season, the average length of the long and the short rains in AEZ 4 is 60—70 days and in AEZ 5/6, about 50 days. With regard to drought, only in the central hill areas (AEZ 2/3, with the highest parts of 4) can adequate rainfall be expected in six or more years in ten (see Figure 2.2).

The breeding problem was to allocate priority to drought escape and drought resistance; it is difficult to meet both objectives in the same genotype. Most drought-resistance mechanisms require some quiescence during dry spells, after which they can resume growth without permanent injury, whereas drought-escape mechanisms require rapid development to maturity (Fisher, 1977). Shortness of season, therefore, calls for a crop that can develop quickly so that, by the time the rains end, it has completed those developmental stages most sensitive to water stress. High probability of drought (including within-season drought) calls for a crop that yields well under drought conditions. According to Mbithi (1967), the success of the Katumani varieties can be attributed to a change in breeding strategy from selecting for drought-resistance to selecting for drought-escaping properties, or early maturity.

The National Dryland Farming Research Station at Katumani was opened in 1956. In 1957, over 500 varieties were collected, and selected for earliness. The first improved variety released was Taboran (see Table 14.1), a member of the Mexican race Salvadoreno, imported from Tabora, Tanzania. Katumani Synthetic II offered a substantial yield improvement in roughly the same maturation time. Further improvement eventually yielded Katumani Composite B (KCB), released in 1968.[2] Later, Makueni Composite was released for areas with less than 250 mm of seasonal rainfall.

Promotion and adoption

From 1963, the new maize varieties were actively promoted by the extension services, along with associated technologies. Multiple methods were used for promoting the new varieties:

> The departments which were involved in the field extension campaigns were the District administration, the Agriculture Department, and Community Development. Agents were appointed by the Agriculture Department in co-operation with the administration; the Information Department got out publicity; and the chiefs were used to round up farmers for barazas. Initially, free seed for the first acre was issued. Farmers who wished to establish demonstration plots received also free fertiliser and free DDT dust. (Mbithi, 1967: 14.)

Later, the emphasis shifted to demonstration plots. In 1965—1966 a maize planting campaign was supported by loans in kind, but repayments were disappointing. Annual 'maize tours' took place to 'good' and 'bad' farmers. But in 1971 it was felt that the messages were still getting through slowly, and extension efforts were focused on the 'unconverted' farmers. However,

TABLE 14.1. Maize varieties released from the Katumani breeding programme

Variety	Year released	Days to 50% silk	Yield (tons/ha)	Remarks
Machakos White	—	76–79	1.8–4.0	Late flowering
Taboran	1961	63	1.83	
Katumani				
Synthetic II	1963	65	2.66	
Composite A	1966	65	2.82	Colour problems
Composite B	1968	65	3.0–4.0	Good husk cover
Makueni Composite	1969 (?)	55	2.5–3.5	Outyields Katumani varieties at <250 mm rainfall

Source: National Dryland Farming Research Station

the campaigns were not helped by seed shortages, nor by the refusal of the Maize and Produce Board to buy the maize produced!

In the short rains of 1975, it was estimated that only 44% of the maize area was planted to Katumani varieties (KNA: Agr/154/Maize/II). Lynam (1978: 177) reported that 89% of farmers in Makaveti, and 71% in Kampi ya Mawe and Kalawa, used them. In 1983–1984, 79% of a sample of 211 farmers used KCB, though 93% knew it by name (Muhammed et al, 1985: 34–36). But only 30 tons of seed were sold annually in the District. According to Carr (1989: 75.6), the drought-escaping varieties have enjoyed limited acceptance because they are particularly sensitive to moisture stress under erratic rainfall distribution. However, sales are not a good measure of use. Katumani's policy of producing open-pollinated composites enables farmers to save seeds from their own harvests and sell to each other. Farmers tend to renew their composite seeds only after every third season. For example, Onchere (1976: 52) reported that 20% of his farmers had planted seed from the previous harvest — a practice that was not then recommended with the new varieties. Frequent crop failures lead to some fresh seed input regularly (Muhammed et al, 1985: 36). Furthermore, there has been extensive on-farm crossing, so that the local varieties are now considered to contain some Katumani strains. The estimates just quoted therefore understate the real impact of Katumani varieties. By 1985, extension messages had adapted to local practice and recommended purchasing KCB every other year.

Adoption also varies among the ecological zones. In AEZ 2/3, Kitale hybrid 511 or 512 maize is often preferred to KCB, having been bred for somewhat wetter and cooler conditions. The highest percentages of farmers using Katumani maize are found in AEZ 5, although Makueni Composite is better adapted to conditions there.

Farmer experimentation

There is some evidence (Onchere, 1976: 52; Rukandema et al, 1981: 18) that seed shortages deterred farmers from using Katumani varieties in some years. But at least as important a reason for the incomplete adoption of KCB is farmer ambivalence, rooted in on-farm evaluation of the performance of local and improved varieties under conditions of uncertain rainfall. Some 33% of Rukandema's farmers, and from 35% to 60% of Onchere's, believed that local varieties were as good. During 1983–1984, 80% of KCB users gave early maturity as a reason for adoption, and only 25% gave high yield (Muhammed et al, 1985: 36). This ambivalence is perhaps surprising in view of optimistic estimates of expected income improvements from the use of the new technology by Heyer (1967) and Lynam (1978) — by 50% on farms of 3 ha and by 70% on farms of 5 ha in AEZ 4.

Group and farmer interviews conducted in five locations in 1990 throw some light on user rationales. In Makueni (AEZ 4/5), during the 1940s and 1950s, settlers tried out various seeds available to them, including a yellow variety (probably imported as food aid: it proved inferior to local white). Early adoption of Taboran maize was a logical response to rainfall conditions there. Later, KCB was adopted in its place, but some farmers have reverted to the older type because KCB is more susceptible to weevil damage. Local varieties, however, are still in use, and no mention was made of the use of Makueni Composite. Of 40 farmers interviewed in five locations, only a third use Katumani varieties (sometimes more than one) exclusively, whilst another third plant Katumani along with local or hybrid varieties, and a third use no Katumani seed at all. It is unlikely that cost is deterring them.

Farmers' experimentation is not confined to evaluating alternative varieties, but extends to adaptive selection and crossing. One woman farmer explained how she plants KCB and her local seeds in blocks — with Katumani on the windward side — so that cross-pollination occurs. She then selects the best cobs from the middle to use as improved seed stock, retaining the seed from the outer lines to repeat the cross the following year. The crossed seeds, she claims, both matured earlier than the local seeds and yielded better than KCB. Some farmers have been formally involved in the maize breeding programme, through hosting on-farm trials and providing varieties for testing. Selected seeds from a farmer's Mwalavu variety, for example, proved to have better cob placement (higher and less susceptible to pest damage) and similar yield potential to KCB, although maturing five days later (J. Kasewa, pers. comm., 1990).

Lessons from the Katumani maize story

It cannot be known with any certainty what percentage of farmers use KCB, how much of the maize area is planted with it, or what proportion of total output it contributes. What is known is that its adoption is incomplete, and is likely to remain so. From a 'green revolution' standpoint, such an outcome appears to qualify the success of the breeding programme. But from the standpoint of the goals of small farmers, it is a measure of some success, for three reasons.

(1) The observed levels of adoption, sustained over two decades, show that KCB is perceived to contribute positively to household subsistence, by maximising yields under the constraint of a variable semi-arid rainfall regime.
(2) KCB strengthens, rather than undermines, the flexibility or adaptive choice that is essential for coping with such a regime and with the range of micro-environments found in the District. That is to say, it extends rather than replaces the menu options.
(3) Its open-pollinating characteristic permits experimentation, which is a major resource of the farming system, and releases the farmer from total dependence on external sources of seed.

In Chapter 6, evidence was presented that food security has improved, notwithstanding an increase in the population, and migration into agroclimatically riskier areas, though large-scale imports are still necessary after prolonged drought. The view that low yields and frequent failures, resulting from extending maize cultivation into drier zones, threaten food security, might predict a 'green revolution' into KCB. This has not occurred. The manner of its adoption into a cropping system characterised by varietal diversity, strategic flexibility, and adaptive experimentation, though perhaps unexpected, suggests that the system is less vulnerable than had been supposed.[3]

HORTICULTURE AND FRUIT

The search for market crops

From 1954, and especially during the 1970s, Akamba farmers gained access to the lucrative export coffee market, but this benefited only those having land in AEZ 2/3. In the lowlands, sisal 'used to be the lifeline of the dry areas' (Mbithi, 1967: 7), but falling prices forced the County Council factory to close in the 1960s. The Government's promotion of cotton, using a combination of incentives and coercion, produced periods of expansion in the 1930s and the 1960s; and there was a third campaign during the period 1976−1985. All three were followed by a collapse of output when prices fell (see Mortimore and Wellard, 1991).

The story of horticulture and fruit production is less well documented, because it was never the major objective of the Government's research and extension efforts. Nevertheless, its impact has been profound, not only in the wetter AEZ 2/3 where it began, but in AEZ 4 and even 5.

Origins

Travelling Akamba brought back seeds and seedlings from Kikuyu country. Small-scale intensive production of hand-cultivated fruit and vegetables is well suited to some micro-environments found in the hill areas of Machakos, and the Northern part of the District was well within reach of the Nairobi market. Strawberries, introduced by the African Inland Mission to Mbooni, and Egyptian onions were popular crops in 1935 (Peberdy, 1958: 14). Pineapples were first introduced about 1930, but grown in commercial quantities from 1952 using imported suckers (Peberdy, 1958: 26, 235, 247). The missions introduced the mango to parts of Mbiuni as recently as the 1950s (Gielen, 1982: 37). According to our informants, missionaries and Asian traders were active in introducing horticultural crops to Kangundo. Coriander, first recorded as a District export in 1943 (Peberdy, 1958: 229), and cited by our informants as a significant market crop in several drier areas in the 1940s, was probably introduced and bought by Asians. Other 'Asian' vegetables were introduced in the same way. Traders supply seed to farmers and guarantee a price for the crop. The method continues to be used; for example, with French beans and spinach.

Research and promotion

Agricultural officers stationed in the District had few resources to direct into the multi-faceted fruit and horticulture sector, but there was a seed farm at Machakos Town, and at the horticultural section of Ngelani farm in Kangundo; variety trials on 22 fruits and nuts and 16 vegetables were in hand or planned in 1959 (Peberdy, 1961). The fragmentation of the sector — in terms of crop varieties, markets, techniques and locations — imparted a completely different character to research and extension efforts. Among 22 vegetables tried successfully in the District by 1958 (Peberdy, 1958: 187, 283−287), the most valuable (per acre) were egg plant, onions, cucumbers, English potatoes, lettuce and tomatoes. All could be grown twice yearly, which made them attractive to farmers.

The Agricultural Department was active in seeking market outlets (see below). Its activity has diminished in recent years — or there is less evidence of it — and in nursery provision for fruit tree growers it has not been effective. Some 11 ministry nurseries were supplying seedlings to a mere 3% of farmers sampled in 1986, and all of them ran at a loss, notwithstanding a strong demand for seedlings (ADEC, 1986). The demand was being met by private sector nurseries.

Adoption

The early popularity of fruit trees is shown by some estimates of their numbers in four AEZ 43/4 locations in the southern hills in 1959.[4] The average numbers (growing and non-growing) amount to four fruit trees per household. Village surveys carried out in three locations in the 1980s (Table 13.2) imply considerable numbers of fruit trees per household. In three villages in Mbiuni Location, 86% of the households grew at least one fruit tree in 1981, though 71% grew less than five (Gielen, 1982: 32). Ecosystems (1985/6, Vol. 4: Table 2.15) reported that, in the District as a whole, the number of fruit trees increased at a rate of 8.6% per year from 1981 to 1985 — notwithstanding a major drought. Only Makueni and Kibwezi Divisions had no increase. A rapid expansion of citrus planting was also reported after 1980 (ADEC, 1986: 5.5), and also of mango and pawpaw. This expansion is confirmed by interviews held in 1990, and is especially noticeable in AEZ 4.

The story of oranges is illustrative. The Chief of Kiteta was given some Washington Navel stock, about 1950, by an agricultural officer. He also acquired the craft of budding, according to informants, from South Africa. He established a nursery and appears to have acted as a centre for the diffusion of the technique; even in 1985 Kiteta was said to be the centre of citrus growing (ADEC, 1986). The first grower of oranges on a commercial scale in Makueni, who planted them in 1972, told us she had gone to Kiteta to learn grafting from the chief there. Other farmers in Makueni learnt from her success.

The information available on the adoption of vegetable crops is inadequate. Onchere (1976) gives data for villages in AEZs 3 and 4 in 1975. Only Irish potatoes and onions had been taken up in AEZ 4, and only by a few households, but in AEZ 3, the numbers adopting potatoes, cabbage and tomatoes exceeded 50% in some villages. The percentage of growing households is now believed to be large in AEZ 3, especially in the north, but plots are nearly always small, indicating a low level of specialisation, relatively high returns per hectare, and high inputs. Ecosystems (1985/6, Vol. 4: 2−15) reported average annual increases (from 1981 to 1985) of 35% in irrigated smallholder vegetables, and of 19% in vegetable gardens and other small plots. These figures confirm that a move into horticulture was occurring on a very significant scale, though these two categories comprised only 1% of the cultivated land in the District. Even in AEZ 3, rainfall variability causes major fluctuations in output from season to season. (Owako (1969: 258−260) quotes a range from K£3400 to K£23 000 in the value of fruit, and from K£9300 to K£76 200 in that of vegetable exports from the District between 1955 and 1965.)

The planting of citrus (especially oranges) has extended beyond AEZ 3 into drier areas of AEZs 4 and even 5. Figure 14.1 shows land being prepared for citrus planting in AEZ 5. The mango thrives in drier areas below 1500 m, and fruits out of season for the Nairobi market. More surprising from a technical standpoint is the growing of bananas and pawpaws on a large scale in AEZ 4, thanks to growing in pits, in diversion channels, and at the backs of terraces

FIGURE 14.1. Hole digging for citrus in AEZ 5, Kamu, Ngwata Location, 1990. The soil is being used to form terraces to trap run-off. The holes look similar in size to those insisted on for coffee in AEZs 2 and 3 in the 1950s and demonstrate the way technologies travel and are adapted. (Photo: D. B. Thomas, reproduced with permission)

where water is within the reach of roots (see Figure 11.4). In 1981 (Ecosystems, 1982, Vol. 1: 78) the average density of bananas in the District was 12/km^2; the highest density was in Northern Division (40/km^2), but even in Makueni Division a density of 8/km^2 was recorded.

Irrigation now permits some vegetable crops (and fruit) to be marketed in the dry seasons when there is no glut. (Horticultural production, though not originally for the external market, may have been the driving force behind several intricate, hand-constructed spring-diversion systems in the hills, a technology that is said to go back 200 years, and which may still be observed.) The Yatta Furrow was originally constructed to support grazing in an area where permanent settlement was forbidden. In 1967 a 50-ha smallholder irrigation scheme was constructed at Matuu (Bottrall, 1969). Local settlers applied for land, and were organised into intake groups sharing the water for a block. Pump-driven sprinklers proved uneconomic, but gravity fed irrigation, first under close DoA supervision, but recently largely self-regulated, continues to support a prosperous enclave of market gardening. Fruit (mango, pawpaw and banana), vegetables (tomatoes, onions, karella) and field crops (maize and cotton) are grown mixed, or in rotations, at the discretion of individual producers. Notwithstanding a favourable assessment in 1968 (KNA: DoA CROP/2/11/235), there have been no major irrigated developments since.

Marketing

Outgrower contracts with Kenya Orchards (for the Kenyan market) and Kenya Canners (for export) were influential in developing horticultural and fruit production (de Wilde, 1967: 104–105). Peberdy (1958: 237) believed that Kenya Orchards' buying activities in the 1930s were responsible for thousands of rough lemons found throughout the District.

During the Swynnerton Plan period, the Agricultural Department, Settlement Board officers, and the canners worked together to formulate policies for contracts and co-operatives to regulate relations between the producers and the canners, to promote cash crops for the new settlement scheme on the Mua Hills, and no doubt to help to secure reliable supplies for the canners. Price fluctuations, and low grade produce (owing to careless growing, picking or grading) were problems; nevertheless, contract growing continues. French beans were reported to us as being very profitable. (For another recent example, sweetcorn, see Ayako et al, 1989.) Organised groups of farmers were in a stronger position to negotiate terms with the canners (Bottrall, 1969: 12). Fruit that are on record as having been purchased by the canners include: strawberries, cape gooseberries, lemons, Seville oranges, plums (from European farms), peaches, figs, passion fruit, guavas and pineapples. The vegetables include green, haricot and French beans, sweetcorn, carrots and tomatoes.

The export vegetable market is now dominated by licensed dealers who have access to air cargo space and market outlets. Attempts by co-operatives to compete have not been successful; their prices and terms, therefore, tend to dictate participation.

The domestic urban marketing system for fruit and vegetables (Bottrall, 1969; Gomez, 1982) is fragmented, diversified and uncontrolled with regard to prices. Asian traders continue to dominate the marketing of 'Asian' vegetables (which are now also exported). In such an uncontrolled and often distant market, variable prices, transport problems, perishability and the need for information provided strong inducements for group marketing initiatives in the late 1960s, which have been described in Chapter 9. Market participation has since increased, according to our interviews (see Table 10.1). Fruit trees may continue yielding when other crops dry up in drought.

Producers' margins in vegetable production have probably been attractive throughout the period, though production and marketing risks were high. Owako (1969: 259) compares returns of Ksh 1400–1800 from a half-acre (0.2 ha) tomato plot at Mbooni, compared with Ksh 900–1200 under coffee and less than Ksh 100 under maize.

Lessons of the fruit and horticulture story

There are important differences between fruit trees and vegetables. Vegetable and field fruit production requires much more labour and purchased inputs than tree crops (perhaps excepting the banana). Vegetables are mainly annuals, and fruit trees are perennials. In relation to intensification in a land-scarce farming system, fruit trees offer a high return per hectare with low inputs of labour, and horticulture offers a higher return per hectare with high inputs of labour.

It is their marketing that they have in common. Its history is largely that of the urban, canning and export markets, and of channels adapted to the diversity and variability of both products and markets. Coffee and cotton required government interventions in extension, the provision of inputs, supervision of production, grading and marketing of output. They have recently run into difficulties, and these can be traced to rigidities in pricing and marketing, which are controlled by state-run monopolies. By contrast, horticultural and fruit crops, developed with far less government involvement (and expense), are sold through more fragmented and less controlled channels, and have been more dynamic over time. Adaptation and innovation are characteristic attributes of Akamba agriculture. With little or no official pressure, the performance of the sector, even in the drier areas, is in sharp contrast to that of cotton.

The high value per hectare of horticultural crops and fruit, when not reduced by drought or other factors, permits optimal use of micro-environments having a favourable moisture balance. The value per hectare also minimises the entry cost in terms of food grain production forgone.

THE OX-PLOUGH

History of adoption

In view of the reputation later acquired by the Akamba for resistance to change in agriculture and livestock husbandry, the early adoption of the ox-plough, if limited in scale, is astonishing. According to Peberdy it was introduced in 1910, and this 'undoubtedly led to the District Commissioner's statement in 1912 that the "Akamba are beginning to cultivate larger areas and disposing of larger quantities for cash (crops) than in former years"' (Peberdy, 1958: 4). The first European settlers arrived in the District in 1903, and though they must have used ox-ploughs, and attracted trade suppliers, seven years was a short lead-time for the innovation to have such a significant impact on the Reserve. Its early association with cash cropping is also noteworthy.

Smallholders in Kangundo are reported to have started buying ploughs, and training their own oxen, by the late 1920s. In 1933, the Agricultural Officer reported that draft implements (ploughs and cultivators) were widespread in the District (Kenya, DoA, 1933); about 600 ploughs were then in use (Kenya Land Commission, 1934). Although this would have been less than 3% of households, the ox-plough's popularity was actually beginning to worry the Administration, who feared that the Akamba would plough more land than they could properly manage, resulting in lower yields and soil erosion (Kenya, DoA, 1935).

Perhaps because of these misgivings, there is no record of systematic promotion of the ox-plough by the Agricultural Department. However, interviews have yielded evidence of one introduction by an agricultural officer (and there may have been more). This case is recorded below as it throws light on the link between livestock ownership and ox-ploughing, and the early evolution of the farming system, as well as on the adoption process:

Mr Thiaka of Muisuni, near Kangundo (see Chapter 4) can remember 'affairs of the world' from about 1915. Digging sticks were used for planting. Around 1920, shifting cultivation began to cease as a result of advice from local missionaries. There was no manuring, though abandoned house sites were recognised as fertile places for cultivation. On grazing land, woody regrowth was controlled by burning.

After marrying in 1928, he began to hire a plough and oxen in Machakos, at a rate of 50 cents per ridge (Ksh 0.5), spaced a yard apart, irrespective of length. Some people in Matungulu had enough cattle in the 1930s to hire out or operate three ploughs. The oxen — four, or six if breaking new land — had been trained by Indians to draw ox-carts, from 1923–1924. He could now cultivate larger areas and produce more grain and cash crops for sale.

In 1943, he bought his own plough and oxen. There were then two trade models on the market. In 1946 the Agricultural Officer introduced a new type which sold for Ksh 40. This plough was not popular, being very large and heavy in beam and mouldboard, and requiring six oxen, or eight when on grassed land. At this time the AOs were promoting contour ploughing, heaping stalks on the contour to stop erosion, and planting sisal on boundaries. They were also promoting row planting of maize and beans, using strings, which replaced irregular sowing with *jembes* (which had by then replaced digging sticks).

With the extension of the cultivated area, the grazing areas became smaller and cattle fewer. The plough he uses today is the lighter one (Victory plough) introduced during the 1940s, which uses two oxen. Its advantage is that in needing fewer oxen it can be supported with less grazing.

Another reason for early uptake, which accelerated during the period 1930–1964, was the experience of plough operation gained on European farms by those who worked on them, and the proximity of such farms to the Reserve. The short-lived cotton boom of 1936–1940 set a premium on plough ownership in the drier areas.

It is likely that the innovation curve was virtually complete by the late 1970s, in terms of usage. Rukandema et al (1981) reported that, in Mwala Location, 78% of farmers owned ox-ploughs and 72% owned oxen. In Makueni in 1975, 91% of farmers owned ploughs and 76% two or more oxen (Heyer, 1975). ADEC (1986) found that, in the District as a whole, 62% of sampled households owned ploughs. Poverty was the main reason for less than 100% ownership (Muchiri, 1979: 198; Rukandema et al, 1981). Farmers owning oxen or bulls generally plant on time, but other farmers may be unable to do so, having to borrow or hire. Sharing or borrowing are reported where one or more of the components (plough and two trained oxen) are lacking.

Ownership is more frequent in AEZs 4 and 5. Our interviews suggest that in the lowland locations of Masii (AEZ 4) and Ngwata (AEZ 5), most farmers are said to own ploughs; in Kangundo (AEZ 3), about half; but in the hills of Mbooni (AEZ 2/3), many farmers are obliged, by reason of their small and intricately terraced holdings, to use the forked *jembe* (itself an innovation, widely marketed only after 1960).

Heyer's farmers in Makueni gave the following reasons for using the ox plough: it is cheaper and more available than a tractor; it saves labour and time; it requires little skill; it gives a good depth of cultivation, and quick germination; it retains soil fertility;[5] and is suitable for most topography and poorly cleared sites. Its disadvantages, however, are: it is slower, requires more labour and can cultivate less land than a tractor; it is susceptible to cattle disease, theft, and shortage of grazing; it calls for extra hand weeding; and (with the oxen) it is expensive. This evidence leaves no doubt why use, if not ownership, is very high; but little work has been done to quantify or prioritise these benefits under smallholder conditions.

Sources of investment[6]

It is worth asking what were the likely sources of investment funds. Early in this history, cattle ownership was greater per capita than now, though possibly no more widespread in the community. Large-scale herders could afford to sell animals to buy ploughs. In the 1940s a plough cost about Ksh 30, roughly equivalent to the cost of a cow. In the early 1930s, ploughs and teams were hired at the rate of one cow, two he-goats, or about Ksh 35 per acre. These relativities would have ensured rapid adoption of the technology.

Ploughs were available from dealers in Machakos and Nairobi. During the famine years of the 1940s, the Government provided ploughs (and dam scoops) for conservation work: dams, terraces, and scratch ploughing for grass planting. After World War II, soldiers who had seen ploughs in India, Burma and Ethiopia returned with the funds necessary for purchasing their own.

During the 1950s improved agricultural prosperity, and a high level of Akamba employment outside the District, made investment funds available in AEZs 2 and 3. Credit was provided by Asian traders, and much of the government's supervised credit was used for ploughs and ox-carts. Horticulture, coffee (after 1950) and cotton (from 1960) brought in cash, and some farmers had earned revenue from selling horticultural produce to Kenya Orchards and Kenya Canners.

In the mid-1970s Lynam, working in AEZ 4, found that only a farm size of 5 ha or more yielded an adequate return to investment from an ox-team (Lynam, 1978: 163). But given that the major factor affecting yields (and incomes) is the ability to plant early, the ownership of ploughs is more widespread than might be expected on purely economic grounds.

Development of types

The Victory mouldboard plough, now ubiquitous, was preceded by heavier types. Many types of plough have been marketed and promoted under different names over the years, and it is not possible, with the information we have recovered, to construct a technical chronology. The early ploughs were very heavy, and there are reports of up to 12 oxen (in Masii) being required for draft. The lighter mouldboard plough came into use in the 1940s, introduced by traders (according to the interview quoted above). It used only one pair of oxen and was more easily manageable, though farmers say it is less strong than the early ploughs.

The significance of the transition to lighter ploughs lies in their compatibility with reduced livestock holdings, smaller grazing areas, and the less frequent need to break new ground as cultivated areas stabilised. It is compatible with the increased participation of women in ploughing work (Figure 14.2). Also, it may be supposed that teams of several span were difficult to manipulate on the terraces that became increasingly common from the 1950s, and on the small fields of the uplands.

The mouldboard plough, however, was not officially judged to be well suited for Machakos conditions. Early planting is essential in order to make optimal use of the rainfall. A district agricultural officer's appraisal in the 1960s considered that it required a tractive effort greater than badly trained and underfed oxen could supply at the end of the dry season (de Wilde, 1967: 104). Correct adjustment was often not understood, or spare adjusters were not available; the share broke the soil but failed to bury trash; the same eight-inch furrow was used for primary cultivation, seedbed preparation and weeding (Alexander, 1975). For example, 60% of farmers in Makueni used ploughs for breaking new land, 83% for first cultivation, 79% for planting and 88% for weeding (Heyer, 1975). The mouldboard plough was judged unable to produce a cloddy structure (for infiltration) or to control weeds, as well as being unsuitable for dry ploughing (and planting) before the rains begin (Johnston and Muchiri, 1975).

Attempts to improve the technology centred on multi-purpose equipment adaptable to the different farm operations performed hitherto by the mouldboard plough. A single tool-bar modified from the Indian Desi plough can be used for chisel ploughing before the rains, opening planting furrows, and weeding (Muchiri and Mutebwa, 1979; Muchiri and Gichuki, 1982; Muchiri, 1983). The weeding equipment requires 5% of the man-hours per hectare to break hard ground prior to the rains, and serve for land preparation, planting and weeding. However, uptake was

FIGURE 14.2. Alice Mulandi and her plough. She is a member of one of the composting groups in Makeveti. Her grain store illustrates one of the reasons why building timber is in demand. (Photo: M. Mortimore)

negligible. Several hundred units were left unsold, and most users preferred their old ploughs, finding the MIDP equipment too heavy for their draft oxen and much more expensive (ODI, 1982). There is no record of farmer participation in research and development. An evaluation report concluded that the problems of the mouldboard plough had been overestimated. The mouldboard plough, slightly modified and available in different sizes, is the one principally used in Machakos today.

Associated practices

Dry planting

Animal power had a considerable impact on cultivation practices. From the 1960s, extension workers advocated dry ploughing and planting (particularly for the Katumani maize varieties). Ox-ploughs enabled farmers to take this up. However, early planting means that stronger oxen are needed for breaking hard ground, when fodder is scarce; two cultivations of the seedbed are necessary; there is a higher risk of seed loss; and weed growth is more dense. Thus by the mid-1970s, acceptance of dry planting was mixed. Its rates of adoption by farmers in Makaveti (AEZ 4) and Makueni (AEZ 4/5) were 78% and 61% respectively, but in Kalawa (AEZ 5), it was less than 25% (Lynam, 1978). Dry planting is now fairly widespread, according to our interviews, but depends on the rainfall pattern and the conditions of animals in a given year. To spread risks and save time, many farmers plant both before and after the rains.

Row planting and inter-row weeding

Row planting and inter-row ox-weeding were promoted by extension workers from the 1950s. In 1963, only a few of the farmers in Masii were practising it (Heyer, 1967). According to our interviews, women farmers in Embui did not learn inter-row weeding until after 1960. By the mid-1970s, however, much of the lowlands were ox-weeded (in the first weeding); up to 86% of farmers in Makueni weeded with oxen (Heyer, 1975), and 90% of the cultivated area surveyed by Lynam (1978) was so weeded.

Ox-weeding reduces labour requirements at a peak time, from 17 to 11 man-days/ha according to Lynam (1978). This was an advantage, especially where farmers had extended their cultivated land in the drier, land-surplus areas. Also, timely weeding conserves moisture by limiting weed competition, reducing run-off and increasing infiltration. These advantages are fully recognised in some ox-weeding systems (for example, Neunhauser et al, 1983: 32−33).

Lessons from the ox-plough story

The ox-plough has proved to be both a durable and a flexible technology. Early adapted to opening new land, with teams of six or eight oxen, it later evolved into a two-oxen instrument suitable for work on small terraced permanent fields. At the same time, average cattle holdings declined, and shortage of grazing dictated a transition to more intensive feeding systems. Today, the need to maintain a viable plough team provides the 'bottom line' keeping many farmers in cattle ownership. Use of the plough spread early on with little government promotion. The sources of investment funds were critical. The 'oxenisation' of Akamba agriculture was, in a measure, a triumph of capitalisation in a capital-scarce, risk-prone and low productive farming system.

The Victory mouldboard plough is criticised as inefficient in several respects, and for being inefficiently used. Yet attempts by the Government and other bodies to intervene in promoting improved technologies have not had a significant impact in the District. An imperfect technology, in the hands of skilful users, is better than a poorly tested innovation, whose adoption, furthermore, calls for major new investment.

The history of the plough in Machakos District is full of paradoxes which support the view (McIntyre et al, 1989) that ox-ploughing is an imperfectly understood technology in tropical Africa. In Kenya, according to Muchiri (1983) there was no definite policy on ox-ploughing before 1975. This is reflected in a sparse research literature, which even now is dominated by technical issues, rather than those of economics or management.

MANURING AND COMPOSTING

Management options

The need to intensify agriculture on permanent fields, with cultivation twice a year, brought about a transformation of the regime of fertility management. What has been achieved falls short of sustainable productivity everywhere, but the direction of change is clear nonetheless.

The soils of the District are deficient in nitrogen and phosphorus (see Chapter 7). Early planting, which is practised in order to take the best advantage of the rainfall, also secures for the crop the benefit of the nitrogen flush that occurs in the first rains. But where phosphorus is seriously deficient, even nitrogen fertiliser may not improve yields significantly.

There are four main soil improvement options: (i) the use of inorganic fertilisers, (ii) the extended use of boma (farmyard) manure; (iii) alternative organic systems (compost, mulches, green manure); and (iv) the extended use of nitrogen fixing legumes as intercrops, rotations or farm trees. Probably none of these alone provides a complete answer to the loss of plant nutrients under cultivation. But in the historical experience of the District, it has been the increased use of boma manure that has provided the main theme in fertility management.

Early promotion of manuring

Official policy favoured boma manure from the start. The Reconditioning Committee (1944–1955) considered that it was 'dangerous to put too much reliance on fertilisers, as they were not real substitutes for farmyard manure and proper rotational measures' (Peberdy, 1958: 21). Behind this 'Better Farming' propaganda, which aimed overtly at intensive mixed farming, may have lain an awareness that the cost of inorganic fertilisers would not recommend them to resource-poor smallholders. Also, where rainfall is unreliable, inorganic fertilisers are not only a risky investment, but may lead to increased water stress. Manure improves the structure of the soil, minimising damage from water splash and improving water retention.

The Department of Agriculture used its model smallholding to demonstrate the advantages of mixed farming. It promoted manure, compost, crop rotations and planted fallows. A Chief's Act was used to encourage the use of manure. Recommendations for manure production and use were given great stress in the 1950s, along with early planting and row cropping (de Wilde, 1967: 102; J. R. Peberdy, pers. comm.). Nitrogen fertiliser was recommended for coffee, but repeated trials with food crops had shown poor and erratic responses. Phosphate fertilisers had given more definite and reliable responses with maize, but these were unspectacular. Manure appears to have had a more marked effect on yields. Experiments at Makueni, for example, gave improvements of 50% in return for a 'moderate' dressing of 5 tons of manure per acre (Kenya, DoA, 1953).

Adoption

It is of some importance to establish when the use of boma manure became widespread. There are reports of the use of manure as a general practice by 1940, but Peberdy (1958: 18) comments that 'when examining these early reports in the light of present practice, it appears that they must have been over-estimated, because it was not until 1950 that widespread manuring became apparent in Kangundo and Matungulu, while in some areas it was still the exception rather than the rule'. In 1946, the Agricultural Officer reported that 80% of a small sample of 26 fields in Kangundo and Matungulu Locations were manured, and the differences between manured and unmanured plots were remarked upon by their owners (Kenya, DoA, 1946). There was a local trade in manure, and Akamba farmers had also been selling it to nearby European farmers for some years. This implies that a turning point may have been passed in these northern Locations some time in the 1930s, though general acceptance of the practice came later.

The information that is available on the adoption of boma manuring in different areas suggests that its use is still spreading. In 1956 it was estimated that 70% of farmers in high-potential areas used it, compared with only 2% in semi-arid areas (Kenya, DoA, 1956). In Masii (AEZ 4) in the early 1960s, manure was used only on some of the nearer fields (Heyer, 1967). In Northern Division in the mid-1970s, more farmers used boma manure in the hill locations than in the plains (Onchere, 1976). But by the 1980s, adoption had reached 90% of farmers in some areas (for example, Yatta: Neunhauser et al, 1983); they were spreading manure over whole fields, in lines or in selected patches. (Placement, to save manure, was taught in the 1950s; J. R. Peberdy, pers. comm., 1992.) In Mwala, about 66% of farmers were using it; in Nzaui, about 50% used it on maize, 33% on beans and fewer on cotton (Rukandema et al, 1981). The ADEC sample survey (ADEC, 1986: 6.34) reported that 87% of farmers in the District used boma manure on crops, and 3% were selling it. Only 10% did not collect it. These figures imply that, in terms of the percentage of users, the adoption curve is almost complete. By contrast, inorganic fertiliser use is minimal, the bulk of it on coffee (ADEC, 1986: 7.6).

The percentage of adopters, of course, tells us nothing of the rates of application, which are known to be highly variable in space (from field to field and within fields) and time (from season to season).

Factors influencing use

The use of boma manure is influenced by (i) yield expectations, (ii) rainfall risk, (iii) supply and (iv) labour and transportation. With regard to expectations, most reports suggest that the best returns from the use of boma manure (especially if it is purchased) can be obtained from coffee, cotton, and improved maize. However, little information has been found on farmers' choices. The residual effects are also recognised.

With regard to risk, the probability of losing a crop through drought deters farmers from using manure (and perhaps other) inputs. Also, it is known that manure may 'burn' the crop,

FIGURE 14.3. Boys transporting waste from Kangundo town to use as manure on the farm. (Photo: D. B. Thomas. Reproduced with permission)

or accentuate water stress, under dry conditions. However, as shown above, manure use has extended steadily into the drier zones, according to the historical record.

Manure supply on the farm is obviously constrained by the size of livestock holdings, which diminished considerably during the period covered by this study, though partly compensated by improvements in the efficiency of collection brought about by stall feeding. Demand has exceeded supply, in some areas, ever since the 1940s, when farmers were buying manure at Ksh 1 for 7−10 bags in Matungulu (Kenya, DoA, 1946). Of those farmers in Mwala who were not applying boma manure around 1980, most cited a lack of livestock as one of their main reasons (Rukandema et al, 1981). In 1990, 40 farmers interviewed in five Locations, in all agro-ecological zones, reported problems of obtaining sufficient manure from their animals, and of cash for purchasing it (or fertilisers). The only ones who said they had few problems in maintaining soil fertility lived in the newest settled location (Ngwata). The better-off farmers buy manure supplies from livestock owners, sometimes Maasai in Kajiado, who do not use it. But at around Ksh 300/ton, the price is now becoming prohibitive. Town refuse is an alternative for some (Figure 14.3).

Labour inputs in manuring have undoubtedly increased with the acceptance of boma management as the normal method of keeping livestock for at least part of the year. Probert et al (1990) report that farmers knowingly delay in moving manure from boma to fields, because they are busy with early planting. With regard to transportation, a shortage of carts and (in hilly areas) difficult terrain may impede the distribution of manure. Transportation problems were cited by some farmers in Mwala as one of the main reasons for not using manure (Rukandema et al, 1981). They may have been referring in oblique form to a labour problem.

Sustainable nutrient cycling

Manure supplies a range of plant nutrients, most critically nitrogen and phosphorus. Field samples from cultivated terraces show that manuring has a marked effect on available phosphorus, which may be limiting even in the presence of nitrogen fertiliser (Okalebo et al, 1990).

Assuming that boma manuring yields 1 ton/year/livestock unit, an average livestock holding of 8.7 units (2.4 oxen, 7.7 cattle, 8.1 goats and 1.3 sheep), kept on 5.1 ha of grazing, could provide an application of 2.5 tons/ha/year on 3.4 ha of cropland, containing 50 kg of nitrogen and 9 kg of phosphorus (Probert et al, 1990). This would support a maize yield of not more than 2 tons/ha, assuming that all residues are recycled as manure, and all nutrients are fully utilised by the crop.

However, land holdings of this size are generally found only in AEZ 4/5. Residues have other uses (especially fodder). The boma system, as it is operated on the majority of farms, is relatively inefficient. The quality of the manure is poor, owing to the incorporation of soil from the floor of the boma; the earth floor also permits the loss of nutrients into the soil beneath. Losses of nitrogen occur through volatilisation, and by denitrification (when the manure is waterlogged). Application to the crops is prone to be left late, and most farmers can only manure a few of their fields each year (Probert et al, 1990).

Improving the efficiency of the boma system should be a target for research. But there will never be enough manure under the constraints of this nutrient cycling system.

Composting

Composting, a closely related technology, was also promoted hard in the 1930s (Peberdy, 1958: 15–19). By 1937, there were reported to be 10 698 compost pits constructed, and over 1000 farmers had tried the technique. It is not known what became of these compost pits. Since dry bedding and uneaten crop residues are normally incorporated in boma manure, it appears possible that the early reports were referring to manure production under a different name. Mr Thiaka, of Kangundo, remembers AOs promoting compost around 1945, but he said that boma manure was preferred by cattle owners who would then have been more numerous than in 1990. Today, farmers with no livestock are said to make compost. Farmers owning livestock cannot, as a rule, afford to use residues for this purpose.

Compost making is being promoted again by NGOs, notably the Kenya Institute of Organic Farming (KIOF).[7] In the Makaveti area there are 56 participating farmers (women and men) organised in five groups. Each group meets twice weekly to provide labour for its members, especially for water carrying. The compost is applied, in handfuls, to each crop stand in the last season's furrows, and buried with the seed by turning in the adjacent ridges with the plough. Considerable quantities are required per hectare.

Compost, which combines manure, vegetation, ash and soil, is preferred to using manure alone because (i) it doubles the quantity of organic matter available; (ii) it reduces the problems associated with insects such as cutworm; and (iii) it does not 'burn' the crops when rainfall is deficient. The first and third of these reasons have the utmost relevance to AEZs 4 and 5, where arable areas are larger than in AEZ 2/3, the soils intrinsically less fertile, and the risk of drought greater.

Compost making may compete for some of the plant materials normally used for feeding livestock. The use of *Lantana camara*, which has few alternative uses, but grows uninvited along roadsides and on abandoned land, and other wild shrubs and hedge plants, sidesteps this potential limitation.

Lessons from the manure and compost story[8]

The growing use of boma manure and composting is entirely consistent with a historical imperative of labour intensification, on holdings diminishing in size, generated by a growing population and increasing land scarcity.

One primary constraint operating on the use of boma manure is supply (livestock holdings). The substitution of compost for manure not only increases the quantity of organic material generated from the boma but also brings into the managed nutrient cycle various fugitive sources such as *Lantana camara*, representing a significant increase in its biological efficiency. The second primary constraint on the use of both manure and compost is labour, especially for transportation (transportation equipment is also sometimes scarce). A general increase in population does not connote an adequate supply of labour on every farm. Manure making and distributing is organised at the household level, but it is significant that the KIOF's composting scheme is predicated on collaborative inter-household use of labour and equipment. Such institutional arrangements achieve increased efficiency in the use of labour and capital in the farming system as a whole. The introduction of compost in the 1930s and 1940s failed because it was premature not only institutionally but also economically, in that a cheaper alternative (manure) was available in AEZs 2 and 3, and there was lack of incentive for intensive farming in AEZ 4 (see Chapter 10).

CONCLUSION

The material is rich in policy implications, but only three general points are made here.

The Machakos experience provides strong support for the idea that technological innovations may originate from multiple sources, in geographical space, in time, and in the institutional sense (Biggs, 1989). The role of the farmers themselves is pre-eminent (Parton, 1990). Among the many examples that could be cited, farmers' experimentation with alternative varieties of maize, and adaptation of the ox-plough to terraced smallholder agriculture are outstanding. However, as both these examples illustrate, farmers did not work in isolation. Government plant breeders diversified the options available to maize growers, and the undocumented activities of traders and European farmers introduced the plough and provided start-up experience. To these three sources must be added travelling Akamba (bringing back ideas from as near as Kikuyu or as far as Burma), commercial fruit and vegetable buyers, and, more recently, NGOs. Others could be added. Given such a multiplicity of sources and promotional agencies, technological change is in 'continuous disequilibrium' (Biggs, 1989) amongst an assortment of interest groups. Interventions in the management of such change cannot sidestep the political economy of these interests, any more than they can avoid the technical implications of the low and erratic rainfall or the properties of the soils.

The motivations for adoption are also diverse. The need to manage risk, in achieving food sufficiency at the household level, has driven technological change. Katumani Composite B maize added to the diversity and flexibility of the cropping system and thereby contributed to meeting this objective.

The imperative of labour intensification in the farming system, in response to an increasing scarcity of land, also drove technological change. The adoption of more efficient methods of cycling scarce nutrients is consistent with such an imperative. Capitalisation of the farming enterprise, illustrated in the adoption of the ox plough, was a necessary concomitant of labour intensification, and facilitated the more productive use of labour and, ultimately, of land.

Market development drove technological change in providing increased incomes from more productive use of the land, illustrated here in the story of horticulture and fruit production.

In consequence of the successful management of technological change, the farming system that was understood to be in a crisis of overgrazing and declining yields in the 1930s and 1940s is now more sustainable and more productive than it has ever been before.

NOTES

1 The literature on Machakos District documents a wealth of production technologies that in one way or another have contributed to the observable changes in primary production systems. An inventory of these technologies is offered in Mortimore and Wellard (1991), where cotton, coffee, livestock and feeding-system technologies are also analysed, in addition to those included here.
2 KCB takes 120 days to reach full physiological maturity at Katumani (AEZ 4), but only 100 days at Kampi ya Mawe (AEZ 5), where the mean annual temperature is 5°C higher (Nadar, 1984).
3 Carr (1989: 75–77) argues that farmers need a drought-tolerant, rather than drought-escaping, variety,

and moreover, one that yields well if planted late, owing to the labour constraint that usually ensures only a small proportion of farmers' fields can be planted early. During the 1980s, breeding policy at Katumani aimed to improve yield without sacrificing earliness and adaptability (Kenya, MoA, 1983: 10). Breeding for the best phenological match between plant development and expected rainfall distribution (Nadar, 1984) has been relatively successful. Keating et al (1990b) conclude that there is little to be gained from further breeding for altered phenology at Katumani (AEZ 4), and only very modest gains at Makindu (AEZ 5). They argue that improving nitrogen supply should be the next major target for research.

4 Kilungu, Kalama, Mukaa and Okia. KNA: DoA Kilome HORT/1/20 (20 September 1959); see Mortimore and Wellard (1991, Table 3).
5 Our interviewees believe that use of the plough improves yields.
6 This section owes much to J. R. Peberdy (1991, pers. comm.).
7 The sources for this account are Rose Maweu and Agnes Mulandi. The method is described in Mortimore and Wellard (1991).
8 This review has paid little attention to the first and fourth management options listed above. Inorganic fertilisers, though applied profitably to commercial crops, compete for scarce capital which will always limit their usefulness. The medium and longer term nutrient requirements of arable soils cannot be met with inorganics alone. Leguminous crops (and trees) already have an established place in the system, but not much research appears to have been done on extending their contribution. They can correct deficiencies of nitrogen, but not of phosphorus.

PART IV

WHAT WORKED AND WHY

15

Interventions and Policies

INTRODUCTION

It is not the purpose of this book to make a general critique of Kenyan policy. However, since it is concerned with the rural environment and its productivity, it is important briefly to review national policies for agricultural extension, research and marketing. We shall also assess two District programmes (ALDEV and MIDP) which brought in temporary infusions of additional funds and staff to deal with the special problems of a semi-arid area. This will enable us to consider the role of special funds in the Machakos story, and also, in relation to the ALDEV programme, the role of compulsion versus persuasion.

MARKETING BOARDS AND CO-OPERATIVES

Although major export crops like cotton and coffee are subject to compulsory marketing through co-operatives, there is a large sphere for private enterprise, particularly in the local grain and livestock trades, in horticulture and in inputs. The situation in domestic marketing from the 1940s to the 1980s remained that the relevant Boards controlled only 'a fraction of the trade' owing to 'a vigorous and aggressive, if somewhat illegal, private marketing system' (Jones, 1972).

Grain

The motivation to control grain has arisen from the costs of imports and distribution in time of shortage. The National Cereals and Produce Marketing Board (NCPB)[1] has aimed to fix the producer price in order to induce an output sufficient to meet national requirements. This has often been higher than the world price, with the loss on exports spread over all suppliers (Heyer, 1976: 317). Purchases are made through an agent, generally one of the general produce buyers/retailers operating in local market centres. A permit from the District headquarters was required for moving more than 10 bags within the District or two bags outside it. (This requirement was only abolished in 1991.) This added to transaction costs, whether by conformity, or by evasion (Wyckoff, 1989: 360; see also Chapter 6). Consumer prices were set by adding processing and distribution costs to the producer price. The gap between producer and consumer prices in rural areas has been large (Chapter 6).

   The Board has been unable to purchase all that is offered in good years, or to control prices and supply to rural areas in bad years. Financial pressures and storage costs mean that it usually has to import in bad years, having exported in good years (Sharpley, 1986) although the maintenance of a national grain reserve was one justification for its control of grain movements. Although Kenya does achieve self-sufficiency in most years, imports are necessary when major food shortages occur. (Imports of the unpopular yellow maize were again necessary in 1992.) Equitable social distribution is achieved (with considerable success in 1984—1985) by a system of famine relief administered through District officials and non-governmental organisations (Borton, 1989) but this does not depend for its success on the movement controls.

The effect of the additional costs on trade and the sharp fluctuations in rural prices have been discussed in Chapter 6. Farmers in Machakos cannot risk specialisation, although they have no comparative advantage in maize production. However, it has been important that the Board has maintained prices at a level where there is an incentive to produce, rather than, as in some countries, depressing farm-gate prices in order to favour urban consumers.

Coffee and cotton

Coffee marketing is the monopoly of the Coffee Board of Kenya. Small-scale producers must market through coffee co-operative societies by means of which the members invest in drying and cleaning factories. The District Co-operative Union pays societies according to the grade delivered; the prices to members therefore vary according to the average quality of coffee produced, and local costs and efficiency in marketing and processing functions. As already noted, Kenya generally obtains an above-average world price for its coffee, as most of it is high quality Arabica. By African standards, taxes and deductions have been low. Coffee producers have resisted price stabilisation and receive a percentage of the world price. Farm-gate smallholder prices averaged 94% of the average world price in the 1970s. (The Kenya price, for quality reasons, would have been higher.) During 1981—1986 this fell to 84% (calculated from Lele and Stone, 1989: Table 12). Thereafter the share fell further: the 3% coffee cess paid to County Councils for road maintenance became a 6% tax, of which 5% went to the Central Government.

Increasing costs and inefficiencies in the Cotton Marketing Board in the 1980s led to late payments to the co-operatives dealing in cotton. This was responsible for the collapse of cotton production at this time, after it had been expensively promoted in the early 1980s by MIDP (see below).

Co-operatives

Co-operatives were initially formed by European farmers for their own purposes. They were promoted in the African farming areas by the new Department of Co-operatives in 1946 (Zeleza, 1990). Only three were registered in Machakos in the period 1946—1953, followed by 46 more in the period of high government activity, 1954—1962. The majority of those dealing in goods where there was private sector competition failed. The coffee societies survived, having both a monopoly and scale advantages in carrying out processing near the farms. Coffee accounted for 75% of co-operative purchases nationally in 1983 (Gyllström, 1991). Coffee areas generally have high population density, dense road coverage, high educational enrolment, and other advantages which favour good performance by either private traders or co-operatives. Societies in Machakos were performing well in the late 1960s, averaging 75% of world price receipts actually delivered to the producer when the best District averaged 77% (Hyden, 1973: 99—100). The scale of their activities is indicated by the Matungulu Co-operative Society which in 1975

TABLE 15.1. Agricultural staff in Machakos District, 1940–1988

YEAR	AO	AAO/TO	TA/AI	JTA/AAI	SCS	LEVELLERS
1940	1	—	16	34	3	29
1950	1	2	36	42	4	N/A
1951	2	4	34	47	2	137
1954	2	8	52	212	4	N/A
1956	4	16	82	256	2	N/A
1962	1	6	56	162	0	—
1976	8	8	47	105	—	—
1988	19	52	135	56	—	—

AO: Agricultural Officer
AAO/TA: Assistant Agricultural Officer or Technical Officer
TA/AI: Technical Assistant or Agricultural Instructor
JTA/AAI: Junior Technical Assistant or Assistant Agricultural Instructor
SCS: Soil Conservation Specialist (professional rank)
N/A: not available
Source: Mbogoh (1991), from Owako (1969) and District Annual Reports

operated seven coffee factories as well as owning two estates. The societies provided inputs to members on credit, deducting costs from receipts, although input purchases were also made from a variety of suppliers for cash (Onchere, 1976). In 1983 the Machakos societies were performing less well than those in better endowed districts, largely because all were in the marginal coffee zone, with lower than average yields per farm and thus higher marketing costs for smaller quantities (Gyllström, 1991). This was after the large expansion in coffee area (Chapter 6). Coffee then provided 85% of the total sales income of the District Union.

Many societies joined the Machakos District Co-operative Union, which provides central services such as book-keeping, accounting, bulk-purchasing of inputs, etc. In 1977, it consisted of 26 societies: 12 coffee, 13 recently-formed for cotton (which also bought maize) and 1 wattle bark. In 1976, the value of coffee production was Ksh 52.6 million while that of cotton was only Ksh 0.6 million, thus giving an idea of their relative importance. The Union was then made responsible for a new national programme, with World Bank finance, to direct credit towards food-crop producers in a combined cash and food crop package. It undertook this unwillingly, complaining that it did not have the necessary staff, facilities and training (ODI, 1982). The Machakos Union was one of several in Kenya that got into difficulties with the programme (Zeleza, 1990), with widespread default, indebtedness and encouragement to corruption affecting the Union's other activities.

Under the MIDP programme in 1978, an expatriate expert was assigned to the Union and funds were made available to improve or extend its rural stores, its lorry fleet, its equipment in weighing machines and pallets, and its communications (VHF radio system) for the cotton and food crop programme. The programme also paid for society secretary-managers and for training in improved financial methods. The Union tried to circulate some of these benefits to its coffee societies, which led to clashes with the MIDP. (There were also those within the Union who had benefitted from previous laxity.) The programme had a temporary beneficial effect on cotton production (Figure 6.3(b)). Rising numbers took credit for cotton, and in 1979/1980 and 1980/1981, 72–74% repayment was achieved (ODI, 1982). However, repayments fell in the subsequent droughts. In 1982–1983 the Union registered a loss of Ksh 1 254 000 (Gyllström,

1991: Table 4.20). By the late 1980s farmers were abandoning cotton due to late payments, high costs of inputs and low prices.

The inputs of capital and skills may have strengthened the Union. In 1987, it was said to have some 80 active societies, with the coffee ones remaining in the lead. Its turnover rose to Ksh 200—333 million during the years 1983—1987, depending on climatic conditions (Kenya, Ministry of Planning, 1988), although in grain it faced strong competition from private traders (Chapter 9). It had established a Machakos maize mill. Minor activities were the exports of crafts and horticultural products.[2] It is undoubtedly the biggest business in Machakos, and is entirely African-managed.

Nationally, the period 1971—1983 saw a huge increase in the Government's Co-operative Department staff, who are supposed to supervise and advise the societies, mainly because new functions such as the delivery of credit necessitated more complex accounting systems (introduced under the influence of various donor programmes).[3] Despite this, the market share of the co-operatives fell nationally, and they remained largely ineffective in the poorer areas with poor private marketing facilities.

We did not attempt to evaluate the role of the co-operatives in sustainable resource management. In the coffee areas they have been one of the institutions through which market information is provided, and through which farmers can have some voice in influencing the Board's policies, as well as a new means of raising capital. The strength of the coffee societies has probably contributed to the relatively favourable price policy pursued by the Kenyan Government, and the weakness of the new cotton societies may be one factor in the greater inefficiency of the responsible Board. It is significant that, as suppliers of inputs, they have always been in competition with a vigorous private sector trade.

AGRICULTURAL EXTENSION AND RESEARCH

Kenya has devoted impressive resources to extension. By 1973 there was one extension agent per 310 farmers on average — high by comparison with other African countries (Heyer and Waweru, 1976). However, in 1977 a generous estimate would be 1 agent to 700 farmers in Machakos (based on Table 15.1). The Ministry of Agriculture was preoccupied with the high potential districts during the period 1962—1978.

Colonial agriculturalists believed that

> The African in Kenya has not yet arrived at the level of education which enables him . . . to plan his agricultural economy successfully . . . In his case, therefore, it is essential that his general farming policy shall, to a large extent, be dictated to him in the light of the experience and knowledge of officers of Government responsible for his welfare . . . (L. H. Brown, 1968, quoting Annual Report of the Agricultural Department, 1945.)

This attitude underlay the compulsory programmes in soil conservation, the attempt at destocking, the forbidding of African experimentation with coffee, which later could only be grown under strict technical supervision. It led to the diagnosis—prescription—intervention mode discussed in Chapter 2, which ignored both discussion with the farmer of priorities, or even detailed studies of his or her activities. The de Wilde report of 1967 called attention to the lack of data of all kinds about farming in the different parts of Machakos District. The first farm-level studies were made for academic purposes in the 1960s. The first to be undertaken with the direct purpose of informing government policy were those of 1978–1981, in connection with programmes supported by FAO and MIDP. They then ceased.

Agricultural and veterinary research in Kenya was orientated towards the needs of the large farm sector, particularly in the high-potential areas. Thus, for coffee, a crop already grown by white farmers, there was a good research base. In the African areas good agricultural officers based their advice on 'what a few more advanced African farmers were doing, augmented by research results where necessary' (Brown, 1968: 79). This had some good results, as we have seen in respect of banana pits and bench terraces, but instructions based on short-term or inadequate experiments made Akamba farmers suspicious and difficult to convince. The advice to build roofed cattle sheds was taken up at first, until the termites got them.

Between 1945 and 1960 several specialised research stations were established, including ones for coffee, fruit and pasture. The establishment of the Katumani Research Station in 1957 gave attention for the first time to agriculture in semi-arid areas and led to the development of Katumani composite varieties of maize. However, programmes at Katumani have reflected fashions amongst a succession of donor organisations, rather than having arisen from farmer representation of their needs. Some programmes have stopped abruptly without follow-through. In 1990 the Director lacked any operational funds unless they were provided by a donor. Under the MIDP, the research–extension link remained unsatisfactory (G.M. Mbate, at the Machakos workshop, 1991). Research–Extension Liaison Committees were established in 1990, with the innovation of some farmer representation, but in the absence of funds were powerless to commission a continuing programme directed at local needs.

On the extension side, staff at Location level were for a long time inadequately trained. In 1951 Hughes Rice broadened the objectives of the Machakos Betterment programme beyond soil conservation and control of grazing to aim at increased productivity. With the special funds available to Machakos under ALDEV he and his successor Peberdy were able to establish a miniature Training and Visit system. Additional staff (Assistant Agricultural Officers with a diploma), almost all European, were posted at the Divisional level. They came in for a monthly review and planning session at District headquarters, and on their return would brief their Agricultural Instructors (AIs) at the Location; Peberdy insisted on four days a week out on tour to accomplish this. Although the AIs still did a lot of pegging of terraces, they were also able to talk to farmers about early planting, manuring by placement, planting in lines, etc. The supervision and briefing were essential since the AIs had only completed a primary education, and Assistant AIs were even less qualified. Machakos did not go in for farm plans for the 'progressive' farmer as elsewhere in Kenya, but concentrated on simple messages for the majority, with some specialised AIs for coffee (J. R. Peberdy, pers. comm. 1992). Hughes Rice also began the recruitment of women AIs. (Machakos has a relatively good record in attention to women. Women farmers formed 44% of participants in Farmer Training Programmes in Machakos in 1977 (Consortium, Report 7, 1978: 167)).

Given the low technical base of the AIs and AAIs, the system depended absolutely on good quality staff at the Divisional level. However, as Table 15.1 shows, the additional staff disappeared with the demise of ALDEV. De Wilde found the quality of the junior staff 'among the lowest in Kenya' (de Wilde, 1967: 99). In the 1970s the older Location staff still had the 'technical rudiments of soil conservation . . . [but they] were much less equipped [for] . . . patient persuasion and proper identification of farmers' problems and needs' (Mbindyo, 1974: 31), as 58% had had 4 months or less of technical training. They suffered from isolation, inadequate supervision and advice from technical specialists, and lack of transport and other aids to efficiency (Mbindyo, 1974).

Extension work was conducted mainly through individual farm visits, demonstrations, *barazas*, agricultural shows and clubs (Heyer and Waweru, 1976). A farm training centre established in 1961 ran short courses for farmers. With the increase in junior staff in the early 1980s there were more demonstrations and more short two-day courses at training centres, (attended by 6700 farmers in 1982/1983) (ODI, 1982).

The qualifications of extension workers had improved by the 1980s. New entrants have a school certificate followed by two years technical training. Numbers of senior staff were increased in the 1980s (Table 15.1) with assistance from various aid programmes. However, the argument as to whether the staff at Location level should be generalists or specialists has not been settled, and various tactics have been tried in the 1980s, sometimes at the cost of undermining existing work. The, thus MIDP had recruited and trained soil conservation staff to work with self-help groups (Chapter 11). Because they were not on the official pay-roll and lacked the requisite qualifications, most were dismissed when MIDP funding ceased and the extension service was reorganised to follow the Training and Visit system under another foreign-aided project (Mwenge, 1988).

The Akamba farmer has found the extension service one useful source of information. A survey of over 1000 farmers, including a substantial proportion from Machakos District, found that 475 said that they would accept a new idea if it was demonstrated to be profitable; 41% would accept if it provided more food. These were overwhelmingly the main influences; reduction of labour or profitability to others earned few responses (Mbithi and Bahemuka, 1981: 47). Asked whom they would turn to for advice on a technical agricultural problem, 40% responded with the agricultural officer, and 42% said friends or relatives (Mbithi and Bahemuka, 1981: 44). It is creditable to the agricultural service that so many see them as the obvious source of advice, but it is equally apparent that many others are also considered expert. Many Machakos farmers have had contact with the service, and have adopted those of its messages that they have thought practical and profitable, but it is impossible to separate the benefits of this extension from the other influences on agricultural production.

ALDEV

Funds and staff resources

Table 15.2 shows ALDEV (African Land Development Board)[4] expenditures in Kenya. Funds were provided first under a post-war Ten Year Development Fund. A new infusion of funding was obtained in 1954 under the Swynnerton Plan from Colonial Development and Welfare funds and a smaller USA grant. Although it comprised only 7% of the area and 8.5% of the population of the Districts benefitting from ALDEV, Machakos obtained 36% of ALDEV grants.

A Board was formed to co-ordinate the departments responsible for projects. The Board initially had eight European and three African members; between 1947 and 1950 this became six Africans, including Jomo Kenyatta, and four Europeans. However, there was a 'radical change' (Kenya, MoA, 1962b: 302) in 1951, and the Board was reduced to five or six members, all European. A minority African membership reappeared in 1955. As already noted, one of the 'unofficial' Europeans serving almost throughout was Major Joyce, a rancher from Machakos District, who also served on the Machakos Reconditioning Committee. However, the people of the Reserve were not represented. Locally, there was some improvement in communication and effective use of local institutions, with the appointment of the first Africans to senior staff status, both of them Akamba with local knowledge (Mr Onesmus Musyoki in Agriculture (Chapter 4) and Mr John Malinda in Community Development (Chapter 9)).

Table 15.2 shows the allocation of funding, according to the Board's final report (Kenya, MoA, 1962b). The 32% 'unlisted' relates to staff costs. It was felt that: 'The way to solve this special problem of "bad" districts was to strengthen the existing district staff with Aldev personnel who would be posted there for several years and would have the specific duty of administering development projects beyond the scope of the district authorities' (Kenya, MoA, 1962b: 2).

The temporary expansion of staff in the Agricultural Department is shown in Table 15.1, together with the abrupt return to much lower levels of staffing after the programme ended.

The programme was initially dominated by the costs of the Makueni settlement, which we have shown to be expensive in its methods and largely unnecessary. The shift to 'betterment' is shown below (Kenya, MoA, 1962b: 17):

	1946–1951	1952–1961
Makueni Settlement	K£167 110	K£157 082
Machakos Betterment	K£54 461	K£372 633

Betterment included the soil conservation, grass-planting and extension programmes which were staff-intensive, taking a considerable share of the unlisted expenditures in Table 15.2. The relatively small expenditures on water supplies had long-lasting effects, particularly in introducing techniques such as sub-surface dams and roof catchments which farmers could adopt themselves. The expensive Yatta Canal, like many of the dams built for the grazing schemes, enabled farmers to settle new lands, although no cost-benefit analysis on it has been performed.

Although total expenditure was large by the standards of the time, it was equivalent only to 88 700 tons of maize at 1957 prices, or 200 kg per person in the Reserve over 15 years. Famine

TABLE 15.2. ALDEV expenditures, 1946–1962 in K£

TOTAL		Grant	Loan	
Kenya		3 920 897	686 313	
Machakos		1 414 039	41 000	
Per cent		36	6	
Machakos breakdown	*Per cent*	*ALDEV grant*	*ALDEV loan*	*ADC loan*
Betterment	30	427 104		
Water supplies	6	83 728		
Sisal	0	4 510	20 500	26 000
Afforestation	6	80 362		
Yatta Canal	23	324 982		
Makueni	23	324 192	11 000	
Grazing schemes	11	150 543	10 000	20 000
Unlisted	32	445 722		
TOTAL	100	1 414 039	41 500	46 000

Source: Kenya, MoA (1962b)

relief in 1960–1961 required over 13 000 tons, plus distribution costs, which Peberdy (1961) thought amounted in total to £1 million. The effort to avert such expenditures through agricultural development was clearly justified, even if not all the means succeeded. Peberdy commented, 'On the face of it, Machakos has done very well out of ALDEV, but on the other hand, we have had little assistance from Central Government or the ADC, and neither has much money been spent on education, roads, veterinary, etc.' (Peberdy, 1958: 50). Interestingly, roads, schools and cattle dips were some of the main targets of self-help in the 1960s (see Chapter 9), which suggests that, had there been greater Akamba representation, expenditures would have been differently targeted.

Compulsion versus persuasion and consultation

A compulsory, large-scale programme was thought necessary by both Barnes and Maher in 1937. They rejected consultation and working through 'native' committees because this might be slow (KNA: Barnes, 1937: 3), and both the Colonial Office and white settler opinion were pressurising for urgent action against the scourge of soil erosion (Chapter 11). The originally-suggested programme of mechanical terracing and wholesale movement of families off endangered hillsides was abandoned in the face of the Akamba reaction to destocking, and the shortage of staff during the war, but the programme of compulsory communal work under government direction for two days a week, supplemented by compulsory closure of grazing areas, lasted some 20 years. At the end of that time, although the Reserve was in a better state than at the beginning, it was still remarkably poor, and still very vulnerable to famine. Owako noted that famine conditions reigned from September 1959 through till February 1962, and again during 1964–1965 (Owako, 1969: Table 21). At the same time, most of the compulsorily-built narrow-base terraces were decaying (Chapter 11). The only independent assessment of achievement, by McLoughlin, quoted in Chapter 2, credited it with only very partial success.

   Although compulsion is no longer an option for most governments, the temptation to promote a rapid attack on environmental problems through investments made under expert direction remains strong in the current climate of world opinion. It is therefore worthwhile to ask what might have happened if the choice to work through locally selected committees, and persuasion, had been made. Would it have achieved more or less in 20 years? What would have been the necessary conditions for the success of such an approach? Barnes gives evidence that some farmers were thinking hard about the reasons for the condition of their lands, that there was keen interest by the 'progressive' farmers around Muisuni and Matungulu in the soil conservation measures being tried out and the results of grassland closures. He did not stop to ask why the Akamba in these two areas were so different from the 'backward' ones elsewhere, described as suspicious about their land tenure rights and the Government's intentions. It is, however, significant that the 'progressive' farmers were the ones enjoying the best connections with markets, and who had had the longest exposure to new ideas through the mission at Muisuni and its schools. It seems likely, therefore, that a persuasive approach, embodying a choice of technologies, and *in the presence of market incentives and tenurial security*, might have succeeded in the same time frame, at least on privately-owned cultivated land.

   The rehabilitation of denuded grazing land might have posed a problem. We do not know from the record how much of the scratch-ploughing and grass-planting was on open-access *weu* and how much on privately owned land. At least some was on private *kisesi*, where people seem to have immediately and readily undertaken hedging, the government only supplying sisal suckers

(Table 11.1). The immediate rewards of further rehabilitation were less under grazing than on cropped land, as shown by Pereira et al (1961), and we have shown that it has been given a lower priority than cropped land, although it seems to be eventually undertaken. Some kind of government subsidy might have been necessary to bring about earlier rehabilitation. However, a lot of this land was converted into conserved cropped land — not an option that was considered in 1937. The effect of the grass-planting programmes on grazing lands was not scientifically assessed, but it may have contributed, in conjunction with their management by private owners, to the situation today, when they are being productively used for arable or grazing purposes.

The closing of denuded open-access grazing land for rest and recovery, and the removal of stock either to more distant and inconvenient grazing land or to labour-intensive stall-feeding, might have needed an element of compulsion. However, an alternative method of reducing the pressure on the land of the Reserve would have been to permit settlement in the Crown Land, as happened as soon as control was removed.

The 1950s are still remembered by older leaders as a time of great hardship and government harshness. Compulsion and mistaken technologies created hostility which the agricultural extension service could only slowly overcome. What has survived best from the 1950s are the roads, the dams and the technologies where government officers were assisting farmers to do what they wanted to do, in achieving better incomes from coffee and horticulture, and more reliable food crops through manuring, row-planting, etc. The remarkably rapid adoption of bench-terracing when market access improved in the early 1950s suggests that in the right circumstances an experimental, consultative approach can in fact bring about more rapid and enduring change than top-down direction. Other technologies, such as silage-making and composting, which did not take account of land:labour ratios at the time, were abandoned till the time was ripe.

THE MACHAKOS INTEGRATED DEVELOPMENT PROGRAMME (MIDP), 1978−1988

Table 15.3 shows funding for the various ASAL (Arid and Semi-Arid Lands) programmes in the period 1978−1991. Machakos received 17% of total expenditures, a figure halfway between its share of the total area (6.1%) and of population (23.6%). On a per capita basis it ranked sixth out of the 12 districts concerned. Expenditure was equivalent, in current prices, to 244 000 tons of maize, or 205 kg maize per head over the 10 years — a little more on a per capita basis than under the ALDEV programme.

The largest share of expenditures (24% in Phase I, 1978−1982, and 60% in Phase 2, 1983−1988) was on water developments, which seem to have been quite successful (Chapter 12). Although this included consultancy, expatriate technical assistance was more visible, and more resented, in Phase I programmes for agriculture, soil conservation, livestock, co-operatives and rural industry. The last had particularly little impact, involving high expenditures for buildings unsuited to many rural industries, in sites that did not necessarily have electricity. Soil conservation received about 6% of the total budget, equivalent to about 16 000 tons of maize. This was spent on staff, tools and operational expenses, and required supplementation, as in the 1950s, by farmers' freely contributed labour. The method adopted was quite effective (Chapter 11). The main useful contribution of the livestock programme was water storage tanks at dips, which made them more effective. The crop development programme, which included the cotton programmes and assistance in the introduction of T and V in Phase II, had no visible impact on yields (Chapter 6), partly because of the weather, and cotton marketing difficulties.

TABLE 15.3. Arid and semi-arid lands programmes, 1978–1991

Programme	Population of area	Total funding to current phase (K£m)	K£ per capita	Per capita rank
Machakos	1 654 486	17.25	10.42	6
Baringo	306 594	23.00	75.02	2
Kitui	723 725	15.00	20.73	4
Kwale	458 202	4.50	9.82	7
Kilifi	684 458	4.50	6.57	9
Laikipia	256 075	1.23	4.80	11
Elgeyo/Marakwet	169 159	1.25	7.39	8
West Pokot	296 611	1.74	5.87	10
Kajiado	267 300	4.10	15.34	5
Taita/Taveta	227 631	8.80	38.66	3
Turkana	145 869	19.60	134.37	1
Embu/Meru/Isiolo	1 815 159	0.35	0.19	12

Source: Kenya, Ministry of Reclamation, ASAL Policy Document (1991)

At the time of the evaluation of Phase I, one achievement was thought to be the improvement of the District planning system, and the better co-ordination of, for example, water, forestry and soil conservation work in particular catchments (ODI, 1982). Planning improved while the MIDP planning unit controlled funds. When external funding diminished or ceased, centrally-controlled programmes and budgets resumed their importance. The people of Machakos participated only to a limited degree (mostly at the stage when they were called upon to take over a water project), since the hierarchy of Planning Committees shown in Figure 9.2 is dominated by officials; the elected County Council is only one voice amongst many more powerful ones in the District Development Committee and has no influence on strategic decisions. Although roads had been identified by local people as one of the main constraints, along with water (Chapter 10), little funding was devoted to this sector, as the donors preferred a more direct approach to agricultural productivity through the support to agricultural programmes. (Most donors dislike the inclusion of roads in integrated development programmes (Adams, 1990), or the inclusion of water and electricity for small towns.)

THE ROLE OF PUBLIC INVESTMENT

The publicly financed programmes of ALDEV took place against a background of low private agricultural investment at a time when private incomes were very low and saving difficult. They could be justified as bringing in capital that was not available locally. Nevertheless, the public investment was supplemented by the considerable private investment of labour in the terracing and grass-planting programmes, through either voluntary *mwethya* groups or compulsory communal work. The MIDP programmes supplemented a level of private investment in conservation and production technologies that had in the meantime risen enormously.

The comparative size of private and public investments in soil conservation can be illustrated. The total estimated length of field terraces and bunds in 1985 was 82 690 km (Ecosystems, 1985/6, Vol 4: 2.3). The minimum cost of a metre of field terrace, according to NGO sources in 1990, was Ksh 4; we were quoted Ksh 20/m for terraces in hill areas (Chapter 7). If the District average is about Ksh 10, the notional replacement or capital value of the 1985 terraces was Ksh 826.9 million, equivalent in 1985 prices to 276 000 tons of maize, and was increasing at a rate of 15% per year, or new constructions worth 40 000 tons of maize. The ALDEV contribution to soil conservation was at most 35% of its total budget, taking into account staff costs, or 79 000 tons of maize. Most of this terracing was later reconstructed. The MIDP contribution was equivalent to about 17 000 tons at current prices. Direct government investment in soil conservation has been helpful to the poorer farmers who had difficulty with tools and capital, and has provided technical advice. However, the private investment has far outweighed the public.

In so far as the people of Machakos have been consulted, they have usually requested investments in roads, water supplies, schools and health services, and they have contributed large amounts of self-help to these. They are beginning to want rural electrification. Water featured in the ALDEV and MIDP programmes, supplementing the private investments made in small dams of various types, roof catchment systems, etc. However, the more important road and water projects require investments and skills of a level that are beyond the reach of individuals, groups or small communities. They present a challenge even to governments and aid agencies, a challenge that has usually been evaded. ALDEV's investment in the Yatta Canal could perhaps be criticised for its excessive expense, but it is still bringing in benefits, and could not have been constructed solely by community effort. It helped to mobilise private labour and investment capital in the formation of many new farms.

Public investments are most productive when they support such a mobilisation of private inputs. They therefore need to be accompanied by pricing and taxation policies which encourage private investments, and these Kenya has generally had. However, there is also another requirement for effectiveness, and that is the existence of institutions and funds capable of their maintenance. In the case of soil conservation works on private land, maintenance is rightly left to the private owner. A feature of both the ALDEV and the MIDP periods was that they recognised the maintenance problem. In the ALDEV period the water projects were supposed to be maintained by water rates raised by the County Council; in the MIDP period, especially in Phase II, training was given to user groups who were elected to be responsible for operation and maintenance. However, during both periods, in the agricultural field, institutions were created which demanded staff and funding of a level that could not be met out of ordinary revenues, thus leading to the collapse of the programmes at the end of the special funding. This is a particularly acute problem in Kenya today; various programmes have encouraged the expansion of government staff without continuing resources for them to perform their job.[5] NGOs have assumed, usefully, some functions previously carried out by government only. However, such NGO activities cannot tackle larger-scale infrastructure improvements, nor alter the policy environment. These remain essential government-led contributions to development.

NOTES

1 The NCPB originated in the Kenya Farmers Association (KFA) which European farmers established in the 1920s to buy and grade maize for bulk export sales. When export prices fell they secured during 1935–1936 the right to trade in the Reserves at posts where all grain was to be brought for inspection and grading. The administration's preference for regulated trade led it to overrule the opposition of Indian traders and emerging African middlemen. The KFA became the agent of the war-time Maize and Produce Control after the food shortages of 1942–1943.

2 The General Manager noted high transaction costs in the latter, due to the amount of paper work required for inspection of produce, securing of export licences and competing for freight space at Nairobi Airport.

This had led to difficulties in competing with Tanzania, which had simplified its procedures (General Manager, 1992, pers. comm.).

3 The Nordic countries provided 600 years of expatriate expert assistance, 1968–1983 (Gyllström, 1991).

4 Successive changes of name reflect its changing functions: 1945–1946, African Settlement Board (ASB); 1946–1947, African Settlement and Land Utilisation Board (ASLUB); 1947–1953, African Land Utilisation and Settlement Board (ALUS); 1953–1955, African Land Development Board (ALDEV); 1957–1960, Land Development Board (Non-Scheduled areas); 1960 Board of Agriculture (Non-Scheduled areas).

5 In Kitui District in 1988–1989 only US$30 was available per professional officer for non-wage operating and maintenance costs (Adams, 1990: footnote 16). This is not unusual.

16

Population Growth and Environmental Degradation: Revising the Theoretical Framework

VICIOUS CIRCLES VERSUS VIRTUOUS INTERACTIONS

The view which this book has taken of the environment—population debate differs from most others. We are not looking for an explanation of why government efforts to reduce environmental degradation in agricultural and pastoral lands have failed. We are seeking to explain why environmental recovery has succeeded, and the role in this of the various actors, including, very importantly, the local inhabitants. We agree with many others that a whole nexus of causalities interact to affect both rates of population growth and increases or decreases in the productivity of land resources.[1] However, some have taken the view that rapid population growth leads inevitably to increased poverty and natural resource degradation, through, amongst other things, land scarcity, falling fallows, deforestation, cultivation of marginal lands, conditions favouring large families and underdeveloped human capital.[2]

Our view has been conditioned by two factors. The first is the evidence we have amassed of the reversal of degradation in Machakos, of rising productivity and living standards, and successful exploitation of lands previously deemed unfit for agricultural use. The second is the knowledge that historically, in many societies, population growth has been accompanied by specialisation, diversification of the economy, rising living standards, and an increasing rate of technological change which has outpaced any threat to the depletion of resources. We therefore see change as positive, not negative.[3] It has been questioned if human adaptability is sufficiently great to cope with population growth rates of 3% per annum, and consequent rapid change in land:labour ratios, as opposed to the 1—2% which were the fastest experienced before this century. The answer, in Machakos, is that so far it has been. This leads us to an alternative nexus of positive interactions, illustrated in Figure 16.1, which derives from our original model in Chapter 2 (Figure 2.5). We shall will use this to consider how far the Machakos experience is replicable, and the policy recommendations that derive from it, in our final chapter.

EVIDENCE FOR A REVERSAL OF ENVIRONMENTAL DEGRADATION

The evidence for a reversal of environmental degradation has been presented in the preceding chapters. In pursuing improvements in their livelihoods, the Machakos people have not destroyed their environment, despite their poverty and the riskiness of their climate. That there was a real environmental problem in the 1930s has been shown in the photographic record. The change that has taken place was not due to changes in rainfall systems (Chapter 3). Chapter 7 has shown

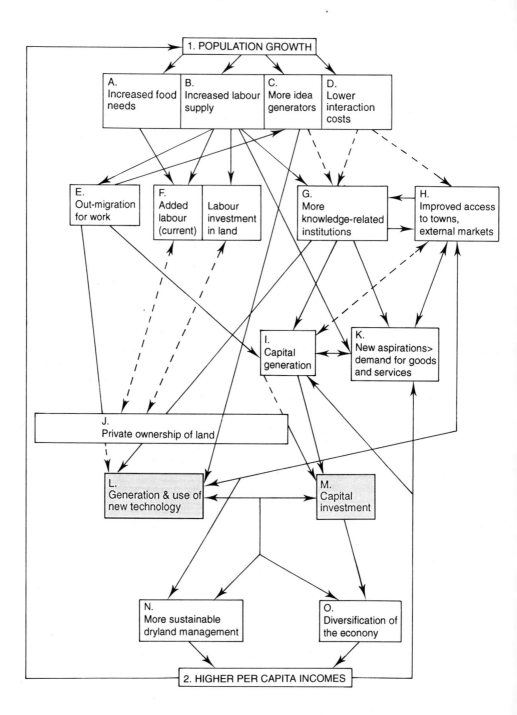

FIGURE 16.1. Positive effects of population growth: ——, autonomous; ----, can be increased or impeded by government action

that soil erosion has been eliminated on much cultivated land, and greatly reduced on others, and that there are beginning to be signs of improvements in grazing lands. Chapter 8 shows that the spread of population and stock into AEZs 5 and 6 has not so far resulted in an irreversible loss of productive capacity, although there has been an increase in woodiness in the vegetation. Some areas formerly under natural vegetation are now conserved and productive arable fields, as are areas that were formerly degraded and almost bare grazing lands in the older settled zones. The fuel shortage, first noted in densely populated areas in 1910, has never reached the often predicted crisis point, and there are now more trees, grown for many different purposes (Chapter 13). Agricultural output on a per head and per hectare basis has increased in value substantially, with food output tracking population growth (Chapter 6). The only area where improvement in resources is in doubt is in the maintenance of soil fertility levels, where we have been unable to reach firm conclusions. However, we have shown that fertility depends on management.

Agricultural incomes are now supplemented by much more non-farm work than was formerly available (Chapter 10). The huge growth in the output of non-subsistence products has developed jobs in marketing, processing and the satisfaction of new consumer demands. Much of the soil conservation was done in the period 1961−1978, when there was least government input (Chapters 5 and 11), although government, and later NGO, programmes have played a part (Chapters 11 and 12). Conservation has been the result of the farmers' own investments of labour and capital into land improvement and development, at times assisted by external advice and capital. The physical changes have been accompanied, and underpinned, by changes in Machakos society which developed its knowledge and management capacity, and which broadened the basis of local leadership (Chapter 9). This enabled it to select, evaluate, develop and use different technologies (Chapter 14) and to react to changes in the markets for its labour, land, and feasible outputs.

THEORIES ON ENVIRONMENT, DEVELOPMENT AND POPULATION INTERACTIONS

Malthus[4] thought that population 'is necessarily limited by the means of subsistence'. It increases exponentially when accidents such as inventions or discoveries temporarily increase the means of subsistence but, because of diminishing returns to capital and labour, the new hands which accompany the new mouths do not produce as much, output declines, the land resource is impoverished, and the population increase is reversed by famines, wars, etc. (misery and vice). Maher echoed this view when he reported on Machakos in 1937 (see Chapter 1).

In later versions of his essay Malthus incorporated Ricardo's view that an expanding population would necessarily have to take in land of lesser quality, giving lower returns to labour. In *The Limits to Growth*, Meadows et al (1972) used similar arguments, pointing to the world's exponential growth rates in the use of raw materials in the period 1900 − 1950. In the agricultural field, this has been linked to the belief that certain agro-ecological zones have fixed human carrying capacities, which, under a given technology, can only be breached at peril to the environmental base. Since Allan (1965) discussed this in relation to Africa, it has been modified to incorporate different levels of agricultural technology (for example, Higgins et al, 1982), but much more rarely by the supposition that technical change and market development will also lead to part of the population being supported by non-farm occupations.[5]

Because additions of increased amounts of the same input (be it seed, weeding labour or whatever) suffer from diminishing returns, according to standard farm management theory

(Upton, 1987), progress in raising output per ha will be dependent on new technologies, and new combinations of inputs and outputs. Technological change becomes a necessity to survival as the land/people ratio changes, which is why Boserup saw increased population density as impelling intensification methodologies (Boserup, 1965). Out-migration, for work or for settlement, is one way of bringing the technology back in balance with the resource base. Boserup saw the new settlement option as usually being preferred while land was available, because it gives a higher return to work than the intensification option.

Malthus regarded new technologies as accidental discoveries, jokers in the pack which could not be relied upon to turn up. Boserup differed from Malthus in seeing the adoption of new technologies as *impelled* by population growth and made feasible by additional labour.[6] In a somewhat similar fashion, technological change has been seen as induced by changes in land—labour or fertiliser—land price ratios, causing a disequilibrium which attracts the attention of scientists, administrators or inventors (Hayami and Ruttan, 1985; Ruttan and Thirtle, 1989). Unlike Boserup, this puts the emphasis on exogenous change agents. Simon (1986) sees invention as a *function* of population growth. He devised a mathematical model for the developed world, taken as a whole, based on additional idea generators in a larger population, and the fact that new inventions and improvements are developed by combining a new thought with existing ideas: 'the more people. . . . the more accidents, more variety, more advances in knowledge and productivity' (Simon, 1986: 28). This stimulates investment and increases output more than proportionately to the increase in numbers. His model depends on a large initial stock of ideas (hence it was limited to the developed world) and showed an increasing labour force implying higher levels of consumption *without limit* (his italics). He accepted that new people imply a capital dilution effect in the short run; the optimum rate of population growth depends on the discount rate accepted, that is, on people's willingness to make present sacrifices for future growth. Simon, like Boserup, sees technological change as arising from endogenous causes.

We accept the view that technological change is both impelled by population growth and facilitated by the increased human interaction to which it gives rise.[7] We see new technologies as coming from many sources (Chapter 14), including, importantly, the farmers themselves. However, we see technology change, adoption and adaptation as more important than invention *per se*.[8] Most economists agree that capital formation and technological progress are the two major tightly linked factors in economic growth. Technical progress makes each input of investment capital more productive, thus making investment more attractive and continually offsetting the tendency to diminishing returns to any single input such as labour (Hagen, 1968: 255, 262; Simon, 1986; Romer, 1989: 12). It is therefore particularly essential when economic growth has to outpace a rapid growth in population. Technology development is linked to education in the widest sense of anything which improves knowledge and organisational capabilities. Technology development and response to market opportunities also depend on security to reap the fruits of investment, particularly, in agriculture, on security of land tenure, but also, more generally, on security and freedom to travel and to seek out information and new opportunities.

In our initial developmental model (Figure 2.5), we regarded the availability of capital and security, knowledge of opportunities and technologies, economic incentives and access to jobs, land, or markets, as necessary conditions to enable people to respond to population pressure either by out-migration to seek jobs, or by settlement of new lands, or by intensification of agriculture and the diversification of the local economy *in situ*. In the integrative developmental model which we now develop (Figure 16.1), we place the generation and use of new technology, in conjunction with capital investments of labour and cash, as the central element in a nexus which leads from our start at population increase (1), via intermediate interactions, to more sustainable dryland management (L), diversification of the economy (M) and the target of development as we have defined it in the Appendix to Chapter 2: (2), higher per capita incomes.

Throughout, we see the Akamba people not as victims of world forces or as passive recipients of government actions, but as people engaged in an on the whole successful struggle with their physical and socio-political environment, who make choices about the use of their talents and their assets. These choices are conditioned by their desire to provide for the essential survival needs of themselves and their families, by the endeavour to avoid risks that would endanger these, and, beyond this, by their wish to improve their level of well-being. Before considering their route to sustainable agricultural intensification, we shall look at the consequences of two other choices which were open to them: out-migration and development of lower-potential land.

CIRCULATION FOR WORK AND SETTLEMENT OF LOWER-POTENTIAL LAND

Circulation for work

At the opening of our study period, farming to produce more than subsistence needs was not profitable in most parts of Machakos (Chapter 10, the Masii study). Further, savings could easily be wiped out by drought or livestock disease, so the investments to make the land more productive could not be generated from agriculture itself. Some intensification could and did occur through labour intensification and the reduction of fallows, but an alternative to this use of labour was out-migration for work — (E) in Figure 16.1. The Akamba recognised early on that out-migration would be most profitable if they first invested in education, since a migrant with skills earns more. Education is provided by both private and social funds and as soon as they gained a little control over taxation, in the 1920s, they invested in schools (Chapter 9). An educated out-migrant could make the savings (I), that would enable not merely family support at times of climatic disaster, but also investment in the farm or in local non-farm business. The association of non-farm incomes with agricultural investment has been demonstrated by studies in Kenya and in sub-Saharan Africa as a whole, and by the specific interviews we have quoted (Mbithi (1971a) including data specifically for Machakos; Bigsten and Collier (1980) for Kenya generally; Haggblade et al (1989) for Sub-Saharan Africa generally). Typically, households have invested heavily in children's education, and one of the sources of farm capital has been the return made by children to the farm in the context of the strong family structure discussed in Chapter 9. However, those working away have transmitted capital home, or brought it with them on retirement. Often it was invested first in a non-farm business, because this generated profit more rapidly, and later, in the farm. The latter has happened, however, only because there is secure private ownership of land (J). Akamba investment strategies demonstrate that they take a very long view.

Working away also led to (L). Workers acquired knowledge, especially by direct observation and experience in their new occupations. We have shown this to be particularly evident with regard to the soldiers who returned from World War II (Chapter 9), but it also applied to those who went to other parts of Kenya, whether they were employed in trade, services or agriculture. The war gave a strong reinforcement to the contacts the Akamba had already made with settlers and missions, in bringing the world stock of knowledge into their purview. This made the process depicted by Simon (1986) more effective: Akamba innovators interacted with a greater stock of existing ideas. It also gave a great stimulus to investment in schools, institutions which store and transmit knowledge.

A final effect of out-migration was that some people — a minority, as the Akamba prefer rural life — became permanent urban residents (Chapter 4). They thus helped build up the population of towns such as Nairobi and Mombasa which became important sources of demand for agricultural products, greatly enhancing the profitability of production for sale.

Settlement of lower potential land

In Kenya, this option has generally been viewed as potentially disastrous, because the land concerned was not deemed fit for mixed farming. It has been interpreted as a further marginalisation of people already in a peripheral economy in world terms, the result of colonial or multinational corporation exploitation, which could only result in further impoverishment and the more frequent occurrence of famine (Wisner, 1977). However, the Akamba elders viewed it circa 1945 as the natural answer to land exhaustion in the older lands (Chapter 11), and they blamed the colonial authorities for the boundaries which had stopped this response (KNA: Lambert, 1945). It was preferred to intensification *in situ* for reasons that Boserup would lead us to expect — it gave a better return to labour in terms of the subsistence products that could be produced, at a time when there were limited markets and low farm-gate prices for goods produced for sale.

The extensive methods adopted by the settlers initially were viewed by external observers as mining the land, and environmentally destructive. Chapters 8 and 11 have shown that this has not been so in the longer term. On the contrary, the settlers, particularly where they have had land security (J), have over time made the savings to invest successively in livestock, terracing and water conservation, and trees. They have derived knowledge of some of the technologies from the experience of intensive agriculture and conservation in the higher potential lands, and where the conditions for intensive agriculture had first developed. The settlers suffered hardships and setbacks imposed by recurrent cyclical droughts, but they have evolved a system which seems to be more resilient than the specialised livestock keeping of the neighbouring Maasai (Chapter 10). Their investments in land development enabled them to produce more than from their original small farms in higher potential land (we have quoted Matingu, 1974, in Chapter 4). They are now in the process of further intensification and income diversification, since new land is no longer available.

THE PROCESSES LEADING TO INTENSIFICATION AND EMPLOYMENT DIVERSIFICATION *IN SITU*

Figure 16.1 shows four positive effects of population growth: (A) increased food needs; (B) increased labour supply; (C) increased interaction of ideas leading to new technologies; (D) economies of scale in the provision of social and physical infrastructure. These effects in the medium or long-term can outweigh the negative effects of population growth, at least at the levels of population density which we have discussed, and if most of the land is owned by smallholders who retain a good proportion of the profits of their work.[9] Boserup's hypothesis that population growth eventually drives intensification relies for its validation on comparisons between contemporary farming systems in different areas and continents. The longitudinal approach of our study, however, permits us to seek validation in the evolution of a single farming system. It makes apparent the importance of two factors given little attention by Boserup: the external market and inflows of new ideas from external sources, both of which reinforced the impetus which population growth gave to local technology generation.

However, both these were in turn facilitated by a factor which Boserup did highlight: as population density increases, the per capita cost of providing infrastructure decreases. Boserup was thinking especially of roads, and the development of internal trade, towns and specialisation; however, roads also connect an economy to the external market (H) which is a source not merely of revenue but also of information (the most obvious example being the activities of the canning factories depicted in Chapter 14). The economies of scale apply also to facilities for the exchange, storage and processing of knowledge, such as schools (where, for example, secondary schools have to be provided as boarding schools when demand for their services is widely scattered), extension services, community development assistance, etc (G). Denser population also makes the activities of the private trader and the co-operative more efficient, leading to higher farm-gate prices (Chapter 15). Population growth also leads to the Simon effect: more idea generators, who in a situation of rising population density spark more ideas off each other, and who spread new ideas through the new facilities created by (D).

Boserup originally argued that most intensification came from additional labour inputs, both into current agricultural activities and into land improvements such as terracing or the creation of irrigation facilities. She recognised that this gave a lower return per labour hour than extensive forms of farming, but, by working longer hours, it could increase total output and per capita income. In a closed economy increased labour inputs will be driven mainly by increased demand if population rises and there are more mouths to be fed (A). (There are examples, such as the Kofyar in Nigeria (Netting, 1965).) However, Machakos in our period was never a closed economy; there was an external demand for labour which made labour migration an alternative and, after the collapse of colonial control over the Crown Lands, there was additional land to settle. Labour migration also provided the needed insurance when harvests fell short of the wants of the family at home. Hence, Chapter 10 has shown intensification proceeding only slowly in Masii in the 1960s, output being constrained by a labour shortage, with many people preferring to form new farms or to work outside the district. Both of these options gave a higher return to labour hours. In the 1970s the increased market demand from the local non-farm sector and coffee farmers made food sales profitable, and there was a continuing need to produce for consumption due to the risk of very high prices in times of local shortage (Chapter 6). The incentives coming from the market (H) thus reinforced the incentives to provide for family subsistence (A) from a farm that was typically becoming smaller, and led to increasing inputs of labour (F) in more careful husbandry and in farm improvements, as described in Chapter 10.

Thus, in a situation where there are alternative uses for labour, intensification is more likely to happen when agricultural production for sale is a more profitable use of labour than out-migration, a situation which is most likely to arise where high population densities have already reduced the cost of roads, which give connections to markets. (High population density will have a two-way effect on roads: it will make it more likely that traders can amass worthwhile quantities from many nearby farmers, creating a pressure for roads, and it will make them cheaper to construct and maintain in relation to the level of usage.) Hence, we find that the leaders in the adoption of new productive technologies, such as the plough, horticulture and the bench terrace, were the high density northern areas which gained a road connection to Nairobi at an early stage, followed by Mbooni as it became connected to the Nairobi–Mombasa route. Hence also, the connection between coffee and terracing. Even now, areas such as Makueni with lower population densities suffer from high-cost roads, lower prices for their products, and high marketing costs for products such as cotton, which cannot be overcome simply by institutional change within organisations such as co-operatives. Our evidence is that they are farmed less intensively than farms in the north of the district, particularly in having more land devoted to grazing. Nevertheless, they are better connected to markets than they were, partly because increased specialisation in the favoured areas on coffee and horticulture has helped to create demand for foodstuffs from specialising farmers and expanding local towns. Farms have also become smaller in the 1980s, with the end of the land frontier, while jobs outside the District have become scarcer. This has encouraged the up-take of conservation technologies, to increase family food availability.

THE MECHANISMS OF INTENSIFICATION

Intensification required both additional labour and capital. Table 4.5 shows that the agricultural labour supply increased more slowly than total population, and at times fell behind the additional supply of land when the Crown Lands were being settled, as shown by the dramatic increase in cropped land per agricultural labour unit in the period 1962–1969. This, and the slower increase during 1930–1962, was probably assisted by investment in the plough. Since 1979 the labour supply in relation to cropped land has increased. We have emphasised, however, that Table 4.5 is based on rough estimates. The labour force increased more slowly than total population because part of it was drawn off by out-migration (Chapter 4), the acquisition of education (Chapter 9) and local off-farm work (Chapter 10). The agricultural labour supply can be expanded at peak times by drawing some of this labour temporarily back to the farm, using family mechanisms.

Although there was more cropped land per labour unit, there is strong inferential evidence that intensification required additional labour hours per hectare, an argument supported by the view, widely held by farmers, that they work harder than their forebears, and by very common observations of necessary farming operations being delayed by labour shortages. The inferential evidence lies in the conversion of grazing lands to arable, of arable land to more efficient methods of double cropping (which required more careful husbandry as well as more work in fertilisation, harvesting, etc.), the planting of more labour-intensive but higher value crops, more careful management of private grazing lands, more intensive methods of livestock production involving tethering, stall-feeding, fodder production, etc. There were also labour investments in soil and water conservation structures, in the enclosure of grazing lands, and the planting of trees. These labour additions are shown in (F) in Figure 16.1 and described in Chapters 10–14. Labour therefore had to be made more productive by working longer hours, and by improving organisation (using *mwethya* groups, for example), improving skills through education and extension, and adding better equipment — ploughs, the forked jembe, carts, roof water catchments, etc. Even so, hired labour was necessary on the larger farms, or those with labour-intensive crops, such as coffee (Chapter 10).

Boserup (1965: 33) argued that, under a given technology, output per manhour must be expected to decline as inputs per hectare increase, and this is compensated for by working longer hours. Pingali et al (1987) argued that, in the absence of labour-saving technology, intensification leads to an increase in agricultural employment. However, neither is borne out in Machakos, where the rate of technological change has been rapid since the 1960s.[10] Our results show that there has been an increase in the value of output per head as well as per hectare (Figures 6.4 and 6.5). Since Table 4.6 shows the agricultural labour force becoming a steadily smaller proportion of the total population, the value of output per worker rose substantially. While part of this is accounted for by working longer hours and better management and skills, the greater part may be due to the switch to higher value crops, and the introduction of the plough — both instances of investment in new technologies.

Agricultural intensification has contributed to the increase in total output: the District has made a small gain in its average ability to feed itself, while transferring some land to the production of higher value crops. Food crop production merely kept pace with local demand (Figures 6.2 and 6.5) since the District has no comparative advantage in its production and transport costs are high in relation to its bulk (a reason why food production to satisfy local demand is likely to continue even after the removal of movement controls). Cropped land per person has remained largely static (Table 4.6), which implies a fall in grazing land per person. The gain in income per person has come in part from increased yields, demonstrated in relation to maize and coffee in Chapter 6, and also very evident in the horticultural field. Livestock output, while not apparently keeping up with population growth, has been intensified.

Higher per capita incomes and higher value output per person engaged in agriculture have come via improved market access (by means of an improved but still low quality road system) D leads to H in Figure 16.1. Because government policy permitted a large percentage of the world price to be passed on to farmers (Chapter 15), this has enormously stimulated L and M, investment in new technologies. Market connections in conjunction with travel and education have not only brought in more technical information, they have also stimulated new aspirations, demand for local services and manufactures, and the information flows that enable these to be met. Thus we show G, H and K interacting with each other and increasing the forces flowing from A and B in stimulating L and M.

Intensification was not restricted to high-potential areas, but spread to areas subject both to aridity and to drought risk. In Kenya, the logic of the Swynnerton Plan's emphasis on the high potential areas of the Highlands was that the returns to labour and investment on such land are superior to those attainable in lower-potential areas. A similar argument in favour of concentrating government resources on high potential lands has recently been made after a national level study of six African countries (Lele and Stone, 1989). Historically, efforts to promote agricultural development in Machakos were constrained by the natural limits of the low-potential areas; thus wattle, coffee, horticulture and fruit were introduced to the hills, but only the low-value crops, sisal and cotton, to the lowlands. The Government's efforts to promote crops it considered suited to the lowlands, such as cassava and sorghum, were not successful. Instead, people preferred to invest in moisture conservation and grow maize. Soil and water conservation, fodder production, stall feeding, fertilisation of arable land, grade livestock and tree planting have been successfully extended from higher to lower potential areas. It must be assumed that the pay-off to these investments justifies the effort. Both crop and livestock production experienced forces deriving both from growth of home demand (A) and from the market (H). As in the higher potential areas, soil and water conservation investments proved mutually reinforcing, with increased cropping per year, and the conversion of grazing land to crops. The techniques used have been examined in Chapters 11 and 12.

Continuing dependence on maize means continued vulnerability to food shortages (Downing et al, 1989). The continuing progress of intensification, however, shows that farmers operate with long- as well as short-term objectives in view. No support has been found for the idea that, in a risky environment, poor farmers discount the future against the present, destroying their resources in order to survive. (Some small farmers, especially if they are poor managers, will have been forced to sell their land. The operation of the land market has not been investigated in any study we have recovered. We know that land purchases occur (Chapter 5) so land sales are implied.)

Soil and water conservation should not be expected to occur on grazing land until the marginal utility of labour or capital invested in improvements on grazing land exceeds their declining marginal utility on arable land. The photographic evidence in Chapter 1 and Figures 9.1, 9.3 and 11.7 illustrate the improvements in grazing land management believed now to be beginning (Chapter 8). The rising price of milk and the increasing number of grade cattle (Chapter 10) accord a higher value to some grazing land, but it is also essential to the plough-oxen which facilitate conservationary farming techniques and improve labour efficiency, and which, along with other stock, provide the manure that enhances both fertility and water penetration. The value of such land is rising, which encourages investment, whereas further incremental investments in conservation on arable lands, it may be surmised, may soon be subject to diminishing returns. On grazing land, investment depended on clear private ownership rights (J); degradation occurred both on state-managed land on the Yatta Plateau before 1960, and on the unclaimed *weu* which was open to everyone. (There appears to have been no strong tradition in Machakos of village institutions managing the grazing land adjacent to them, though there are occasional references to elders asking men to cut their *kisesi* down to reasonable size. The *weu* was open access land, not communally managed.)

Early coercive programmes were unsuccessful in winning wide acceptance of new methods, though they had a secondary role in familiarising the population with conservationary objectives and technologies. The narrow-based terrace, promoted by Maher during the 1940s, gave place to the bench terrace in the 1950s. Farmers, when convinced of the need for conservation, were prepared to pay the higher labour costs because of its technical superiority and economic benefits. Community-based schemes promoted by the Government gave way likewise to private works on individual farms (Chapter 11), through *mwethya* or hired labour.

In forestry policy, the Government's practice of reserving lands exclusively for centrally controlled forestry plantations and reserves was always unpopular because land appropriation was feared and no benefits to the community were realised. The switch to farm-tree promotion that took place under the MIDP recognised the value placed on privately owned economic trees (Chapter 13). A quiet revolution in farm tree management has increased the value of output per hectare and is consistent with the imperative of intensification.

Organic manure now drives the fertilisation regime and its lack is considered a severe disadvantage, which is driving some farmers to labour-intensive composting techniques. The use of inorganic fertiliser has increased, particularly in connection with coffee, and in the higher potential areas, but is not perceived as a substitute for manure by many farmers, on account of its cost and riskiness in the event of rainfall failure.

Increased productivity has proved to be consistent with sustainability, since farmers need to maintain or enhance the productivity of their land, for the sake of themselves and their heirs (J). It has been enabled by the investment of capital and labour (F and M) driven by both the necessity of supporting more people and the attraction of the market. The considerable investments made by farmers in conservation structures, farm boundaries, dams, tree-planting, improved livestock and farm equipment have gone unnoticed. They are not incorporated in the national accounts, and neglected even by those who make farm-level surveys (Chapter 10). However, without these investments, productivity would not have increased. We are not in a position to quantify how much was provided by direct cash investment and how much by leisure forgone, but our record has shown the frequency with which hired labour is used for conservation structures and for farm operations, the purchase of manure by those who do not have enough of their own, the acquisition of equipment, for which cash has been a necessity. We have also shown the high reward to those who spend on non-labour cash inputs (Table 10.5).

GETTING THE PROCESS STARTED

In view of the mutually reinforcing interactions that are shown in Figure 16.1, it can reasonably be asked why the lands of the Akamba were allowed to degenerate in the first place, and why the process of recovery took several decades. There are several reasons. Firstly, with low densities, shifting cultivation and migratory grazing represented a more productive use of scarce labour, and the Akamba were frustrated by the knowledge that there was vacant land they were not allowed to settle.

Secondly, Figure 16.1 shows that, while certain effects of population growth are autonomous, others can be impeded or assisted by government interventions and policies. This will be considered further in our final chapter, but some unhelpful policy restrictions in the colonial period can be noted here. The Akamba were forbidden until the 1950s from entering the profitable coffee business; their cattle trade was frequently impeded by quarantine restrictions; the security of their tenure of land was frequently put in doubt and private appropriation of large areas such as the Yattas forbidden. Hence, some of the interactions which depended on (H) and (J) either did not take place, or were seriously weakened.

Thirdly, it appears to be beyond doubt that low levels of population density are inimical to technology change. Access to markets and knowledge depends on social and physical infrastructure, especially roads, schools, and extension. The per capita cost of provision remains high until there has been quite a marked increase in density. We place particular importance on population density, because it transforms both access to markets and the multiplication rate of technological knowledge and adoption (G and H in Figure 16.1). Density is more important than a population growth rate which ignores the starting position.[11] At low densities, communication, both intellectual and physical, is difficult and the market for most products is limited. Innovations spread more slowly when villages are widely separated. Mbithi noted in the 1960s their association with villages having roads, and facilities for interaction, such as bars, shops, markets, schools, etc. (Mbithi, 1971b). Without markets, it is only worthwhile to keep pace with local consumption needs, earning cash by migratory labour.[12] The forces deriving from (C) and (D) in Figure 16.1 are weak initially and grow in strength as densities increase.

In Figure 16.2 we have graphed output per head against population density in AEZ 4 — the middle zone in terms of potential, and also an area which has not expanded as much in size as the District as a whole. The population density axis also represents time, from 1925 to 1988.[13] Historical evidence suggests that the Akamba began seeking work outside the District only from about 1924, and it would accord with Boserup's theory that they would have had a higher return to labour while land was plentiful and extensive methods possible. We have therefore assumed that output per head was higher in 1925 than in 1930, and that it went on falling at least until 1943, which from all accounts saw Machakos at its nadir, before beginning a gradual rise. This rise speeded up and gathered force as population density crossed a threshold which in AEZ 4 may have been at around 80/km^2. As population density increased above this,

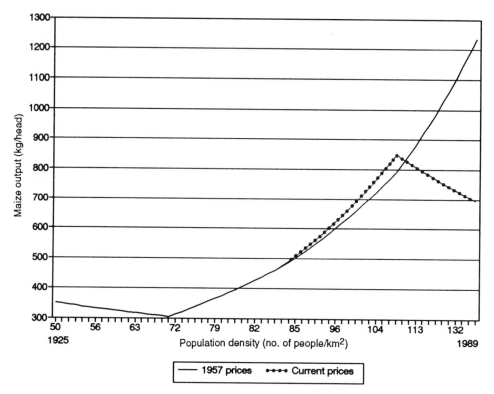

FIGURE 16.2. Population density and farm output per head, 1925–1988

growth accelerated. In terms of value per head in current prices as opposed to constant prices there was a fall-off between 1977 and 1987 which happened when densities were about 110/km². We have seen this to coincide with a fall in world coffee prices, with increasing inefficiencies in cotton marketing, with poor maintenance of infrastructure and the continuance of restrictions which discouraged change away from coffee and maize production. This indicates the importance of supportive policies at high population densities. The volume of output continued to rise, but in terms of income benefit to the farmers, there was a reduction, which must have also affected his or her ability to save and invest.

In northern Nigeria, very high densities have been found to be compatible with sustainable environmental management (in the Kano close-settled zone), and a theory of transition has been advanced to suggest that low-density systems are more likely to show indicators of degradation under population increase than higher-density, more sustainable systems (Mortimore, 1989b, 1991, in press; Cline-Cole et al, 1990). Non-farm incomes there as in Machakos play an important role in assisting the transition to stable or improving fertility, as survival strategies which compensate for droughts and other causes of falling outputs, and as sources of capital for rebuilding herds, and for making other investments in the farm (Mortimore, in press). Although our study calls into question the negative linkage, commonly supposed, between population growth and environmental degradation, the linkage needs to be investigated empirically in more studies of *both* high- and low-density situations. We are not able to forecast the final shape of the curve in Figure 16.2 because the policy situation and world price movements in the 1980s were leading to falling purchasing power per head, despite an increase in the volume of output per head (Chapter 6).

CONCLUSION

The replicability, continuity and policy issues are considered in the next chapter. However, the discussion here has shown the importance of attention to population density and to access to markets and knowledge, which increasing population density helps to facilitate. What is appropriate at a high level of population density may be a misuse of scarce labour resources at low population densities. At low densities, population growth assists development, by providing labour and facilitating access to markets and to information. In Machakos, rising output volume has accompanied a rise in densities to over 400/km^2 in the higher potential areas. The people who have the best knowledge of the changing costs of land and labour and of the market opportunities for products and labour are the inhabitants, for the changes may be slow and often imperceptible to outsiders. Governments have too often concentrated their attention on the symptoms of a problem (under-investment in land improvement and intensification technologies) while failing to grapple with the need to provide security for these investments through their tenure policies, and to provide incentives in the form of high farm-gate prices through their pricing policies and transport investments, and the knowledge enhancement that increases people's ability to evaluate and develop alternative technologies. The Akamba themselves seem always to have emphasised the importance of government investment in schools and roads, but political structures have not given them much influence over the strategic decisions on state investments.

NOTES

1 Well expressed in relation to soil erosion by Blaikie (1989) and Blaikie and Brookfield (1987).
2 A study of population and the environment in Malawi (Shanmugaratnam et al, draft, 1992) produced a nexus diagram illustrating the negative interactions. This was one of a series commissioned by the World Bank in a search for policy guidance on the means to combat this degradational spiral (Cleaver and Schreiber, 1992).
3 Thus, Bernard (in Consortium, Report 6, 1978) saw the reduction of fallows and the breakdown of 'old indigenous farming systems as indicators of land degradation. We interpret them as part of a movement to more intensive systems. Bernard, like Wisner (1977), saw increasing use of marginal lands as an indicator of degradation. We have shown it led to successful methods of exploitation.
4 In successive editions, 1798–1824.
5 In addition to the diminishing returns effect, economists blame rapid population growth for the diversion of resources from investment to consumption, an increase in the ratio of dependents to producers, and/or a declining per capita share in social infrastructure such as schools and health facilities (e.g. Elkan, 1973, amongst many others).
6 In a recent summary (Boserup, 1990: 11–20) makes the following points which readers unfamiliar with her work may find helpful:

   - Population growth entails larger demand for food and other products. This leads to greater frequency of cropping, a higher labour requirement, and a larger output per unit of land, but a reduced reward per labour day (links between A and F in Figure 16.1). Therefore, people do not intensify a farm system while additional land of equal quality is available.
   - Increased frequency of cropping demands increased labour inputs, not merely into current farming activities, but also into labour investments to conserve and improve farm productivity (terracing, soil improvement, irrigation, etc.), F in Figure 16.1.

- As frequency of cropping increases, so tenure develops from a tribal or feudal basis towards private property, thus affording more security for investments (J in Figure 16.1).
- As population increases, the cost of transport infrastructure per head decreases (D), leading to specialisation and the emergence of market towns (H). The increase in market demand leads to higher prices at the farm gate, providing greater incentives to invest labour and capital (M) in improving output.
- New mechanical and chemical technologies, which become necessary as population growth continues, make the raising of output more heavily dependent on cash rather than labour investment, and, therefore, on the continued improvement of rural infrastructure. This is shown in the two-way interaction H $<->$ I in Figure 16.1.

Boserup's original work is complemented by that of Ruthenberg on the development of agricultural systems (most recently revised in Ruthenberg, 1980). It has been taken up and re-examined by Pingali et al (1987), and others.

7   Simon's predicted outcome could not occur in semi-arid Africa while population density was kept low by intermittent famine and the ravages of disease, as was the case in Machakos until this century. Isolated self-sufficient communities had limited need for new technologies because of the availability of land; the means of storing and communicating knowledge and travelling were also limited.

8   Agreeing with Romer that 'the real advantage lies in being able to buy a new good like a personal computer, not in being able to design or produce it' (Romer, 1989: 18).

9   Baldwin (1964) and North (1964) were amongst the first to draw attention to the differential effects of agricultural development in economies dominated by relatively small family farms, which generated demand for goods that could be produced locally, and estate agriculture, which tends to generate demand for luxury or other imported goods. The other two provisos will be discussed later in the chapter.

10 Although there was a continuous absolute increase in the agricultural work force, the cropped area per labour unit, as emphasised above, only fell after 1979 (see Table 4.6).

11 Simon and Gobin (1980) called attention to a statistical linkage between countries with high population densities and high economic growth rates. However, Simon (1986) uses population growth rates and population size in his model, not density.

12 Simon (1977) quotes Haswell and Clark that food was rarely transported more than 15 km in 18th century France. In the 1960s in Nigeria the most expensive lorry transport on the worst roads was eight times less expensive than human porterage, and three times less expensive than donkeys (Tiffen, 1976: 44).

13 We obtained a density figure for each year by applying the known inter-census growth rate. We have made similar entries for value of production per head and in current prices, by taking the District values shown in Figures 6.4 and 6.5, and applying an average growth rate between the known points — with some exceptions. First, we have assumed that production in 1959 was the average of the 1957 and 1960−1961 figures (for reasons given in Chapter 6). Our known points are therefore 1930, 1959, 1977 and 1987.

17

Replicability, Sustainability and Policy

INTRODUCTION

A historical case study of successful environmental recovery inevitably raises questions of how unique the area is, in terms of its experience and its physical and social conditions. On this depends whether its lessons can be applied elsewhere, by those responsible for designing policies or the allocation of funds, whether in government, aid agencies or NGOs. The coordinators of this study are also frequently asked whether sustainable increases in production and welfare can continue if population growth rates remain high, given the present level of population density in Machakos.

UNIQUE OR REPLICABLE?

In several respects, Machakos differs from semi-arid areas in many other African countries. It has a bimodal rainfall regime. Though divided into two short, risky seasons, the total growing period per year is longer than found under unimodal regimes with a similar annual rainfall. In some part of the District altitude and lower temperatures increase the effectiveness of the rainfall by reducing rates of evaporation, relative to places with hotter climates. Its relatively compressed ecological gradients facilitate the exploitation of several different environments by the same communities, increasing the livelihood options available. The District's history as a former Reserve, surrounded by alienated or Crown Land, imposed a set of constraints on its development which were not shared by countries without a white settler population. However, this also meant that unoccupied land was available after independence.

Kenya's history also provided a strong economic base in export agriculture, with supporting institutions and infrastructure. This enhanced the market opportunities open to Akamba farmers. Machakos retained a strong social structure at village level, in which family loyalties and mutual help organisations have adapted to modern circumstances. Although it went through periods of social stress, recurrent drought and the necessity of food relief, participation in World War II and the political cleavages associated with Mau Mau and the run up to independence, it has never suffered a major breakdown of law and order or the horrors of civil war. Hence, it is not comparable with countries like Somalia, in which development has been forced into reverse.

However, the differences are in most cases relative rather than substantive. Even colonial compression and the subsequent availability of new land are not unique. We feel justified, therefore, in seeking lessons of wider applicability. And in major variables, Machakos has a low and variable rainfall, low average soil fertility, increasing population densities, and rapid socio-economic change in common with other African semi-arid regions.

Comparative reviews of farming systems show that increasing population density correlates with crop—livestock integration, as well as with intensification, in all the major ecological zones of tropical Africa (Pingali et al, 1987; McIntyre et al, 1989), and in particular, in the semi-arid zone of west, east and southern Africa (Mortimore, 1991). The growth of the non-farm sector is also common (Haggblade et al, 1989). Such comparative studies indicate that the Machakos experience is being replicated elsewhere and is likely to have wide applicability.

SUSTAINABILITY AND EQUITY

Machakos has sustained agricultural intensification, improved conservation and increased output through several decades of population growth in excess of 3% per annum. The rapidity of population growth was alleviated by the conversion of Crown Land into farm land between 1960 and 1980, so that, from 1960 to 1979, population growth in the old heartland of the Reserve was 1.5—2.5% rather than 3% per annum. It was during this period that intensification and conservation in the old Reserve areas proceeded most rapidly. However, both have continued in the 1980s and spread into the areas of new settlement, when population growth was everywhere around 3%. This suggests that high rates of population growth are not *intrinsically inimical* to sustainable environmental management, and that they were not exceeding 'the capacity of the system to evolve, and the capacity of the institutions to cope' (Flint, 1991).

Several generations of farmers, with government officers and others, in turn learnt, made evaluations, and took decisions. Most important, farmers have always had to cope with unpredictable rainfall. This constraint compels the Akamba to develop an adaptive system of production. It follows that, being adaptive, the systems's future evolution cannot be reliably predicted. It is as risky to attempt a technical assessment of potential productivity now as it was when the 'carrying capacity' of the Machakos Reserve was said to have been exceeded in the 1930s. Admittedly, more is known today on the ecological side. But to the ingenuity of the indigenous resource managers of the future we must add the imperfectly known potential of agricultural research, public and private, to develop new solutions, as well as the uncertain future of the Kenyan and global economies, with which Machakos is now integrated.

Machakos has as yet only a small urban population and a very poor network of rural market towns (Chapters 4 and 9). While there are clearly further opportunities for agricultural intensification, particularly if unexploited water rights are brought into play (Chapter 12), and the adoption of improved livestock breeds continues (Chapter 10), the full strength of symbiotic relationships between small towns and their hinterlands, observable elsewhere in Kenya, has yet to be mobilised. It will depend on government support and investment in such things as electrification and better roads. There are some things which are beyond the scope of communities, even with the assistance of NGOs (Chapter 15).

Human capacity to adapt has clearly been underestimated. There remains, however, the possibility of diminishing returns in the future, and we cannot extrapolate a continuously rising line for value of output, particularly if supportive policies are not followed at the national level in such matters as price and taxation policies, infrastructure investment, etc. Figure 16.2 illustrates the dangers clearly. Land and water become dearer as they become scarcer, which could alter the economies of scale in infrastructure development which population increase has so far brought. Sustainable management will depend in the future on new technologies and ingenious management both in agriculture and an increasing non-farm sector, in order to outpace the inevitable rise in population which the present age structure ensures.

However, future population growth rates are another unknown. These usually decline, as is now happening in Kenya, when per capita incomes and education increase, and we have added a possible feed-back loop from (2) to (1) in Figure 16.1. More directly, our interviews showed that parents are feeling the increased costs of education to equip children with the means to a living now that free land is no longer available, and are discussing or adopting family limitation. We can recount the past, and indicate the policies that facilitate change, but we cannot predict the future on the available data.

It may be asked whether the general improvement in incomes and welfare, through the increased commercialisation of the economy, has increased inequality and the relative poverty of certain groups, such as women or the landless or near landless. We are unable to give a definitive answer. The studies we have seen have demonstrated the existence of inequality of land resources and other assets such as livestock, both in the 1960s and at present, but they are inadequate to demonstrate trends. Rocheleau (1990) argues that the appropriation of individual rights over what used to be common resources has weakened the rights of women to collect wild food, fuel and other products. But this does not address the question of whether they have been able to replace or even improve their incomes by the adoption of other strategies, in the light of the different opportunities offered by more secure individual land rights and the diversification of income opportunities. At least one study showed those with the smallest farms having the largest non-farm income, and the greatest ability to invest in improvements — enhancing productivity per hectare (Chapter 10).

POLICIES TO ENCOURAGE INVESTMENT AND TECHNOLOGY DEVELOPMENT

An inevitable consequence of population growth is a changed land:labour relationship and an increase in demand for food and other goods ((A) in Figure 16.1). The increasing scarcity of land leads to investments in its improvement. The development model in Figure 16.1 emphasises the importance of the mainly unrecorded investments (M) which farmers make in response to changing circumstances, provided government policies do not shut them off from incentives, opportunities and new sources of knowledge and capital, and provided that peace and security are maintained to facilitate trade, travel and investment. These investments pay off most highly when made in new, appropriate technologies (L) which meet the changing dynamics of the situation in which people find themselves. The model also shows the importance of supportive government policies and investments by the broken lines which demonstrate where governments can stimulate or impede investment and change. We now consider some of these in more detail.

Encouraging private investment through market growth

Private investment in agricultural intensification is unlikely to be sufficiently stimulated now by subsistence agriculture, since people have aspirations which require cash and, in a semi-arid environment, need to make provision against risk through a diversity of income sources. If agriculture is unprofitable, they are likely to migrate out. Conservation and intensification require the incentive of profit.

In smallholder areas with secure tenure, policies that raise farm-gate prices are therefore the single most important action required from governments that want to encourage good land management, since they provide both the means and the incentives for investment. Governments need to do all they can to ensure that the forces flowing from accessible markets act as strongly as possibly on investment and technology (L) and (M). This means, on the one hand, taxing exports at a modest level and ensuring that the bulk of the world market price reaches the farm-gate and, on the other, ensuring that marketing costs are as low as possible, which usually implies a competitive structure having either many private buyers, or both government and private alternatives, rather than any form of monopsony. It means removing controls which increase costs to the buyer or seller, or which prevent the seller from switching into more profitable commodities when circumstances change. Machakos would be assisted by the removal of the ban on coffee uprooting, just as it once was by the ending of the ban on coffee planting. Regional specialisation in products having comparative advantage is likely to increase profitability, and the decision of how far to aim at self-sufficiency in food at the farm level should be left to individuals' judgment of their particular circumstances. It is likely that they will maintain a diversity of crops that provide some safeguard against the vagaries of both the weather and the market.

Trade and marketing, and the general flow of information, can be encouraged by a variety of other means, such as encouraging the development of financial services such as those provided by banks and Post Offices, particularly in the context of more small market towns.

Increasing knowledge, management capacity and skills

The main requirements are, firstly, increasing access to sources of knowledge and secondly, increasing capabilities in using technologies, selecting and evaluating them, judging market opportunities and managing institutions in which people combine to raise capital or to organise trade.

The study has shown that the Akamba themselves took a leading role in the search for new technologies and new opportunities, for example, wanting to go in for coffee before it was permitted, adopting the plough without any official encouragement, perceiving the benefits of bench terraces in association with horticulture, using Katumani composite varieties to cross with others, and devising a mixed farming system for AEZs 5 and 6. The top-down approach of the Colonial Government placed the Akamba in a passive role and measured success in terms of their compliance with the Government's directives. Inevitably, this ran into conflict with the way Akamba farmers saw their own objectives, in terms of household survival and welfare, and the transmission of secure land rights to their heirs. The finding of appropriate technologies is, therefore, assisted by the existence of mechanisms whereby local farmers participate in the definition of problems and their research and development. This is facilitated by representative institutions and handicapped by their absence. Consultation, demonstration and modification can seem slow processes compared with a top-down approach, which at its worst involves compulsion, and at its best is a single message carried by an extension worker. However, the washed-out narrow-base terraces of 1961 — at the culmination of 20 years of top-down activity — remind us that the expert approach can lead to the waste of time as well as resources.

The bench-terrace story is one illustration amongst many of the wisdom of offering farmers not one 'best' technology, but several, which they can evaluate and select in accordance with their needs. (The lesson of Machakos does *not* imply that the bench terrace should be adopted everywhere.) The selection of a cheap and sufficiently adaptable plough came mainly through market forces. A diversity of technologies is supported by a diversity of sources of information, which in Machakos has included personal observations and experiments, traders and missionaries, extension services, and more recently, a variety of NGOs. It is supported, therefore, by a policy of openness to outside influences. Kenya has allowed foreign NGOs or trading companies to bring in new ideas, market information, and technologies.

The capacity to select, evaluate and manage can be increased by both formal and informal educational experience. On the formal side, this means support to schools, adult education classes, agricultural extension, and a community development service that brings knowledge and management skills to groups who want to develop amenities or non-farm businesses.

On the informal side, while population densities are low, and marketing opportunities few, migration for work or small-scale trade provides information and capital flows to the home farm. Kenya has not on the whole impeded free movement of people to jobs, and has provided, generally, conditions of peace and security. This has enabled the generation of ideas through observation, and the development of new skills through practice in new situations. This emphasises the importance of supporting education in disadvantaged regions with low population densities and poor market connections. Kenya has supported the creation of informal enterprises through the development of village polytechnics. However, the poorer members of society are inevitably the least able to afford educational costs and, therefore, the most dependent on the informal education that comes from experience. Restrictions on the often-despised 'hawking' block an avenue whereby such people can travel, make useful observations, and from that, develop an enterprise. Policies that place restrictive licensing requirements in the way of enterprise establishment or trading movements diminish the beneficial interactions between (G), (H), (K) and (I) which we have shown in Figure 16.1.

Investment security, savings and credit

Governments have often attempted to tackle the capital shortage directly by providing credit, or building up co-operatives. However, in a semi-arid environment the capital shortage can better be tackled by indirect methods which facilitate savings, and provide security for investments.

Facilitating saving

Savings are essential to investment. However, in a semi-arid environment, savings may be literally eaten up after crop failure. Government can minimise these losses, and its own expenditures on famine relief, by ensuring that marketing is efficient so that farmers can buy grain cheaply when the deficit is purely local; and by having an efficient drought warning system so that contingency plans can be activated for food imports, food relief, etc. Government can also provide research and advice on minimising crop loss in the field or in store from disease, pests, etc., and direct research to drought-resistant varieties and appropriate husbandry and other techniques for soil moisture conservation.

As farmers hold some capital in the form of livestock, good veterinary services help savings by preventing disease losses. Farmers are generally willing to pay for these, and this may be important for the Government's ability to maintain the service. We were struck by the extent of animal loss in some places where we interviewed, although there have been considerable improvements in the situation in regard to rinderpest, trypanosomiasis and East Coast Fever. Savings also take the form of money, and can be facilitated by such institutions as Post Office Savings Banks, or rural branch banks.

Land tenure policies
Secure land tenure is essential to encourage farmers to undertake investment in permanent improvements. This can be provided either by allowing custom to develop in this direction, or by a change in the legal environment. The greatest uncertainties can be caused by conflict between a developing customary law and statutory law that gives ownership to government, or which conflicts with strongly entrenched customs on inheritance. Therefore legal change should be preceded by careful consideration of the implications, and preferably, at rare intervals. Women should be consulted on whether they prefer secure rights as wives or as daughters before instituting change in custom.

An economy with many small holdings rather than a few large estates is more likely to develop an active local non-farm sector. Such an economy can be encouraged, for example by laws that promote inheritance of many rather than one heir, or by taxes on undeveloped land, but these policies have to be devised with the overriding necessity of creating security for investment in land improvement in mind, and the avoidance of clashes with strongly entrenched social or religious customs that mean that the law will be evaded.

The Machakos story has shown that small farmers from crowded 'high-potential' areas can effectively develop 'marginal' land, but it is a process which requires time and capital. The speed with which they invest in land and water conservation depends on the ease with which they can provide for all their urgent capital needs, and on the speed of settlement, which increases the value of land. Therefore, declaring an uncultivated, unsettled area open for settlement, and encouraging a rush of settlers who can obtain rights only by cultivation, is more likely to result in small, intensively cultivated and tree-planted farms than prescribing large farms (inevitably under-capitalised) based on notions of proper land use (as at Makueni). Where government action can help is in providing some of the community investments such as water supply and roads.

Credit
Credit in a semi-arid, risky environment is apt to create debt rather than productive assets. Machakos farmers are nervous of taking credit on the basis of their title deeds and risking loss of their land. Credit has not played an important part in the Machakos story, except perhaps for the coffee farmers who have a tree crop and a somewhat less risky rainfall. In the semi-arid areas credit for the major cotton programme resulted in a waste of government resources. Farmers would be assisted in finding their own working capital if they had prompt payment for their output.

Community investments: self-help and co-operatives
Kenya's orientation to self-help and the spirit of *harambee* has encouraged households and communities to realise that the Government cannot do everything, and that much depends on their own efforts. Self-help can be stimulated and made more efficient by community development techniques and management training, which in Kenya are part of the equipment of the churches, the very active NGO community, and the Government's own locally-based community development assistants. The efficiency of a community development service depends on good training, and it is unfortunate that the course that used to provide initial training to Council CDA staff has been closed down. *Harambee* has mobilised not merely community work, but also community savings. The latter has been assisted by the general improvement in literacy and numeracy brought about by the schools, which have themselves been a main target of local community effort.

Grants of tools and topping up grants of equipment and materials to self-help groups have helped the poorer members of society, particularly when stressed by crop failure. They work particularly well when they assist a project designed and managed by the beneficiaries who have the necessary technical and management knowledge, or who have been equipped with this. Food for work has played a part in relieving hardship, but runs the risk of inappropriate investments that are carried out to get relief, rather than because lasting benefits are expected.

Co-operatives can succeed only in a suitable environment with educated members to check the management, and an infrastructural situation which reduces marketing and transport costs and risks to a reasonable level in relation to the cost of the product. In this situation private traders are also likely to provide reasonable services. However, a co-operative can in the right circumstances be a way of raising capital to provide processing facilities which add value to the product. They have succeeded in Machakos in relation to the densely populated coffee areas with relatively good roads; they have failed to be very effective in processing milk in Makueni where there is poor infrastructure and a more scattered population. Government and aid donors should beware of overloading their capacity, and of giving them functions from the top-down which may be in conflict with the objectives of the members' own elected management. This seems to have happened in Machakos when a cotton programme was imposed on a union consisting largely of coffee societies.

Small towns and income diversity

The growth of marketed production has created more non-farm jobs, in processing, transport and trade, and in meeting the needs of farmers with new aspirations. In turn, non-farm jobs have helped to reduce the uncertainty of a family income entirely dependent on climatic vagaries, to provide investment funds, and to provide livings for those who inherit non-viable plots. Government can assist income diversification by investment in infrastructure at the level of secondary and tertiary towns, providing water supplies, electricity, sanitation, Post Offices, etc. Governments can also assist the growth of small market towns by giving them municipal status (as the Kenyan Government is increasingly doing), so that they have taxing and revenue raising capacity to provide and maintain essential community amenities. Market towns with a collection of mutually stimulating services will in turn improve the reach of traders into the countryside, the spread of information, the stabilisation of prices in times of shortage, and the raising of the farm-gate prices of products in demand. However, such towns will grow only if they have good transport connections, their priority need.

Some services and industries will best be provided from national centres. This need not be regretted, since it both provides opportunities for migrants and an increased urban market which stimulates agriculture. We are not advocating a return to the policy of investing in industry at the expense of agriculture, which proved a policy failure of the 1960s in many countries. Rather, we are arguing for investments in infrastructure, both social and physical, which enable agriculture to become profitable and to increase its demands for services and consumer goods from national, regional and local centres.

Population growth will inevitably raise still further the price of land, as it becomes correspondingly more scarce, and the price of water, as all the cheaper sources are developed. But for the Akamba people the District will remain home, still to be valued and cherished even if they themselves derive their income increasingly from non-farm sources.

DIRECT INTERVENTIONS IN AGRICULTURE

Our policy recommendations have focused on the generation of conditions that will encourage investments in land improvement and the adoption of technologies that enhance both incomes and conservation. There is, of course, also a role for direct government promotion of improved farming and livestock methods, provided it goes hand in hand with local consultation and the encouragement of access to diverse sources of information.

Government promotion of technologies will succeed best if correctly timed. At very low densities, intensive agriculture is unattractive, unsuited to the land:labour ratio. Market links are likely to be weak and expensive in terms of per capita cost and in relation to usage. In such circumstances, emigration to seek work should not be discouraged, for it may widen people's experience, and enable them to raise the capital which farming cannot initially generate. Assistance to education is one way to assist the out-migrants to get the good jobs that may enable some of them to invest in new farm technologies.

The first marketable output is likely to be livestock. People are likely to respond to innovations that increase their health, productivity and marketability. As early as the 1920s, the Akamba welcomed, and paid for, rinderpest inoculations. As livestock numbers increase, and difficulties arise in pasture management, they are likely to devise, and to welcome help in devising, methods of increasing household control over specific areas. In some cases, in some areas, there will be traditions of group control that are still strongly active, and in this case, after consultation, the government may wish to work with such groups in devising methods of increasing the productive capacity of the range. However, the Machakos experience shows the futility of trying to impose ideas of group or tribal control of land on people whose custom has already evolved in the direction of more individualised land rights. It is also apparent that there has to be a quite high degree of land scarcity before planted fodder, and cut and carry methods of feeding, become more attractive than open grazing. Some methods of range land improvement, including hedging, bush and indigenous tree management and scratch ploughing and reseeding or replanting become attractive at a fairly early stage, and have the additional advantage that they can be carried out mostly by forgoing leisure and direct labour, an advantage in a situation where cash is likely to be scarce.

In semi-arid areas with variable rainfall, food prices will always rocket in bad seasons, and even at low population densities, people will have an interest in reducing the risk to their food supplies. Generally, this will mean finding ways to harvest and conserve what rainfall there is. Water management is likely to have a more direct impact on output than the management of soil erosion only. Fortunately, better water management goes hand in hand with erosion control where water is the chief cause of soil erosion. The Machakos farmer has become an expert in the use of cut-off drains, bench terraces, etc., to conserve water for crops as well as to reduce erosion, and it is time that researchers took a stronger interest in such dual purpose technology.

Choices between maintaining fertility by fallowing, manuring, or the use of chemical fertiliser will be dictated by population density (land scarcity), livestock density and chemical fertiliser availability and cost at a given time (Tiffen, 1974, for a Nigerian example). Manure is the natural next stage to fallowing, when land for grazing is still relatively plentiful. It is also preferable in a semi-arid area because of its improvement to the water-retention capacity of the soil. This implies a continued role for livestock, which are all the more important because many water-harvesting techniques depend on the use of the plough (e.g. early planting, contour ridging, early weeding). On small farms, with terraces, the ox-plough is likely to remain a preferable instrument to the tractor. Hence, as farms become smaller, with a higher proportion of arable, it becomes necessary to find ways to intensify the keeping of cattle. At this stage, research directed at alternative feeds for cattle which are kept in stalls for at least part of the year becomes appropriate. On even smaller farms, there may be only small stock and poultry; research then on using their droppings, perhaps in association with composting, will become appropriate.

The need to get high returns to water may in fact drive some farmers out of livestock and into those tree crops which can, if well managed with appropriate water-conserving techniques, survive the inevitable drought years. They will be looking to get from their trees not merely subsistence fuel needs, but also satisfaction for their multifarious cash wants. In addition, they will be balancing other requirements, for building poles, boundary delimitation, shade and decoration, livestock-feed, etc. Some needs will be satisfied with a few scattered trees in the arable and grazing lands, or a variety of trees near the house. Others will best be satisfied by dedicating a patch of land to a tree crop. Moving into tree crops will bring its own risks, such as disease. Farmers in Machakos are already worried, for example, at the threat of what they call the greening disease which blights citrus. Given the limited resources available for research, it will be difficult to keep ahead of farmers who have already reached this diversity of practice and utilisation of trees. This again emphasises the need for consultation with the farmer as to what are the major problems that should be given priority.

Fruit tree crops with horticulture generally represent later stages of intensification, when there is a local and/or accessible external market for these higher value food products. It requires a more sophisticated research and extension service than is generally available to keep up with the multiplicity of products in such an environment, and suggests that the Government should actively encourage commercial enterprises and NGOs to join in meeting farmers' needs and listening to both their problems and the results of their experimentations.

These are only some examples of the way in which interventions, to be successful, have to be in conformity with the changing dynamics of farming systems evolving in response to population growth and increased market access.

GOVERNANCE

Much of the above highlights the importance of investment, by government or by communities, in physical and social infrastructure such as roads, electricity, water, schools, financial services, veterinary and extension services, research services, etc. However, investment alone is not enough, since these facilities, to be useful, have to be operated and maintained, and funding has to be available, not merely for staff salaries, but also for the means by which staff can operate and maintain. Given the limitations on government and community resources, this means providing

(1) a cost-effective service;
(2) a revenue base from
    — centrally raised taxes or,
    — locally raised taxes, or
    — user fees and contributions, or
    — a combination of the above;
(3) a monitoring and accounting system in which those using the facilities have a role, either as voters, or as people who can choose whether or not to buy the service.

Few governments solve all these problems ideally. Kenya has a relatively satisfactory system in regard to schooling (although it could certainly be improved), and very unsatisfactory systems in regard to roads. Services are seldom cost-effective, because staff are employed who have not the means to be effective. Aid agencies have been blameworthy in encouraging policies that have led to staff expansion without considering revenue sources and limitations.

The choice of policies, and the oversight of their implementation, depend on the extent to which rural people are able to influence the agenda, and the disposition of resources. Chapter 9 has implied an important role for elected local authorities at the District and municipal level, which can provide at least some of the services that are required in a fashion dictated by the needs and wishes of their electorate. It is easier for local people to communicate with and monitor a local authority than a centrally-controlled government department, and in Kenya Location Councillors are active in seeing that the County Council shares out limited resources fairly. There is the further advantage that Councils employ staff who are likely to come from the District itself, whose formal qualifications are enhanced by local knowledge. Policies that deprive such Councils of funds, professional skills and functions are therefore likely to detract from the matching of policies to local needs, and accountability.

There is an important role for central government in drawing up macroeconomic policies, in maintaining law and order and the stability of the currency, in establishing fair and equitable taxation, and in setting minimum acceptable standards in matters that will affect the community as a whole. They also have to provide the national infrastructure with which local social and physical infrastructure links up. However, central authorities should not seek to dictate the precise technologies that individuals should use, or the precise crops that they should grow. Choice should be left to the users, remembering that what is suited to the assets and resources of one family will not necessarily be best for their neighbour. 'Governments should try to create a distortion-free environment that allows farmers to choose the most cost-effective alternatives' (Binswanger and Pingali, 1989; the authors are writing about mechanisation, but the conclusion has general applicability).

POPULATION POLICIES

The Machakos experience between 1930 and 1990 lends no support to the view that population growth, even rapid population growth, leads inexorably to environmental degradation. It is impossible to show that a reduced rate of population growth might have had a more beneficial effect on the environment. On the contrary, it might have made less labour available for conservation technologies, resulted in less market demand and incentives for investment, and reduced the speed at which new land was demarcated and conserved after being cleared. Population growth has made land a scarce and increasingly valued asset.

Falling fertility, reflected in a lower rate of population growth, suggests a spontaneous response to changed economic conditions in the period 1979—1989. An extreme shortage of land in some parts of the District, diminished opportunities for income diversification with the national economy in recession, and the high educational and other costs of raising children appear to be leading to voluntary family limitation. The provision of family planning information and the making accessible of supplies can be justified as adding to peoples' choices and the control which they have over their circumstances. To argue for population limitation on environmental grounds weakens the case for it both theoretically and practically.

CONCLUSION

The adaptive capability of the Akamba people has been underestimated in the past, and makes it difficult to predict their future. They are not unique, and it is equally likely that the capabilities of others have been similarly underestimated. Given suitable policies and attention to water conservation, the semi-arid lands can support larger populations and become more productive. The direction of undue proportions of government attention and resources to high potential areas (as suggested, for example, by Lele and Stone, 1989) is, therefore, not justifiable on the grounds that the semi-arid areas cannot repay investment. Direct dictation of what farmers should do to limit their families or to develop their land is not the way to assist them to retain the necessary flexibility to face the future. Rather, government support is required in increasing access to knowledge and to markets, and in maintaining the infrastructure that is provided, in order to encourage people to make informed choices in their private investments and innovations in response to changing circumstances. The best policies are likely to derive from institutions which permit communication on policy needs between the experts who know and live in the District (i.e. the farmers), and those who derive expertise from their professional studies and knowledge of the national and international situation. It is the latter who need to learn the virtues of humility.

Population growth has in itself helped to impel Machakos society to change, and facilitated the interactions that develop capability to respond to challenge. It has been immensely helped by the openness of Akamba society to new influences coming from the churches, trade and travel. At the same time the Akamba have retained the strength of their basic social institutions and values in the family and in mutual help groups, while modernising these to meet new needs, and drawing more fully on the talents of all to provide the required leadership. Education and community development approaches have helped to enhance the management capacity with which they are now facing the challenges of the future.

As we write this book, the people of Kenya have made choices in an election which may influence the use of national resources in the future. Unfortunately, Kenya has already incurred debts which will ensure that some policies will be determined by its creditors and those who provide aid funds. We hope this study will assist in the national and international debates which will take place in future.

References

ARCHIVAL SOURCES

Two main sources were used: Kenya National Archives in Nairobi (KNA) and the Rhodes House Library, Oxford (RH). File references are given in the text. However, major reports are referred to by the author's name. These include:

Kenya National Archives, Nairobi

Barnes, R. O. (1937). 'Soil erosion, Ukamba Reserve. Report to the Department of Agriculture', Memorandum, July, DC/MKS/10a/29/1.
Bolton, B. D. (1953). 'Forest activity — Machakos', Memorandum to the Machakos Reconditioning Committee.
Cowley, G. S. (1947/8?) — undated, but from internal evidence late 1947 or early 1948. 'Reconditioning: A review of the Machakos problems', 1/DC/MKS/8.2.
Hopkins, G. (1943?) — undated, but from internal evidence late 1943, or perhaps early 1944. Report on Machakos District, DC/MKS/8/3.
Lambert, H. E. (1945). 'A note on native land problems in the Machakos District with particular references to reconditioning', DC/MKS/7/1
Logan, W. E. M. (1948). 'Forest reservation in Machakos Native Reserve', Report to the Conservator of Forests, DC/MKS/26/1/1.
Parsons, B. T. (1952). 'Makueni vegetation', DC/MKS/Recond/40/65).
Trapnell, C. G. (1958). 'Notes on ecological zones in North Machakos'.
Waterer, B. R. (1951). 'Conservator of Forests, B. R. Waterer, to District Commissioner, Machakos, J. W. Howard, 8 May, 1951'.

Rhodes House Library, Oxford

Barnes, R. O. (1960). 1. Soil conservation: Lecture notes used over a period of years up to 1960. 2. Soil water conservation: Notes for agricultural department 1960 (map, diagrams, rainfall graph), Mss. Brit. Emp. T1.
Brown, G. R. B. (1945). Agricultural Service, Machakos District, Mss. Afr. S.545.
Maher, C. (1937). 'Soil erosion and land utilisation in the Ukamba Reserve (Machakos)', report to the Department of Agriculture, Mss. Afr. S.755
Penwill, D. J. (1953). 'Machakos District Development Plan', pp. 15—34 in the papers of T. Hughes Rice, Mss. Afr. S.531.

BOOKS, JOURNALS, THESES AND REPORTS

Abel, N. O. J. and Blaikie, P.M. (1990). *Land Degradation, Stocking Rates and Conservation Policies in the Communal Rangelands of Botswana and Zimbabwe*, ODI Pastoral Development Network paper 29a, Agricultural Administration Unit, Overseas Development Institute, London.

Ackello-Ogutu, C. (1991). 'Livestock production', In *Environmental Change and Dryland Management in Machakos District, Kenya 1930–90: Production Profile*, (Ed M. Tiffen) pp. 45–89, ODI Working Paper no. 55, Overseas Development Institute, London.

Adams, M. E. (1990). 'Slow progress with integrated rural development programmes in Kenya's arid and semiarid lands', *Land Degradation and Rehabilitation*, **2**, 285–299.

ADEC (African Development and Economic Consultants Ltd.) (1986). 'Machakos Integrated Development Programme Socio-Economic Survey: Final report. Volume 1: Main report', Mimeo from ADEC, Nairobi, to MIDP, Ministry of Planning and National Development, Machakos.

Alexander, E. N. (1975). 'Increasing the efficiency of the traditional systems of ox cultivation', in *Proceedings of a Workshop on Farm Equipment Innovations for Agricultural Development and Rural Industrialisation*. (Eds S. B. Westley and B. F. Johnston), Occasional Paper 16, Institute of Development Studies, University of Nairobi, Nairobi.

Allan, W. A. (1965). *The African Husbandman*, Oliver and Boyd, Edinburgh.

Anderson, D. M. (1984). 'Depression, dustbowl, demography and drought: the colonial state and soil conservation in East Africa during the 1930s'. *African Affairs*, **83**(332), 321–343.

Asamba, I. and Thomas-Slayter, B. P. (1991). *From cattle to coffee: Transformation in rural Machakos*, ECOGEN Case Study Series, Worcester, MA: Clark University.

Ayako, A. B., Awiti, L. M., Makanda, D. M., Okech-Owiti and Mwabu, G. M. (1989). 'Contract farming and outgrower schemes in Kenya: Case studies', *Eastern Africa Economic Review*, August.

Baldwin, R. E. (1964). 'Patterns of development in newly settled regions', in *Agriculture in Economic Development*, (Eds C. K. Eicher and L. W. Witt) pp. 238–251, McGraw-Hill, New York.

Barber, R. G., Moore, T. R. and Thomas, D. B. (1979). 'The erodibility of two soils from Kenya', *Journal of Soil Science*, **30**(3), 579–591.

Bates, R. H. (1989). *Beyond the Miracle of the Market: The Political Economy of Agrarian Development in Kenya*, Cambridge University Press, Cambridge.

Beckley, V. A. (1935). *Soil erosion*. Bulletin no. 1, Department of Agriculture, Nairobi.

Behnke, R. H. (1985). 'Measuring the benefits of subsistence versus commercial livestock production in Africa', *Agricultural Systems*, **16**, 109–135.

Biggs, S. D. (1989). *A Multiple Source of Innovation Model of Agricultural Research and Technology Promotion*, Agricultural Administration (Research and Extension) Network Paper 6, Overseas Development Institute, London.

Bigsten, A. and Collier, P. (1980). *Education, Innovation and Income in Rural Kenya*,Institute for Development Studies, University of Nairobi, Nairobi.

Binswanger, H. P. and McIntire, J. (1987). 'Behavioural and material determinants of production relations in land abundant tropical agriculture', *Economic Development and Cultural Change*, **36**(1), 73–100.

Binswanger, H. and Pingali, P. (1989). 'Technological priorities for farming in Sub-Saharan Africa', *Journal of International Development*, **1**(1), 46–65.

Blaikie, P. (1989). 'Explanation and policy in land degradation and rehabilitation for developing countries', *Land Degradation and Rehabilitation*, **1** (July–August), 23–37.

Blaikie, P. and Brookfield, H. (1987). *Land Degradation and Society*,Methuen, London.

Borton, J. (1989). 'Overview of the 1984/85 National Drought Relief Program', in *Coping with Drought in Kenya: National and Local Strategies*, (Eds T. E. Downing, K. Gitu and C. Kamau), pp. 24 64, Lynne Rienner, Boulder, CO and London.

Boserup, E. (1965). *The Conditions of Agricultural Growth: The Economics of Agrarian Change under Population Pressure*, Allen and Unwin, London (Republished 1993: Earthscan Publications, London).

Boserup, E. (1981). *Population and Technological Change: A Study of Long-term Trends*, University of Chicago Press, Chicago.

Boserup, E. (1990). *Economic and Demographic Relationships in Development/Ester Boserup: Essays Selected and Introduced by T. Paul Schultz*, The Johns Hopkins University Press, Baltimore, MD.

Bottrall, A. F. (1969). *The marketing of fruit and vegetables in Kenya. Case Study No. 4, Machakos District of Eastern Province*, unpublished report for the Tropical Studies Institute, University of Nairobi.

Bradley, P. N. (1991). *Woodfuel, Women and Woodlots: Vol 1. A Basis for Effective Research and Development in East Africa*, Macmillan Educational, London.

Brown, L. H. (1968). 'Agricultural change in Kenya', *Food Research Institute Studies*, **8**, 33–90.

CARE International (1991). 'Kibwezi Environmental Management Project (KEMP)', Mimeo, project proposal for period 1991–1997 submitted by CARE International in Kenya.

Carr, S. J. (1989). *Technology for Small-Scale Farmers in Sub-Saharan Africa. Experience with Food Crop Production in Five Major Ecological Zones*, World Bank Technical Paper 109. The World Bank, Washington, DC.

Chapman, M. and Prothero, R. M. (Eds) (1985). *Circulation in Population Movement: Substance and Concepts from the Melanesian Case*, Routledge and Kegan Paul, London.

Churchill, W. S. *The Second Word War, Volume 3. The Grand Alliance*. Cassel, London, 1950.

Clayton, E. (1964). *Agrarian Development in Peasant Economies: Some Lessons from Kenya*, Pergamon Press, London; Macmillan, New York.

Cleaver, K. M. and Schreiber, G. A. (1992). *The Population, Agriculture and Environment Nexus in Sub-Saharan Africa*, Agriculture and Rural Development Series No. 1, The World Bank, Technical Department, Africa Region, Washington, DC.

Cline-Cole, R. A., Falola, J. A., Main, H. A. C., Mortimore, M. J., Nichol, J. E. and O'Reilly, F. D. (1990). *Wood Fuel in Kano*, United Nations University Press, Tokyo.

Collier, P. and Lal, D. (1980). *Poverty and Growth in Kenya*. World Bank Staff Working Paper No. 389. The World Bank, Washington, DC.

Consortium for International Development; Hash, C. T and Mbatha, B. (1978). [Report 3] 'Kenya Marginal/Semi-Arid Lands Pre-Investment Inventory, Report No. 3: Economics: the economics of smallholder agriculture in two areas of the semiarid lands of Kenya: Final report', Mimeo prepared for Government of Kenya.

Consortium for International Development (1978). [Report 5] 'Kenya Marginal/Semi-Arid Lands Pre-Investment Inventory, Report No. 5: Forestry', prepared for the Government of Kenya.

Consortium for International Development; Thom, D. J. (1978). [Report 6] 'Kenya Marginal/Semi-Arid Lands Pre-Investment Inventory: Human resources and social characteristics. Final report: Machakos/Kitui/Embu — Baringo/Kerio Valley', Report No. 6, Mimeo prepared for Government of Kenya.

Consortium for International Development; Mutiso, G. C. M. (1978). [Report 7] 'Kenya Marginal/Semi-Arid Lands Pre-Investment Inventory: Institutions', Report No.7, Mimeo prepared for Government of Kenya.

Consortium for International Development; Ottley, R. A., Wanjaiya, J. K. and Martin, N. L. (1978). [Report 8] 'Kenya Marginal/Semi-Arid Lands Pre-Investment Inventory: Report No. 8: Livestock and range management: Final report', prepared for the Government of Kenya.

Coppock, D. L., McCabe, J. T., Ellis, J. E., Galvin, K. A. and Swift, D. M. (1985). 'Traditional tactics of resource exploitation and allocation among nomads in an arid African environment', paper presented at International Rangelands Resources Development Symposium, Salt Lake City, Utah, USA.

Cossins, N. J. (1984). 'Resource conservation and productivity improvement under communal land tenure', paper presented at Fourth International Rangelands Congress, Adelaide, Australia.

Cossins, N. J. (1985). 'The productivity and potential of pastoral systems', *ILCA Bulletin*, (International Livestock Centre for Africa), **21**, 10−15.

Crawley, J. M. (1983). *Herbivory: The Dynamics of Animal−Plant Interactions*, University of California Press, Lanham, MD.

de Leeuw, P. N. and Tothill, J. C. (1990). *The Concept of Rangeland Carrying Capacity in Sub-Saharan Africa, Myth or Reality?* Pastoral Development Network Paper 29b, Overseas Development Institute, London.

de Wilde, J. C., assisted by McLoughlin, P. F. M., Guinard, A., Scudder, T. and Maubouché, R. (1967). *Experiences with Agricultural Development in Tropical Africa, Vol. 2: The Case Studies*,The Johns Hopkins Press, Baltimore, MD.

Dewees, P. A. (1989). 'The woodfuel crisis reconsidered: Observations on the dynamics of abundance and scarcity', *World Development,* **17**(8), 1159−1172.

Downing, T. E., Mungai, D. N. and Muturi, H. R. (1988a). 'Drought climatology and development of the climatic scenarios', in *The Impact of Climatic Variations on Agriculture: Vol 2: Assessments in Semi-arid Regions (Eds M. L. Parry, T. R. Carter and N. T. Konijn)* pp. 149−174, Kluwer Academic Publishers, Dordrecht, Netherlands.

Downing, T. E., Akong'a, J., Mungai, D. N., Muturi, H. R. and Potter, H. L. (1988b). 'Introduction to the Kenya case study', in *The Impact of Climatic Variations on Agriculture: Vol. 2: Assessments in Semi-arid Regions* (Eds M. L. Parry, T. R. Carter and N. T. Konijn) pp. 129−148, Kluwer Academic

Publishers, Dordrecht, Netherlands.

Downing, T. E., Gitu, K. W. and Kamau, C. (Eds) (1989). *Coping with Drought in Kenya: National and Local Strategies*, Lynne Rienner, Boulder, CO and London.

Ecosystems (1982). *Survey of Agriculture and Land Use February 1981. Final Report. Vol.1: Land Use Inventory. Vol.2: Land Use Analysis. Vol.3: Soil Erosion in Machakos District* (Consultant: Leslie Reid), Ecosystems Ltd for Government of Kenya (Ministry of Economic Planning and Development, Machakos Integrated Development Programme), Nairobi.

Ecosystems (1985/6). *Baseline survey of Machakos District, 1985. Report No. 2: Results of the 1985 photographic aerial survey. Sectorial analysis for the District Planning Unit. Report No. 3: Reinterpretation of the 1981 land use survey. Report No. 4: Land use changes in Machakos District 1981–1985*, Ecosystems Ltd for Government of Kenya (Ministry of Finance and Planning, Machakos Integrated Development Programme), Nairobi.

Edwards, D. C. (1940). 'A vegetation map of Kenya with particular reference to grassland types', *Journal of Ecology*, **28**, 377–385.

Edwards, K. A. (1979). 'Regional contrasts in rates of soil erosion and their significance with respect to agricultural development in Kenya', in *Soil Physical Properties and Crop Production in the Tropics* (Eds R. Lal and D. Greenland), John Wiley, Chichester.

Elkan, W. (1958). 'The East African trade in woodcarvings', *Africa*, **28**, 314–323.

Elkan, W. (1973). *An Introduction to Development Economics*, Penguin, Harmondsworth.

Ellis, J. E. and Swift, D. M. (1988). 'Stability of African pastoral ecosystems: Alternate paradigms and implications for development', *Journal of Range Management*, **41**(6), 450–459.

English, J., Tiffen, M. and Mortimore, M. (in press). *Resource Management in Machakos District, Kenya 1930–1990*, Bank Environment Paper no. 5, The World Bank, Washington, DC.

Evans, H. E. (1992). 'A virtuous circle model of rural-urban development: Evidence from a Kenyan small town and its hinterland', *The Journal of Development Studies*, **28**(4), 640–667.

FAO (1979). *A Provisional Methodology for Estimating Soil Degradation*. Land and Water Development Division, FAO, Rome.

Farah, K. O. (1991). 'Natural vegetation', in *Environmental Change and Dryland Management in Machakos District, Kenya 1930–1990: Environmental Profile* (Ed. M. Mortimore), ODI Working Paper No. 53, Overseas Development Institute, London, UK.

Farmer, G. and Wigley, T. M. L. (1985). 'Climatic trends for tropical Africa: A research report for the Overseas Development Administration', Climatic Research Unit, School of Environmental Sciences, University of East Anglia, Norwich, UK.

Figueiredo, P. (1986). *The Yield of Food Crops on Terraced and Non-terraced Land — A Field Survey of Kenya: Report from a Minor Research Task*, Working Paper No. 35, Swedish University of Agricultural Sciences, Uppsala.

Fisher, N. M. (1977). 'Toward more efficient water use for crop production in Kenya', in *Role of Water Resources in Development. Proceedings of the 13th Annual Symposium of the East African Academy.*

Fisher, N. M. (1978). 'Cropping systems for soil conservation in Kenya', In *Soil and Water Conservation in Kenya. Report of a Workshop, University of Nairobi, 21–23 September, 1977*. Occasional Paper No. 27, pp. 47–55, Institute for Development Studies, University of Nairobi, Nairobi.

Fliervoet, E., (1982). *An Inventory of Trees and Shrubs in the Northern Division of Machakos District, Kenya*, Wageningen Agricultural University, Netherlands and ICRAF (International Council for Research in Agroforestry), Nairobi.

Flint, M. (ODA) (1991). 'Population, environment and development: An issues paper for the Third UNCED Preparatory Committee, Geneva, August, 1991', Overseas Development Administration, London.

Gichuki, F. N. (1991). *Environmental Change and Dryland Management in Machakos District, Kenya 1930–90: Conservation Profile*, ODI Working Paper No. 56, Overseas Development Institute, London.

Gielen, H. (1982). *Report on an Agroforestry Survey in Three Villages of Northern Machakos, Kenya*, Wageningen Agricultural University, Netherlands and ICRAF (International Council for Research in Agroforestry), Nairobi.

Gomez, M. I. (1982). 'The evaluation of fruit and vegetable resources in Machakos District', unpublished report, Machakos Integrated Development Programme.

Gregory, J. W. (1896). *The Great Rift Valley*, Frank Cass, London.

Gupta, D. (1973). 'A brief economic history of the Akamba, with particular reference to labour supplies',

Journal of Eastern African Research and Development, 3(1), 65−74.

Gyllström, B. (1991). *State Administered Rural Change: Agricultural Cooperatives in Rural Kenya*, Routledge, London.

Hagen, E. E. (1968). *The Economics of Development*, Richard D. Irwin Inc., Homewood, IL and Irwin-Dorsey Ltd, Nobleton, Ontario.

Haggblade, S., Hazell, P. and Brown, J. (1989). 'Farm-nonfarm linkage in rural sub-Saharan Africa', *World Development,* 17(8), 1173−1202.

Harrington, G. N., Wilson, A. D. and Young, M. A. (1984). *Management of Australia's Rangelands*, Commonwealth Scientific and Industrial Research Organization, Australia.

Harrison, P. (1987). *The Greening of Africa: Breaking Through in the Battle for Land and Food*, Paladin Grafton Books, Collins, London.

Hayami, Y. and Ruttan, V. W. (1985). *Agricultural Development: An International Perspective*,The Johns Hopkins University Press, Baltimore, MD.

Hayes, J. J. (1986). 'Not enough wood for the women: How modernization limits access to resources in the domestic economy of rural Kenya', MA thesis, Clark University, Worcester, MA.

Heady, H. F. (1975). *Rangelands Management*, McGraw Hill, New York.

Heyer, J. (1966). 'Agricultural development and peasant farming in Kenya', PhD thesis, University of London.

Heyer, J. (1967). *The Economics of Small-Scale Farming in Lowland Machakos*, Occasional Paper No. 1, Social Science Division, Institute of Development Studies, University of Nairobi, Nairobi.

Heyer, J. (1975). 'Preliminary report on farm surveys: Tractor and ox cultivation in Makueni and Bungoma', in *Proceedings of a Workshop on Farm Equipment Innovations for Agricultural Development and Rural Industrialization* (Eds S. B. Westley and B. F. Johnston), pp. 68−89, Occasional Paper 16, Institute of Development Studies, University of Nairobi, Nairobi.

Heyer, J. (1976). 'The marketing system', In *Agricultural Development in Kenya: An Economic Assessment* (Eds J. Heyer, H. K. Maitha and W. M. Senga), Oxford University Press, Nairobi.

Heyer, J. and Waweru, J. K. (1976). 'The development of the small farm areas', in *Agricultural Development in Kenya: An Economic Assessment* (Eds J. Heyer, J. K. Maitha and W. M. Senga), Oxford University Press, Nairobi.

Hicks, U. K. (1961). *Development from Below*, Clarendon Press, Oxford.

Higgins, G. M., Kassam, A. H., Naiken, L., Fischer, G. and Shah, M. M. (1982). *Potential Population Supporting Capacities of Lands in the Developing World*, Technical Report of Project FPA/INT/513, Land Resources for the Populations of the Future. Food and Agriculture Organization of the United Nations, United Nations Fund for Population Activities and International Institute for Applied Systems Analysis, FAO, Rome.

Hill, M. J. D. (1991). 'Harambee movement in Kenya: Self-help, development and education among the Kamba of Kitui District, *Monographs in Social Anthropology no. 64*, Athlone Press, London School of Economics.

Hoekstra, D. A., with Torres, F., Raintree, J. B., Darnhofer, T. and Kariuki, E. (1984). 'Agroforestry systems for the semiarid areas of Machakos District, Kenya', Working Paper 19, ICRAF, Nairobi.

Hollings, C. S. (1973). 'Resilience and stability of ecological systems', *Annual Review of Ecological Systems,* 4, 1−23.

Holmberg, G. (1990). 'An economic evaluation of soil conservation in Kitui District, Kenya', in *Dryland Management: Economic Case Studies* (Eds J. A. Dixon, D. E. James and P. B. Sherman), Earthscan Publications Ltd, London.

Holmgren, E. and Johansson, G. (1987). 'Comparisons between terraced and non-terraced land in Machakos District, Kenya', *Machakos Report 1987*, Soil and Water Conservation Branch, Ministry of Agriculture, Nairobi.

Hussain, Shirin Ali, Landstra, W., Manda, D. R. B., Medland, J., Paraico, E. G. S. and Schnabel, J. (1982). *The Farming System in Makueni Location, Machakos, Kenya*, ICRA Bulletin No. 8, ICRA, Wageningen, Netherlands.

Huxley, E. (1937). 'The menace of soil erosion', *Journal of the Royal African Society*. 36, 357−370.

Hyden, G. (1973). *Efficiency Versus Distribution in East African Cooperatives: A Study in Organizational Conflict*, East African Literature Bureau, Nairobi.

Jaetzold, R. and Schmidt, H. (1983). *Farm Management Handbook of Kenya, Vol.2: Natural Conditions and Farm Management Information, Part IIc: East Kenya (Eastern and Coast Province)*, Ministry of Agriculture, Niarobi.

Jama, B., Nair, P.K.R. and Kuriva, P. W. (1989). 'Comparative growth performance of some multipurpose trees and shrubs grown at Machakos, Kenya', *Agroforestry Systems*, **9**(1), 17–27.

Johnston, B. F. and Muchiri, G. (1975). 'Equipment and tillage innovations for Kenya's medium potential (semi-arid) farming regions', *Proceedings of a Workshop on Farm Equipment Innovations for Agricultural Development and Rural Industrialisation (Eds S. B. Westley and B. F. Johnston)*, pp. 200–214, Occasional Paper 16, Institute of Development Studies, University of Nairobi, Nairobi.

Jones, P. H. (1959). *The Marketing of African Livestock*, Ministry of Agriculture, Animal Husbandry and Water Resources, Nairobi.

Jones, W. O. (1972). *Marketing Staple Food Crops in Tropical Africa*, Cornell University Press, Ithaca, NY.

Kaluli, J. W. (1992). 'NGOs and technological change', in *Environmental Change and Dryland Management in Machakos District, Kenya, 1930–90. Institutional Profile* (Ed. M. Tiffen), ODI Working Paper 62, Overseas Development Institute, London

Keating, B. A., Godwin, D. C. and Watiki, J. M. (1990b). 'Optimization of nitrogen inputs under climatic risk', KARI-ACIAR-CSIRO Symposium, A search for strategies for sustainable dryland cropping in semi-arid eastern Kenya, Nairobi, 10–11 December 1990.

Keating, B. A., Wafula, B. M. and Watiki, J. M. (1990a). 'Development of a modelling capability for maize in Kenya', paper presented at KARI-ACIAR-CSIRO Symposium, A Search for Strategies for Sustainable Dryland Cropping in Semi-Arid Eastern Kenya, Nairobi, 10–11 December 1990.

Kelley, A. C. and Nobbe, C. E. (1990). *Kenya at the Demographic Turning Point? Hypotheses and a Proposed Research Agenda*, World Bank Discussion Paper No. 107, The World Bank, Washington, DC.

Kenya Forest Department (1984). 'Rural afforestation in Kenya', paper for workshop on planning fuelwood projects, held at Lilongwe, Malawi, 12–30 November 1984.

Kenya Land Commission (1934). *Report*. 3 vols, Her Majesty's Stationery Office, London.

Kenya, Agricultural Dept, Southern Province (1953, 1954). Annual Reports.

Kenya, ALDEV (1961). *Report of the Land Development Board (Non-scheduled Areas) for the period 1st July, 1959 to 31st December, 1960*, African Land Development in Kenya, Kenya.

Kenya, ALUS (1953). 'Annual Report 1952', Mimeo with photographs, from African Land Utilisation and Settlement Board.

Kenya, CBS (1977). *Integrated Rural Survey, 1974–75: Basic Report*, Central Bureau of Statistics, Nairobi.

Kenya, CBS (1979). *Statistical Abstract*, Central Bureau of Statistics, Nairobi.

Kenya, CBS (1983). *Third Rural Child Nutrition Survey, 1982*, Central Bureau of Statistics, Nairobi.

Kenya, CBS (1985). *Social Indicators: Selected Data on Social Conditions in Kenya*, Central Bureau of Statistics, Nairobi.

Kenya, CBS (1988). *Economic survey*, Central Bureau of Statistics, Ministry of Finance and Planning, Nairobi.

Kenya, CBS (1989). *Economic Survey*. Central Bureau of Statistics, Ministry of Finance and Planning, Nairobi.

Kenya, DoA (1930). *Agricultural Census 1930*, Department of Agriculture, Nairobi.

Kenya, DoA (1927–1961). *Annual report*, Department of Agriculture, Nairobi.

Kenya, Hall, A. D., Chairman, Agricultural Commission Kenya (1929). *Report*, Government Printer, Nairobi.

Kenya, Ministry of Animal Husbandry and Water Resources (1959). *Survey of the grazing schemes*, Nairobi.

Kenya, Ministry of Planning and National Development (1988). *Machakos District Development Plan 1989–1993*, Government Printer, Nairobi.

Kenya, MoA (1962a). *Kenya agricultural census, 1962*, Ministry of Agriculture, Kenya.

Kenya, MoA (1962b). *African Land Development in Kenya, 1946–62*, Ministry of Agriculture, Animal Husbandry and Water Resources, Nairobi.

Kenya, MoA (1969). 'National coffee policy plan', prepared for International Coffee Organisation Diversification Fund (Mimeo).

Kenya, MoA (1971). 'Agricultural development in cotton growing areas: Description of the proposed project area (Makueni, Nzaui and Mbitini)', unpublished report from Economic Planning Division, Ministry of Agriculture, Kenya, prepared for World Bank.

Kenya, MoA (1983). *National Dryland Farming Research Station (Katumani). Visitors Guide*, Ministry of Agriculture, Machakos.

Kenya, Ministry of Water Development (1991). 'National water master plan'.

Kilewe, A. M. (1987). 'Prediction of erosion rates and the effect of topsoil thickness on soil productivity', PhD thesis, University of Nairobi, Nairobi.

Kimambo, I. (1970). 'The economic history of the Kamba, 1850–1950', in *Hadith 2* (Ed. B. A. Ogot), East African Publishing House, Nairobi.

Kitching, G. (1980). *Class and Economic Change in Kenya: The Making of an African Petite Bourgeoisie, 1905–1970*, Yale University Press.

Kliest, T. (1985). *Regional and Seasonal Food Problems in Kenya*, Food and Nutrition Studies Programme, African Studies Centre, Leiden.

Kolkena, T. F. M. and Pronk, A. (1975). 'Report on a socio-economic survey in two rural areas of Machakos District, Kenya', Mimeo from Royal Tropical Institute, Amsterdam.

Konijn, N. T. (1988). 'The effects on maize yields', in *The Impact of Climatic Variations on Agriculture. Vol 2: Assessments in Semi-arid Regions* (Eds M. L. Parry, T. R. Carter and N. T. Konijn), pp. 191–202, Kluwer Academic Publishers, Dordrecht, Netherlands.

Kusin, J. A. and Jansen, A. A. J. (1984). 'Overview of the nutrition studies', in *Maternal and Child Health in Rural Kenya: Epidemiological Study* (Eds J. K. van Ginneken and A. S. Muller), pp. 207–212, Croom Helm, London.

Lang, B. (1974). 'Migrants, commuters and townsmen: Aspects of urbanisation in a small town in Kenya', PhD thesis, University of Edinburgh, Edinburgh.

Lele, U. and Stone, S. W. (1989). *Population Pressure, the Environment and Agricultural Intensification in Sub-Saharan Africa: Variations on the Boserup Hypothesis*, MADIA Discussion Paper 4. The World Bank, Washington.

Leslie, A. and Mitchell, A. J. B. (1979). 'Geomorphology, soils and land use of Utangwa, Iiuni, Kitui and Kune catchment areas. Report to the Institute of Hydrology, Wallingford', Vol. 1, Project Record 32: Kenya-03/REC-32/79, from Land Resources Development Centre, Surbiton, UK, unpublished report (restricted document).

Leys, C. (1975). *Underdevelopment in Kenya: The Political Economy of Neo-colonialism, 1964–1971*, Heineman, London.

Lindblom, K. G. (1920). *The Akamba of British East Africa*, Appelborgs Boktrycheri Aktieborg, Uppsala.

Lindgren, B. M. (1988). *Machakos Report 1988: Economic Evaluation of a Soil Conservation Project in Machakos District, Kenya*, Ministry of Agriculture, Nairobi.

Livingstone, I. (1986). *Rural Development, Employment and Incomes in Kenya*, ILO Jobs and Skills Programme for Africa, Gower, Aldershot, Hants.

Low, A. (1988). 'Farm household-economics and the design and impact of biological research in Southern Africa', *Agricultural Administration and Extension*, **29**(1), 23–34.

Lubega, A. M. (1987). 'Economic feasibility of rural projects in semiarid areas of developing countries: A case study of agroforestry in Kenya', PhD dissertation, State University of New York.

Lynam, J. K. (1978). 'An analysis of population growth, technical change, and risk in peasant, semi-arid farming systems: A case study of Machakos District, Kenya', PhD dissertation, Stanford University.

Mace, R. (1991). 'Overgrazing overstated', *Nature*, **349**, 280–281.

Matingu, M. N. (1974). 'Rural to rural migration and employment: A case study in a selected area of Kenya', MA thesis, University of Nairobi, Nairobi.

Mbindyo, J. M. (1974). 'The effect of extension workers' role-orientation in rural development', MA thesis, University of Nairobi, Nairobi.

Mbithi, P. (1967). *Famine Crises and Innovation: Physical and Social Factors Affecting New Crop Adoptions in the Marginal Farming Areas of Eastern Kenya*, RDR Paper 52, Department of Rural Economy and Extension, Makerere University College, Uganda.

Mbithi, P. M. (1971a). 'The intervention and explication models: Their application as strategies for rural development', in *Strategies for Improving Rural Welfare* (Eds M. E. Kempe and L. D. Smith), IDS Occasional Paper No.4, University of Nairobi, Nairobi.

Mbithi, P. M. (1971b). 'Social differentiation and agricultural development in East Africa', PhD thesis, Cornell University, Ithaca, NY.

Mbithi, P. M. (1971c). *Non Farm Occupation and Farm Innovation in Marginal, Medium and High Potential Regions of Eastern Kenya and Buganda*, IDS Staff Paper No.114, University of Nairobi, Nairobi.

Mbithi, P. M. (1972). ' "Harambee" self-help: The Kenyan approach', *The African Review*, 2(1), 146−166.
Mbithi, P. M. and Bahemuka, J. (1981). 'Socio-economic factors influencing technical farm development in the ASAL', Mimeo report for the Ministry of Agriculture, Kenya.
Mbithi, P. and Barnes, C. (1975). *The Spontaneous Settlement Problem in Kenya*, East African Literature Bureau, Nairobi.
Mbithi, P. M. and Kayongo-Male, D. (1978). 'Local environmental perception and soil and water conservation practices', in *IDS and Faculty of Agriculture, University of Nairobi Soil and water conservation in Kenya: Report of a workshop held at University of Nairobi, 21−23 Sept 1977*, pp. 102−124, IDS Occasional Paper No. 27, Institute of Development Studies, University of Nairobi, Nairobi.
Mbithi, P. M. and Wisner, B. (1972). *Drought in Eastern Kenya: Comparative observations of Nutritional Status and Farmer Activity at 17 Sites*, IDS Discussion Paper No. 167, Institute of Development Studies, University of Nairobi, Nairobi.
Mbiti, J. S. (1971). *New Testament Eschatology in an African Background: A Study of the Encounter between New Testament Theology and African Traditional Concepts*, SPCK, London.
Mbogoh, S. G. (1991). 'Crop production', In *Environmental Change and Dryland Management in Machakos District, Kenya 1930−90: Production Profile* (Ed M. Tiffen), ODI Working Paper No. 55, Overseas Development Institute, London.
Mbula, J. (1974). 'Penetration of Christianity into Akamba traditional family', MA thesis, University of Nairobi, Nairobi.
Mbula, J. (1977). 'The impact of Christianity on family structure and stability: The case of the Akamba of Eastern Kenya', PhD dissertation, University of Nairobi, Nairobi.
Mbula, J. (1986). 'How to reach farmers through better extension methods', FAO-SIDA Cooperative Programme Workshop, Arusha.
Mbula Bahemuka, J. (1986). 'Social anthropological survey of small-scale farming in Kenya', On-Farm Grain Storage Project, Ministry of Agriculture, Kenya.
Mbula Bahemuka, J. and Tiffen, M. (1992). 'Akamba institutions and development, 1930−90', in *Environmental change and dryland management in Machakos District, Kenya, 1930−90. Institutional Profile* (ed. M. Tiffen), ODI Working Paper 62, Overseas Development Institute, London.
Mburu, D. M. (1990). 'The role of sand dams in water supply in arid areas', MSc thesis, University of Nairobi, Nairobi.
Mbuvi, J. P. (1991). 'Soil fertility', in *Environmental Change and Dryland Management in Machakos District, Kenya 1930−90. Environmental Profile* (Ed. M. Mortimore), ODI Working Paper No. 53, Overseas Development Institute, London.
McIntire. J., Bourzat, D. and Pingali, P. (1989). *Crop−livestock interactions in sub-Saharan Africa*, International Livestock Commission for Africa, Addis Ababa.
McNaughton, S. J. (1979). 'Grazing as an optimization process: Grass−ungulate relationships in Serengeti', *American Naturalist*, 113, 691−703.
Meadows, D. H., Meadows, D. L., Randers, J. and Behrens III, W. W. (1972). *The Limits to Growth: A Report for the Club of Rome's Project on the Predicament of Mankind*, Earth Island, London.
Meyers, L. R. (1981). 'Organization and administration of integrated rural development in semi-arid areas: The Machakos Integrated Development Program', A report prepared for the Office of Rural Development and Development Administration Development Support Bureau, Agency for International Development, Contract no. AID/DSAN-C-0212.
Meyers, L. R. (1982). 'Socioeconomic determinants of credit adoption in a semiarid district of Kenya', PhD dissertation, Cornell University, Ithaca, NY.
Moock, J. L. (Ed.) (1986). *Understanding Africa's Rural Households and Farming Systems*, Westview Press, Boulder, CO and London.
Moore, T. R., Thomas, D. R. and Barber, R. G. (1979). 'The influence of grass cover on runoff and soil erosion in the Machakos area, Kenya', *Tropical Agriculture (Trinidad)*, 56(4), 339−344.
Morgan, W. T. W. (Ed.) (1967). *Nairobi City and Region*, Oxford University Press, Nairobi.
Morgan, W. T. W. and Shaffer, N. M. (1966). *Population of Kenya: Density and Distribution: A Geographical Introduction to the Kenya Population Census, 1962*, Oxford University Press, Nairobi.
Moris, J. R. (1972). 'Administrative authority and the problem of effective agricultural administration in East Africa', *The African Review*, 2(1), 105−146.

Mortimore, M. (1989a). *The Causes, Nature, and Rate of Soil Degradation in the Northernmost States of Nigeria*, Environment Department Working Paper No. 17, The World Bank, Washington, DC.

Mortimore, M. (1989b). *Adapting to Drought: Farmers, Famines and Desertification in West Africa*, Cambridge University Press. Cambridge, UK.

Mortimore, M. (1991). 'Land transformation under agricultural intensification in Northern Nigeria', Conference paper for the Workshop on Population Change and Land Use in Developing Countries, 5–6 December 1991. National Research Council, Washington, DC.

Mortimore, M. (1992). *Environmental Change and Dryland Management in Machakos District, Kenya 1930–1990: Tree Management*, ODI Working Paper No. 63, Overseas Development Institute, London.

Mortimore, M. (in press). 'Population growth and land degradation', *Geojournal*.

Mortimore, M. and Wellard, K. (1991). *Profile of Technological Change: Environmental Change and Dryland Management in Machakos District, Kenya 1930–1990*. ODI Working Paper No. 57, Overseas Development Institute, London.

Muchena, F. N. et al (in preparation). 'Soils of Makueni area', Reconnaissance Soil Survey Report No. 5, Kenya Soil Survey, Nairobi.

Muchiri, G. (1979). 'Development of tillage and equipment systems for small-holder semi-arid agriculture in Kenya', Progress Report No. 1, submitted to the Director of Research, Ministry of Agriculture, Nairobi.

Muchiri, G. (1980). 'Tillage and equipment development for small-holder semi-arid agriculture (TEDSSA) with special reference to Kenya', Seminar paper given to Operations Research Group of the Institute of Agricultural Engineering, Wageningen.

Muchiri, G. (1983). 'Production and use of agricultural machinery in Kenya', *Industry and Development*, (UNIDO) No. 9, 13–38.

Muchiri, G. and Gichuki, F. N. (1982). 'Conservation tillage in semi-arid areas of Kenya', paper presented at the Soil and Water Conservation Workshop, 10–13 March, 1982, at the Faculty of Agriculture, University of Nairobi, Nairobi.

Muchiri, G. and Mutebwa, A. (1979). 'Mechanisation and energy in agriculture', paper presented at the Seminar on Natural Resource Aspects on Environmental Management, Naivasha, 26–30 November 1979.

Muhammed, L., Scott, F. H. C. and Steeghs, M. H. C. G. (1985). 'Seed availability, distribution and use in Machakos District, short rains 1983 — short rains 1984', Draft Report, Ministry of Agriculture and Livestock Development, District Agricultural Office, Machakos/National Dryland Farming Research Station, Katumani.

Mukhebi, A. W. (1981). 'Income and employment generation in Kenyan smallscale agriculture', PhD dissertation, Washington State University, Pullman, WA.

Mukhebi, A. W., Gitunu, M., Kavoi, J. and Iroha, J. (1985). *Impact of the 1983/4 Drought on Cattle, Sheep and Goats in Kenya*, Technical Report No. 3, Kiboko National Range Research Station, Ministry of Agriculture and Livestock Development, Makindu, Kenya.

Mung'ala, P. and Openshaw, K. (1984). 'Estimation of present and future demand for woodfuel in Machakos District, Kenya', in *Wood, Energy and Households: Perspectives on Rural Kenya* (Eds C. Barnes, J. Ensminger, and P. O'Keefe), Stockholm/Uppsala: The Beijer Institute/Scandinavian Institute of African Studies.

Munro, J. F. (1975). *Colonial Rule and the Kamba: Social Change in the Kenya Highlands 1889–1939*, Clarendon Press, Oxford.

Musyoki, A. K. (1986). 'The spatial structure of internal trade in staple foodstuffs in Machakos District, Kenya', PhD dissertation, Howard University, Washington DC.

Musyoki, A. K. (1987). 'The hierarchy of centres and the rural-urban balance strategy in Kenya: The case of Machakos District', *Journal of Eastern African Research and Development*, **17**, 74–89.

Mutiso Consultants Ltd. (1986). 'NGOs in Machakos', Mimeo, Nairobi.

Mutiso, C. G. M. (1975). *Kenya: Politics, Policy and Society*, East African Literature Bureau, Kampala and Nairobi.

Mutiso, S. K. (1988). 'Water resources and crop production in Machakos District, Kenya', PhD thesis, University of Reading, Reading.

Mutiso, S. K., Mortimore, M. and Tiffen, M. (1991). 'Rainfall', in *Environmental Change and Dryland Management in Machakos District, Kenya 1930–90: Environmental Profile* (Ed. M. Mortimore), pp. 3–25, ODI Working Paper No. 53, Overseas Development Institute, London.

Muya, F. S. (1990). 'Reservoir sedimentation and catchment land use', MSc thesis, University of Nairobi, Nairobi.

Mwanjila, D. N. (1989). 'Food crop monitoring and reporting by the Ministry of Agriculture', in *Coping with Drought in Kenya: National and Local Strategies* (Eds T. E. Downing, K. W. Gitu and C. M. Kamau), Lynne Rienner, Boulder, CO and London.

Mwenge International Associates (1988). 'Evaluation of Machakos Integrated Development Programme. Final Report', Mwenge International Associates, Nairobi.

Nadar, H. M. (1984). 'Intercropping and intercrop component interaction under varying rainfall conditions in eastern Kenya: 1. Maize/bean intercrop; 2. Maize/cowpea intercrop; 3. Maize and pigeon pea intercrop', *East African Agricultural and Forestry Journal*, Special issue on dryland farming research in Kenya, **44**, 166–175, 176–181, 182–188.

Ndeti, K. (1972). *Elements of Akamba Life*, East African Publishing House, Nairobi.

Nelson, R. (1990). *Dryland Management: The 'Desertification Problem'*, Technical Paper No. 116, The World Bank, Washington, DC.

Netting, R. M. (1965). 'Household organisation and intensive agriculture: The Kofyar case', *Africa*, **35**, 422–429.

Neunhauser, P., Bayreuther, H., Engel, A. et al (1983). *Appropriate Land Use Systems for Smallholder Farms: A Survey of Ecological and Socio-economic Conditions in the Machakos District (Kenya)*, Centre for Advanced Training in Agricultural Development, Technical University of Berlin, Berlin.

Newman, J. R. (1974). *The Ukamba Members Association*. Transafrica Historical Papers No. 3, Transafrica Publishers, Nairobi.

Nicholson, J. W. and Walter, A., (no date). 'The influence of forests on climate and water supply in Kenya', Forest Department Pamphlet No. 2, Colony and Protectorate of Kenya.

Nida, E. A. (1962). 'Akamba initiation rights and culture themes', *Practical Anthropology*, **9**(4), 145–155.

Njui, K. and Daines, S. H. (1977). 'Domestic and livestock water supplies', in *Interim Resources Inventory Reports*, prepared by the Marginal/Semi-arid Land Study Team, for the Mid-point Review, Nairobi, 29 November–2 December 1977.

Norman, D. W. and Baker, D. C. (1986). 'Components of farming systems research, FSR credibility, and experiences in Botswana', in *Understanding Africa's Rural Households and Farming Systems* (Ed. J. L. Moock), Westview Press, Boulder, CO.

North, D. C. (1964). 'Agriculture in regional economic growth', in *Agriculture in Economic Development* (Eds C. K. Eicher and L. W. Witt), pp. 569–78, McGraw-Hill, New York.

North, D. C. (1990). *Institutions, Institutional Change and Economic Performance*, Cambridge University Press, Cambridge, UK.

Nzioka, C. B. K. (1986). 'Vocational training and rural employment: An investigation into some factors which influence the local employment of Youth Polytechnic graduates in Machakos District, Kenya', MA thesis, University of Nairobi, Nairobi.

Ockwell, A. P., Parton, K.A., Nguw, S. and Muhammad, L. 'Relationship between the farm household and adoption of improved practices in the semi-arid tropics of eastern Kenya', paper prepared for the 'Dryland Farming Symposium. A search for strategies for sustainable dryland cropping in semi-arid eastern Kenya' held in conjunction with the review of the KARI/ACIAR/CSIRO Dryland Project, Nairobi, Kenya, 10–11 December 1990.

Odera, J. A. (1981). 'Forest resources in the semiarid lands of Kenya', in *The Development of Kenya's Semi-arid Lands* (Eds D. Campbell and S. E. Migot-Adholla), pp. 127–149, Occasional Paper No. 36, Institute of Development Studies, Nairobi.

ODI (1982). 'Machakos Integrated Development Programme: Phase 1: Evaluation', unpublished report (by M. Adams, R. M. Doake, S. E. Lister, A. D. McKay and M. Tiffen) prepared for the Ministry of Economic Planning and Development by Overseas Development Institute under assignment by the Commission of the European Communities.

Okalebo, J. R., Simpson, J. R. and Probert, M. E. (1990). 'Phosphorus status of cropland soils in the semi-arid areas of Machakos and Kitui Districts (Kenya)', paper prepared for the Dryland Farming Symposium, A search for strategies for sustainable dryland cropping in semi-arid eastern Kenya' held in conjunction with the review of the KARI/ACIAR/CSIRO Dryland Project, Nairobi, Kenya, 10–11 December 1990.

O'Leary, M. F. (1984). *The Kitui Akamba: Economic and Social Change in Semi-arid Kenya*, Heinemann,

Nairobi.

Oliver, S. C. (1965). 'Individuality, freedom of choice and cultural flexibility of the Kamba', *American Anthropologist,* **67**(2), 421–428.

Ominde, S. H. (1968). *Land and Population Movements in Kenya,* Northwestern University Press, Evanston.

Onchere, S. R. (1976). 'Structure and performance of agricultural product and input markets in the Northern Division of Machakos District, Kenya', MSc thesis, Nairobi University, Nairobi.

Onchere, S. R. (1982). 'The pattern of food production, availability and intakes of the people of Eastern Kenya; The case of North Western Machakos', MSc thesis, University of Reading, Reading.

Ondiege, P. O. (1992). 'Local coping strategies in Machakos District, Kenya', in *Development from Within: Survival in Rural Africa* (Eds D. R. F. Taylor and F. Mackenzie), pp. 125–147, Routledge, London and New York.

Otieno, A. K. (1984). 'Soil erosion in Ukambani: A geographical and historical perspective', MA thesis, Ohio University, Athens, OH.

Oucho, J. O. (1988). 'Spatial population change in Kenya: A district-level analysis', in *Kenya's Population Growth and Development to the Year 2000* (Ed. S. H. Ominde), pp. 131–139, James Currey, London.

Owako, F. N. (1969). 'The Machakos problem: A study of some aspects of the agrarian problems of Machakos District of Kenya', PhD thesis, University of London, London.

Parry, M. L., Carter, T. R. and Konijn, N. (Eds) (1988). *The Impact of Climatic Variations on Agriculture. Vol.2: Assessments in Semi-arid Regions,* Kluwer Academic Publishers, Dordrecht, The Netherlands.

Parton, K. A. (1990). 'Central issues in the development of technologies for resource-poor farmers: A socio-economic perspective', Paper given at the KARI-ACIAR-CSIRO Symposium, A search for strategies for sustainable dryland cropping in semi-arid eastern Kenya, Nairobi, 10–11 December, 1990.

Peberdy, J. R. (1958). *Machakos District Gazetteer,* Machakos District Office, Department of Agriculture.

Peberdy, J. R. (1961). 'Notes on some economic aspects of Machakos District', Mimeo, report for Ministry of Agriculture.

Penwill, D. J. (1951). *Kamba Customary Law: Notes Taken in the Machakos District of Kenya Colony,* East African Literature Bureau, Nairobi and Macmillan, London.

Pereira, H. C. and Beckley, V. R. S. (1952). 'Grass establishment on eroded soil in a semi-arid African reserve', *Empire Journal of Experimental Agriculture,* **21**(81), 1–14.

Pereira, H. C., Hosegood, P. and Thomas, D. B. (1961). 'The productivity of tropical semi arid and thorn scrub country under intensive management', *Empire Journal of Experimental Agriculture,* **29**, 269–286.

Perham, M. (Ed.) 1959). *The Diaries of Lord Lugard,* Vol.1, Faber & Faber, London.

Perrier, G. K. (1990). *The Contextual Nature of Range Management,* Pastoral Development Network Paper 30c, Overseas Development Institute, London.

Philp, H. R. A. (1936). *A New Day,* Oxford University Press, London.

Pingali, P., Bigot, Y. and Binswanger, H. P. (1987). *Agricultural Mechanization and the Evolution of Farming Systems in sub-Saharan Africa,* The Johns Hopkins University Press, Baltimore.

Pole-Evans, I. B. (1939). *Report on a Visit to Kenya,* Government Printer, Nairobi.

Pollard, S. J.; Kenya, Ministry of Agriculture, Land Development Division, Agricultural Mechanisation Station (1981). 'Report on the Nzaui/Machakos Farming Systems Study, November 1980 to February 1981', Agricultural Economics Unit report.

Pomery, D. and Service, M. W. (1986). *Tropical Ecology,* Longman, Harlow.

Porter, P. (1965). 'Environment potentials and economic opportunities: A background for cultural adaptation', *American Anthropologist* **67**, 409–420.

Potter, H. L. (1988). 'The effects on livestock production', in *The impact of climatic variations on agriculture. Vol 2: Assessments in semiarid regions* (Eds M. L. Parry, T. R. Carter and N. T. Konijn), pp. 209–220, Kluwer Academic Publishers, Dordrecht, Netherlands.

Pratt, D. J. and Gwynne, M. D. (1977). *Rangeland Management and Ecology in East Africa,* Hodder and Stoughton, London.

Probert, M. E., Okalebo, J. R. and Simpson, J. R. (1990). 'The role of farmyard manure for improving soil fertility', Paper given at the KARI-ACIAR-CSIRO Symposium, A search for strategies for sustainable dryland cropping in semi-arid eastern Kenya, Nairobi, 10–11 December 1990.

Rabeneck, S. (1982). 'The determinants of protein-energy malnutrition among preschool children in Kenya with respect to cash cropping and self-sufficiency in staple food production', PhD dissertation, Cornell University, Ithaca, NY.

Reid, L. (1982). *Soil Erosion in Machakos District*, Ecosystems Ltd, Nairobi.

Rocheleau, D. (1985). *Criteria for Re-appraisal and Re-design: Intra-household and Between-household Aspects of FSRE in Three Kenya Agroforestry Projects*, Working Paper 37, ICRAF, Nairobi.

Rocheleau, D. (1990). 'Gender complementarity and conflict in sustainable forestry development: a multiple user approach', paper presented to IUFRO World Congress Quinquennial, 5–11 August 1990, Montreal.

Rocheleau, D. (1991). 'Gender, ecology and the science of survival: stories and lessons from Kenya', *Agriculture and Human Values*, **8**/1, 156–164.

Rocheleau, D. and van den Hoek, A. (1984). *The Application of Ecosystems and Landscape Analysis in Agroforestry Diagnosis and Design: A Case Study from Kathama Sub-location, Machakos District, Kenya*, Working Paper 11, ICRAF, Nairobi.

Rocheleau, D. and Malaret, L. (1987). 'Use of ethnoecology in agroforestry systems research: an example of AF technology and pest management research in Kenya', paper presented to the Annual Symposium on Farming Systems Research, University of Arkansas, Fayetteville, Arkansas, 18–21 October 1987.

Rocheleau, D., Wachira, K., Malaret, L. and Wanjohi, B. (1989). 'Local knowledge, innovations, and ethnological methods for agroforestry and indigenous plants', in *Farmer First: Farmer Innovation and Agricultural Research* (Eds R. Chambers, A. Pacey and L. Thrupp), pp. 14–23, Intermediate Technology Publications, London.

Romer, P. M. (1989). *What Determines the Rate of Growth and Technological Change?* Country Economics Department WPS 279, The World Bank, Washington.

Rostom, R. S. and Mortimore, M. (1991). *Environmental Change and Dryland Management in Machakos District, Kenya 1930–90: Land Use Profile*, ODI Working Paper No. 58, Overseas Development Institute, London.

Rukandema, M., Mavua, J. K. and Audi, P. O. (1981). *The Farming System of Lowland Machakos, Kenya: Farm Survey Results from Mwala*. Farming Systems Economic Research Programme Technical Report (Kenya) No. 1, Ministry of Agriculture, Nairobi.

Ruthenberg, H. (1966). *African Agricultural Production Development Policy in Kenya 1952–1965* (IFO Afrika-Studien no. 10), Springer-Verlag, Berlin.

Ruthenberg, H. (1980). *Farming Systems in the Tropics*, Clarendon Press, Oxford.

Ruttan, V. W. and Thirtle, C. (1989). 'Induced technical and institutional change in African agriculture', *Journal of International Development*, **1**(1),1–45.

Scoones, I. (1989). *Economic and Ecological Carrying Capacity Implications for Livestock Development in the Dryland Communal Areas of Zimbabwe*, ODI Pastoral Development Network Paper No. 27b, Agricultural Administration Unit, Overseas Development Institute, London.

Shanmugaratnam, N., Mossige, A., Nyborg, I. and Jensen, A.-M. (1992). 'From natural resource degradation and poverty to sustainable development in Malawi: A study of the population–environment–agriculture nexus', a report from Norwegian Centre for International Agricultural Development, Agricultural University of Norway, for The World Bank, (Draft).

Sharpley, J. (1986). *Economic Policies and Agricultural Performance: The Case of Kenya*, OECD Development Centre Papers, OECD, Paris.

Shepherd, G. (1989). *Assessing Farmers' Tree Use and Tree-Planting Priorities. A Report to Guide the ODA/Government of Kenya Embu–Meru–Isiolo Forestry Project*, Overseas Development Institute, London.

Shorter, A. (1974). *East African Societies*, pp. 120–145, Library of Man series, Routledge and Kegan Paul, London.

Silberfein, M. (1989). *Rural Change in Machakos, Kenya: A Historical Geography Perspective*, University Press of America, Lanham, MD and London.

Simon, J. L. (1977). *The Economics of Population Growth*, Princeton University Press, Princeton, NJ.

Simon, J. L. (1986). *Theory of Population and Economic Growth*, Basil Blackwell, Oxford.

Simon, J. L. and Gobin, R. (1980). 'The relationship between population and economic growth in LDC's', in *Research in Population Economics: A Research Annual. Vol. 2* (Eds J. L. Simon and J. DaVanzo), Jai Press, Greenwich, CT.

Sketchley, H. R., Mbuvi, J. P., Wokabi, S. M. and Scilley, F. M. (1979). *Reconnaissance Soil Survey of Portions of Machakos–Kitui–Embu Area*, Soil Conservation Service, United States Department of Agriculture, Washington, DC.

Sombroek, W. G., Braun, H. M. H. and Van der Pouw, B. J. A. (1982). *Exploratory Soil Map and Agro-climatic Zone Map of Kenya, 1980, scale 1:1,000,000*, Kenya Soil Survey, Nairobi.

Stewart, J. I. (1980). 'Effective rainfall analysis to guide farm practices and predict yields', paper presented at the 4th Annual General Meeting of the Soil Science Society of East Africa, held in Arusha, Tanzania, 27–28 October 1980.

Stewart, J. I. (1991). 'Principles and performance of response farming', in *Climatic Risk in Crop Production: Models and Management from the Semiarid Tropics and Subtropics* (Eds R. C. Muchow and J. A. Bellamy), pp. 361–382, CAB International, Wallingford, Oxon, UK.

Stichter, S. B. (1982). *Migrant Labour in Kenya: Capitalism and African Response, 1895–1975*, Longman, London.

Stocking, M. (1984). *Erosion and Soil Productivity: A Review*, FAO Manuals and Reports Series No. 22, Land and Water Development Division, FAO, Rome.

Stocking, M. (1986). *A Working Model for the Estimation of Soil Loss Suitable for Underdeveloped Areas*, Occasional Paper No. 15, Centre for Development Studies, University of East Anglia, Norwich, UK.

Stocking, M. and Peake, L. (1985). *Erosion Induced Loss in Soil Productivity: Trends in Research and International Cooperation*, Land and Water Development Division, FAO, Rome.

Stoddart, L. A., Smith, A. D. and Box, T. W. (1975). *Range Management*, McGraw Hill, New York.

Styczen, M. (1983). *Research Activities carried out by the Soil and Water Conservation Section*, National Dryland Farming Research Centre, Katumani, Kenya.

Swynnerton, R. J. M. (1954). *A Plan to Intensify the Development of African Agriculture in Kenya*, Government Printer, Nairobi.

Thomas, D. B. (1956). 'Annual report of the agricultural officer (experimentation), Southern Province', in *Annual report 1956*, Ministry of Agriculture, Nairobi.

Thomas, D. B. (1974). 'Air photo analysis of trends in soil erosion and land use in part of Machakos District. MSc thesis, University of Reading, Reading.

Thomas, D. B. (1977). 'Soil conservation methods', Technical supplement 1, Evaluation of Machakos Manual Terracing Programme by Mwethia groups, unpublished manuscript.

Thomas, D. B. (1978). 'Some observations on soil conservation in Machakos District, with special reference to terracing', in *Soil and Water Conservation in Kenya: Report of a workshop held at University of Nairobi 21–23 Sept. 1977*, pp. 25–39, Occasional Paper No. 27, Institute for Development Studies and Faculty of Agriculture, University of Nairobi, Nairobi.

Thomas, D. B. (1991). 'Soil erosion', in *Environmental Change and Dryland Management in Machakos District, Kenya 1930–90: Environmental Profile* (Ed. M. Mortimore), pp. 24–43, ODI Working Paper No. 53, Overseas Development Institute, London.

Thomas, D. B. and Barber, R. G. (1983). 'The control of soil and water losses in semi-arid areas: Some problems and possibilities', *The Kenyan Geographer*, **5**, 1–2, 72–79.

Thomas, D. B., Edwards, K. A., Barber, R. G. and Hogg, I. C. G. (1981). 'Runoff, erosion and conservation in a representative basin in Machakos District, Kenya', in *Tropical Agricultural Hydrology and Watershed Management* (Eds R. Lal and E. W. Russell), pp. 395–417, John Wiley, Chichester, UK.

Throup, D. W. (1987). *Economic and social origins of Mau Mau, 1945–53*, James Currey, London.

Tiffen, M. (1974). 'Timing as a factor in the success of extension work: A Nigerian case-study', *Agricultural Administration*. **1**, 125–139.

Tiffen, M. (1976). *The Enterprising Peasant: A Study of Economic Development in Gombe Emirate, North Eastern State, Nigeria*, HMSO, London.

Tiffen, M. (1985). 'Peasant participation in district water planning: An example from Machakos District, Kenya', in *Les Politiques de l'Eau en Afrique* (Eds. G. Conac, C. Savonnet-Guyot and F. Conac), pp. 363–375, Economica, Paris.

Tiffen, M. (1990). *Socio-economic Parameters in Designing Small Irrigation Schemes for Small Scale Farmers: Nyanyadzi Case Study. Report IV: Summary and Conclusions*, Report OD 117, Hydraulics Research, Wallingford, Oxfordshire, UK.

Tiffen, M. (1991). *Environmental Change and Dryland Management in Machakos District, Kenya 1930–90: Population Profile*, ODI Working Paper No. 54, Overseas Development Institute, London.

Tiffen, M. (1992). *Environmental Change and Dryland Management in Machakos District, Kenya 1930–90: Farming and Income Systems*, ODI Working Paper No. 59, Overseas Development Institute, London.

Ulsaker, L. G. and Kilewe, A. M. (1983). 'Runoff and soil erosion for an alfisol in Kenya', *East African Agriculture and Forestry Journal*, **44**, 210–241.

United Nations Centre for Human Settlements (Habitat) (1990). *Women of Kibwezi: A Case Study of the Kibwezi Women's Integrated Rural Development Programme*, Nairobi.

Upton, M. (1987). *African Farm Management*, Cambridge University Press, Cambridge.

Valentine, J. F. (1981). *Range Development and Improvements*, Brigham Young University Press, Utah.

Van Ginneken, J. K., Omondi-Odhiambo and Muller, A. S. (1986). 'Mobility patterns in a rural area of Machakos District, Kenya in 1974−1980', *Tijdschrift voor Economische und Sociale Geografie*, **77**(2), 82−91.

Van der Weg, R. F. and Mbuvi, J. P. (Eds) (1975). *Soils of the Kindaruma Area*, Reconnaissance Soil Survey Report No. 1, Kenya Soil Survey, Nairobi.

Van Zwanenberg, R. M. A. (1974). 'The development of peasant production in Kenya, 1920−1942', *The Economic History Review*, No. 27, 442−454.

Van Zwanenberg, R. M. A. with King, A. (1975). *An Economic History of Kenya and Uganda, 1800−1970*, Macmillan, London.

Wain, A. S. (1983). 'Athi River sediment yields and the significance for water resource development', in *Soil and Water Conservation in Kenya: Proceedings of the second national workshop, Nairobi, 10−16 March 1982* (Eds D. B. Thomas and W. M. Senga), pp. 274−293, IDS Occasional Paper No. 42, Institute of Development Studies, University of Nairobi, Nairobi.

Walker, B. H. and Noy-Meyer, I. (1982). 'Aspects of the stability and resilience of savanna ecosystems', in *Ecology of Tropical Savannas* (Eds B. J. Huntley and R. M. Peterman), Springer-Verlag, Berlin.

Walker, B. H., Ludwig, D., Hollings, C. S. and Peterman, R. M. (1981). 'Stability of semi-arid savanna grazing systems', *Journal of Ecology*, **69**, 473−498.

Wallis, M. (1990). 'District planning and local government in Kenya', *Public Administration and Development*, **10**, 437−452.

Warren, A. and Agnew, C. (1988). *An Assessment of Desertification and Land Degradation in Arid and Semi-arid Areas*, Paper No. 2, Dryland Programme, International Institute for Environment and Development, London.

Wilmot, C. *The Struggle for Europe*, Collins, London, 1952.

Wisner, B. (1977). 'Man-made famine in eastern Kenya: The interrelationship of environment and development', in *Land Use and Development* (Eds P. O'Keefe and B. Wisner), pp. 194−215, African Environment Special Report 5, International African Institute, London.

Wyckoff, J. B. (1989). 'Drought and food policy in Kenya', in *Coping with Drought in Kenya: National and Local Strategies* (Eds T. E. Downing, K. W. Gitu and C. Kamau), pp. 355−368, Lynne Rienner, Boulder, CO and London.

Young, A. (1989). *Agroforestry for Soil Conservation*, Commonwealth Agricultural Bureau International, Wallingford, UK and International Council for Research in Agroforestry, Nairobi.

Young, A. (1991). 'Soil monitoring: A basic task for soil survey organizations', *Soil Use and Management*, **7**, 126−130.

Young, F. W. and Young, R. (1963). 'Towards a theory of community development', Social problem and urbanization, vol. 8 of *Science, Technology and Development*, United Nations, New York.

Zeleza, T. (1990). 'The development of the cooperative movement in Kenya since Independence', *Journal of East African Research and Development*, **20**, 68−94.

Zöbisch, von M. A. (1986). 'Erfassung und Bewertung von Bodenerosionsprozessen auf Weideflächen im Machakos-Distrikt von Kenia [Registration and evaluation of soil erosion processes of grazing land in Machakos District, Kenya]', *Der Tropenlandwirt*, **27**.

Index

Index

Index compiled by Margaret Cornell